JEPPESEN®
Sanderson Training Products

COMMERCIAL PILOT

FAA

AIRMEN KNOWLEDGE

TEST GUIDE

for
COMPUTER TESTING

- Questions, Answers, Explanations, References
- Keyed to GFD Instrument/Commercial Manual
- Explanations Adjacent to Each Question
- Organized by Topic, Includes Full-Color Charts
- Unique Sliding Mask for Self-Testing
- Perforated and 3-Hole Punched Pages
- Includes All FAA Airplane Questions

JS312402-009

PREFACE_____

Thank you for purchasing this Commercial Pilot FAA Airmen Knowledge Test Guide. This Test Guide will help you understand the answers to the test questions so you can take the FAA computer test with confidence. It contains all the FAA Commercial Pilot airplane test questions. Included are the correct answers and explanations, along with study references. Explanations of why the other choices are wrong have been included where appropriate. Questions are organized by topic, with explanations conveniently located adjacent to each question. The three-hole punched, perforated pages provide flexibility so you can select and remove specific pages for effective study. Full-color charts identical to those on the FAA test are included, plus our unique sliding mask for self-testing. Please note that this Test Guide is intended to be a supplement to your instructor-led flight and ground training, not a stand alone learning tool.

THE JEPPESEN SANDERSON TRAINING PHILOSOPHY

Flight training in the developing years of aviation was characterized by the separation of academics from flight training in the aircraft. For years, ground and flight training were not integrated. There were lots of books on different subjects, written by different authors, which produced a general lack of continuity in training material. The introduction of **Jeppesen Sanderson Training Products** changed all this. Our proven, professionally integrated training materials include extensive research on teaching theory and principles of how people learn best and most efficiently. Effective instruction includes determining objectives and completion standards. We employ an important principle of learning a complex skill using a step-by-step sequence known as the **building block principle**. Another important aspect of training is the principle of **meaningful repetition**, whereby each necessary concept or skill is presented several times throughout the instructional program. Jeppesen training materials incorporate these principles in our syllabi, textbooks, videos, computer-based training (CBT), exercises, exams, PCATD Desktop Simulator, and this Test Guide. When these elements are combined with an instructor's class discussion and the skills learned in the simulator and airplane, you have an ideal integrated training system, with all materials coordinated.

Observation and research show that people tend to retain 10% of what they read, 20% of what they hear, 30% of what they see, and 50% of what they both hear and see together. These retention figures can be increased to as high as 90% by including active learning methods. Videos and textbooks are generally considered passive learning materials. Exercises, stage exams, student/instructor discussions, CBT, and practice in the simulator and airplane are considered to be active learning methods. Levels of learning include rote, understanding, application, and correlation. One of the major drawbacks with test preparation courses that concentrate only on passing the test is that they focus on rote learning, the lowest level of learning. Students benefit from Jeppesen's professional approach through standardized instruction, a documented training record, increased learning **and** increased passing rates. Our materials are challenging and motivating, while maximizing knowledge and skill retention. Nearly 3 million pilots have learned to fly using our materials, which include:

MANUALS — Our training manuals contain the answers to many of the questions you may have as you begin your training program. They are based on the study/review concept of learning. This means detailed material is presented in an uncomplicated way, then important points are summarized through the use of bold type and color. The best results can be obtained when the manual is studied as an integral part of the coordinated materials. The manual is the central component for academic study and is cross-referenced to video presentations.

VIDEOS — These motivating, high-quality ground school videos are professionally produced with actual inflight video and animated graphics. They allow you to review and reinforce essential concepts presented in the manual. The videos are available for viewing at flight and ground schools which subscribe to the Jeppesen Sanderson Guided Flight Discovery (GFD) Training System. Call 1-800-621-JEPP for the names of our Training System dealers in your area.

SUPPORT COMPONENTS — Supplementary items include a training syllabus, stage and end-of-course exams, CBT, PCATD Desktop Simulator, FAR/AIM Manual, FARs Explained, airmen knowledge test and practical test study guides, test preparation software and videos, question banks and computer testing supplements, an aviation weather book, student record folder, computer, plotter, and logbook. Jeppesen Sanderson's training products are the most comprehensive pilot training materials available. In conjunction with your instructor, they help you prepare for the FAA exam and practical test; and, more importantly, they help you become a more proficient and safer pilot.

You can purchase our products and services through your Jeppesen dealer. For product, service, or sales information call **1-800-621-JEPP, 303-799-9090, or FAX 303-328-4153**. If you have comments, questions, or need explanations about any component of our GFD Training System, we are prepared to offer assistance at any time. If your dealer does not have a Jeppesen catalog, please request one and we will promptly send it to you. Just call the above telephone number, or write:

Manager, Training and Courseware
Jeppesen Sanderson, Inc.
55 Inverness Drive East
Englewood, CO 80112-5498

Please direct inquiries from Europe, Africa, and the Middle East to:
Jeppesen & Co., GmbH
Frankfurter Strasse 233
63263 Neu-Isenburg, Germany
Tel: 011-49-6102-5070
Fax: 011-49-6102-507-999

UPDATES OF FAA QUESTIONS — You can obtain free updates for the FAA questions in this Test Guide by visiting Jeppesen's web site. These updates are generally valid within one year of book publication; if you are using an older Test Guide, the web site may not update all questions that have changed since the book was printed.

To find updated questions, go to www.jeppesen.com, click Online Publications and then click FAA Test Prep Updates. Due to improvements and ongoing reorganization of the web site, the exact location of the updates is subject to change.

Jeppesen Briefing Bulletin

The FAA is changing your test. We want you to be ready.
The FAA is concerned that many students are memorizing the answers to the FAA knowledge test. As a result, they are regularly shuffling around the answer choices to most questions in the FAA databases. This means if you have learned the answer to a question based on the letter of the correct answer, or based on the correct answer's position below the question, you will likely miss the question when you take the test. We believe the shuffle will continue on a regular basis, and it will not be possible for test preparation courses to match the sequence of the answer choices.

Jeppesen has never encouraged its students to memorize answers to FAA questions. We provide comprehensive, no-nonsense study material that teaches you what you need to know to determine the correct answers to the tests. And our test prep materials always tell you why the correct answer is correct and if it is not obvious, why the other answers are incorrect. We want you to know the material, not memorize it.

So, be careful how you study this material. While it is possible to memorize the letter and position of the correct answer, it is not in your best interest, either when taking the test, or further in your flight career when this knowledge will be tested in the cockpit. When answering an FAA question, carefully read and evaluate each answer choice and choose the correct answer based on what you know from your study, not from that answer's position.

Jeppesen thanks you for choosing our test preparation materials. We are confident you will be better prepared to pass the FAA test.

TABLE
OF CONTENTS

INTRODUCTION

The Commercial Pilot FAA Airmen Knowledge Test Guide is designed to help you prepare for the Commercial Pilot Computer Test. It covers FAA exam material that applies to airplanes, including pertinent Federal Aviation Regulations (FARs). Questions and answers pertaining to rotorcraft, gliders, balloons, powered-lift, and airships have been omitted.

We recommend that you use this Test Guide in conjunction with the Guided Flight Discovery (GFD) Pilot Training System. The Test Guide is organized like the Instrument/Commercial Pilot Manual, with fifteen chapters and distinctive sections within each chapter. Questions are covered in the Test Guide in the same sequence as the material in the manual. References to applicable chapter and section in the manual are included along with the answers. A separate chapter (Chapter 15) in the Test Guide is devoted to FAR questions and answers.

Within the chapters, each section contains a brief introduction. FAA test questions appear in the left column and answers and explanations are in the right column. Below is an example of a typical reference for a question.

[1]   [2]   [3]   [4]   [5]   [6]
3-41 **J05**   **3-41. Answer C. GFDICM 3A (AIM)**
(FAA Question)   *(Explanation of FAA Question)*

[1]   Jeppesen designated test guide question number. The first number is the chapter where the question is located in the Test Guide. In most cases, this corresponds to the chapter in the GFD manual. The second number is the question number within the chapter. This number may or may not be in sequential order. In this example, the question is in Chapter 3 of the Test Guide and it is the 41st question.

[2]   FAA subject matter knowledge code. The reference to this code can be found in the appendix of the Test Guide.

[3]   The Jeppesen test guide number is repeated in the right hand column above the explanation.

[4]   Correct answer to the question, in this case answer C is correct.

[5]   The location where the question is covered in the GFD manual. In this case, the question is covered in Chapter 3, Section A in the Instrument/Commercial Pilot Manual.

[6]   Abbreviation for the FAA or other authoritative source document. In this case, the reference is the Aeronautical Information Manual (AIM). Abbreviations used in the Test Guide are as follows:

AC	—	Advisory Circulars
A/FD	—	Airport/Facility Directory
AIM	—	Aeronautical Information Manual
AW	—	Aviation Weather, AC 00-6A
AWS	—	Aviation Weather Services, AC 00-45
FAR	—	Federal Aviation Regulation
AFH	—	Airplane Flying Handbook, FAA-H-8083-3
IAP	—	Instrument Approach Procedure
IFH	—	Instrument Flying Handbook, FAA-H-8083-15
GFDICM	—	Guided Flight Discovery Instrument/Commercial Manual
GFDPPM	—	Guided Flight Discovery Private Pilot Manual
NAVWEPS	—	Aerodynamics for Naval Aviators
PHB	—	Pilot's Handbook of Aeronautical Knowledge, AC 61-23
WBH	—	Aircraft Weight and Balance Handbook, FAA-H-8083-1
TPRS	—	U.S. Standard for Terminal Instrument Procedures

Below the reference line is the FAA question in the left column and the explanation in the right column. The explanation includes the correct answer followed by an explanation of why the answer is correct and why the other answers are wrong. In some cases, the incorrect answers are not explained. Examples include instances where the answers are calculated, or when the explanation of the correct answer obviously eliminates the wrong answers.

The answers in this Test Guide are based on official reference documents and, in our judgment, are the best choices of the available answers. Some questions which were valid when the FAA test was developed may no longer be appropriate due to ongoing changes in regulations or official operating procedures. However, with the computer test format, timely updating and validation of questions is anticipated. Therefore, when taking the FAA test, it is important to answer the questions according to the latest regulations or official operating procedures.

Two appendices from the FAA test materials are included in the back of the Test Guide. These are Appendix 1, Subject Matter Knowledge Codes, which also lists reference material, and Appendix 2, which consists of legend information from the National Aeronautical Charting Office (NACO) Airport/Facility Directory (A/FD). You will need to refer to this legend to answer some questions concerning A/FD information. Appendix 3 in the Test Guide contains a numerical listing of all airplane questions. Included in this listing is a tabulation with the Jeppesen test guide question number, FAA question number, correct answer, and the page number where the question appears in the Test Guide.

Figures in the Test Guide are the same as those that are used in the FAA Computerized Testing Supplement. These figures, that are referred to in many of the questions, are placed throughout the Test Guide as close as practical to the applicable questions. When a figure is not on the same page or facing page, a note will indicate the page number where you can find that figure. In addition, pages in this Test Guide are three-hole punched and perforated to allow you to easily remove any figure for reference while answering a specific question.

HOW TO PREPARE FOR THE FAA TEST

It is important to realize that to become a safe, competent pilot, you need more than just the academic knowledge required to pass a test. For a comprehensive ground training program, we recommend a structured ground school with a qualified flight or ground instructor. An organized course of instruction will help you complete the course in a timely manner, and you will be able to have your questions answered. The additional instruction will be beneficial in your flight training.

Regardless of whether or not you are in a structured ground training program, you will find this Test Guide is an excellent training aid to help you prepare for the FAA computerized test. The Test Guide contains all of the airplane questions as they are presented in the FAA computerized test format. By reviewing the questions and studying the Guided Flight Discovery Pilot Training materials, you should be well equipped to take the test.

You will also benefit more from your study if you test yourself as you proceed through the Test Guide. Cover the answers in the right-hand column, read each question, and choose what you consider the best answer. A sliding mask is provided for this purpose. Move the sliding mask down and read the answer and explanation for that question. You may want to mark the questions you miss for further study and review prior to taking the exam.

The sooner you take the exam after you complete your study, the better. This way, the information will be fresh in your mind, and you will be more confident when you actually take the FAA test.

WHO CAN TAKE THE TEST

When you are ready to take the FAA computerized test, you must present evidence that you have completed the appropriate ground instruction or a home study course. This proof may be in the form of a graduation certificate from a pilot training course, a written statement, or a logbook entry by a certified ground or flight instructor. Although you are encouraged to obtain ground instruction, a home study course may be used. If you cannot provide one of the abo documents, you may present evidence of a completed home study course to an FAA aviation safety inspector for approval.

You also must provide evidence of a permanent mailing address, appropriate identification, and proof of your age. The identification must include a current photograph, your signature, and your residential address, if different from your mailing address. You may present this information in more than one form of identification, such as a driver's license, government identification card, passport, alien residency (green) card, or a military identification card.

GENERAL INFORMATION — FAA COMPUTER TESTS

Detailed information on FAA computer testing is contained in FAA Order 8080.6B, Conduct of Airmen Knowledge Tests. This FAA order provides guidance for Flight Standards District Offices (FSDOs) and personnel associated with organizations that are participating in, or are seeking to participate in, the FAA Computer-Assisted Airmen Knowledge Testing Program. You also may refer to FAA Order 8700.1, General Aviation Operations Inspector's Handbook, for guidance on computer testing by 14 CFR Parts 141 and 142 pilot schools that hold examining authority.

As an applicant, you don't need all of the details contained in FAA Orders, but you will be interested in some of the general information about computer testing facilities. A **Computer Testing Designee (CTD)** is an organization authorized by the FAA to administer FAA airmen knowledge tests via the computer medium. A **Computer Testing Manager (CTM)** is a person selected by the CTD to serve as manager of its national computer testing program. A **Testing Center Supervisor (TCS)** is a person selected by the CTM, with FAA approval, to administer FAA airmen knowledge tests at approved testing centers. The TCS is responsible for the operation of the testing center. A **Special Test Administrator (STA)** is a person selected by a CTD to administer FAA airmen knowledge tests in unique situations and remote or isolated areas. A test proctor is a properly trained and qualified person, appointed by a TCS, authorized to administer FAA airmen knowledge tests.

CTDs are selected by the FAA's Airmen Testing Standards Branch. Those selected may include companies, schools, universities, or other organizations that meet specific requirements. For example, they must clearly demonstrate competence in computer technology, centralized database management, national communications network operation and maintenance, national facilities management, software maintenance and support, and technical training and customer support. They must provide computer-assisted testing, test administration, and data transfer service on a national scale. This means they must maintain a minimum of 20 operational testing centers geographically dispersed throughout the United States. In addition, CTDs must offer operational hours that are convenient to the public. An acceptable plan for test security is also required.

TEST MATERIALS, REFERENCE MATERIALS, AND AIDS

You are allowed to use aids, reference materials, and test materials within specified guidelines, provided the actual test questions or answers are not revealed. All models of aviation-oriented computers, regardless of manufacturer, may be used, including hand-held computers designed expressly for aviation use, and also small electronic calculators that perform arithmetic functions. Simple programmable memories, which allow addition to, subtraction from, or retrieval of one number from the memory, are acceptable. Simple functions such as square root or percent keys are also acceptable.

In addition, you may use any reference materials provided with the test. You will find that these reference materials are the same as those in your Test Guide. They include a printed Computerized Testing Supplement with the legend data and the applicable figures. You also may use scales, straight-edges, protractors, plotters, navigation computers, log sheets, and, as already mentioned, electronic or mechanical calculators that are directly related to the test. Permanently inscribed manufacturer's instructions on the front and back of these aids, such as, formulas, conversions, regulations, signals, weather data, holding pattern diagrams, frequencies, weight and balance formulas, and ATC procedures, are permissible.

WHAT TO EXPECT ON A COMPUTER TEST

Computer testing centers are required to have an acceptable method for the "on-line" registration of test applicants during normal business hours. They must provide a dual method, for example, keyboard, touch screen, or mouse, for answering questions. Features that must be provided also include an introductory lesson to familiarize you with computer testing procedures, the ability to return to a test question previously answered (for the purpose of review or answer changes), and a suitable display of multiple-choice and other question types on the computer screen in one frame. Other required features include a display of the time remaining for the completion of the test, a "HELP" function which permits you to review test questions and optional responses, and provisions for your test score on an Airman Computer Test Report.

On computer tests, the selection of questions is done for you, and you will answer the questions that appear on the screen. You will be given a specific amount of time to complete the test, which is based on past experience with others who have taken the exam. If you are prepared, you should have plenty of time to complete the test. After you begin the test, the screen will show you the time remaining for completion. When taking the test, keep the following points in mind:

1. Answer each question in accordance with the latest regulations and procedures. If the regulation or procedure has recently changed, you will receive credit for the affected question. However, these questions will normally be deleted or updated on the FAA computerized exams.

2. Read each question carefully before looking at the possible answers. You should clearly understand the problem before attempting to solve it.

3. After formulating an answer, determine which of the alternatives most nearly corresponds with that answer. The answer chosen should completely resolve the problem.

4. From the answers given, it may appear that there is more than one possible answer; however, there is only one answer that is correct and complete. The other answers are either incomplete or are derived from popular misconceptions.

5. Make sure you select an answer for each question. Questions left unanswered will be counted as incorrect.

6. If a certain question is difficult for you, it is best to proceed to other questions. After you answer the less difficult questions, return to those which were unanswered. The computer-aided test format helps you identify unanswered questions, as well as those questions you wish to review.

7. When solving a calculator problem, select the answer nearest your solution. The problem has been checked with various types of calculators; therefore, if you have solved it correctly, your answer will be closer to the correct answer than the other choices.

8. Generally, the test results will be available almost immediately. Your score will be recorded on an Airman Computer Test Report form. [Figure 1]

1
2
3
4
5
6
7
8
9
10
11
12
13
14
15
16
17
18
19
20
21
22
23
24
25
26
27
28
29
30
31
32
33
34
35
36
37
38
39
40
41
42
43
44
45
46
47
48
49
50
51
52
53
54

Federal Aviation Administration
Airmen Computer Test Report

EXAM TITLE: Commercial Pilot — Airplane

NAME: Jones David John

ID NUMBER: 123456789   TAKE: 1

DATE: 08/14/—   SCORE: 82   GRADE: Pass

Knowledge area codes in which questions were answered incorrectly.
See Appropriate FAA-CT-8080 test book. A code may represent more
than one incorrect response.

A21 B08 B09 H04 H05 H06 I04 I05 J58 K01 M51

EXPIRATION DATE: 08/31/—

DO NOT LOSE THIS REPORT

Authorized Instructor's Statement. (If Applicable)

I have given Mr./Mrs._____additional instruction in
each subject area shown to be deficient and consider the applicant competent to pass the
test.

Last _____ Initial _____ Cert. No. _____ Type _____
(Print Clearly)

Signature _____

CTD's Embossed Seal

Figure 1. This sample Airman Computer Test Report shows the applicants test results. Take 1 indicates this is
the first time the applicant has taken this test. Knowledge area codes for incorrect answers are listed in the
center portion of the report, and an additional instruction section is included in the last part.

The Airmen Computer Test Report includes subject matter knowledge codes for incorrect answers. To determine the knowledge area in which a particular question was incorrectly answered, compare the subject matter knowledge codes on this report to Appendix 1, Subject Matter Knowledge Codes.

Computer testing designees must provide a way for applicants, who challenge the validity of test questions, to enter comments into the computer. The test proctor should advise you, if you have complaints about test scores, or specific test questions, to write directly to the appropriate FAA office. In addition to comments, you will be asked to respond to a critique form which may vary at different computer testing centers. The TCS must provide a method for you to respond to critique questions projected on the computer screen. [Figure 2]

1. Did the test administration personnel give you an adequate briefing on testing procedures?

2. Was the "sign-on" accomplished efficiently?

3. Did you have any difficulty reading the computer presentation of test questions?

4. Was the test supplementary material (charts, graphs, tables, etc.) presented in a usable manner?

5. Did you have any difficulty using the "return to previous question for review" procedures?

6. Was the testing room noise level distracting?

7. Did you have adequate work space?

8. Did you have adequate lighting?

9. What is your overall evaluation of the computer testing experience?

    a. Unsatisfactory.

    b. Poor.

    c. Satisfactory.

    d. Highly satisfactory.

    e. Outstanding.

FIGURE 2. Critique forms used at different computer testing centers may vary. This sample form contains typical questions.

RETESTING AFTER FAILURE

The applicant shall surrender the previous test report to the test proctor prior to retesting. The original test report shall be destroyed by the test proctor after administering the retest. The latest test taken will reflect the official score.

As stated in 14 CFR section 61.49, an applicant may apply for retesting after receiving additional training and an endorsement from an authorized instructor who has determined the applicant has been found competent to pass the test.

WHERE TO TAKE THE FAA TEST

Almost all testing is now administered via computer at FAA-designated test centers. As indicated, these CTDs are located throughout the U.S. You can expect to pay a fee and the cost varies at different locations. The following is a listing of the approved computer testing designees at the time of publication of this Test Guide. You may want to check with your local FSDO for changes.

Computer Assisted Testing Service (CATS)
1-800-947-4228
Outside U.S. (650) 259-8550

LaserGrade Computer Testing
1-800-211-2754
Outside U.S. (360) 896-9111

BUILDING PROFESSIONAL EXPERIENCE

This textbook chapter introduces some of the training requirements and the opportunities for pilots with instrument ratings and commercial certificates. It presents highlights of aviation history as well.

Each chapter and section in the Commercial Pilot Airmen Knowledge Study Guide directly corresponds to the same chapter and section in Jeppesen's *Instrument/Commercial Manual*, part of the Guided Flight Discovery Pilot Training System. The manual explores in depth each topic presented in this guide, and covers many areas not tested in the computer exam. This additional information is vital to your commercial pilot preparation, and we strongly encourage you to study the manual, in addition to this guide.

Although certain textbook chapters cover material not directly tested in the knowledge test, those chapters are referenced in this study guide and comments provided that may be useful in preparing for the oral portion of your practical test.

SECTION A
INSTRUMENT/COMMERCIAL TRAINING AND OPPORTUNITIES

There are no commercial FAA test questions assigned to this section.

Commercial Pilot Certificate

1. For you to be eligible for a commercial pilot certificate, you must be at least 18 years of age, hold a private pilot certificate, be able to read, write, speak, and understand the English language, and meet specific training and flight time requirements described in the FARs, as well as pass a knowledge and practical test. Under Part 141, you must hold an instrument rating or be concurrently enrolled in an instrument rating course.

Commercial Pilot Privileges

2. Although you need at least a third-class medical certificate to be eligible for a commercial pilot certificate, you must have a second-class medical certificate to exercise commercial pilot privileges.

3. As part of the commercial pilot training requirements, you must receive 10 hours of flight training in a complex airplane (an airplane with retractable landing gear, flaps, and a controllable pitch propeller).

4. A high performance airplane is defined as an airplane having an engine of more than 200 horsepower.

5. FAR Parts 119, 121, 125, and 135 govern operations ranging from scheduled air carriers to on-demand charters.

6. Under FAR Part 91, you may not engage in common carriage which involves holding out, or advertising your services, to furnish transportation for any member of the public.

7. Student instruction, certain nonstop sightseeing flights within limited areas, crop dusting, banner towing, aerial photography or survey, fire fighting, and some types of corporate flights are examples of operations which are not governed by FAR Parts 121, 125, and 135.

8. A person who applies for a commercial pilot certificate with an airplane category rating, and does not hold an instrument rating in the same category and class, will be issued a commercial pilot certificate that contains the limitation, "The carriage of passengers for hire in airplanes on cross-country flights in excess of 50 nautical miles or at night is prohibited."

Requirements for Commercial Pilot Certification

9. The addition of a multi-engine rating to your private or commercial certificate does not require a minimum number of ground or flight instruction hours under FAR Part 61. Under FAR Part 141, a multi-engine rating course must include the ground and flight instruction hours in accordance with the applicable Part 141 appendices.

SECTION B
ADVANCED HUMAN FACTORS CONCEPTS

From your previous training and pilot experience, you know that flying requires a continuous series of decisions. If you are at your best, you should be able to plan effectively and safely handle most situations that occur during a flight.

Aeronautical Decision Making

1. Aeronautical decision making is a systematic approach to the mental process used by aircraft pilots to consistently determine the best course of action in response to a given set of circumstances.

2. Approximately 75% of all aviation accidents are attributed to human factors-related causes. Studies have identified five hazardous attitudes which can interfere with a pilot's ability to make sound decisions and exercise authority properly.

Pilot-In-Command Responsibility

3. As pilot in command, you are the final authority in the airplane you are flying. When only one pilot is in the cockpit, the PIC is obvious, but when two pilots are present, each pilot's responsibilities must be defined before the flight. Within the cockpit, one person is pilot in command, and the other serves to assist the PIC.

Resource Use

4. Resource use is an important part of human factors training. Cockpit resources increase as you fly more complex aircraft with advanced systems. If you are not thoroughly familiar with the equipment in your aircraft or you rely on it so much that you become complacent, flight safety is compromised.

5. The focus of crew resource management (CRM) programs is the effective use of all available resources: human resources, hardware, and information. CRM training helps flight crews understand the limitations of human performance, especially under stressful situations, and makes them aware of the importance of crew coordination to combat error.

Communication

6. When flying with another pilot, it is important to use standard terminology and verify that your meaning is understood. A breakdown in communication can cause friction and frustration, detracting from important tasks, or lead to a hazardous situation where one pilot believes the other is controlling the airplane, but in reality, neither pilot has control.

Workload Management

7. Effective workload management directly impacts safety by ensuring that you are prepared for the busiest segments of the flight through proper use of down time. Organizing charts in the order of use, setting radio frequencies, and writing down expected altitudes and route clearances will help you visualize and mentally prepare for what comes next.

Situational Awareness

8. Controlled flight into terrain (CFIT) occurs when an aircraft is flown into terrain or water with no prior awareness on the part of the crew that the crash is imminent.

Aviation Physiology

9. The study of aviation physiology is an important part of human factors training. How you feel, physically, has a direct impact on how well you fly.

Disorientation

10. When there is a conflict between the information relayed by your central vision and your peripheral vision, you may suffer from spatial disorientation. When subjected to the various forces of flight, the vestibular system can send misleading signals to the brain resulting in vestibular disorientation.

11. A pilot is more subject to spatial disorientation if body signals are used to interpret flight attitude. The sensations which lead to spatial disorientation during instrument flight conditions must be suppressed and complete reliance placed on the indications of the flight instruments.

Motion Sickness

12. Nausea, sweating, dizziness, and vomiting are some of the symptoms of motion sickness. To overcome motion sickness without outside visual references, you should focus on the instrument panel, since it is your only source of accurate position information.

Hypoxia

13. Hypoxia occurs when the tissues in the body do not receive enough oxygen. It can be caused by an insufficient supply of oxygen, inadequate transportation of oxygen, or the inability of the body tissues to use oxygen. Hypoxic hypoxia occurs when there are not enough molecules of oxygen available at sufficient pressure to pass between the membranes in your respiratory system.

14. If you are planning a flight with a cruise altitude over 12,500 feet MSL, you should review FAR Part 91 for the requirements regarding supplemental oxygen. Prior to operating a pressurized aircraft with a service ceiling or maximum operating altitude higher than 25,000 feet MSL, you must complete high-altitude training.

15. Hypemic hypoxia occurs when your blood is not able to carry a sufficient amount of oxygen to your body's cells. Since it attaches itself to the hemoglobin about 200 times more easily than does oxygen, carbon monoxide (CO) prevents the hemoglobin from carrying sufficient oxygen. Even without considering the dangers of incapacitating the flight crew, carbon monoxide poisoning can be fatal. Frequent inspections should be made of aircraft exhaust manifold-type heating systems to minimize the possibility of exhaust gases leaking into the cockpit.

16. Hypoxia is particularly dangerous during flights with one pilot because symptoms of hypoxia may be difficult to recognize before the pilot's reactions are affected.

17. Stagnant hypoxia is an oxygen deficiency in the body due to the poor circulation of the blood. It can result from pulling excessive positive Gs. The inability of the cells to effectively use oxygen is defined as histotoxic hypoxia. This can be caused by alcohol and other drugs such as narcotics and poisons.

Hyperventilation

18. Hyperventilation is a physiological disorder that develops when too much carbon dioxide (CO_2) has been eliminated from the body, usually caused by breathing too rapidly or too deeply. To overcome the symptoms of hyperventilation, you should slow your breathing rate. Some of the symptoms include dizziness, tingling of hands and feet, muscle spasms, coolness, feelings of suffocation, drowsiness, weakness or numbness, rapid heart rate, apprehension and mental confusion, and finally, loss of consciousness.

Decompression Sickness

19. Decompression sickness (DCS) is a painful condition that can occur if flying too soon after diving. It is very important that you allow enough time for the body to rid itself of excess nitrogen absorbed during diving.

Fitness for Flight

20. Stress is the body's reaction to the physical and psychological demands placed upon it, and it can adversely affect your ability to fly safely. When you are fatigued, you are more prone to error in the cockpit. Getting adequate rest and improving your overall fitness will help you perform at your best.

21. Preflight use of the I'm Safe Checklist will help ensure you are fit for flight. Consider illness and medication that might affect your safety as a pilot. Factors such as rest, a good breakfast, and issues at work can interfere with your concentration level in the airplane. If you have any reservations about your ability to make the flight, save the trip for another time.

22. Judgment and decision-making abilities can be adversely affected by even small amounts of alcohol.

Vision

23. Effective traffic scanning is accomplished by allowing time for the eyes to focus at 10 degree increments across the sky.

24. The best night vision is achieved by allowing the rods of the eyes to adapt to the night environment, which usually takes 30 minutes in the dark.

1-1   **H351**

Frequent inspections should be made of aircraft exhaust manifold-type heating systems to minimize the possibility of

A — exhaust gases leaking into the cockpit.
B — a power loss due to back pressure in the exhaust system.
C — a cold-running engine due to the heat withdrawn by the heater.

1-2   **J31**

As hyperventilation progresses, a pilot can experience

A — decreased breathing rate and depth.
B — heightened awareness and feeling of well being.
C — symptoms of suffocation and drowsiness.

1-3   **J31**

To scan properly for traffic, a pilot should

A — concentrate on any peripheral movement detected.
B — slowly sweep the field of vision from one side to the other at intervals.
C — use a series of short, regularly spaced eye movements that bring successive areas of the sky into the central visual field.

1-4   **J31**

Which is a common symptom of hyperventilation?

A — Drowsiness.
B — Decreased breathing rate.
C — Euphoria — sense of well-being.

1-1. Answer A. GFDICM 1B (AC 91-59)

FAA studies show that approximately 50% of exhaust system failures occurred in the exhaust gas-to-air heat exchanger, resulting in carbon monoxide gas entering the cabin through the aircraft heater. Because of this, the owner/operator should make frequent inspections on the exhaust system. Answer (B) is wrong because a visual inspection of the exhaust will not reveal this problem. Answer (C) is incorrect because using the heater doesn't affect the engine temperature.

1-2. Answer C. GFDICM 1B (AIM)

Some of the symptoms of hyperventilation include dizziness, tingling of hands and feet, muscle spasms, coolness, suffocation, drowsiness, weakness or numbness, rapid heart rate, apprehension and mental confusion, and finally, loss of consciousness. Answer (A) is wrong because hyperventilation is a result of an excessive breathing rate. Answer (B) is incorrect because a heightened awareness and feeling of well-being is not associated with hyperventilation.

1-3. Answer C. GFDICM 1B (AIM)

Effective traffic scanning must be accomplished by using a series of short, regularly spaced eye movements that bring successive areas of the sky into the central, or foveal, area of vision. A series of 10-degree movements while pausing in between each for approximately 1 second is most effective. Answer (A) is incorrect because peripheral vision does not provide the clear, sharp images required for identifying and avoiding potential collision hazards. Answer (B) is incorrect because the eyes need time to focus on each segment of airspace.

1-4. Answer A. GFDICM 1B (AIM)

Some of the symptoms of hyperventilation include dizziness, tingling of hands and feet, muscle spasms, coolness, suffocation, drowsiness, weakness or numbness, rapid heart rate, apprehension and mental confusion, and finally, loss of consciousness. Answer (B) is wrong because hyperventilation is the result of an excessive breathing rate. Answer (C) is incorrect because hyperventilation usually results from anxiety and fear; euphoria and a sense of well-being are normally associated with hypoxia.

1-5 **J31**
Which would most likely result in hyperventilation?

A — Insufficient oxygen.
B — Excessive carbon monoxide.
C — Insufficient carbon dioxide.

1-5. Answer C. GFDICM 1B (AIM)
Hyperventilation is caused by a breathing rate that is too rapid and too deep. This process forces too much carbon dioxide from your body and creates a chemical imbalance in the blood. Answer (A) is wrong because insufficient oxygen causes hypoxia, not hyperventilation. Answer (B) is incorrect because excessive carbon monoxide can produce symptoms which are similar to hypoxic hypoxia and can lead to total incapacitation or even death.

1-6 **J31**
Hypoxia is the result of which of these conditions?

A — Excessive oxygen in the bloodstream.
B — Insufficient oxygen reaching the brain.
C — Excessive carbon dioxide in the bloodstream.

1-6. Answer B. GFDICM 1B (AIM)
Hypoxia occurs when the tissues in your body do not receive enough oxygen. It is considered to be the most lethal factor of all physiological causes of accidents. Answers (A) and (C) are wrong because excessive oxygen (or more appropriately, a lack of carbon dioxide) causes hyperventilation, not hypoxia.

1-7 **J31**
To overcome the symptoms of hyperventilation, a pilot should

A — swallow or yawn.
B — slow the breathing rate.
C — increase the breathing rate.

1-7. Answer B. GFDICM 1B (AIM)
Hyperventilation is caused by a breathing rate that is too rapid and too deep. Restoring the proper carbon dioxide level in the body is the treatment for hyperventilation. Breathing normally is the best prevention and the best cure. Answer (A) is wrong because swallowing or yawning is a method for equalizing ear pressure with the surrounding atmosphere. This will not slow breathing long enough to stop hyperventilation. Answer (C) is incorrect because increasing the breathing rate will further elevate your carbon dioxide levels.

1-8 **J31**
Which is true regarding the presence of alcohol within the human body?

A — A small amount of alcohol increases vision acuity.
B — An increase in altitude decreases the adverse effect of alcohol.
C — Judgment and decision-making abilities can be adversely affected by even small amounts of alcohol.

1-8. Answer C. GFDICM 1B (AIM)
Under the influence of alcohol, you experience a dulling of the senses, a decrease in good judgment, and a reduced sense of responsibility. Answer (A) is wrong because even small amounts of alcohol dull the senses. Answer (B) is incorrect because alcohol reduces the amount of oxygen that can be absorbed in the blood and altitude will amplify the effects of alcohol.

1-9 **J31**
Hypoxia susceptibility due to inhalation of carbon monoxide increases as

A — humidity decreases.
B — altitude increases.
C — oxygen demand increases.

1-9. Answer B. GFDICM 1B (AC 20-32B)
As altitude increases, air pressure decreases and the body has difficulty getting enough oxygen. Add carbon monoxide, which further deprives the body of oxygen, and the situation can become critical. Answer (A) is wrong because a decrease in humidity provides only a very slight increase in the availability of oxygen. Answer (C) is incorrect because the oxygen demanded by the body while flying an aircraft is a relatively fixed amount. As altitude increases, the availability of oxygen is reduced.

1-10   **H351**

To best overcome the effects of spatial disorientation, a pilot should

A — rely on body sensations.
B — rely on aircraft instrument indications.
C — increase the breathing rate.

1-10. Answer B. GFDICM 1B (AIM)

To avoid overcome spatial disorientation, you must learn to disregard false body sensations and rely on the flight instruments. The flight instruments are the only unbiased indicators of what the airplane is really doing. FORCE YOURSELF to believe them no matter what things "feel" like.

CHAPTER 2

PRINCIPLES OF INSTRUMENT FLIGHT

SECTION A
FLIGHT INSTRUMENT SYSTEMS

The major portion of this section is for instrument rating applicants. An instrument rating is required to exercise most commercial airplane pilot privileges. Although the FAA will not test you on instrument knowledge for the commercial test, you may wish to review some of the instrument basics.

Heading Indicator

1. You must align the heading indicator with the magnetic compass before flight and recheck it periodically during flight.

Turn Indicator

2. Turn indicators allow you to establish and maintain standard-rate turns of three degrees per second, or in the case of certain high performance aircraft, half-standard-rate turns. At three degrees per second, a 360° turn will be completed in two minutes.

3. Both turn coordinators and turn-and-slip indicators indicate rate of turn, but because of the improved design of the turn coordinator, this instrument also indicates rate of roll as you enter a turn.

4. One advantage of an electric turn coordinator is that it serves as a backup in case of vacuum system failure.

5. During a constant-bank level turn, an increase in airspeed results in a decreased rate of turn, and an increased turn radius.

Magnetic Compass

6. Magnetic deviation is error due to magnetic interference with metal components in the aircraft, as well as magnetic fields from aircraft electrical equipment. It varies for different headings of the same aircraft.

Pitot-Static Instruments

7. The pitot-static instruments are the airspeed indicator, altimeter, and vertical speed indicator. Blockages in either the pitot or static systems affect the airspeed indicator, while the remaining instruments are affected only by static system blockage.

8. The altimeter and pitot-static system, as well as the transponder, must have been inspected within the preceding 24 calendar months before flying.

9. Standard temperature and pressure at sea level are 15°C (59°F) and 29.92 inches of Hg. (1013.2 Mb.). Pressure altitude is indicated on the altimeter when 29.92 is set in the altimeter setting window.

Airspeed Indicator

10. Calibrated airspeed (CAS) is indicated airspeed corrected for installation and instrument errors. Equivalent airspeed (EAS) is calibrated airspeed corrected for compressibility. True airspeed (TAS) is the actual speed your airplane moves through undisturbed air. Mach is the ratio of the aircraft's true airspeed to the speed of sound at the temperature and altitude in which the aircraft is flying.

11. V_{S1} is defined as stalling speed or minimum steady flight speed in a specified configuration.

12. You should use the same indicated airspeed at higher elevation airports that you use at lower elevations for take-off, approach, and landing at higher elevation airports, even though the corresponding groundspeeds are faster.

13. If, while maintaining a constant indicated altitude, you are able to maintain constant power as outside air temperature increases, true airspeed will increase.

14. Design maneuvering speed, V_A, is one important value not shown by the color coding of an airspeed indicator. During operations in turbulence, you should slow the airplane below this speed. Other values can be identified by the color coding on the indicator, like the red line denoting V_{NE}, never-exceed speed.

15. V speeds are defined in Part 1 of the FARs. V_F indicates design flap speed. V_X is the best angle of climb speed while, V_Y is the best rate of climb speed. V_{NO} is the maximum structural cruising speed.

Altimeter

16. The most common altimeter error is failure to keep it set to the current barometric pressure.

17. The altimeter indicates high when the actual pressure is lower than what is set in the window. The altimeter also indicates high when in colder than standard temperature conditions.

18. It is your responsibility as pilot in command to make sure that an altimeter system check has been made within the preceding 24 calendar months. You must also make sure that the required instruments for VFR are functioning properly.

19. Pressure altitude is displayed on the altimeter when it is set to the standard sea level pressure of 29.92 in. Hg. However, to provide for proper vertical separation of aircraft up to 17,999 feet MSL, all pilots should use the local altimeter setting so that their altimeters approximately indicate true altitude. At or above 18,000 feet MSL, all pilots must set their altimeters to 29.92 in. Hg.

2-1   A02
Which is the correct symbol for the stalling speed or the minimum steady flight speed in a specified configuration?

A — V_S.
B — V_{S1}.
C — V_{S0}.

2-2   A02
Which is the correct symbol for the stalling speed or the minimum steady flight speed at which the airplane is controllable?

A — V_S.
B — V_{S1}.
C — V_{S0}.

2-3   A02
14 CFR part 1 defines V_F as

A — flap operating speed.
B — maximum flap extended speed.
C — design flap speed.

2-4   A02
14 CFR part 1 defines V_{NO} as

A — maximum operating speed.
B — maximum structural cruising speed.
C — normal operating speed.

2-1. Answer B. GFDICM 2A (FAR 1.2)
V_{S1} is defined as stalling speed or minimum steady flight speed in a specified configuration. Answer (A) is incorrect because it defines the stalling speed or the minimum steady flight speed at which the airplane is controllable. Answer (C) defines the stalling speed or the minimum steady flight speed in the landing configuration.

2-2. Answer A. GFDICM 2A (FAR 1.2)
V_S defines the stalling speed or the minimum steady flight speed at which the airplane is controllable. Answer (B) defines the stalling speed or minimum steady flight speed in a specified configuration and is incorrect. Answer (C) is incorrect because it defines the stalling speed or the minimum steady flight speed in the landing configuration.

2-3. Answer C. GFDICM 2A (FAR 1.2)
V_F is the design flap speed. V_{FE} is the maximum flap extended speed. Flap operating speed is not defined in 14 CFR part 1.

2-4. Answer B. GFDICM 2A (FAR 1.2)
According to FAR 1.1, V_{NO} is defined as the maximum structural cruising speed of an aircraft.

2-5 **A02**
14 CFR part 1 defines V_{NE} as

A — never-exceed speed.
B — maximum nose wheel extend speed.
C — maximum landing gear extended speed.

2-5. Answer A. GFDICM 2A (FAR 1.2)
According to FAR 1.1, V_{NE} is defined as the never-exceed speed of an aircraft.

2-6 **A02**
14 CFR part 1 defines V_Y as

A — speed for best angle of climb.
B — speed for best rate of climb.
C — speed for best rate of descent.

2-6. Answer B. GFDICM 2A (FAR 1.2)
According to FAR 1.1, V_Y is defined as the speed for the best rate of climb of an aircraft.

2-7 **B08**
What altimeter setting is required when operating an aircraft at 18,000 feet MSL?

A — Altimeter setting at the departure or destination airport.
B — Current reported altimeter setting of a station along the route.
C — 29.92" Hg.

2-7. Answer C. GFDICM 2A (FAR 91.121)
Up to 17,999 feet MSL, you must use the current reported altimeter setting of a station along the route within 100 nautical miles. At or above 18,000 feet MSL, your altimeter must be set to 29.92" Hg.

2-8 **H312**
Which airspeed would a pilot be unable to identify by the color coding of an airspeed indicator?

A — The never-exceed speed.
B — The power-off stall speed.
C — The maneuvering speed.

2-8. Answer C. GFDICM 2A (PHB)
The maneuvering speed, V_A, is the speed at which the airplane will stall before excessive G-forces can build up. However, V_A varies with weight and is, therefore, not depicted on the airspeed indicator. Never-exceed speed, V_{NE}, (answer A) is depicted as the red line on the airspeed indicator. The power-off stall speed (answer B) is depicted as the bottom of the green arc in the clean configuration, and bottom of the white arc with flaps and landing gear in the landing configuration.

2-9 **H314**
Which statement is true about magnetic deviation of a compass? Deviation

A — varies over time as the agonic line shifts.
B — varies for different headings of the same aircraft.
C — is the same for all aircraft in the same locality.

2-9. Answer B. GFDICM 2A (PHB)
Magnetic deviation is the compass error that is caused by the magnetic fields which are produced by the metal and electrical accessories within the airplane. This error distorts the lines of magnetic force produced by the earth and causes the compass to swing away from the correct heading. The amount of error varies from one heading to the next because the lines of force interact at different angles. The agonic line (answer A) is a line that charts the area around the earth where magnetic north and true north are the same. This line shifts slightly over time (same as isogonic lines). Answer (C) is incorrect because compass deviation varies from airplane to airplane depending on equipment installed and compass location.

2-10   H66

At higher elevation airports the pilot should know that indicated airspeed

A — will be unchanged, but groundspeed will be faster.
B — will be higher, but groundspeed will be unchanged.
C — should be increased to compensate for the thinner air.

2-10. Answer A. GFDICM 2A (AFH)

The airspeed indicator displays the speed of your airplane through the air by comparing ram air pressure with static air pressure. The greater the differential, the greater the indicated airspeed. When an indicated airspeed is specified by the manufacturer for a given situation, such as takeoff or landing, you normally should use that speed, regardless of the elevation. At higher elevations the air is less dense so the aircraft must move through the air faster to get the same pressure differential (indicated airspeed). Thus you will have a greater true airspeed resulting in a greater groundspeed. Answers (B) and (C) are incorrect because you use the same indicated airspeed regardless of altitude.

2-11   I04

What is an operational difference between the turn coordinator and the turn-and-slip indicator? The turn coordinator

A — is always electric; the turn-and-slip indicator is always vacuum-driven.
B — indicates bank angle only; the turn-and-slip indicator indicates rate of turn and coordination.
C — indicates roll rate, rate of turn, and coordination; the turn-and-slip indicator indicates rate of turn and coordination.

2-11. Answer C. GFDICM 2A (IFH)

The gyros in both the turn coordinator and turn-and-slip indicator are mounted so that they rotate in the vertical plane. The gimbal in the turn coordinator is set at an angle which means precession allows the gyro to sense both rate of roll and rate of turn. The gimbal in the turn-and-slip indicator is horizontal. In this case, precession allows the gyro to sense only rate of turn. Both the turn coordinator and turn-and-slip indicator have inclinometers which indicate coordination of a turn. Answer (A) is wrong because both the turn coordinator and turn-and-slip indicator can be electric or vacuum-driven. Answer (B) is wrong because the turn coordinator does not indicate the angle of bank.

2-12   I04

What is an advantage of an electric turn coordinator if the airplane has a vacuum system for other gyroscopic instruments?

A — It is a backup in case of vacuum system failure.
B — It is more reliable than the vacuum-driven indicators.
C — It will not tumble as will vacuum-driven turn indicators.

2-12. Answer A. GFDICM 2A (IFH)

On most light airplanes, the vacuum system supplies power to the attitude and heading indicators, while the electrical system powers the turn coordinator. This configuration provides a backup in case one system fails. Answer (B) is not correct because both systems are reliable. Answer (C) is wrong because neither system will cause a gyro to tumble.

2-13   I05

If a standard rate turn is maintained, how long would it take to turn 360°?

A — 1 minute.
B — 2 minutes.
C — 3 minutes.

2-13. Answer B. GFDICM 2A (IFH)

A standard-rate turn is a turn at a rate of three degrees per second. At this rate, you will complete a 360° turn in two minutes. To complete a 360° turn in one minute (answer A), you would have to turn at a rate twice that of standard. A 360° turn completed in three minutes (answer C) requires a turn rate less than standard.

2-14   I22

What are the standard temperature and pressure values for sea level?

A — 15°C and 29.92″ Hg.
B — 59°F and 1013.2″ Hg.
C — 15°C and 29.92 Mb.

2-14. Answer A. GFDICM 2A (AW)

The standard temperature and pressure at sea level are 15°C (59°F) and 29.92 inches of Hg. (1013.2 Mb.) respectively. Answer (B) is wrong because 1013.2 is a Mb. pressure, not a pressure in inches of Hg. Answer (C) is wrong because 29.92 is pressure in inches of Hg. not Mb.

2-15   **H312**

Calibrated airspeed is best described as indicated airspeed corrected for

A — installation and instrument error.
B — instrument error.
C — non-standard temperature.

2-16   **H312**

True airspeed is best described as calibrated airspeed corrected for

A — installation or instrument error.
B — non-standard temperature.
C — altitude and non-standard temperature.

2-17   **I04**

To determine pressure altitude prior to takeoff, the altimeter should be set to

A — the current altimeter setting.
B — 29.92″ Hg and the altimeter indication noted.
C — the field elevation and the pressure reading in the altimeter setting window noted.

2-15. Answer A. GFDICM 2A (AFH)

Calibrated Airspeed (CAS) is the airspeed indicator reading corrected for position (or installation), and instrument errors. CAS is equal to TAS at sea level in standard atmosphere. Answer (B) is incomplete, and Answer (C) is incorrect because temperature does not account for any of the difference between CAS and IAS.

2-16. Answer C. GFDICM 2A

True airspeed is the actual speed the aircraft moves through the airmass. It is what you get when you correct calibrated airspeed for temperature and altitude. Answer (A) is incorrect because it describes the difference between indicated and calibrated airspeed. Answer (B) is incomplete because reduced air density is the reason CAS is less than TAS, and temperature is only part of this.

2-17. Answer B. GFDICM 2A (PHB)

Pressure altitude is indicated on the altimeter when 29.92 is set in the altimeter setting window. You can also determine pressure altitude arithmetically from the current altimeter setting and field elevation. However, if you use only the current altimeter setting (answer A), the altimeter will show indicated altitude. Answer (C) describes a method to obtain an approximate altimeter setting if none other is available, but it does not give you pressure altitude.

SECTION B
ATTITUDE INSTRUMENT FLYING

Chapter 2, Section B, reviews the basic technique and concepts of attitude instrument flying, or controlling an aircraft solely through the use of flight instruments. While this was the cornerstone of your instrument training, it is not a major part of the preparation for your commercial airplane certificate.

SECTION C
INSTRUMENT NAVIGATION

As a commercial pilot, you will refine your instrument interpretation skills to the point where you can easily visualize your position in relation to ground stations. In addition, you will more likely be flying complex or high performance airplanes with more sophisticated navigation equipment and instrumentation.

VOR Navigation

1. There are various types of indicators for VOR navigation, including the basic VOR indicator, the horizontal situation indicator (HSI) and the radio magnetic indicator (RMI).

2. Flying a heading that is the reciprocal to the bearing selected on the OBS would result in reverse sensing on a conventional VOR indicator.

3. An HSI solves nearly all reverse sensing and other visualization problems associated with a conventional VOR indicator. The HSI display combines the VOR indicator with a heading indicator, so the display is automatically rotated to the correct position for you.

4. Each dot on an HSI or conventional VOR course deviation scale is 2° deviation, or 200 feet per nautical mile, when tuned to a VOR. Station passage is indicated by the first positive, complete reversal of the TO/FROM indicator. Unlike a conventional VOR indicator, an HSI gives information about your aircraft heading and its relationship to your intended course.

Time and Distance to a Station

5. You can calculate the time and distance to a station by turning perpendicular to the direct course to the station and measuring the time to move a specific number of degrees to a new radial. [Time to the station] = [Time to move to the new radial x 60] ÷ [Degrees to the new radial]. This formula also works when timing the degrees of change in the magnetic bearing to or from an NDB. EXAMPLE: If it takes 3 minutes to traverse 10 degrees of DME arc, the time to the station is 3 minutes x 60 ÷ 10 = 18 minutes. If your speed is 120 knots (2 n.m. per minute), the distance to the station is 18 x 2 = 36 n.m.

6. To determine time to a station using the isosceles triangle method, turn 10° (or any angle) to the side of your course and twist your course selector the same amount in the opposite direction. Time to station is the same as the time it takes for your CDI to center (assuming no wind).

ADF Navigation

7. To determine time to a station using the isosceles triangle method with an ADF, simply measure the time it takes for the relative bearing (left or right of the aircraft nose) to double while holding a constant heading.

8. The angle between the nose of the aircraft and an NDB is the relative bearing. Magnetic heading (MH) plus relative bearing (RB) equals magnetic bearing to the station (MB).

9. Because a radio magnetic indicator (RMI) has a slaved compass card that automatically rotates to the correct heading, it always displays the bearing to a station at the head of the arrow, and the bearing from a station at the tail of the arrow.

10. A movable card ADF also directly indicates bearing to a station when its compass card is adjusted to agree with the aircraft's actual heading.

11. Most RMIs have two bearing pointer needles, either one of which can be set to point to an NDB or VOR station. The tail of an RMI needle set to a VOR station indicates the radial you are on FROM the station, and the arrowhead indicates the course TO the station.

12. Intercepting a bearing to an NDB is easiest if you choose an angle, such as 45°, that is easy to read on the compass card. To establish a 45° intercept, turn so that the bearing to be intercepted appears over the heading indicator reference mark 45° to the left or right of the aircraft nose. Precisely maintain this heading and look for the ADF needle to also point 45° to the left or right of the aircraft's nose.

13. When turned parallel to the course to the station, the needle indicates any deviation by pointing left or right toward the course. If you simply home to the station with a crosswind, you will fly a curved path to the station.

14. If tracking on course to a station and holding a wind correction, the needle indicates the amount of wind correction, but in the opposite direction. If correcting 10° left, the needle points 10° right of the nose. When homing to a station in high wind conditions, the result is a curved flight path until a direct headwind is reached.

15. When on the desired track outbound with the proper drift correction established, the ADF pointer will be deflected to the windward side of the tail position.

Radio Navigation Operational Considerations

16. At altitudes between 14,500 and 18,000 feet MSL, an (H) Class VORTAC has a usable signal range of 100 nautical miles. Therefore, for direct routes off established airways at these altitudes, the facilities should be no farther apart than 200 nautical miles.

17. A VOR receiver check is required within 30 days prior to an IFR flight. Written documentation of this check is required.

18. When checking your VOR using a VOT, the CDI should be centered and the OBS should indicate that the aircraft is on the 360° radial, ±4°.

19. When using a VOR ground checkpoint, the CDI must center within ±4°. The allowable error using an airborne checkpoint is ±6°. When you conduct a dual system check, the difference between VOR systems should not exceed 4°.

20. VOR and DME facilities transmit their identifiers on a time sharing basis, with the VOR transmitting several identifiers for each one from the DME. If, when tuning to a VORTAC, you receive a single coded identification approximately once every 30 seconds, it means the DME component is operative and the VOR component is inoperative. The reverse is true if you hear the 1,020 Hz VOR signal several times and the 1,350 Hz DME tone is missing over a 30-second interval.

21. If a station is not transmitting an identifier, it means the station is undergoing maintenance and is unreliable, even if you are receiving navigation indications from that station.

Area Navigation

22. Area navigation (RNAV) allows you to fly direct to your destination without the need to overfly VORs or other ground facilities. These systems include VOR/DME RNAV, inertial navigation system (INS), LORAN, and the global positioning system (GPS).

23. GPS provides a 95% probability of horizontal accuracy within 100 meters (328 feet), and a 99.99% probability of accuracy within 300 meters (984 feet).

2-18 **B10**

What is the maximum bearing error (+ or -) allowed for an operational VOR equipment check when using an FAA-approved ground test signal?

A — 6 degrees.

B — 8 degrees.

C — 4 degrees.

2-18. Answer C. GFDICM 2C (FAR 91.171)

A VOR Test (VOT) facility provides the most accurate VOR check. The maximum allowable bearing error with this test is ± 4°.

2-19   **B10**

When must an operational check on the aircraft VOR equipment be accomplished to operate under IFR? Within the preceding

A — 30 days or 30 hours of flight time.
B — 30 days.
C — 10 days or 10 hours of flight time.

2-20   **B10**

Which data must be recorded in the aircraft logbook or other record by a pilot making a VOR operational check for IFR operations?

A — VOR name or identification, place of operational check, amount of bearing error, and date of check.
B — VOR name or identification, amount of bearing error, date of check, and signature.
C — Date of check, place of operational check, bearing error, and signature.

2-21   **H348**

The ADF is tuned to a radiobeacon. If the magnetic heading is 040° and the relative bearing is 290°, the magnetic bearing TO that radiobeacon would be

A — 150°.
B — 285°.
C — 330°.

2-22   **H348**

If the relative bearing to a nondirectional radiobeacon is 045° and the magnetic heading is 355°, the magnetic bearing to that radiobeacon would be

A — 040°.
B — 065°.
C — 220°.

2-19. Answer B. GFDICM 2C (FAR 91.171)
There must be a written record of a VOR accuracy check within the previous 30 days, containing the date and place of the check, the error and signature of the person performing the check.

2-20. Answer C. GFDICM 2C (FAR 91.171)
There must be a written record of a VOR accuracy check within the previous 30 days, containing the date and place of the check, the error and signature of the person performing the check.

2-21. Answer C. GFDICM 2C (IFH)
With a fixed-card ADF indicator, the magnetic bearing TO the station equals your magnetic heading plus your relative bearing TO the station. If the result is greater than 360°, subtract 360°.

MH + RB =MB
040° + 290° = 330°

2-22. Answer A. GFDICM 2C (IFH)
With a fixed-card ADF indicator, the magnetic bearing TO the station equals your magnetic heading plus your relative bearing TO the station. If the result is greater than 360°, subtract 360°.

MH + RB =MB
355° + 045° = 400° - 360° = 040°

2-23   **H348**
(Refer to figure 16 on page 2-10.) If the aircraft continues its present heading as shown in instrument group 3, what will be the relative bearing when the aircraft reaches the magnetic bearing of 030° FROM the NDB?

A — 030°.
B — 060°.
C — 240°.

2-24   **H348**
(Refer to figure 16 on page 2-10.) At the position indicated by instrument group 1, what would be the relative bearing if the aircraft were turned to a magnetic heading of 090°?

A — 150°.
B — 190°.
C — 250°.

2-23. Answer C. GFDICM 2C (IFH)
With a fixed-card ADF indicator, the magnetic bearing TO the station equals your magnetic heading plus your relative bearing TO the station. To figure this relationship, use the standard formula for magnetic bearing TO the station. First, convert the 30° magnetic bearing FROM the NDB to 210°, the magnetic bearing TO the station.

MH + RB = MB (TO)
330° + (unknown) = 030° (TO)
330° + (unknown) = 030° + 180 (FROM)
330° + (unknown) = 210° (FROM)

Next, you solve for relative bearing.

RB = 210° - 330°
RB = -120
RB = -120° + 360°
RB = 240

Note: You must add 360° to convert the relative bearing to a positive value. Answer (A) is wrong because it would place the aircraft due south of the station. Answer (B) is wrong because it would place the aircraft on a 210° bearing FROM the station.

2-24. Answer C. GFDICM 2C (IFH)
With a fixed-card ADF indicator, the magnetic bearing TO the station equals your magnetic heading plus your relative bearing TO the station. If the result is greater than 360°, subtract 360°.

MH + RB = MB
300° + 040° = 340°

When MH is changed from 300° to 090° the MB will not change.

MH + RB = MB
090° + RB = 340°
RB = 340° - 090°
RB = 250°

Answer (A) is incorrect because a relative bearing of 150° would mean the aircraft would have to be on the 240° magnetic bearing TO the station. Answer (B) is incorrect because a relative bearing of 190° would mean the aircraft would have to be on the 280° magnetic bearing TO the station.

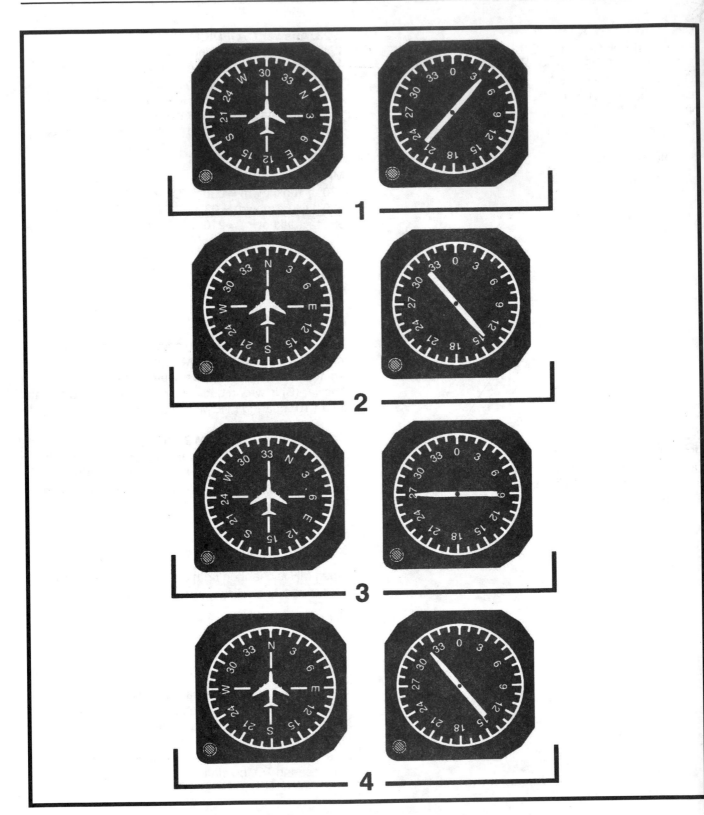

FIGURE 16.—Magnetic Compass/ADF

2-25   **H348**

(Refer to figure 16.) At the position indicated by instrument group 1, to intercept the 330° magnetic bearing to the NDB at a 30° angle, the aircraft should be turned

A — left to a heading of 270°.
B — right to a heading of 330°.
C — right to a heading of 360°.

2-26   **H348**

Which situation would result in reverse sensing of a VOR receiver?

A — Flying a heading that is reciprocal to the bearing selected on the OBS.
B — Setting the OBS to a bearing that is 90° from the bearing on which the aircraft is located.
C — Failing to change the OBS from the selected inbound course to the outbound course after passing the station.

2-27   **H348**

To track outbound on the 180 radial of a VOR station, the recommended procedure is to set the OBS to

A — 360° and make heading corrections toward the CDI needle.
B — 180° and make heading corrections away from the CDI needle.
C — 180° and make heading corrections toward the CDI needle.

2-28   **H348**

To track inbound on the 215 radial of a VOR station, the recommended procedure is to set the OBS to

A — 215° and make heading corrections toward the CDI needle.
B — 215° and make heading corrections away from the CDI needle.
C — 035° and make heading corrections toward the CDI needle.

2-29   **I08**

(Refer to figure 17 on page 2-12.) Which illustration indicates that the airplane will intercept the 060 radial at a 60° angle inbound, if the present heading is maintained?

A — 6.
B — 4.
C — 5.

2-25. Answer C. GFDICM 2C (IFH)
Only two magnetic headings will intercept 330° at a 30° angle, 300° and 360°. In order to intercept the 330° bearing TO the station, a heading of 360° must be flown. A heading of 300° would take you away from the 330° bearing at a 30° angle. Answer (A) is incorrect because a heading of 270° will take you away from the 330° bearing TO the station. Answer (B) is incorrect because a heading of 330° will parallel the 330° bearing.

2-26. Answer A. GFDICM 2C (IFH)
When your course selector is in general agreement with your heading indicator in an off course situation, the CDI will be deflected toward the selected course. However, if you mistakenly set your course selector to the reciprocal of the desired course, your CDI will be deflected away from the course you want to follow. This is known as reverse sensing. Answer (B) is incorrect because a difference of 90° between the radial you are on and that set in the bearing selector should not result in reverse sensing. When tracking a radial inbound with proper sensing, no change is necessary to continue flying outbound with proper CDI sensing (answer C).

2-27. Answer C. GFDICM 2C (IFH)
When tracking a VOR radial, it is important that the course selector indicates the approximate heading (allowing for wind correction) of the airplane. When tracking outbound on the 180° radial, you should have a FROM indication with 180° selected. This will result in proper sensing. If 360° is set (answer A), reverse sensing will exist and corrections will have to be made away from the CDI. Answer (B) is wrong because corrections should be made toward the CDI.

2-28. Answer C. GFDICM 2C (IFH)
When tracking a VOR radial, it is important that the course selector indicates the approximate heading (allowing for wind correction) of the airplane. When tracking inbound on the 215° radial, you should have a TO indication with 035° selected. This will result in proper sensing. If 215° is set (answer A), reverse sensing will exist and corrections will have to be made away from the CDI. Answer (B) is wrong because corrections should be made toward the CDI.

2-29. Answer A. GFDICM 2C (IFH)
To intercept the 060° radial inbound at a 60° angle, the HSI course arrow must be pointing at 240° with a TO indication, and the aircraft's heading needs to be either 300° or 180° (240° + 60° = 300°) or (240° - 60° = 180°).

Answer (B) indicates that you are going to intercept the 060° radial inbound at a 15° angle, and answer (C) shows that you will intercept the 060° radial outbound at a 75° angle.

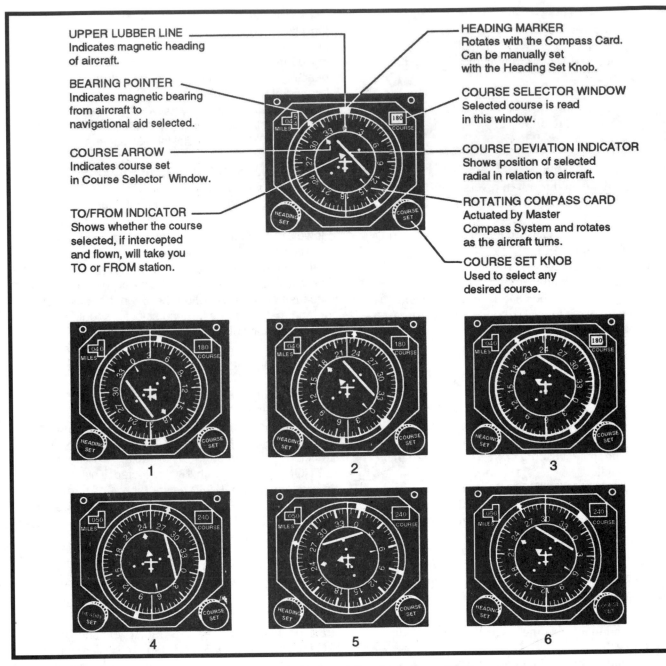

FIGURE 17.—Horizontal Situation Indicator (HSI).

2-30   I08

(Refer to figure 17.) Which statement is true regarding illustration 2, if the present heading is maintained? The airplane will

A — cross the 180 radial at a 45° angle outbound.
B — intercept the 225 radial at a 45° angle.
C — intercept the 360 radial at a 45° angle inbound.

2-30. Answer A. GFDICM 2C (IFH)

The bearing indicator shows that the VOR station is approximately 10° right of the aircraft's nose. If the present heading is maintained (225°), you will intercept the 180° radial outbound with a 45° angle (225° - 180° = 45°). (Note: the magnetic heading of the aircraft appears to be closer to 226° than 225°). Answer (B) is wrong because 225° is the aircraft's heading not the course selected. Since the aircraft will pass south of the station, answer (C) could not be correct.

2-31 **I08**

(Refer to figure 17.) Which illustration indicates that the airplane will intercept the 060 radial at a 75° angle outbound, if the present heading is maintained?

A — 4.
B — 5.
C — 6.

2-32 **I08**

(Refer to figure 17.) Which illustration indicates that the airplane should be turned 150° left to intercept the 360 radial at a 60° angle inbound?

A — 1.
B — 2.
C — 3.

2-33 **I08**

(Refer to figure 17.) Which is true regarding illustration 4 if the present heading is maintained? The airplane will

A — cross the 060 radial at a 15° angle.
B — intercept the 240 radial at a 30° angle.
C — cross the 180 radial at a 75° angle.

2-34 **I08**

(Refer to figure 18 on page 2-14.) To intercept a magnetic bearing of 240° FROM at a 030° angle (while outbound), the airplane should be turned

A — left 065°.
B — left 125°.
C — right 270°.

2-35 **I08**

(Refer to figure 18 on page 2-14.) If the airplane continues to fly on the heading as shown, what magnetic bearing FROM the station would be intercepted at a 35° angle outbound?

A — 035°.
B — 070°.
C — 215°.

2-31. Answer B. GFDICM 2C (IFH)
The TO/FROM indicator in illustration 5 shows that once you intercept the 060° radial, a heading of 240° will take you TO the station. Since your indicated heading is 345°, you will intercept the 060° radial outbound at a 75° angle. Illustration 4 (answer A) shows the aircraft intercepting the 240° radial at a 15° angle, and illustration 6 (answer C) shows the aircraft intercepting the 060° radial at a 120° angle.

2-32. Answer A. GFDICM 2C (IFH)
In order to intercept the 360° radial inbound at a 60° angle, the aircraft must be on a heading of 240° (180° + 60° = 240°) and the course arrow must be pointing at 180° with a TO indication. Illustration 1 is the only illustration that, after completing a 150° turn, would indicate this. Illustrations 2 and 3 (answers B and C) are inappropriate since both would take you away from the 360° radial.

2-33. Answer C. GFDICM 2C (IFH)
The bearing indicator shows you are on the 095° radial. If you maintain the present heading (255°), you will intercept the 180° radial outbound with a 75° angle (255° - 180° = 75°). Answer (A) is wrong because you will never intercept the 060° radial with a 255°. Answer (B) is incorrect because when you intercept the 240° radial, it will be at a 15° angle not 30°.

2-34. Answer B. GFDICM 2C (IFH)
The tail of the bearing indicator shows that you are on the 165° bearing (southeast) FROM the station (130° + 35° = 165°). To intercept the 240° bearing (southwest) FROM the station, you must first turn left. The heading required to intercept the 240° bearing FROM can be calculated by adding the intercept angle (030°) to 240°. Your new heading is 270° (30° + 240° = 270°). To determine the number of degrees to turn calculate the difference between your present heading (035°) and your new heading (270°). The answer is 125°.

2-35. Answer B. GFDICM 2C (IFH)
You are currently on the 165° bearing FROM the station (130° + 35° = 165°) heading 035°. Since you are southeast of the station, you can determine the bearing you will intercept by adding the angle of intercept to your heading. The answer is 070° (35° + 35° = 70°). You would intercept the 035° bearing FROM (answer A) if your heading was 360°, and you would intercept the 215° bearing FROM (answer C) if your heading was 250°.

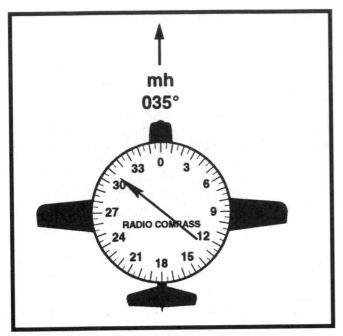

FIGURE 18.—Magnetic Heading/Radio Compass.

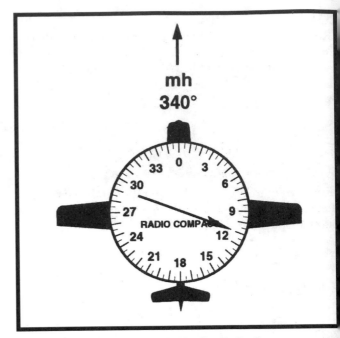

FIGURE 19.—Magnetic Heading/Radio Compass.

2-36   **I08**

(Refer to figure 19.) If the airplane continues to fly on the magnetic heading as illustrated, what magnetic bearing FROM the station would be intercepted at a 35° angle?

A — 090°.
B — 270°.
C — 305°.

2-37   **I08**

(Refer to figure 19.) If the airplane continues to fly on the magnetic heading as illustrated, what magnetic bearing FROM the station would be intercepted at a 30° angle?

A — 090°.
B — 270°.
C — 310°.

2-38   **I08**

The relative bearing on an ADF changes from 265° to 260° in 2 minutes of elapsed time. If the groundspeed is 145 knots, the distance to that station would be

A — 26 NM.
B — 37 NM.
C — 58 NM.

2-36. Answer C. GFDICM 2C (IFH)
You are on the 270° bearing FROM the station (340° - 70° = 270°) heading 340°. Since you are northwest of the station, you can determine the bearing you will intercept by subtracting the intercept angle (35°) from your heading. The answer is 305° (340° - 35° = 305°). Answers (A) and (B) are inappropriate.

2-37. Answer C. GFDICM 2C (IFH)
You are on the 270° bearing FROM the station (340° - 70° = 270°) heading 340°. Since you are northwest of the station, you can determine the bearing you will intercept by subtracting the intercept angle (30°) from your heading. The answer is 310° (340° - 30° = 310°). Answers (A) and (B) are inappropriate.

2-38. Answer C. GFDICM 2C (IFH)
You can estimate the distance to an NDB by using the formula (TAS x minutes flown) ÷ degrees of bearing change. To solve this problem, you have to assume that your groundspeed is equal to your true airspeed. The answer is 58 n.m. (145 x 2) ÷ 5 = 58. Answers (A) and (B) are substantially less than the actual distance.

2-39　　　　I08
The ADF indicates a wingtip bearing change of 10° in 2 minutes of elapsed time, and the TAS is 160 knots. What is the distance to the station?

A — 15 NM.
B — 32 NM.
C — 36 NM.

2-40　　　　I08
With a TAS of 115 knots, the relative bearing on an ADF changes from 090° to 095° in 1.5 minutes of elapsed time. The distance to the station would be

A — 12.5 NM.
B — 24.5 NM.
C — 34.5 NM.

2-41　　　　I08
GIVEN:

Wingtip bearing change..5°
Time elapsed between bearing change................5 min
True airspeed..115 kts

The distance to the station is

A — 36 NM.
B — 57.5 NM.
C — 115 NM.

2-42　　　　I08
The ADF is tuned to a nondirectional radiobeacon and the relative bearing changes from 095° to 100° in 1.5 minutes of elapsed time. The time en route to that station would be

A — 18 minutes.
B — 24 minutes.
C — 30 minutes.

2-43　　　　I08
The ADF is tuned to a nondirectional radiobeacon and the relative bearing changes from 270° to 265° in 2.5 minutes of elapsed time. The time en route to that beacon would be

A — 9 minutes.
B — 18 minutes.
C — 30 minutes.

2-39. Answer B. GFDICM 2C (IFH)
You can estimate the distance to an NDB by using the formula (TAS x minutes flown) ÷ degrees of bearing change. The answer is 32 n.m. (160 x 2) ÷ 10 = 32.

2-40. Answer C. GFDICM 2C (IFH)
You can estimate the distance to an NDB by using the formula (TAS x minutes flown) ÷ degrees of bearing change. The answer is 34.5 (115 x 1.5) ÷ 5 = 34.5.

2-41. Answer C. GFDICM 2C (IFH)
You can estimate the distance to an NDB by using the formula (TAS x minutes flown) ÷ degrees of bearing change. The answer is 115 n.m. (115 x 5) ÷ 5 = 115.

2-42. Answer A. GFDICM 2C (IFH)
You can calculate the estimated time to an NDB station by using the formula (time in seconds ÷ degrees of bearing change). The answer is 18 minutes (90 ÷ 5 = 18).

2-43. Answer C. GFDICM 2C (IFH)
You can calculate the estimated time to an NDB station by using the formula (time in seconds ÷ degrees of bearing change). The answer is 30 minutes (150 ÷ 5 = 30).

2-44 I08

The ADF is tuned to a nondirectional radiobeacon and the relative bearing changes from 085° to 090° in 2 minutes of elapsed time. The time en route to the station would be

A — 15 minutes.
B — 18 minutes.
C — 24 minutes.

2-44. Answer C. GFDICM 2C (IFH)
You can calculate the estimated time to an NDB station by using the formula (time in seconds ÷ degrees of bearing change). The answer is 24 minutes (120 ÷ 5 = 24).

2-45 I08

If the relative bearing changes from 090° to 100° in 2.5 minutes of elapsed time, the time en route to the station would be

A — 12 minutes.
B — 15 minutes.
C — 18 minutes.

2-45. Answer B. GFDICM 2C (IFH)
You can calculate the estimated time to an NDB station by using the formula (time in seconds ÷ degrees of bearing change). The answer is 15 minutes (150 ÷ 10 = 15).

2-46 I08

The ADF is tuned to a nondirectional radiobeacon and the relative bearing changes from 090° to 100° in 2.5 minutes of elapsed time. If the true airspeed is 90 knots, the distance and time en route to that radiobeacon would be

A — 15 miles and 22.5 minutes.
B — 22.5 miles and 15 minutes.
C — 32 miles and 18 minutes.

2-46. Answer B. GFDICM 2C (IFH)
You can estimate the distance to an NDB by using the formula (TAS x minutes flown) ÷ degrees of bearing change. The answer is 22.5 miles (90 × 2.5) ÷ 10 = 22.5.

To determine the time to an NDB station use the formula (time in seconds ÷ degrees of bearing change). The answer is 15 minutes (150 ÷ 10 = 15).

2-47 I08
GIVEN:

Wingtip bearing change ....10°
Elapsed time between bearing change ....4 min
Rate of fuel consumption ....11 gal/hr

Calculate the fuel required to fly to the station.

A — 4.4 gallons.
B — 8.4 gallons.
C — 12 gallons.

2-47. Answer A. GFDICM 2C (IFH)
To solve this problem you must first calculate the time to the station. You can do this by using the formula (time in seconds ÷ degrees of bearing change). The estimated time enroute (ETE) is 24 minutes (240 ÷ 10 = 24).

To determine the fuel required, multiply your ETE by the fuel consumption rate (11 gal/hr). The fuel required is 4.4 gallons (0:24:00 × 11 = 4.4).

2-48 I08
GIVEN:

Wingtip bearing change ....5°
Elapsed time between bearing change ....6 min
Rate of fuel consumption ....12 gal/hr

The fuel required to fly to the station is

A — 8.2 gallons.
B — 14.4 gallons.
C — 18.7 gallons.

2-48. Answer B. GFDICM 2C (IFH)
To solve this problem you must first calculate the time to the station. You can do this by using the formula (time in seconds ÷ degrees of bearing change). The estimated time enroute (ETE) is 72 minutes (360 ÷ 5 = 72).

To determine the fuel required, multiply your ETE by the fuel consumption rate (12 gal/hr). The fuel required is 14.4 gallons (0:72:00 × 12 = 14.4).

2-49 I08

GIVEN:

Wingtip bearing change ....15°
Elapsed time between bearing change ....6 min
Rate of fuel consumption ....8.6 gal/hr

Calculate the approximate fuel required to fly to the station.

A — 3.44 gallons.
B — 6.88 gallons.
C — 17.84 gallons.

2-50 I08

GIVEN:

Wingtip bearing change ....15°
Elapsed time between bearing change ....7.5 min
True airspeed ....85 kts
Rate of fuel consumption ....9.6 gal/hr

The time, distance, and fuel required to fly to the station is

A — 30 minutes; 42.5 miles; 4.80 gallons.
B — 32 minutes; 48 miles; 5.58 gallons.
C — 48 minutes; 48 miles; 4.58 gallons.

2-51 I08

While maintaining a constant heading, a relative bearing of 15° doubles in 6 minutes. The time to the station being used is

A — 3 minutes.
B — 6 minutes.
C — 12 minutes.

2-52 I08

While maintaining a constant heading, the ADF needle increases from a relative bearing of 045° to 090° in 5 minutes. The time to the station being used is

A — 5 minutes.
B — 10 minutes.
C — 15 minutes.

2-49. Answer A. GFDICM 2C (IFH)
To solve this problem you must first calculate the time to the station. You can do this by using the formula (time in seconds ÷ degrees of bearing change). The estimated time enroute (ETE) is 24 minutes (360 ÷ 15 = 24).

To determine the fuel required, multiply your ETE by the fuel consumption rate (8.6 gal/hr). The fuel required is 3.44 gallons (0:24:00 × 8.6 = 3.44).

2-50. Answer A. GFDICM 2C (IFH)
To solve this problem you must calculate the estimated time enroute (ETE), the distance to the station, and the fuel required.

To determine the ETE to the station use the formula (time in seconds ÷ degrees of bearing change). The answer is 30 minutes (450 ÷ 15 = 30).

You can estimate the distance to the NDB by using the formula (TAS x minutes flown) ÷ degrees of bearing change. The answer is 42.5 miles (85 x 7.5) ÷ 15 = 42.5.

To determine the fuel required, multiply your ETE by the fuel consumption rate (9.6 gal/hr). The answer is 4.80 gallons (0:30:00 x 9.6 = 4.80).

2-51. Answer B. GFDICM 2C (IFH)
When not on a heading perpendicular to a bearing or radial, the estimated time enroute to the station will equal the time it takes to double the relative bearing. You can tell you are not perpendicular to the station because your relative bearing is less than 90°. The answer is 6 minutes. Answers (A) and (C) are inappropriate.

2-52. Answer A. GFDICM 2C (IFH)
When not on a heading perpendicular to a bearing or radial, the estimated time enroute to the station will equal the time it takes to double the relative bearing. The answer is 5 minutes.

2-53   I08

While cruising at 135 knots and on a constant heading, the ADF needle decreases from a relative bearing of 315° to 270° in 7 minutes. The approximate time and distance to the station being used is

A — 7 minutes and 16 miles.
B — 14 minutes and 28 miles.
C — 19 minutes and 38 miles.

2-54   I08

While maintaining a constant heading, a relative bearing of 10° doubles in 5 minutes. If the true airspeed is 105 knots, the time and distance to the station being used is approximately

A — 5 minutes and 8.7 miles.
B — 10 minutes and 17 miles.
C — 15 minutes and 31.2 miles.

2-55   I08

When checking the course sensitivity of a VOR receiver, how many degrees should the OBS be rotated to move the CDI from the center to the last dot on either side?

A — 5° to 10°.
B — 10° to 12°.
C — 18° to 20°.

2-56   I08

An aircraft 60 miles from a VOR station has a CDI indication of one-fifth deflection, this represents a course centerline deviation of approximately

A — 6 miles.
B — 2 miles.
C — 1 mile.

2-57   I08

(Refer to figure 20 on page 2-19.) Using instrument group 3, if an aircraft makes a 180° turn to the left and continues straight ahead, it will intercept which radial?

A — 135 radial.
B — 270 radial.
C — 360 radial.

2-53. Answer A. GFDICM 2C (IFH)

When not on a heading perpendicular to a bearing or radial, the estimated time enroute to the station will equal the time it takes to double the relative bearing. A relative bearing of 315° is equivalent to having the station 45° off the nose. When you reach the 270° relative bearing, the station will be 90° off the nose. In essence, you double the relative bearing (45° to 90°) in 7 minutes. The answer is 7 minutes.

You can estimate the distance to the NDB by multiplying the time to the station by the aircraft's speed. The answer is 16 miles (0:07:00 × 135 = 15.75).

2-54. Answer A. GFDICM 2C (IFH)

When not on a heading perpendicular to a bearing or radial, the estimated time enroute to the station will equal the time it takes to double the relative bearing. The answer is 5 minutes.

You can estimate the distance to the NDB by multiplying the time to the station by the aircraft's speed. The answer is 8.7 miles (0:05:00 × 105 = 8.7).

2-55. Answer B. GFDICM 2C (IFH)

Course sensitivity may be checked by noting the number of degrees of change in the course selected as you rotate the course selector to move the CDI from the center to the last dot on either side. This should be between 10° and 12°. Answer (A) is wrong because VOR sensitivity is between 10° and 12°, not 5° and 10°. Answer (C) is wrong because it substantially exceeds the 10° to 12° sensitivity range.

2-56. Answer B. GFDICM 2C (IFH)

In addition to telling you the number of degrees off course you are, the course deviation dots may also be used to estimate your lateral distance TO or FROM a selected radial. To make this computation, multiply your distance from the VOR by 200 feet per dot of deflection and divide by 6,076 (feet per n.m.). Each dot equals about a one-fifth deflection. The answer is 2 miles (60 x 200 = 12,000 ÷ 6,076 = 1.97). Answer (A), 6 miles, represents the distance off course with a three-dot deflection, and answer (C), 1 mile, represents the off-course distance with a half-dot deflection.

2-57. Answer A. GFDICM 2C (IFH)

Prior to making the turn, the RMI indicates you are on a heading of 300° and the tail of the VOR needle indicates that you are on the 135° radial. After making a 180° turn, you will be heading 120° which will reintercept the 135° radial outbound. To intercept the 270° radial (answer B) you would have to continue straight ahead, and to intercept the 360° radial (answer C) you would have to make a 20° to 60° right turn.

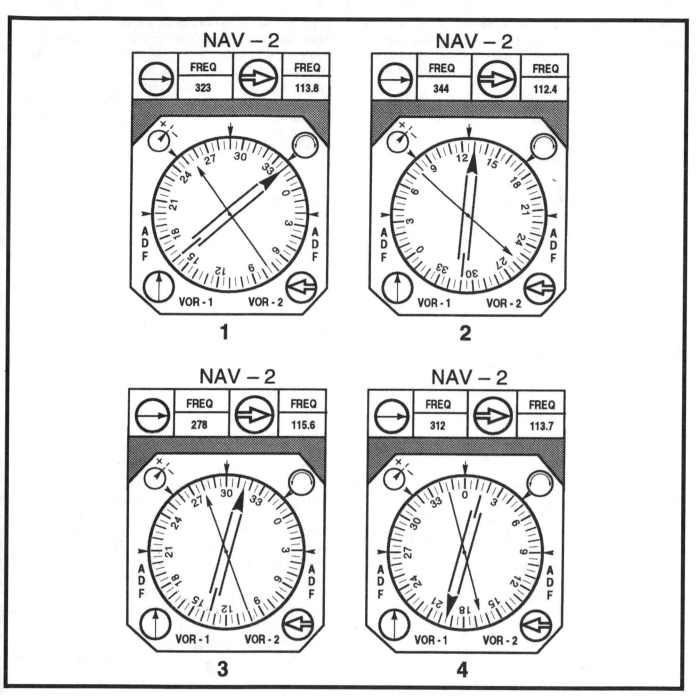

FIGURE 20.—Radio Magnetic Indicator (RMI).

2-58   **I08**
(Refer to figure 20.) Which instrument shows the aircraft in a position where a 180° turn would result in the aircraft intercepting the 150 radial at a 30° angle?

A — 2.
B — 3.
C — 4.

2-58. Answer C. GFDICM 2C (IFH)
To intercept the 150° radial at a 30° angle after making the turn, you would have to fly on a heading of 180° or 120°. The only illustrations that would indicate either of these headings are illustrations 3 and 4. After the turn, illustration 4 would indicate you are heading south (180°) towards the 150° radial. Illustration 3 (answer B) would indicate that you are heading southeast (120°) away from the 150° radial. Answer (A) is inappropriate.

2-59   I08

(Refer to figure 20 on page 2-19.) Which instrument shows the aircraft in a position where a straight course after a 90° left turn would result in intercepting the 180 radial?

A — 2.
B — 3.
C — 4.

2-60   I08

(Refer to figure 20 on page 2-19.) Which instrument shows the aircraft to be northwest of the VORTAC?

A — 1.
B — 2.
C — 3.

2-61   I08

(Refer to figure 20 on page 2-19.) Which instrument(s) show(s) that the aircraft is getting further from the selected VORTAC?

A — 4.
B — 1 and 4.
C — 2 and 3.

2-62   I08

While maintaining a magnetic heading of 270° and a true airspeed of 120 knots, the 360 radial of a VOR is crossed at 1237 and the 350 radial is crossed at 1244. The approximate time and distance to this station are

A — 42 minutes and 84 NM.
B — 42 minutes and 91 NM.
C — 44 minutes and 96 NM.

2-59. Answer B. GFDICM 2C (IFH)
After a 90° left turn, illustration 3 would indicate that you are southeast of the station (135° radial) heading 210° towards the 180° radial. Answer (A), illustration 2, would indicate you are northwest of the station (310° radial) heading 035° away from the 180° radial. Answer (C), illustration 4, would indicate you are northeast of the station (015° radial) heading 270° away from the 180° radial.

2-60. Answer B. GFDICM 2C (IFH)
You can identify the radial you are on by looking at the tail of VOR bearing indicator. Illustration 2 indicates that you are on the 310° radial (northwest). Answers (A) and (C) indicate you are on the 160° and 135° radials southeast of the station.

2-61. Answer A. GFDICM 2C (IFH)
The head of the VOR indicator always points directly to the VOR station. In these examples, illustration 4 is the only indicator that shows you are heading away from the station. Illustrations 1 (answer B), and 2 and 3 (answer C) indicate that you are getting closer to the VOR.

2-62. Answer A. GFDICM 2C (IFH)
To solve this problem you must calculate the estimated time enroute (ETE), the distance to the station.

To determine the ETE to the station use the formula (time in seconds ÷ degrees of bearing change). The answer is 42 minutes (420 ÷ 10 = 42).

You can estimate the distance to the VOR by using the formula (TAS × minutes flown) ÷ degrees of bearing change. The answer is 84 n.m. (0:42:00 × 120 = 84). Answer (B) is wrong because you are only 84 n.m. from the VOR, not 91 n.m., and answer (C) is inappropriate.

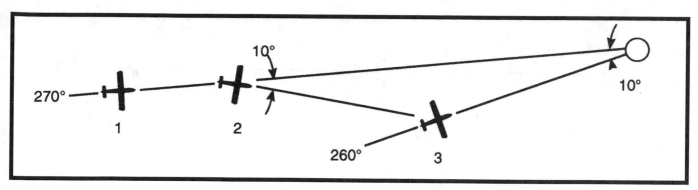

FIGURE 21.—Isosceles Triangle.

2-63   **I08**

(Refer to figure 21.) If the time flown between aircraft positions 2 and 3 is 13 minutes, what is the estimated time to the station?

A — 13 minutes.
B — 17 minutes.
C — 26 minutes.

2-63. Answer A. GFDICM 2C (IFH)
When not on a heading perpendicular to a bearing or radial, the time to the station equals the time required to double the relative bearing. Figure 21 shows aircraft 2 has a relative bearing of 10°. Prior to turning inbound, aircraft 3 would have a relative bearing of 20°. The estimated time to the station is 13 minutes. Answers (B) and (C) substantially exceed the 13 minutes required.

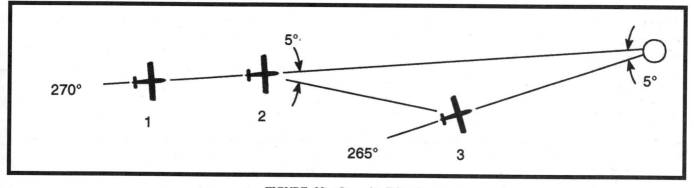

FIGURE 22.—Isosceles Triangle.

2-64   **I08**

(Refer to figure 22.) If the time flown between aircraft positions 2 and 3 is 8 minutes, what is the estimated time to the station?

A — 8 minutes.
B — 16 minutes.
C — 48 minutes.

2-64. Answer A. GFDICM 2C (IFH)
When not on a heading perpendicular to a bearing or radial, the time to the station equals the time required to double the relative bearing. The relative bearing to the station for aircraft 2 is 5°. The relative bearing of aircraft 3 prior to turning is 10°. The estimated time to the station is 8 minutes.

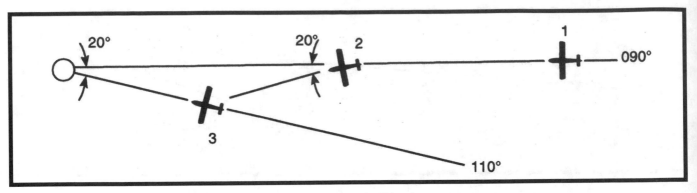

Figure 23.—Isosceles Triangle.

2-65   I08
(Refer to figure 23.) If the time flown between aircraft positions 2 and 3 is 13 minutes, what is the estimated time to the station?

A — 7.8 minutes.
B — 13 minutes.
C — 26 minutes.

2-65. Answer B. GFDICM 2C (IFH)
When not on a heading perpendicular to a bearing or radial, the time to the station equals the time required to double the relative bearing. The relative bearing to the station for aircraft 2 is 20°. The relative bearing of aircraft 3 prior to turning is 40°. The estimated time to the station is 13 minutes.

2-66   I08
(Refer to figure 24.) If the time flown between aircraft positions 2 and 3 is 15 minutes, what is the estimated time to the station?

A — 15 minutes.
B — 30 minutes.
C — 60 minutes.

2-66. Answer A. GFDICM 2C (IFH)
When not on a heading perpendicular to a bearing or radial, the time to the station equals the time required to double the relative bearing. The relative bearing to the station for aircraft 2 is 15°. The relative bearing of aircraft 3 prior to turning is 30°. The estimated time to the station is 15 minutes.

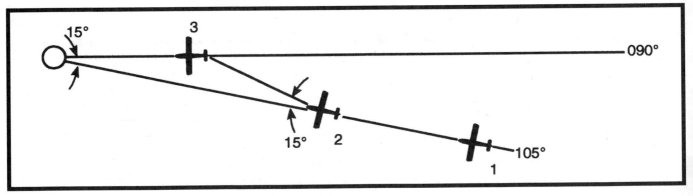

FIGURE 24.—Isosceles Triangle.

2-67   I08
Inbound on the 040 radial, a pilot selects the 055 radial, turns 15° to the left, and notes the time. While maintaining a constant heading, the pilot notes the time for the CDI to center is 15 minutes. Based on this information, the ETE to the station is

A — 8 minutes.
B — 15 minutes.
C — 30 minutes.

2-67. Answer B. GFDICM 2C (IFH)
When not on a heading perpendicular to a bearing or radial, the time to the station equals the time required to double the relative bearing or, in this case, the time required to achieve a 15° radial change. The heading change and the radial change must be the same. The estimated time to the VOR is 15 minutes.

2-68   I08

Inbound on the 090 radial, a pilot rotates the OBS 010° to the left, turns 010° to the right, and notes the time. While maintaining a constant heading, the pilot determines that the elapsed time for the CDI to center is 8 minutes. Based on this information, the ETE to the station is

A — 8 minutes.
B — 16 minutes.
C — 24 minutes.

2-68. Answer A. GFDICM 2C (IFH)

When not on a heading perpendicular to a bearing or radial, the time to the station equals the time required to double the relative bearing or, in this case, the time required to achieve a 10° radial change. The heading change and radial change must be the same. The estimated time to the VOR is 8 minutes.

2-69   I08

Inbound on the 315 radial, a pilot selects the 320 radial, turns 5° to the left, and notes the time. While maintaining a constant heading, the pilot notes the time for the CDI to center is 12 minutes. The ETE to the station is

A — 10 minutes.
B — 12 minutes.
C — 24 minutes.

2-69. Answer B. GFDICM 2C (IFH)

When not on a heading perpendicular to a bearing or radial, the time to the station equals the time required to double the relative bearing or, in this case, the time required to achieve a 5° radial change. The heading change and radial change must be the same. The estimated time to the VOR is 12 minutes.

2-70   I08

Inbound on the 190 radial, a pilot selects the 195 radial, turns 5° to the left, and notes the time. While maintaining a constant heading, the pilot notes the time for the CDI to center is 10 minutes. The ETE to the station is

A — 10 minutes.
B — 15 minutes.
C — 20 minutes.

2-70. Answer A. GFDICM 2C (IFH)

When not on a heading perpendicular to a bearing or radial, the time to the station equals the time required to double the relative bearing or, in this case, the time required to achieve a 5° radial change. The heading change and radial change must be the same. The estimated time to the VOR is 10 minutes.

2-71   J01

How should the pilot make a VOR receiver check when the aircraft is located on the designated checkpoint on the airport surface?

A — Set the OBS on 180° plus or minus 4°; the CDI should center with a FROM indication.
B — Set the OBS on the designated radial. The CDI must center within plus or minus 4° of that radial with a FROM indication.
C — With the aircraft headed directly toward the VOR and the OBS set to 000°, the CDI should center within plus or minus 4° of that radial with a TO indication.

2-71. Answer B. GFDICM 2C (IFH)

When making a VOR receiver check at a designated ground checkpoint, you must set the course selector to the specified radial and the CDI must center within ± 4° of the radial. If you are at the correct location, the TO/FROM will indicate FROM. You can find a list of designated ground checkpoints in the Airport/Facility Directory. Answer (A) is wrong because 180° is not the only radial that may be used. In addition, if you are using a VOR test facility (VOT) with 180°, the TO/FROM indicator will display TO. Answer (C) is wrong because it doesn't matter what the aircraft's heading is and 000° is not the only radial used. In addition, if using a VOT with 000°, the indicator will be FROM.

2-72   J01

When using VOT to make a VOR receiver check, the CDI should be centered and the OBS should indicate that the aircraft is on the

A — 090 radial.
B — 180 radial.
C — 360 radial.

2-72. Answer C. GFDICM 2C (AIM)

A VOR test facility (VOT) emulates a 360° radial. Therefore, when conducting a VOT, the course selector should indicate 360° with a FROM indication, or 180° with a TO indication. Answer (A) is wrong because a VOT is never made on the 090° radial, and answer (B) is wrong because although the course selector can show 180°, the TO indication means you are on a simulated 360° radial.

2-73   **J01**

When the CDI needle is centered during an airborne VOR check, the omnibearing selector and the TO/FROM indicator should read

A — within 4° of the selected radial.
B — within 6° of the selected radial.
C — 0° TO, only if you are due south of the VOR.

2-73. Answer B. GFDICM 2C (AIM)

Airborne check points consist of certified radials that should be received at specific points over predetermined landmarks in the immediate vicinity of an airport. When making an airborne check, the course selector must indicate the designated radial and the CDI must be within 6° of the selected radial with a FROM indication. Answer (A) is wrong because it indicates the permissible error for ground checks. Answer (C) is inappropriate.

THE FLIGHT ENVIRONMENT

SECTION A
AIRPORTS, AIRSPACE, AND FLIGHT INFORMATION

Chapter 3, Section A of the Instrument Commercial Manual contains essential information for instrument and commercial pilots. It emphasizes IFR operations and does not include VFR chart information, since this is considered private pilot knowledge. Nonetheless, a number of FAA commercial questions covering VFR charts appear here, since this material is most closely related to airports, airspace, and flight information.

Airport Markings

1. Mandatory instruction signs, such as those marking hold lines consist of white lettering on a red background. A hold line painted on the pavement consists of four yellow lines, with the two dashed lines nearest the runway.

2. A mandatory instruction sign has white lettering on a red background.

3. Remain outside of the ILS hold line if asked to hold short of the ILS critical area, and completely pass this line when exiting the runway during ILS operations.

Airspace

Controlled Airspace

4. Controlled airspace includes Class A, B, C, D, and Class E airspace. It is where air traffic control service is available to pilots. When you are operating under IFR, you must comply with ATC clearances.

5. You must have an operating transponder with Mode C (or Mode S) capability in Class A and B airspace and within 30 nautical miles of Class B primary airports. This equipment is also required in and above Class C airspace, and at or above 10,000 feet MSL, except at and below 2,500 feet AGL.

6. Below 10,000 feet MSL, basic VFR visibility is 3 statute miles in controlled airspace and 1 mile in uncontrolled airspace. Cloud clearance requirements within 1,200 feet of the surface in uncontrolled airspace, and in Class B airspace, is simply clear of clouds. Otherwise, you must maintain 1,000 feet above, 500 feet below, and 2,000 feet horizontal distance from clouds. Above 10,000 feet MSL and more than 1,200 feet above the surface, required flight visibility increases to 5 miles in both controlled and uncontrolled airspace with 1 mile horizontal and 1,000-foot vertical separation required from clouds.

Class A Airspace

7. Most Class A airspace extends from 18,000 feet MSL up to and including FL600. You are required to use an altimeter setting of 29.92 in. Hg., you must be rated and current for instrument flight, your aircraft must be equipped for IFR and you must be operating on an IFR clearance at an altitude assigned by ATC. DME is required at or above FL 240 where a VOR is required, with exceptions for in-flight failure.

Class B Airspace

8. Most Class B airspace is from the surface to 10,000 feet MSL. You must be at least a private pilot, or a student pilot with the appropriate endorsement, and must receive an ATC clearance before entering this airspace. Some Class B areas completely prohibit student pilot operations. Among other requirements for flight within Class B airspace, your aircraft must be equipped with either a Mode S or a 4096-code transponder that has Mode C altitude reporting equipment.

Class C Airspace

9. Class C airspace normally resides in 5 and 10 nautical mile circles extending outward from a primary airport. An outer area with radar coverage outside Class C airspace extends to 20 n.m. From 5 to 10 n.m. from the airport, Class C airspace generally begins at about 1,200 feet above the primary airport surface and extends to approximately 4,000 feet above the airport. Within 5 n.m. of the primary airport, Class C airspace is from the surface to about 4,000 feet AGL.

10. Radio contact is encouraged within the 20 n.m. outer area and required prior to entering Class C airspace. If you depart a satellite airport within Class C airspace, you must establish two-way communication with ATC as soon as practicable after takeoff.

Class D Airspace

11. Class D airspace exists at airports with operating control towers which are not associated with Class B or C airspace. Normally, the upper limit of Class D airspace is about 2,500 feet above the surface of the primary airport and the lateral limits are approximately 4 nautical miles from the primary airport.

12. Two-way radio communication with the control tower must be established prior to entering this airspace or taking off from the primary airport. Pilots taking off from satellite airports within Class D airspace must check in with the tower as soon as practicable.

13. At part-time tower locations, Class D airspace normally becomes Class E airspace when the tower is closed, or Class G if weather observations and reporting are not available.

Class E Airspace

14. The remaining controlled airspace includes Federal airways, which are normally 8 nautical miles wide, begin at 1,200 feet AGL and extend up to 17,999 feet MSL. Transition areas are depicted with magenta shading on sectional charts, for certain airports with approved instrument approach procedures. These areas of Class E airspace typically begin at 700 feet AGL and extend to the overlying controlled airspace.

15. At some nontower airports, Class E airspace extends upward from the surface, and typically encompasses a 4 n.m. circle around the airport, in addition to extensions to accommodate arrivals and departures. These are depicted with dashed magenta lines on VFR charts.

16. At almost all remaining U.S. locations where Class E airspace is not designated at a lower altitude, it begins at 14,500 feet MSL (except within 1,500 feet of the surface) and extends up to 17,999 feet MSL.

Special VFR

17. When the weather is below basic VFR minimums, as indicated by daytime operation of a rotating beacon, you may obtain a special VFR (SVFR) clearance from the ATC facility controlling the airspace at selected airports. Ground (or flight) visibility must be at least 1 statute mile and you must remain clear of clouds. An instrument rating and IFR equipped airplane are required for SVFR after sunset and it is not allowed at airports indicating "No SVFR" on aeronautical charts.

Class G Airspace

18. Class G airspace is that area which has not been designated as Class A, B, C, D, or E airspace. It is uncontrolled by ATC. For example, the airspace below a Class E airspace area or below a Victor airway is normally uncontrolled. Most Class G airspace terminates at the base of Class E airspace at 700 or 1,200 feet AGL, or at 14,500 feet MSL.

Aircraft Speed Limits

19. The speed limit is 250 knots indicated airspeed (KIAS) below 10,000 feet MSL and 200 KIAS within 4 nautical miles of the primary airport of Class C or Class D airspace within 2,500 feet of the surface. The 200 KIAS limit also applies to the airspace underlying Class B airspace or in a VFR corridor through such airspace. Aircraft that cannot safely operate at these speeds are exempt.

Special Use Airspace

20. Military operations areas (MOAs) separate certain military training activities from IFR traffic. You may be cleared IFR through an active MOA only if ATC can provide separation.

21. Military training routes (MTRs) are depicted as thin, black, shaded lines on VFR charts. You could encounter military traffic exceeding 250 knots below 10,000 feet MSL along these routes.

Other Airspace Areas

22. An airport advisory area is within 10 statute miles of an airport with an FSS but no control tower. At these locations, the FSS provides local airport advisory (LAA) service.

Obstruction Lighting

23. Red or white beacons/flashing lights are used to mark man-made obstructions and hazards to aerial navigation when the obstruction is not in the vicinity of an airport. Steady red lights are used to mark obstructions and hazards in the vicinity of an airport, including end-of-runway lights.

Land and Hold Short Operations (LAHSO)

24. LASHO clearances can be issued by ATC when the ceiling and visibility limits are above basic VFR minimums of 1,000 feet and 3 statute miles. It is the responsibility of the pilot-in-command to determine if the clearance can be safely executed, including determining that the available length of runway is adequate to adhere to the clearance.

Flight Information

Airport/Facility Directory

25. The *Airport/Facility Directory* (A/FD) is a series of regional books with FAA information for public-use civil airports, associated terminal control facilities, air route traffic control centers, and radio aids to navigation.

26. When planning night cross-country flights, airport and enroute lighting should be considered. This should include determining the availability and type of lighting at the destination, enroute, and alternate airports.

Aeronautical Information Manual

27. The *Aeronautical Information Manual* (AIM) contains fundamental information required for both VFR and IFR flight operations within the National Airspace System. It is a major reference for this Study Guide.

Notices To Airmen

28. NOTAM(D) information is disseminated for all navigational facilities that are part of the National Airspace System, all public use airports, seaplane bases, and heliports listed in the *Airport/Facility Directory*. NOTAM(L) information is distributed locally and includes items such as taxiway closures, construction activities near runways, snow conditions, and changes in the status of airport lighting, such as VASI, that do not affect instrument approach criteria. FDC NOTAMs are used to disseminate information that is regulatory in nature. Examples are amendments to aeronautical charts, changes to instrument approach procedures, and temporary flight restrictions.

3-1   **J08**

What designated airspace associated with an airport becomes inactive when the control tower at that airport is not in operation?

A — Class D, which then becomes Class C.
B — Class D, which then becomes Class E.
C — Class B.

3-1. Answer B. ICM 3A (FAR 1.1)
An Airport Traffic Area (Class D Airspace) exists only when the control tower is in operation. When the tower closes the airspace becomes Class E.

3-2   A66
Excluding Hawaii, the vertical limits of the Federal Low Altitude airways extend from

A — 700 feet AGL up to, but not including, 14,500 feet MSL.
B — 1,200 feet AGL up to, but not including, 18,000 feet MSL.
C — 1,200 feet AGL up to, but not including, 14,500 feet MSL.

3-3   B11
A coded transponder equipped with altitude reporting equipment is required for

A — Class A, Class B, and Class C airspace areas.
B — all airspace of the 48 contiguous U.S. and the District of Columbia at and above 10,000 feet MSL (including airspace at and below 2,500 feet above the surface).
C — both answers.

3-4   B11
In the contiguous U.S., excluding the airspace at and below 2,500 feet AGL, an operable coded transponder equipped with Mode C capability is required in all airspace above

A — 10,000 feet MSL.
B — 12,500 feet MSL.
C — 14,500 feet MSL.

3-5   B11
What transponder equipment is required for airplane operations within Class B airspace? A transponder

A — with 4096 code or Mode S, and Mode C capability.
B — is required for airplane operations when visibility is less than 3 miles.
C — with 4096 code capability is required except when operating at or below 1,000 feet AGL under the terms of a letter of agreement.

3-6   B08
What is the maximum indicated airspeed authorized in the airspace underlying Class B airspace?

A — 156 knots.
B — 200 knots.
C — 230 knots.

3-2. Answer B. ICM 3A (FAR 71.5c)
Low altitude airways begin at 1,200 feet AGL, unless otherwise indicated on sectional charts, and end at the overlying Class A Airspace.

3-3. Answer A. ICM 3A (FAR 91.215b)
A Mode C transponder is required in Class A, B, and C airspace, and everywhere above 10,000 feet and excluding the airspace at and below 2,500 feet above the surface.

3-4. Answer A. ICM 3A (FAR 91.215b)
Encoding transponders are required in all airspace above 10,000 feet (except within 2,500 feet of the surface).

3-5. Answer A. ICM 3A (FAR 91.215)
Airplanes, helicopters, and any aircraft, must have an encoding transponder to operate in Class B Airspace.

3-6. Answer B. ICM 3A (FAR 91.117c)
No person may operate an aircraft in the airspace underlying Class B airspace or in a VFR corridor designated through such Class B airspace at an indicated airspeed of more than 200 knots.

3-7   B11

Unless otherwise authorized or required by ATC, the maximum indicated airspeed permitted when at or below 2,500 feet AGL within 4 NM of the primary airport within Class C or D airspace is

A — 200 knots.
B — 180 knots.
C — 230 knots.

3-8   B08

Which is true regarding flight operations in Class B airspace?

A — The pilot must receive an ATC clearance before operating an aircraft in that area.
B — Solo student pilot operations are not authorized.
C — Flight under VFR is not authorized unless the pilot in command is instrument rated.

3-9   B08

Which is true regarding pilot certification requirements for operations in Class B airspace?

A — The pilot in command must hold at least a private pilot certificate with an instrument rating.
B — The pilot in command must hold at least a private pilot certificate.
C — Solo student pilot operations are not authorized.

3-10   B08

Which is true regarding flight operations in Class B airspace?

A — The aircraft must be equipped with an ATC transponder and altitude reporting equipment.
B — The pilot in command must hold at least a private pilot certificate with an instrument rating.
C — The pilot in command must hold at least a student pilot certificate.

3-11   B09

When operating an airplane for the purpose of takeoff or landing within Class D airspace under special VFR, what minimum distance from clouds and what visibility are required?

A — Remain clear of clouds, and the ground visibility must be at least 1 SM.
B — 500 feet beneath clouds, and the ground visibility must be at least 1 SM.
C — Remain clear of clouds, and the flight visibility must be at least 1 NM.

3-7. Answer A. ICM 3A (FAR 91.157)
Unless otherwise authorized or required by ATC, you may not operate an aircraft at or below 2,500 feet above the surface within 4 nautical miles of the primary airport of a Class C or Class D airspace area at a speed greater than 200 KIAS.

3-8. Answer A. ICM 3A (FAR 91.131)
An ATC clearance is required prior to penetrating Class B airspace.

3-9. Answer B. ICM 3A (FAR 91.131)
Generally, the pilot in command must hold at least a private pilot certicate to operate an aircraft in Class B airspace.

3-10. Answer A. ICM 3A (FAR 91.131b)
An encoding transponder with mode C is required in all Class B airspace. With limited exceptions allowing student pilot operations, a private pilot certificate, but not an instrument rating, is required.

3-11. Answer A. ICM 3A (FAR 91.157)
You may take off or land an airplane under special VFR with a ground visibility of at least 1 statute mile. If ground visibility is not reported, then flight visibility must be at least 1 statute mile.

3-12   B09

At some airports located in Class D airspace where ground visibility is not reported, takeoffs and landings under special VFR are

A — not authorized.
B — authorized by ATC if the flight visibility is at least 1 SM.
C — authorized only if the ground visibility is observed to be at least 3 SM.

3-12. Answer B. ICM 3A (FAR 91.157d)
If ground visibility is not reported then flight visibility is used.

3-13   B09

To operate an airplane under SPECIAL VFR (SVFR) within Class D airspace at night, which is required?

A — The Class D airspace must be specifically designated as a night SVFR area.
B — The pilot must hold an instrument rating, but the airplane need not be equipped for instrument flight, as long as the weather will remain at or above SVFR minimums.
C — The pilot must hold an instrument rating, and the airplane must be equipped for instrument flight.

3-13. Answer C. ICM 3A (FAR 91.157e)
Special VFR is not permitted between sunset and sunrise unless you have a current instrument rating and the aircraft is equipped for instrument flight. In addition, special VFR clearances are not issued to fixed-wing aircraft (day or night) at the nation's busier airports which are listed in Section 3 of Appendix D of FAR 91.

3-14   B08

When operating an aircraft in the vicinity of an airport with an operating control tower, in Class E airspace, a pilot must establish communications prior to

A — 8 NM, and up to and including 3,000 feet AGL.
B — 5 NM, and up to and including 3,000 feet AGL.
C — 4 NM, and up to and including 2,500 feet AGL.

3-14. Answer C. ICM 3A (FAR 91.127c)
Sometimes, control towers are established in Class E airspace. These are normally non-FAA facilities and often exist on a temporary basis, such as managing traffic for a special event at the airport. You are obligated to communicate with these towers over about the same area as if Class D airspace existed there, establishing contact prior to approaching within 4 NM of the airport below 2,500 feet AGL.

3-15   B08

When approaching to land at an airport with an ATC facility, in Class D airspace, the pilot must establish communications prior to

A — 10 NM, up to and including 3,000 feet AGL.
B — 30 SM, and be transponder equipped.
C — 4 NM, up to and including 2,500 feet AGL.

3-15. Answer C. ICM 3A (FAR 91.129)
Communications must be established prior to 4 nautical miles from the airport, up to and including 2,500 feet AGL. There is no transponder requirement for Class D airspace.

3-16   B08

Which is true regarding flight operations to or from a satellite airport, without an operating control tower, within the Class C airspace area?

A — Prior to takeoff, a pilot must establish communication with the ATC controlling facility.
B — Aircraft must be equipped with an ATC transponder and altitude reporting equipment.
C — Prior to landing, a pilot must establish and maintain communication with an ATC facility.

3-16. Answer B. ICM 3A (FAR 91.130)
An altitude encoding transponder is required within Class C airspace. Communication with ATC is not always possible when on the ground at a satellite airport, which is why the regulations state that two-way radio communications with ATC must established as soon as practicable after departing.

3-17   B08

Which is true regarding flight operations to or from a satellite airport, without an operating control tower, within the Class C airspace area?

A — Prior to takeoff, a pilot must establish communication with the ATC controlling facility.

B — Prior to entering that airspace, a pilot must establish and maintain communication with the ATC serving facility.

C — Aircraft must be equipped with an ATC transponder.

3-17. Answer B. ICM 3A (FAR 91.130)

Each person must establish two-way radio communications with the ATC facility prior to entering Class C airspace and thereafter, maintain those communications while within that airspace. Communication with ATC is not always possible when on the ground at a satellite airport, therefore two-way radio communications with ATC must established as soon as practicable after departing.

3-18   B08

Which is true regarding flight operations in Class A airspace?

A — Aircraft must be equipped with approved distance measuring equipment (DME).

B — Aircraft must be equipped with an approved ATC transponder.

C — Must conduct operations under instrument flight rules.

3-18. Answer C. ICM 3A (FAR 91.135)

Each person operating an aircraft in Class A airspace must conduct that operation under instrument flight rules (IFR) and must receive an ATC clearance prior to enter the airspace. Obviously, each pilot must maintain two-way communications with ATC while operating in Class A airspace. DME is only required at or above FL240 where VOR is required.

3-19   B08

Which is true regarding flight operations in Class A airspace?

A — Aircraft must be equipped with approved distance measuring equipment (DME).

B — Aircraft must be equipped with an ATC transponder and altitude reporting equipment.

C — May conduct operations under visual flight rules.

3-19. Answer B. ICM 3A (FAR 91.135)

Each person operating an aircraft in Class A airspace must conduct that operation under instrument flight rules (IFR) and must receive an ATC clearance prior to enter the airspace. Each aircraft must be equipped with an altitude encoding transponder. DME is only required at or above FL240 where VOR is required.

3-20   H568

Light beacons producing red flashes indicate

A — end of runway warning at departure end.

B — a pilot should remain clear of an airport traffic pattern and continue circling.

C — obstructions or areas considered hazardous to aerial navigation.

3-20. Answer C. GFDICM 3A (AIM)

Flashing red lights, or beacons, are used to indicate obstructions or other areas considered hazardous to aerial navigation. End of runway warning lights at some airports are steady red while a flashing red light from a control tower indicates that an airport is unsafe- do not land.

3-21   H568

When planning a night cross-country flight, a pilot should check for the availability and status of

A — all VORs to be used en route.

B — airport rotating light beacons.

C — destination airport lighting system.

3-21. Answer C. ICM 3A

It is recommended that prior to a night flight, and particularly a cross-country night flight, the pilot check the availability and status of lighting systems at the destination airport. This information can be found on aeronautical charts and in the Airport/Facility Directory.

3-22   J37
Which is true concerning the blue and magenta colors used to depict airports on Sectional Aeronautical Charts?

A — Airports with control towers underlying Class A, B, and C airspace are shown in blue, Class D and E airspace are magenta.
B — Airports with control towers underlying Class C, D, and E airspace are shown in magenta.
C — Airports with control towers underlying Class B, C, D, and E airspace are shown in blue.

3-22. Answer C. PPM 4C
Airports with operating control towers are depicted in blue symbols, and underlie Class B, C, or D airspace. For questions regarding chart symbology, refer to a chart legend panel.

3-23   J37
(Refer to figure 52, point 1.) The floor of the Class E airspace above Georgetown Airport (Q61) is at

A — 3,823 feet MSL.
B — the surface.
C — 700 feet AGL.

3-23. Answer A. PPM 4C
Class E airspace begins at 1,200 feet AGL on the UNshaded side of magenta areas. The airport elevation is 2,623 feet MSL. For questions regarding chart symbology, refer to a chart legend panel.

3-24   J37
(Refer to figure 52, point 7.) The floor of Class E airspace over the town of Woodland is

A — 700 feet AGL over part of the town and no floor over the remainder.
B — 1,200 feet AGL over part of the town and no floor over the remainder.
C — both 700 feet and 1,200 feet AGL.

3-24. Answer C. PPM 4C (AIM)
The floor is 700 feet AGL inside the magenta shaded area and 1,200 feet AGL outside it.

3-25   J37
(Refer to figure 52, point 5.) The floor of the Class E airspace over University Airport (0O5) is

A — the surface.
B — 700 feet AGL.
C — 1,200 feet AGL.

3-25. Answer B. PPM 4C (AIM)
This airport is inside a magenta shaded area, where the floor of controlled (Class E) airspace is 700 feet AGL.

3-26   J37
(Refer to figure 52.) The floor of the Class E airspace over the town of Auburn is

A — 1,200 feet MSL.
B — 1,200 feet AGL.
C — 700 feet AGL.

3-26. Answer C. PPM 4C (AIM)
Auburn is inside a magenta shaded area. Here, the floor of Class E (controlled) airspace is 700 feet AGL.

3-27   J37
(Refer to figure 53, point 1 on page 3-10.) This thin black shaded line is most likely

A — an arrival route.
B — a military training route.
C — a state boundary line.

3-27. Answer B. PPM 4C (AIM)
State boundaries a thinner than this and solid black. This is actually a gray line, which depicts a military training route.

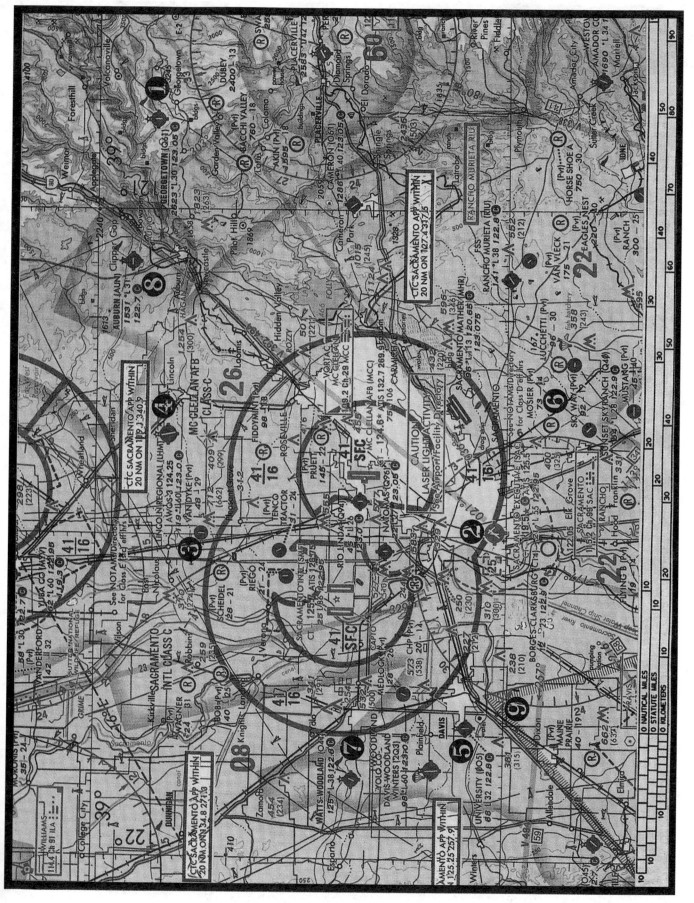

Figure 52. — Sectional Chart Excerpt.

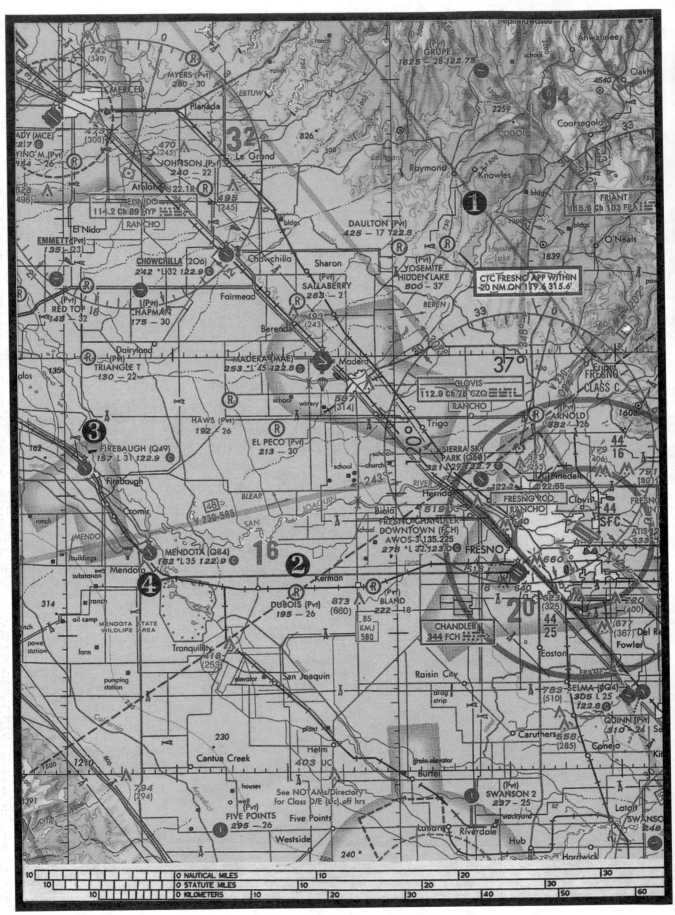

Figure 53. — Sectional Chart Excerpt

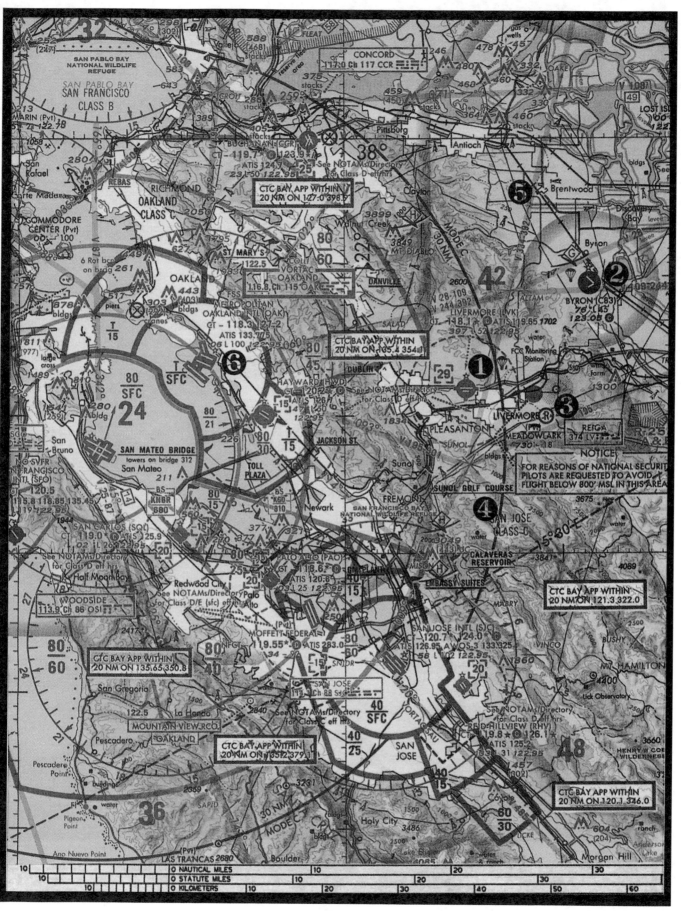

Figure 54. — Sectional Chart Excerpt.

3-28   **J37**
(Refer to figure 53, point 2 on page 3-10.) The 16 indicates

A — an antenna top at 1,600 feet AGL.
B — the maximum elevation figure for that quadrangle.
C — the minimum safe sector altitude for that quadrangle.

3-28. Answer B. PPM 4C (AIM)
This is the maximum elevation MSL including terrain and obstacles in the quadrangle bounded by ticked lines of latitude and longitude. It includes 200-300 feet safety margin for altimeter error. For questions regarding chart symbology, refer to a chart legend panel.

3-29   **J37**
(Refer to figure 54, point 1 on page 3-11.) What minimum altitude is required to avoid the Livermore Airport (LVK) Class D airspace?

A — 2,503 feet MSL.
B — 2,901 feet MSL.
C — 3,297 feet MSL.

3-29. Answer B. PPM 4C (AIM)
The top of the Class D airspace is indicated by the number [29] within the blue dashed circle.

3-30   **J37**
(Refer to figure 52, point 9 on page 3-9.) The alert area depicted within the blue lines is an area in which

A — there is a high volume of pilot training activities or an unusual type of aerial activity, neither of which is hazardous to aircraft.
B — the flight of aircraft is prohibited.
C — the flight of aircraft, while not prohibited, is subject to restriction.

3-30. Answer A. PPM 4C (Chart Legend)
An alert area is established to inform pilots of a specific area wherein a high volume of pilot training or an unusual type of aeronautical activity is conducted. However, unlike prohibited or restricted areas, there are no restrictions to flight in alert areas.

3-31   **J37**
When a dashed blue circle surrounds an airport on a sectional aeronautical chart, it will depict the boundary of

A — Special VFR airspace.
B — Class B airspace
C — Class D airspace.

3-31. Answer C. ICM 3A (AIM)
A dashed blue circle indicates Class D airspace. Although a special VFR clearance is required here when certain weather conditions exist, there is no such designation as Special VFR airspace. For questions regarding chart symbology, refer to a chart legend panel.

3-32   **J37**
(Refer to figure 52, point 4 on page 3-9.) The highest obstruction with high intensity lighting within 10 NM of Lincoln Regional Airport (LHM) is how high above the ground?

A — 1,254 feet.
B — 662 feet.
C — 299 feet.

3-32. Answer C. PPM 4C
The only obstruction with high intensity lighting is 3 NM south of the airport. The top of the obstruction is at 409 feet MSL, and it is 299 feet high.

3-33   **J37**
(Refer to figure 52, point 6 on page 3-9.) Mosier Airport is

A — an airport restricted to use by private and recreational pilots.
B — a restricted military stage field within restricted airspace.
C — a nonpublic use airport.

3-33. Answer C. PPM 4C
Airports identified with the letter "R" enclosed in an open circle are non-public use (private) airports. Although landing at a private airport requires the owner's permission, you could use one in an emergency. For questions regarding chart symbology, refer to a chart legend panel.

3-34   **J37**

(Refer to figure 54, point 2 on page 3-11.) After departing from Byron Airport (C83) with a northeast wind, you discover you are approaching Livermore Class D airspace and flight visibility is approximately 2 1/2 miles. You must

A — stay below 700 feet to remain in Class G and land.
B — stay below 1,200 feet to remain in Class G.
C — contact Livermore ATCT on 119.65 and advise of your intentions.

3-35   **J37**

(Refer to figure 52, point 4 on page 3-9.) The terrain at the obstruction approximately 8 NM east southeast of the Lincoln Airport is approximately how much higher than the airport elevation?

A — 376 feet.
B — 835 feet.
C — 1,135 feet.

3-36   **J37**

(Refer to figure 54, point 6 on page 3-11.) The Class C airspace at Metropolitan Oakland International (OAK) which extends from the surface upward has a ceiling of

A — both 2,100 feet and 3,000 feet MSL.
B — 8,000 feet MSL.
C — 2,100 feet AGL.

3-37   **J37**

(Refer to figure 53 on page 3-10.)
GIVEN:
Location -Madera Airport (MAE)
Altitude ....1,000 ft AGL
Position.........................7 NM north of Madera (MAE)
Time..3 p.m. local
Flight visibility ....1 SM
You are VFR approaching Madera Airport for a landing from the north. You

A — are in violation of the CFR's; you need 3 miles of visibility under VFR.
B — may descend to 800 feet AGL (Pattern Altitude) after entering Class E airspace and continue to the airport.
C — are required to descend to below 700 feet AGL to remain clear of Class E airspace and may continue for landing.

3-34. Answer A. ICM 3A (FAR 91.155)
If you climb above 700 feet AGL, you will be in Class E airspace, where required visibility is 3 miles. You could request a special VFR clearance from Livermore ATCT, but that frequency is 118.1, not 119.65.

3-35. Answer B. PPM 4C (FAR 91.95)
The obstruction extends to 1,254 feet MSL. If you subtract the obstruction's AGL height (300 feet) from the MSL height, you can determine the MSL elevation of the terrain. The answer is 954 (1,254 - 300 = 954). The difference between this elevation and the airport elevation is 835 feet (954 - 119 = 835). For questions regarding chart symbology, refer to a chart legend panel.

3-36. Answer A. ICM 3A
The "T/SFC" indicates the ceiling of the Oakland Class C airspace is at the overlying San Francisco Class B airspace. The Class B sectors here have altitudes "80/21" and "80/30."

3-37. Answer C. ICM 3A (FAR 91.155)
Class E airspace begins at 700 feet AGL over this airport. You can operate VFR clear of clouds and land with 1 mile of visibility during daylight hours if you stay below this controlled airspace.

3-38   J13

Who has the final authority to accept or decline any "land and hold short" (LAHSO) clearance?

A — Pilot-in-command.
B — ATC tower controller.
C — Airplane owner/operator.

3-39   J13

When should pilots decline a "land and hold short" (LAHSO) clearance?

A — When it will compromise safety.
B — If runway surface is contaminated.
C — Only when the tower controller concurs.

3-38. Answer A. ICM 3A (AIM)
The Pilot-in-Command (PIC) of an aircraft has the final authority to accept or decline any LAHSO clearance. If the PIC elects to decline the clearance, ATC must be notified as soon as possible.

3-39. Answer A. ICM 3A (AIM)
The Pilot-in-Command (PIC) of an aircraft has the final authority to accept or decline a LAHSO clearance. If the PIC determines that the LAHSO may compromise safety in any way, the pilot should advise ATC that the clearance is declined.

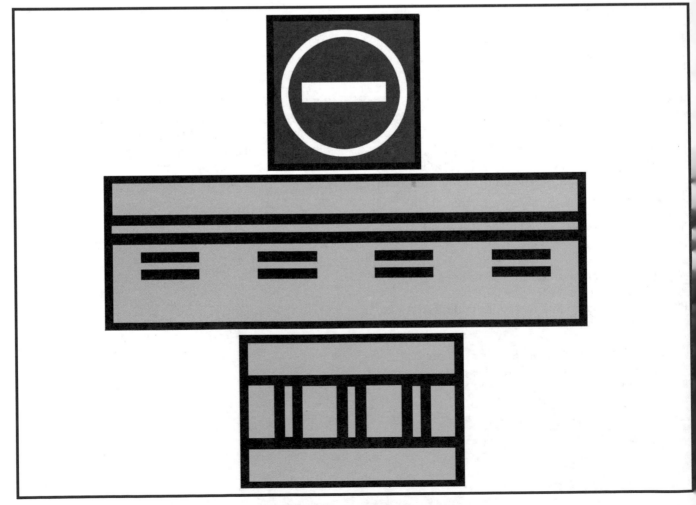

Figure 51. — Airport Signs.

3-40   **J13**

What is the minimum visibility and ceiling required for a pilot to receive a "land and hold short" clearance?

A — 3 statute miles and 1,500 feet.
B — 3 nautical miles and 1,000 feet.
C — 3 statute miles and 1,000 feet.

3-41   **J05**

(Refer to figure 51.) The pilot generally calls ground control after landing when the aircraft is completely clear of the runway. This is when the aircraft

A — is on the dashed-line side of the middle symbol.
B — passes the red symbol shown at the top of the figure.
C — is past the solid-line side of the middle symbol.

3-42   **J05**

(Refer to figure 51.) The red symbol at the top would most likely be found

A — near the approach end of ILS runways.
B — at an intersection where a roadway may be mistaken as a taxiway.
C — upon exiting all runways prior to calling ground control.

3-43   **J05**

(Refer to figure 51.) While clearing an active runway, you are most likely clear of the ILS critical area when you pass which symbol?

A — Top red
B — Middle yellow
C — Bottom yellow

3-44   **J05**

(Refer to figure 51.) When taxiing up to an active runway, you are likely to be clear of the ILS critical area when short of which symbol?

A — Top red.
B — Middle yellow.
C — Bottom yellow.

3-45   **J05**

(Refer to figure 51.) Which symbol does not directly address runway incursion with other aircraft?

A — Top red.
B — Middle yellow.
C — Bottom yellow.

3-40. Answer C. ICM 3A (AIM)
Pilots should only receive a LAHSO clearance when there is a minimum ceiling of 1,000 feet and 3 statute miles visibility. The intent of having "basic" VFR weather conditions is to allow pilots to maintain visual contact with other aircraft and ground vehicle operations.

3-41. Answer C. ICM 3A (AIM)
Runway Safety Area/OFZ boundary signs and runway approach area boundary signs (middle example) are used at controlled airports on taxiways where the controller commonly asks the pilot to report "clear of the runway." The middle symbol is a hold line. The aircraft should always be positioned on the solid line side of the hold line.

3-42. Answer B. ICM 3A (AIM)
The "No Entry Sign" prohibits you from entering an area. Typically, this sign is located on a taxiway intended to be used in only one direction or at the intersection of vehicle roadways with runways, taxiways or aprons where the roadway may be mistaken as a taxiway or other aircraft movement surface area.

3-43. Answer C. ICM 3A (AIM)
You know when you have cleared an ILS critical area when you pass the bottom sign in figure 51.

3-44. Answer C. ICM 3A (AIM)
The middle symbol is the hold line closest to the runway. The bottom symbol is a second hold line farther from the runway, which is used during ILS operations.

3-45. Answer A. ICM 3A (AIM)
The "No Entry Sign" prohibits you from entering an area. Typically, this sign is located on a taxiway intended to be used in only one direction or at the intersection of vehicle roadways with runways, taxiways, or aprons where the roadway may be mistaken as a taxiway or other aircraft movement surface area.

SECTION B
AIR TRAFFIC CONTROL SYSTEM

Although no specific commercial FAA test questions are included in this section, important information pertaining to your commercial training is covered. Some of these topics are: ATC services, separation requirements, and the function of automatic terminal information service (ATIS).

Procedures at Tower-Controlled Airports

1. Automatic terminal information service (ATIS) broadcasts are updated upon receipt of any official weather information. The absence of the sky condition and visibility on an ATIS broadcast specifically implies the ceiling is more than 5,000 feet AGL and the visibility is more than 5 statute miles.

2. To relieve congestion on ground control frequencies, clearance delivery is used for ATC clearances at busier airports.

3. At airports with an operating control tower, you are required to obtain a clearance before operating in a movement area, which is an area on the airport, other than a parking area and loading ramp, used for taxiing, takeoff, and landing. When departing from a runway intersection, always state your position when calling the tower for takeoff.

Terminal Procedures

4. Terminal radar service for VFR aircraft includes basic radar service, terminal radar service area (TRSA) service, Class C service, and Class B service.

5. Basic radar service for VFR aircraft includes safety alerts, traffic advisories, and limited radar vectoring. Sequencing also is available at certain terminal locations.

6. Departure control provides separation of all aircraft within Class B and Class C airspace.

7. When calling out traffic, controllers describe the position of the traffic in terms of the 12-hour clock. For example, "traffic at 3 o'clock" indicates the aircraft lies off your right wing. Traffic advisories from ATC are based on your aircraft's actual ground track, not on your aircraft's heading.

8. A local airport advisory (LAA) is provided by flight service at FSS airports not served by an operating control tower, or when the tower is closed. Although VFR participation LAA service is not mandatory, it is strongly encouraged that you report your position, aircraft type, and intentions when 10 miles from the airport, and request an airport advisory from the FSS.

SECTION C
ATC CLEARANCES

Chapter 3, Section C of the *Instrument Commercial Manual* contains information that is useful to both instrument and commercial pilots. Although this section emphasizes IFR operations, some clearances, such as to operate in Class B airspace, are also relevant to VFR operations. There no FAA commercial questions assigned to this section.

1. An ATC clearance is an authorization for you to proceed under a specified set of conditions within controlled airspace.

2. You may not deviate from an ATC clearance unless you experience an emergency or the clearance will cause you to violate a rule or regulation. If you deviate from an ATC clearance, you must notify ATC as soon as possible. If you are given priority over other aircraft you may be requested to submit a written report to the manager of the ATC facility within 48 hours.

3. While operating under VFR, if ATC assigns an altitude or heading that will cause you to enter clouds, you should avoid the clouds and inform ATC that the altitude or heading will not permit VFR.

4. Anytime you are in VFR conditions, it is your responsibility to see and avoid all other traffic, even if you have filed a flight plan.

5. You must receive an ATC clearance before entering Class A or B airspace regardless of the weather and Class C, D, and E airspace when the weather is below VFR minimums.

6. You may cancel a flight plan anytime you are operating under VFR conditions.

CHAPTER 4

DEPARTURE

Chapter 4 covers such areas as IFR departure charts, IFR departure procedures, and IFR departure considerations. Most of this information is directed toward those preparing for an instrument rating.

SECTION A
DEPARTURE CHARTS

Chapter 4, Section A, covers IFR departure charts. Since this information is directed toward those preparing for an instrument rating, there are no commercial airplane FAA test questions assigned to this section.

SECTION B
DEPARTURE PROCEDURES

1. When taxiing in a quartering headwind, turn the control yoke into the wind. When taxiing with a quartering tailwind, turn the control yoke away from the wind and push forward. Remember the saying "climb into the wind, dive away." Although it is not necessary to pull back on the yoke when taxiing a tricycle gear airplane into a headwind it is okay to do so and it is recommended for tailwheel airplanes.

2. If an aircraft is equipped with anti-collision lights, the lights are required to be on anytime that the aircraft is operated both day and night. However, the lights may be turned off, if the pilot-in-command determines that, because of operating conditions, it would be in the interest of safety to do so.

4-1 **J13**
Pilots are required to have the anti-collision light system operating

A — during all types of operations, both day and night.
B — anytime the pilot is in the cockpit.
C — anytime an engine is in operation.

4-1. Answer A. GFDICM 4B (FAR 91.209) (AIM 4-3-23)
Anti-collision lights are required to be operated during all types of operations (day and night) except when the pilot in command determines that, because of operating conditions, it would be in the interest of safety to turn the lights off.

ENROUTE

SECTION A
ENROUTE AND AREA CHARTS

Chapter 5, Section A, covers such areas as IFR enroute and area charts. Since this information is directed toward those preparing for an instrument rating, there are no commercial airplane FAA test questions assigned to this section.

SECTION B
ENROUTE PROCEDURES

Chapter 5, Section B, covers such areas as IFR enroute procedures. However, there are several items relevant to the commercial pilot certificate and there are several FAA commercial airplane questions.

1. The rate at which an airplane climbs is dependent on several factors. The most accurate way to determine a climb rate for a specific type of aircraft is to refer to the manufacturer's POH. The POH will provide graphical and textual information concerning the configuration, airspeed, and other factors affecting the rate of climb.

2. You can determine if you are on a collision course with another aircraft if there is no apparent relative motion between your aircraft and the other aircraft.

3. If you inadvertently drift off course during the enroute portion of your flight, first find the angle to correct back to a course paralleling your original course, then add to that the angle to converge back on course. Use the formula, Angle = (Miles Off Course x 60) ÷ Miles Flown.

5-1   **L34**
How can you determine if another aircraft is on a collision course with your aircraft?

A — The nose of each aircraft is pointed at the same point in space.
B — The other aircraft will always appear to get larger and closer at a rapid rate.
C — There will be no apparent relative motion between your aircraft and the other aircraft.

5-1. Answer C. GFDPPM 4A (AIM)
If there is no apparent relative motion between your aircraft and another aircraft, you are probably on a collision course. Answer (A) is wrong because the nose of each aircraft does not have to be pointed at the same point in space in order for the danger of a collision to be present. Answer (B) is wrong because your eye may not always pick up the increase in size or closure rate of opposing aircraft.

5-2   H341

You have flown 52 miles, are 6 miles off course, and have 118 miles yet to fly. To converge on your destination, the total correction angle would be

A — 3°.
B — 6°.
C — 10°.

5-2. Answer C. GFDICM 5B

The correction angle to fly directly to your destination can be easily determined with the calculator side of a mechanical flight computer, or by using two formulas. Using a mechanical computer, first set the distance off course (outer scale) over the distance flown (inner scale). Then find the degree of correction necessary to parallel the course under the speed index (7°). Next, set the distance off course (outer scale) over the distance remaining (inner scale). Then, find the additional degrees of correction to return to course (3°). The sum of the two correction angles is 10°.

You also can compute the correction angle arithmetically. An important rule of thumb for off-course problems is that one mile off course in 60 miles equals approximately one degree of drift. First, you must determine the correction angle that would parallel the original course using the following equation.

$$\frac{Distance\ Off\ Course}{Distance\ Flown} \times 60 = \frac{Degrees\ of\ turn\ to}{parallel\ original\ course}$$

$$\frac{6\ n.m.}{52\ n.m.} \times 60 = 6.92°$$

Second, you must determine the additional correction angle necessary to fly direct to the destination using the formula:

$$\frac{Distance\ Off\ Course}{Distance\ Remaining} \times 60 = \frac{Additional\ degrees\ of\ turn}{to\ fly\ directly\ to\ destination}$$

$$\frac{6\ n.m.}{118\ n.m.} \times 60 = 3.05°$$

The sum of these correction angles is approximately 10.0° (6.92 + 3.05 = 9.97). Answers (A) and (B) are wrong since they represent the additional angle needed to converge on the course (A) and the angle needed to parallel the course.

5-3   H341

GIVEN:

Distance off course..9 mi
Distance flown ....95 mi
Distance to fly ....125 mi

To converge at the destination, the total correction angle would be

A — 4°.
B — 6°.
C — 10°.

5-3. Answer C. GFDICM 5B

See explanation for Question 5-2. The sum of these correction angles is approximately 10° (5.7° + 4.3° = 10.0°). Answers (A) and (B) are wrong since they represent the angle needed to parallel the course (answer A) and the additional angle needed to converge on the course (answer B).

5-4   **H567**

What is the general direction of movement of the other aircraft if during a night flight you observe a steady white light and a rotating red light ahead and at your altitude? The other aircraft is

A — headed away from you.

B — crossing to your left.

C — approaching you head-on.

5-4. Answer A. GFDPPM 4A (AFH)

By interpreting the position lights on other aircraft, you can determine which direction the aircraft is heading. For example, if you see only a white light and a rotating beacon, you know an aircraft is heading away from you. If an aircraft were crossing to your left (answer B), you would see a red wing light and rotating beacon. If an aircraft were approaching you head-on (answer C), you would see a red wing light on your right, a green wing light on your left, and a rotating beacon.

5-5   **J14**

When in the vicinity of a VOR which is being used for navigation on VFR flights, it is important to

A — make 90° left and right turns to scan for other traffic.

B — exercise sustained vigilance to avoid aircraft that may be converging on the VOR from other directions.

C — pass the VOR on the right side of the radial to allow room for aircraft flying in the opposite direction on the same radial.

5-5. Answer B. GFDPPM 4A (AIM)

When flying in the vicinity of a VOR, you should be vigilant for other aircraft that may be converging on the VOR. This pertains to both VFR and IFR operations. Answer (A) is wrong because the area can be sufficiently cleared without making 90° turns. In addition, whenever flying on an established airway, you should always stay on its centerline, not to one side (answer C).

SECTION C
HOLDING PROCEDURES

Chapter 5, Section C, covers IFR holding procedures. Since this information is directed toward those preparing for an instrument rating, there are no commercial airplane FAA test questions assigned to this section.

CHAPTER 6

ARRIVAL

Chapter 6 covers IFR arrival charts and procedures. Since this information is directed toward those preparing for an instrument rating, there are no commercial airplane FAA test questions assigned to this chapter.

CHAPTER 7

APPROACH

Chapter 7 covers IFR approach charts and procedures. Since this information is directed toward those preparing for an instrument rating, there are no commercial airplane FAA test questions assigned to this chapter.

CHAPTER 8

INSTRUMENT APPROACHES

Chapter 8 covers VOR, NDB, ILS, GPS, and RNAV approach procedures. Since this information is directed toward those preparing for an instrument rating, there are no commercial airplane FAA test questions assigned to this chapter.

CHAPTER 9

METEOROLOGY

SECTION A
WEATHER FACTORS

The Atmosphere

1. The atmosphere commonly is divided into a number of layers according to its thermal characteristics. The lowest layer, the troposphere, is where most weather occurs.

2. In the troposphere, temperatures decrease with altitude up to the tropopause, where an abrupt change in the temperature lapse rate occurs. The average height of the troposphere in the middle latitudes is 36,000 to 37,000 feet. The temperature in the lower part of the stratosphere (up to approximately 66,000 feet) experiences relatively small changes in temperature with an increase in altitude.

Atmospheric Circulation

3. Uneven heating of the earth's surface is the driving force behind all weather. The special characteristics of water also affect the release of heat into the atmosphere, and dramatically affect the weather.

4. Atmospheric circulation patterns are caused by differences in pressure. Wind flows outward from high pressure areas to low pressure areas.

5. Above the friction layer, the wind does not flow directly from a high to a low because of Coriolis force, which deflects air to the right in the northern hemisphere. The result is a wind that flows in a clockwise direction leaving a high and in a counterclockwise, or cyclonic, direction when entering a low.

6. Near the surface, friction reduces the effects of Coriolis force and causes the wind to flow more directly from a high to low pressure area. This causes the wind to cross the isobars at an angle, rather than flowing parallel to them.

7. A low pressure area, or trough, is an area of rising air, which results in generally unfavorable weather conditions. A high pressure area, or ridge, is characterized by descending air, which encourages dissipation of clouds and results in generally favorable weather conditions. Because of the wind circulation patterns, you will most likely experience a crosswind from the left when flying from a high to a low in the northern hemisphere, with stronger winds as you approach the low.

8. Convective circulation patterns associated with sea breezes are caused by land absorbing and radiating heat faster than water. Cool air must sink to force warm air upward.

9. Moisture is added to a parcel of air by evaporation and sublimation. The amount of water vapor that air can hold increases with temperature. When the temperature cools to the dewpoint, the air is saturated.

10. At 100% humidity, water vapor condenses, forming clouds, fog or dew. Frost forms when the temperature of the collecting surface is below the dewpoint and the dewpoint is below freezing.

11. Precipitation occurs when water vapor condenses out of the air and becomes heavy enough to fall to earth. The type of precipitation is influenced by the temperature and other conditions under which condensation occurs. Upward currents enhance the growth rate of precipitation.

12. The presence of ice pellets normally indicates freezing rain at higher altitudes. The presence of wet snow indicates the temperature is above freezing at your flight altitude.

13. Virga is best described as streamers of rain trailing beneath clouds which evaporate before reaching the ground.

Stability

14. When unsaturated air is forced to ascend a mountain slope, it cools at the rate of approximately 3°C per 1,000 feet. When saturated air is lifted, it cools at a lower rate, which could cause it to be warmer than the surrounding air. The standard temperature of the surrounding air at sea level is 15°C, and it decreases at an average rate of 2°C per 1,000 feet.

15. Stability is the atmosphere's resistance to vertical motion. Air is stable when a lifted parcel of air is cooler than the ambient air. Dry air tends to cool more when lifted and tends to be more stable. The ambient lapse rate allows you to determine atmospheric stability.

16. Ambient air with a low or inverted lapse rate tends to be stable. A common type of ground- or surface-based temperature inversion is that which is produced by ground radiation on clear, cool nights with calm or light wind. When humidity is high you can expect poor visibility due to fog, haze, or low clouds.

Clouds

17. Clouds occur when water vapor condenses. They are divided into four basic families: low, middle, high, and clouds with vertical development.

18. Cumulus clouds are formed when unstable air is lifted. Stratiform clouds are formed when stable air is lifted. The lifting of moist, unstable air results in good visibility outside the cloud, showery precipitation, and turbulence. However, the lifting of moist, stable air results in continuous precipitation, little or no turbulence, and poor visibility.

19. Towering cumulus clouds indicate convective turbulence. Fair weather cumulus clouds indicate turbulence at and below the cloud level. To estimate the bases of cumulus clouds, in thousands of feet, divide the temperature/dewpoint spread at the surface by 2.5°C (4.4°F). If using the quick estimate method, divide the temperature/dewpoint spread by 4°F (2.2°C).

20. The suffix nimbus, used in naming clouds, means a rain cloud.

21. High clouds are composed mostly of ice crystals.

Airmasses and Fronts

22. An airmass is a large body of air that covers an extensive area and has fairly uniform temperature and moisture content. A front is a discontinuity between two airmasses. A cold front occurs when cold air displaces warmer air. A warm front occurs when warm air overruns colder air.

23. Cooling from below increases the stability of an airmass and warming from below decreases it. Steady precipitation, in contrast to showers, preceding a front is an indication of stratiform clouds with little or no turbulence.

24. When a cold airmass moves over, or is heated by, a warm surface, the result is cumuliform clouds, turbulence, and good visibility. When the air is moist and unstable, the updrafts are particularly strong, resulting in cumulonimbus clouds.

25. An occlusion occurs when a cold front overtakes another front. In a cold front occlusion, the air ahead of the warm front is warmer than the air behind the overtaking cold front.

26. A frontal cyclone starts as a slow-moving cold front or stationary front and can end as a cold front occlusion with potentially severe weather.

High Altitude Weather

27. A jetstream is defined as wind of 50 knots or greater. They are found in bands of strong westerly winds that occur at breaks in the tropopause in the northern hemisphere. While they can provide beneficial winds when flying west to east, they also can be associated with strong turbulence.

28. The strength and location of the jetstream is normally weaker and farther north in the summer. During the winter months in the middle latitudes, the jet stream shifts toward the south and speed increases.

9-1   I21

Every physical process of weather is accompanied by, or is the result of,

A — a heat exchange.
B — the movement of air.
C — a pressure differential.

9-1. Answer A. GFDICM 9A (AW)

Every physical process of weather is accompanied by, or is the result of, a heat exchange. This process happens as the earth's surface is cooled or heated, and when water changes from one physical state to another. Answers (B) and (C) are wrong because the movement of air is a result of pressure differentials which are caused by uneven heating of the earths surface.

9-2   I21

What is the standard temperature at 10,000 feet?

A — -5°C.
B — -15°C.
C — +5°C.

9-2. Answer A. GFDICM 9A (AW)

Standard temperature at sea level is 15°C. The standard, or average, lapse rate is approximately 2°C per 1,000 feet of altitude. To determine the standard temperature at 10,000 feet, multiply 10 by the lapse rate (2°C) and subtract the result from the sea level standard (15°C). The answer is -5°C (15 - (10 x 5). Answer (B), -15°C, is the standard temperature at 15,000 feet, and answer (C), +5°C, is the standard temperature at 5,000 feet.

9-3   I21

What is the standard temperature at 20,000 feet?

A — -15°C.
B — -20°C.
C — -25°C.

9-3. Answer C. GFDICM 9A (IFH)

See explanation for Question 9-2. The answer is -25°C (15 - (20 x 2) = -25). Answers (A) and (B) are wrong because they represent the standard temperatures at 15,000 feet and 17,500 feet respectively.

9-4   I21

Which conditions are favorable for the formation of a surface based temperature inversion?

A — Clear, cool nights with calm or light wind.
B — Area of unstable air rapidly transferring heat from the surface.
C — Broad areas of cumulus clouds with smooth, level bases at the same altitude.

9-4. Answer A. GFDICM 9A (AW)

When temperature increases with altitude, a temperature inversion exists. One of the most familiar types of ground- or surface-based inversions forms in stable conditions from radiation cooling just above the ground on clear, cool nights with little wind. Answers (B) and (C) are wrong because they both indicate unstable conditions.

9-5   I23

What causes wind?

A — The Earth's rotation.
B — Air mass modification.
C — Pressure differences.

9-5. Answer C. GFDICM 9A (AW)

The uneven heating of the earth's surface creates circulation patterns, resulting in pressure differences. In an attempt to equalize the pressure between systems, air flows from system to system creating wind. The speed of the resulting wind depends on the strength of the pressure gradient. The earth's rotation (answer A), causes the wind to deflect to the right, in the northern hemisphere, and airmass modification (answer B), identifies a change in characteristics of an airmass.

9-6   I23

In the Northern Hemisphere, the wind is deflected to the

A — right by Coriolis force.
B — right by surface friction.
C — left by Coriolis force.

9-6. Answer A. GFDICM 9A (AW)

The earth's rotation induces what is known as Coriolis force. This force deflects the wind to the right in the northern hemisphere and to the left in the southern hemisphere. Surface friction (answer B) opposes Coriolis force reducing its effect near the surface. Answer (C) is wrong because Coriolis force deflects the wind to the right, not left.

9-7   **I23**

Why does the wind have a tendency to flow parallel to the isobars above the friction level?

A — Coriolis force tends to counterbalance the horizontal pressure gradient.
B — Coriolis force acts perpendicular to a line connecting the highs and lows.
C — Friction of the air with the Earth deflects the air perpendicular to the pressure gradient.

9-8   **I23**

The wind system associated with a low-pressure area in the Northern Hemisphere is

A — an anticyclone and is caused by descending cold air.
B — a cyclone and is caused by Coriolis force.
C — an anticyclone and is caused by Coriolis force.

9-9   **I23**

What prevents air from flowing directly from high-pressure areas to low-pressure areas?

A — Coriolis force.
B — Surface friction.
C — Pressure gradient force.

9-10   **I23**

While flying cross-country, in the Northern Hemisphere, you experience a continuous left cross-wind which is associated with a major wind system. This indicates that you

A — are flying toward an area of generally unfavorable weather conditions.
B — have flown from an area of unfavorable weather conditions.
C — cannot determine weather conditions without knowing pressure changes.

9-11   **I23**

Which is true with respect to a high- or low-pressure system?

A — A high-pressure area or ridge is an area of rising air.
B — A low-pressure area or trough is an area of descending air.
C — A high-pressure area or ridge is an area of descending air.

9-7. Answer A. GFDICM 9A (AW)
When pressure gradient force and Coriolis are balanced, airflow circulation aloft is parallel to the isobars. Within about 2,000 feet of the ground, surface friction slows the wind, and Coriolis force is weakened. Pressure gradient force then predominates, causing the wind to flow at an angle to the isobars. Answer (B) is wrong because Coriolis force does not act perpendicular to a line connecting highs and lows. Answer (C) is wrong because friction tends to cause the wind to flow perpendicular to the pressure gradient.

9-8. Answer B. GFDICM 9A (AW)
See explanation for Question 9-7. In the northern hemisphere, Coriolis force causes low-pressure areas to circulate in a counterclockwise, or cyclonic, direction, while high-pressure areas circulate in a clockwise, or anticyclonic (answers A and C), direction.

9-9. Answer A. GFDICM 9A (AW)
If the earth did not rotate, the pressure gradient force would propel wind directly from highs to lows. Instead, the earth's rotation introduces Coriolis force which deflects the wind to the right in the northern hemisphere. Surface friction (answer B) acts with the pressure gradient force (answer C) to oppose Coriolis force and prevents the wind from flowing directly between pressure systems.

9-10. Answer A. GFDICM 9A (AW)
High pressure systems circulate in a clockwise (anticyclonic) direction and are usually associated with favorable flying conditions. On the other hand, low pressure areas circulate in a counterclockwise direction and are associated with unfavorable flying conditions. If you experience a continuous left crosswind when flying, you are generally flying from an area of high pressure and good weather to an area of low pressure and bad weather. Answer (B) is wrong because when flying from an area of low pressure (bad weather), you will experience a right crosswind. Answer (C) is wrong because you do not need to know the degree of pressure change to determine general weather conditions.

9-11. Answer C. GFDICM 9A (AW)
In high-pressure systems, air is moving outward, depleting the quantity of air. As a result, a high or ridge is characterized by descending air which favors generally good flying conditions. In low-pressure systems, the air is moving inward, converging to the center and rising. As a result, a low or trough is characterized by ascending air which generally produces unfavorable flying conditions. Answer (A) is wrong because air descends in a high-pressure area, and answer (B) is wrong because air rises in a low-pressure area.

9-12 I23

Which is true regarding high- or low-pressure systems?

A — A high-pressure area or ridge is an area of rising air.
B — A low-pressure area or trough is an area of rising air.
C — Both high- and low-pressure areas are characterized by descending air.

9-13 I23

When flying into a low-pressure area in the Northern Hemisphere, the wind direction and velocity will be from the

A — left and decreasing.
B — left and increasing.
C — right and decreasing.

9-14 I24

Which is true regarding actual air temperature and dewpoint temperature spread? The temperature spread

A — decreases as the relative humidity decreases.
B — decreases as the relative humidity increases.
C — increases as the relative humidity increases.

9-15 I24

The general circulation of air associated with a high-pressure area in the Northern Hemisphere is

A — outward, downward, and clockwise.
B — outward, upward, and clockwise.
C — inward, downward, and clockwise.

9-16 I24

Virga is best described as

A — turbulent areas beneath cumulonimbus clouds.
B — wall cloud torrents trailing beneath cumulonimbus clouds which dissipate before reaching the ground.
C — streamers of precipitation trailing beneath clouds which evaporates before reaching the ground.

9-12. Answer B. GFDICM 9A (AW)
See explanation for Question 9-11.

9-13. Answer B. GFDICM 9A (AW)
See explanation for Question 9-10. When flying into a low-pressure system, the wind direction will always be from the left and the wind speed will increase as you fly toward the system's center. When flying into a high-pressure system, the wind direction will always be from the right (answer C) and the speed will decrease (answers A and C) as you fly towards the center.

9-14. Answer B. GFDICM 9A (AW)
The difference between air temperature and dewpoint temperature is popularly called the "spread." As spread becomes less, relative humidity increases, and it is 100 when temperature and dew point are the same. Answers (A) and (C) are wrong because the relative humidity percentage moves opposite to the temperature/dewpoint spread.

9-15. Answer A. GFDICM 9A (AW)
In high-pressure systems, air circulates in a clockwise direction and moves outward, depleting the quantity of air. As a result, a high or ridge is characterized by descending air which favors generally good flying conditions. In low-pressure systems, the air circulates in a counterclockwise direction as it converges and rises. As a result, a low or trough is characterized by ascending air which generally produces unfavorable flying conditions. Answer (B) is wrong because air descends in a high-pressure area, and answer (C) is wrong because air flows inward in a low-pressure area, not a high-pressure area.

9-16. Answer C. GFDICM 9A
Virga are streamers of precipitation that trail below the clouds, but evaporate before reaching the ground.

9-17   I24
Moisture is added to a parcel of air by

A — sublimation and condensation.
B — evaporation and condensation.
C — evaporation and sublimation.

9-17. Answer C. GFDICM 9A (AW)
Water vapor is added to the atmosphere by the process of evaporation or sublimation. Evaporation is the process of a liquid changing to a gaseous state, and sublimation describes the process of solid moisture (ice) changing to a gas. Condensation (answers A and B) refers to a process which removes moisture from the atmosphere as water vapor condenses to a liquid.

9-18   I25
When conditionally unstable air with high-moisture content and very warm surface temperature is forecast, one can expect what type of weather?

A — Strong updrafts and stratonimbus clouds.
B — Restricted visibility near the surface over a large area.
C — Strong updrafts and cumulonimbus clouds.

9-18. Answer C. GFDICM 9A (AW)
When unstable, moist air exists over a warm surface, convective activity tends to force the moisture aloft producing cumulus and/or cumulonimbus clouds. Answer (A) is wrong because stratonimbus clouds typically form in stable conditions. Answer (B) is wrong because unstable air usually results in good surface visibility.

9-19   I25
What is the approximate base of the cumulus clouds if the temperature at 2,000 feet MSL is 10°C and the dewpoint is 1°C?

A — 3,000 feet MSL.
B — 4,000 feet MSL.
C — 6,000 feet MSL.

9-19. Answer C. GFDICM 9A (AW)
To determine the base of a cloud layer, compute the difference between the temperature and dewpoint and divide the difference by the rate at which the temperature and the dewpoint converge. In convective conditions, the convergency rate is about 2.5°C per 1,000 feet. The result will approximate cloud bases in thousands of feet. The answer is 6,000 feet (10 - 1 = 9 ÷ 2.5 = 3.6 or 3,600 + 2,000 = 5,600 feet) or approximately 6,000 feet MSL.

9-20   I25
If clouds form as a result of very stable, moist air being forced to ascend a mountain slope, the clouds will be

A — cirrus type with no vertical development or turbulence.
B — cumulus type with considerable vertical development and turbulence.
C — stratus type with little vertical development and little or no turbulence.

9-20. Answer C. GFDICM 9A (AW)
Stable and unstable air have predictable characteristics in terms of cloud types, precipitation, visibility, turbulence, and icing. If either a stable or unstable layer of air is lifted, the associated characteristics remain. For example, if stable air is forced up a slope, stratus-type clouds with little or no turbulence typically form. If the same air is unstable, clouds with extensive vertical development and turbulence (answer B) usually develop. Answer (A) is wrong because cirrus clouds form at very high altitudes.

9-21   I25
What determines the structure or type of clouds which will form as a result of air being forced to ascend?

A — The method by which the air is lifted.
B — The stability of the air before lifting occurs.
C — The relative humidity of the air after lifting occurs.

9-21. Answer B. GFDICM 9A (AW)
See explanation for Question 9-19.

9-22   **I25**

Refer to the excerpt from the following METAR report:

KTUS.....08004KT 4SM HZ 26/04 A2995 RMK RAE36

At approximately what altitude AGL should bases of convective-type cumuliform clouds be expected?

A — 17,600 feet.
B — 4,400 feet.
C — 8,800 feet.

9-23   **I25**

What are the characteristics of stable air?

A —Good visibility; steady precipitation; stratus clouds.
B — Poor visibility; steady precipitation; stratus clouds.
C — Poor visibility; intermittent precipitation; cumulus clouds.

9-24   **I25**

Which would decrease the stability of an air mass?

A — Warming from below.
B — Cooling from below.
C — Decrease in water vapor.

9-25   **I25**

From which measurement of the atmosphere can stability be determined?

A — Atmospheric pressure.
B — The ambient lapse rate.
C — The dry adiabatic lapse rate.

9-26   **I25**

What type weather can one expect from moist, unstable air and very warm surface temperature?

A — Fog and low stratus clouds.
B — Continuous heavy precipitation.
C — Strong updrafts and cumulonimbus clouds.

9-27   **I25**

Which would increase the stability of an air mass?

A — Warming from below.
B — Cooling from below.
C — Decrease in water vapor.

9-22. Answer C. GFDICM 9A (AW)
Temperature and dewpoint converge at 2.5°C per 1,000 feet of altitude. The temperature/dewpoint spread at the surface, according to the METAR, is 26°C − 4°C = 22°C. The bases of cumulus clouds are at the altitude where the spread is zero:

22°C ÷ (2.5°C/1,000 feet) = 8,800 feet AGL.

9-23. Answer B. GFDICM 9A (AW)
Stable and unstable air each have identifiable characteristics. For example, stable air is generally smooth, with layered or stratiform clouds. Visibility usually is restricted, with widespread areas of clouds and steady rain or drizzle. Unstable air is usually turbulent, with cumulus clouds (answer C) and good surface visibility (answer A) outside of scattered rain showers.

9-24. Answer A. GFDICM 9A (AW)
As an airmass moves over a warmer surface, its lower layers are heated, and vertical movement of the air develops. This typically results in extreme instability. On the other hand, when an airmass is cooled from below (answer B), stability increases. Answer (C) is wrong because a decrease in the amount of water vapor lowers the dewpoint.

9-25. Answer B. GFDICM 9A (AW)
The ambient lapse rate can be used to determine the stability of the atmosphere. For example, moist air has less stability and a lower lapse rate than dry air. Answer (A), atmospheric pressure, is incorrect because stable or unstable air can exist at any atmospheric pressure. Answer (C), the dry adiabatic lapse rate, is incorrect because it measures the rate at which dry air cools with altitude.

9-26. Answer C. GFDICM 9A (AW)
When moist, unstable air exists over a warm surface, convective activity will tend to force the moisture aloft producing cumulus and/or cumulonimbus clouds. Answers (A) and (B) are wrong because fog, low stratus clouds, and heavy precipitation are characteristics of stable air.

9-27. Answer B. GFDICM 9A (AW)
See explanation for Question 9-24.

9-28   I26

The conditions necessary for the formation of stratiform clouds are a lifting action and

A — unstable, dry air.
B — stable, moist air.
C — unstable, moist air.

9-29   I26

Which cloud types would indicate convective turbulence?

A — Cirrus clouds.
B — Nimbostratus clouds.
C — Towering cumulus clouds.

9-30   I27

The formation of either predominantly stratiform or predominantly cumuliform clouds is dependent upon the

A — source of lift.
B — stability of the air being lifted.
C — temperature of the air being lifted.

9-31   I27

Which combination of weather-producing variables
would likely result in cumuliform-type clouds, good
visibility, and showery rain?

A — Stable, moist air and orographic lifting.
B — Unstable, moist air and orographic lifting.
C — Unstable, moist air and no lifting mechanism.

9-32   I27

What is a characteristic of stable air?

A — Stratiform clouds.
B — Fair weather cumulus clouds.
C — Temperature decreases rapidly with altitude.

9-33   I27

A moist, unstable air mass is characterized by

A — poor visibility and smooth air.
B — cumuliform clouds and showery precipitation.
C — stratiform clouds and continuous precipitation.

9-28. Answer B. GFDICM 9A (AW)
Stratiform clouds are layered clouds that form in stable, moist air. Cumulus clouds, on the other hand, form
in unstable, moist air (answer C) and unstable, dry air
(answer A) does not promote cloud formation.

9-29. Answer C. GFDICM 9A (AW)
Towering cumulus clouds develop in moist, unstable air
that is lifted. The combination of instability and the lifting action typically produce moderate to heavy convective turbulence with icing conditions. Answers (A) and
(B) are wrong because cirrus and nimbostratus clouds
indicate little or no turbulence.

9-30. Answer B. GFDICM 9A (AW)
The formation of either stratiform or cumuliform clouds
is dependent upon the stability of the air before it's lifted.
For example, when stable air is lifted, stratiform clouds
typically form, and when unstable air is lifted, cumuliform clouds usually form. Neither the source of lifting
(answer A) nor the temperature of the air being lifted
(answer C) will determine the types of clouds that form.

9-31. Answer B. GFDICM 9A (AW)
Both stable and unstable airmasses have distinguish-
able characteristics. Stable air is generally smooth, with
layered or stratiform clouds, and visibility usually is
restricted with widespread areas of clouds and steady
rain or drizzle (answer A). Unstable air is typically turbulent, with cumuliform type clouds and good surface visibility outside areas of showery rain. When either type of
airmass is lifted, their associated characteristics usually
persist. If no lifting force is present (answer C) the formation of clouds or precipitation is unlikely.

9-32. Answer A. GFDICM 9A (AW)
See explanation for Question 9-31.

9-33. Answer B. GFDICM 9A (AW)
See explanation for Question 9-31. Both answers (A)
and (C) indicate characteristics of a stable airmass.

9-34   **I27**

When an air mass is stable, which of these conditions are most likely to exist?

A — Numerous towering cumulus and cumulonimbus clouds.

B — Moderate to severe turbulence at the lower levels.

C — Smoke, dust, haze, etc., concentrated at the lower levels with resulting poor visibility.

9-35   **I27**

Which is a characteristic of stable air?

A — Cumuliform clouds.

B — Excellent visibility.

C — Restricted visibility.

9-36   **I27**

Which is a characteristic typical of a stable air mass?

A — Cumuliform clouds.

B — Showery precipitation.

C — Continuous precipitation.

9-37   **I27**

Which is true regarding a cold front occlusion? The air ahead of the warm front

A — is colder than the air behind the overtaking cold front.

B — is warmer than the air behind the overtaking cold front.

C — has the same temperature as the air behind the overtaking cold front.

9-38   **I27**

Which are characteristics of a cold air mass moving over a warm surface?

A — Cumuliform clouds, turbulence, and poor visibility.

B — Cumuliform clouds, turbulence, and good visibility.

C — Stratiform clouds, smooth air, and poor visibility.

9-34. Answer C. GFDICM 9A (AW)

A stable airmass is characterized by smooth air, stratiform clouds, and poor visibilities. The poor visibilities can be the result of extensive areas of continuous rain or a low level temperature inversion creating widespread areas of fog, haze, and low clouds. Answers (A) and (B) are wrong because they indicate conditions associated with unstable airmasses.

9-35. Answer C. GFDICM 9A (AW)

See explanation for Question 9-34. Cumuliform clouds (answer A) and excellent visibility (answer B) are characteristics of unstable air.

9-36. Answer C. GFDICM 9A (AW)

See explanation for Question 9-34. A stable airmass with sufficient moisture will typically create widespread areas of continuous precipitation. Answers (A) and (B) are properties of unstable airmasses.

9-37. Answer B. GFDICM 9A (AW)

A frontal occlusion occurs when a fast-moving cold front catches up to a slow-moving warm front. The difference in temperature within each frontal system is a major factor that influences the type of front that develops. A cold front occlusion develops when the air ahead of the warm front is warmer than the overtaking cold front. A warm front occlusion takes place when the air ahead of the slow-moving warm front is colder than the air within the fast-moving cold front (answer A). Answer (C) is not a likely possibility in this weather system.

9-38. Answer B. GFDICM 9A (AW)

The speed of a cold front usually dictates the type of weather associated with the front. However, there are some general weather characteristics that are found in most cold fronts. These include the development of cumulus clouds, turbulence, showery precipitation, strong, gusty winds, and good visibility after the front passes. In contrast, the common weather patterns found in a warm front include the development of stratus clouds, little turbulence, steady, widespread precipitation, and poor visibility (answer C). Answer (A) is wrong because poor visibility is not a characteristic of a cold front.

9-39   I32
Which feature is associated with the tropopause?

A — Constant height above the Earth.
B — Abrupt change in temperature lapse rate.
C — Absolute upper limit of cloud formation.

9-40   I32
During the winter months in the middle latitudes, the jet stream shifts toward the

A — north and speed decreases.
B — south and speed increases.
C — north and speed increases.

9-41   I32
The strength and location of the jet stream is normally

A — weaker and farther north in the summer.
B — stronger and farther north in the winter.
C — stronger and farther north in the summer.

9-42   I35
Which is true regarding the development of convective circulation?

A — Cool air must sink to force the warm air upward.
B — Warm air is less dense and rises on its own accord.
C — Warmer air covers a larger surface area than cooler air; therefore, the warmer air is less dense and rises.

9-43   I35
Convective circulation patterns associated with sea breezes are caused by

A — water absorbing and radiating heat faster than the land.
B — land absorbing and radiating heat faster than the water.
C — cool and less dense air moving inland from over the water, causing it to rise.

9-39. Answer B. GFDICM 9A (AW)
The tropopause is a thin layer that acts as a boundary between the troposphere and the stratosphere and is characterized by an abrupt change in the temperature lapse rate. Answer (A) is wrong because the height of the tropopause changes with latitude and seasonal variations. Answer (C) is wrong because clouds have been known to penetrate the tropopause.

9-40. Answer B. GFDICM 9A (AW)
As the core of the jet stream moves south in the winter, its core rises, and its average speed usually increases. Answers (A) and (C) are wrong because the jet stream does not move north during the winter months. In addition, the speed of the jet stream does not decrease during the winter.

9-41. Answer A. GFDICM 9A (AW)
See explanation for Question 9-40.

9-42. Answer A. GFDICM 9A (AW)
Convective circulation results from cool, dense air sinking to the surface and forcing warm, less dense air upward. Answer (B) is wrong because warm air is forced upward, it does not rise on its own accord. Answer (C) is wrong because warmer air does not always cover a larger area than cooler air, and warm air does not rise on its own.

9-43. Answer B. GFDICM 9A (AW)
Land surfaces warm and cool faster than water surfaces; therefore, land is warmer than water during the day. This creates the sea breeze, which is a wind that blows from the cool water to the warmer land. Answer (A) is wrong because water does not absorb and radiate heat faster than the land. Answer (C) is wrong because convective heating causes the inland air to rise, not the movement of cooler air inland.

SECTION B
WEATHER HAZARDS

Thunderstorms

1. When sufficient moisture is present, cumulus cloud build-ups indicate the presence of convective turbulence.

2. Thunderstorm formation requires an unstable lapse rate, a lifting force, and a relatively high moisture level.

3. The life cycle of a thunderstorm consists of three distinct stages. The cumulus stage is characterized by continuous updrafts. Thunderstorms reach the greatest intensity during the mature stage, which is signaled by the beginning of precipitation at the surface. As the storm dies during the dissipating stage, updrafts weaken and downdrafts become predominant.

4. Airmass thunderstorms are relatively short-lived storms and are usually isolated or scattered over a large area. They form in convective currents, which are most active on warm summer afternoons when the winds are light. Severe thunderstorms contain wind gusts of 50 knots or more, hail 3/4 inch in diameter or larger, and/or tornadoes.

5. Cumulonimbus clouds by themselves indicate severe turbulence. Other indications of turbulence are very frequent lightning and roll clouds.

6. Some weather hazards associated with thunderstorms, such as lightning, hail, and turbulence, are not confined to the cloud itself. Wind shear areas can be found on all sides of a thunderstorm, as well as directly under it.

7. Embedded thunderstorms are particularly dangerous to IFR pilots. Because they are obscured by massive cloud layers, they are more difficult to avoid.

8. Airborne weather radar can help you avoid thunderstorms. However, it provides no assurance of avoiding IFR weather conditions. If using radar, avoid intense radar echoes by at least 20 miles and do not fly between them if they are less than 40 miles apart.

9. A squall line is a narrow band of active thunderstorms that often forms 50 to 200 miles ahead of a fast moving cold front and contains some of the most severe types of weather-related hazards.

10. If you encounter turbulence during flight, establish maneuvering or penetration speed, maintain a level flight attitude, and accept variations in airspeed and altitude. If encountering turbulence during the approach to a landing, it is recommended that you increase the airspeed slightly above normal approach speed to attain more positive control.

Wake Turbulence

1. Wake turbulence is created when an aircraft generates lift. The greatest vortex strength occurs when the generating aircraft is heavy, slow, in a clean configuration, and at a high angle of attack.

2. Wingtip vortices can exceed the roll rate of an aircraft, especially when flying in the same direction as the generating aircraft.

3. Wingtip vortices tend to sink below the flight path of the aircraft which generated them. They are most hazardous during light, quartering tailwind conditions. You should avoid the area below and behind an aircraft generating wake turbulence, especially at low altitude where even a momentary wake encounter could be hazardous.

4. A helicopter can produce vortices similar to wingtip vortices of a large fixed-wing airplane.

Other Turbulence

5. Turbulence that momentarily causes slight, erratic changes in altitude and/or attitude should be reported as light. Moderate turbulence causes noticeable changes in altitude and/or attitude, but aircraft control remains positive.

6. Mechanical turbulence is often experienced in the traffic pattern when wind forms eddies as it blows over hangars, stands of trees, or other obstructions.

7. Any front traveling at a speed of 30 knots or more produces at least a moderate amount of turbulence.

8. Turbulence that is encountered above 15,000 feet AGL that is not associated with cumuliform cloudiness, including thunderstorms, is reported as clear air turbulence. Clear air turbulence often develops in or near the jet stream, which is a narrow band of high altitude winds near the tropopause.

19. A common location of clear air turbulence is in an upper trough on the polar side of a jet stream. The jet stream and associated clear air turbulence can sometimes be visually identified in flight by long streaks of cirrus clouds.

20. Strong mountain wave turbulence can be anticipated when the winds across a ridge are 40 knots or more, and the air is stable. The crests of mountain waves may be marked by lens-shaped, or lenticular, clouds. The presence of rotor clouds on the lee side of the mountain also indicates the possibility of strong turbulence.

21. The greatest turbulence normally occurs as you approach the lee side of mountain ranges, ridges, or hilly terrain in strong headwinds.

Wind Shear

22. Wind shear is a sudden, drastic change in wind speed and/or direction. It can exist at any altitude and may occur in a vertical or horizontal direction.

23. Wind shear is often associated with a strong low-level temperature inversion with strong winds above the inversion, a jet stream, a thunderstorm, or a frontal zone.

24. Wind shear can also occur prior to the passage of a warm front and following the passage of a cold front.

25. During an approach, monitoring the power and vertical velocity required to remain on the proper glideslope is the most important and most easily recognized means of being alerted to possible wind shear. When the wind changes to more of a headwind, the aircraft initially tends to balloon above the glidepath, and then drop below the glidepath because of lower groundspeed. To correct, reduce power momentarily, and then increase it once established in the headwind conditions. The reverse actions are needed if flying into conditions of less headwind or more tailwind.

26. Microbursts are one of the most dangerous sources of wind shear. A microburst is an intense, localized downdraft seldom lasting longer than 15 minutes from the time the burst first strikes the ground until dissipation. The maximum downdrafts encountered in a microburst may be as strong as 6,000 feet per minute.

27. In a microburst, strong wind flows outward in every direction at the surface. An aircraft entering a microburst initially experiences a headwind, with increasing performance, and then a tailwind, with decreasing performance combined with a strong downdraft. If encountering a headwind of 45 knots within a microburst, you would expect a total shear across the microburst of 90 knots.

28. When a squall is reported, you can expect a sudden increase in wind speed of at least 16 knots to a sustained wind speed of 22 knots or more for at least 1 minute.

Restrictions to Visibility

29. Restrictions to visibility can include fog, haze, smoke, smog, and dust.

30. Formation of fog is encouraged by the presence of small particles in the air on which condensation can occur. Industrial areas typically produce more fog since the burning of fossil fuels produces more of these condensation nuclei.

31. Radiation fog forms over fairly flat land on clear, calm nights when the air is moist and there is a small temperature/dewpoint spread.

32. Advection fog is most likely to form in coastal areas when moist air moves over colder ground or water. It can appear suddenly during the day or night and is more persistent than radiation fog.

33. Advection fog and upslope fog are both dependent upon wind for their formation. However, surface winds stronger than 15 knots tend to dissipate or lift advection fog into low stratus clouds.

34. Volcanic ash clouds are highly abrasive to aircraft and engines, and they also restrict visibility.

35. Precipitation-induced fog is most commonly associated with warm fronts and is a result of saturation due to evaporation of precipitation.

36. Steam fog forms when very cold air moves over a warmer water surface.

37. Restrictions to visibility, such as haze, create the illusion of being at a greater distance above the runway, which can cause a pilot to fly a lower-than-normal approach.

38. When flying cross-country at night, the gradual disappearance of ground lights while at altitude indicates clouds and areas of reduced visibility below the aircraft.

Icing

39. The three types of structural ice are rime, clear, and mixed.

40. The accumulation of ice on an aircraft increases drag and weight and decreases lift and thrust.

41. Ice pellets usually indicate the presence of freezing rain at a higher altitude. Freezing rain is hazardous because it is most likely to have the highest rate of accumulation of structural icing. The presence of freezing rain at your altitude indicates the temperature is above freezing at some higher altitude and could indicate that a warm front is about to pass.

42. Since high clouds typically do not consist of liquid water, they are least likely to contribute to aircraft structural icing.

43. The freezing level is where the temperature is 0°C. You can estimate the freezing level by dividing the temperature in °C above zero, by the lapse rate of 2°C per 1,000 feet.

44. If frost is not removed from the wings before flight, it may cause an early airflow separation which decreases lift and increases drag. This causes the airplane to stall at a lower-than-normal angle of attack.

Hydroplaning

45. Hydroplaning occurs when the tires float on top of a thin layer of water on the runway. It results in poor or nil braking action at high speeds, and may result in an aircraft skidding off the side or end of the runway.

46. High aircraft speed, standing water, slush, and a smooth runway texture are factors conducive to hydroplaning.

Cold Weather Operations

47. During preflight in cold weather, crankcase breather lines should receive special attention because they are susceptible to being clogged by ice from crankcase vapors that have condensed and subsequently frozen.

48. It is recommended that during cold weather operations, you should preheat the cabin, as well as the engine.

9-44   H572

When operating VFR at night, what is the first indication of flying into restricted visibility conditions?

A — A gradual disappearance of lights on the ground.
B — Cockpit lights begin to take on an appearance of a halo or glow around them.
C — Ground lights begin to take on an appearance of being surrounded by a halo or glow.

9-44. Answer A. GFDICM 9B

When operating VFR at night, one of the first indications of flying into areas of restricted visibility is the gradual disappearance of lights on the ground. The appearance of halos or a glow around ground lights indicates areas of ground fog or haze, which may obstruct visibility during the landing phase.

9-45   H303

The need to slow an aircraft below V_A is brought about by the following weather phenomenon:

A — High density altitude which increases the indicated stall speed.
B — Turbulence which causes an increase in stall speed.
C — Turbulence which causes a decrease in stall speed.

9-45. Answer B. GFDICM 9B (PHB)

When an airplane is flying at a high airspeed with a low angle of attack, and suddenly encounters a vertical current of air moving upward, the relative wind changes to an upward direction as it meets the wing. This increases the angle of attack of the wing, and can cause a momentary stall. High density altitude has no effect on indicated airspeed including stall speed (answer A). A decrease in stall speed caused by turbulence (answer C) or vertical wind shear is not the best reason for slowing the airplane to V_A.

9-46   **I24**

Ice pellets encountered during flight normally are evidence that

A — a warm front has passed.
B — a warm front is about to pass.
C — there are thunderstorms in the area.

9-46. Answer B. GFDICM 9B (AW)

In order for ice pellets to form, moisture (rain) must fall through colder air. Because of this, the presence of ice pellets at your altitude always indicates freezing rain aloft. This situation is most common just prior to the passage of a warm front when warm air extends up over the cold air preceding the front. Typically, once a warm front passes (answer A), temperatures at the surface are warmer than those aloft. Answer (C) is wrong because, typically, the air temperature in a thunderstorm cools with an increase in altitude.

9-47   **I24**

What is indicated if ice pellets are encountered at 8,000 feet?

A — Freezing rain at higher altitude.
B — You are approaching an area of thunderstorms.
C — You will encounter hail if you continue your flight.

9-47. Answer A. GFDICM 9B (AW)

See explanation for Question 9-46.

9-48   **I24**

Ice pellets encountered during flight normally are evidence that

A — a cold front has passed.
B — there are thunderstorms in the area.
C — freezing rain exists at higher altitudes.

9-48. Answer C. GFDICM 9B (AW)

See explanation for Question 9-46.

9-49   **I26**

The presence of standing lenticular altocumulus clouds is a good indication of

A — lenticular ice formation in calm air.
B — very strong turbulence.
C — heavy icing conditions.

9-49. Answer B. GFDICM 9B (AW)

Standing lenticular clouds form on the crests of waves created by barriers to wind flow such as mountain ranges. The clouds show little movement but can contain strong winds. The presence of these clouds is a good indication of very strong turbulence and should be avoided. Answers (A) and (C) are inappropriate because the nature of lenticular clouds usually preclude the formation of ice.

9-50   **I27**

The conditions necessary for the formation of cumulonimbus clouds are a lifting action and

A — unstable, dry air.
B — stable, moist air.
C — unstable, moist air.

9-50. Answer C. GFDICM 9B (AW)

There are three conditions necessary to create cumulonimbus (thunderstorm) clouds. They include unstable air, a lifting force, and a high moisture content. Without sufficient moisture (answer A), clouds and precipitation may not form. If the air is stable (answer B), stratus clouds are more likely to form.

9-51   **I27**

Fog produced by frontal activity is a result of saturation due to

A — nocturnal cooling.
B — adiabatic cooling.
C — evaporation of precipitation.

9-51. Answer C. GFDICM 9B (AW)

Precipitation fog typically forms as a result of frontal activity. As a cold front advances, warm air is pushed aloft over the cooler air below. If precipitation begins to fall through the cooler air, evaporation from the precipitation will saturate the cool air and fog typically will form. Nocturnal fog (answer A) forms on clear, calm nights when the air cools to the dewpoint. Answer (B) is inappropriate because adiabatic cooling results from the expansion of vertically moving air.

9-52   **I28**
What is an important characteristic of wind shear?

A — It is present at only lower levels and exists in a horizontal direction.
B — It is present at any level and exists in only a vertical direction.
C — It can be present at any level and can exist in both a horizontal and vertical direction.

9-53   **I28**
Hazardous wind shear is commonly encountered

A — near warm or stationary frontal activity.
B — when the wind velocity is stronger than 35 knots.
C — in areas of temperature inversion and near thunderstorms.

9-54   **I28**
Low-level wind shear may occur when

A — surface winds are light and variable.
B — there is a low-level temperature inversion with strong winds above the inversion.
C — surface winds are above 15 knots and there is no change in wind direction and windspeed with height.

9-55   **I28**
If a temperature inversion is encountered immediately after takeoff or during an approach to a landing, a potential hazard exists due to

A — wind shear.
B — strong surface winds.
C — strong convective currents.

9-56   **I28**
GIVEN:

Winds at 3,000 feet AGL ....30 kts
Surface winds ....calm
While on approach for landing, under clear skies with convective turbulence a few hours after sunrise, one should

A — keep the approach airspeed at or slightly below normal to compensate for floating.
B — not alter the approach airspeed; these conditions are nearly ideal.
C — increase approach airspeed slightly above normal to avoid stalling.

9-52. Answer C. GFDICM 9B (AW)
Wind shear is a sudden, drastic shift in wind speed and/or direction that may occur at any altitude in a vertical or horizontal plane. Answer (A) is wrong because wind shear can occur at any altitude and in both a vertical or horizontal direction. Answer (B) is wrong because wind shear is not limited to just the vertical plane.

9-53. Answer C. GFDICM 9B (AW)
Hazardous wind shear is most commonly associated with temperature inversions, the jet stream, and thunderstorms and is less common in warm and stationary front activity (answer A). Answer (B) is wrong because strong winds do not necessarily indicate the presence of wind shear.

9-54. Answer B. GFDICM 9B (AW)
When a temperature inversion forms with strong winds above, a wind shear zone can develop between the calm air in the inversion and stronger winds above. Eddies in the shear zone can cause airspeed fluctuations as you climb or descend through them. Light surface winds (answer A) and winds above 15 knots with no change in direction or speed (answer C) do not indicate the presence of low-level wind shear.

9-55. Answer A. GFDICM 9B (AW)
See explanation for Question 9-54. If you encounter a temperature inversion after takeoff or during an approach to landing, the abrupt change in wind direction and/or speed above the inversion can create a potential wind shear hazard. Answers (B) and (C) are wrong because strong surface winds and convective currents are not associated with a temperature inversion.

9-56. Answer C. GFDICM 9B
The conditions indicated can create a wind shear hazard. When approaching to land in these conditions, it is recommended that the approach be flown at an airspeed slightly higher than normal to avoid stalling. If the wind shears from a strong headwind to no wind during descent, you could stall dangerously close to the ground.

9-57   I28

Convective currents are most active on warm summer afternoons when winds are

A — light.
B — moderate.
C — strong.

9-58   I28

When flying low over hilly terrain, ridges, or mountain ranges, the greatest potential danger from turbulent air currents will usually be encountered on the

A — leeward side when flying with a tailwind.
B — leeward side when flying into the wind.
C — windward side when flying into the wind.

9-59   I28

During an approach, the most important and most easily recognized means of being alerted to possible wind shear is monitoring the

A — amount of trim required to relieve control pressures.
B — heading changes necessary to remain on the runway centerline.
C — power and vertical velocity required to remain on the proper glidepath.

9-60   I28

During departure, under conditions of suspected low-level wind shear, a sudden decrease in headwind will cause

A — a loss in airspeed equal to the decrease in wind velocity.
B — a gain in airspeed equal to the decrease in wind velocity.
C — no change in airspeed, but groundspeed will decrease.

9-61   I29

Which situation would most likely result in freezing precipitation? Rain falling from air which has a temperature of

A — 32°F or less into air having a temperature of more then 32°F.
B — 0°C or less into air having a temperature of 0°C or more.
C — more than 32°F into air having a temperature of 32°F or less.

9-57. Answer A. GFDICM 9B (AW)

Convective currents are created as the surface releases heat into the air. These currents are most common during hot summer afternoons when winds are light. Moderate (answer B) or strong (answer C) winds tend to inhibit convective activity.

9-58. Answer B. GFDICM 9B (AW)

Turbulence created due to interference with normal wind flow is called mechanical turbulence. This type of turbulence is typically encountered when flying low on the leeward side of hilly terrain, ridges, or mountain ranges with a headwind. Answer (A) is wrong since you would be flying away from rising terrain. Answer (C) is wrong because the windward side is an area of predominate updrafts.

9-59. Answer C. GFDICM 9B (AC 00-54)

On every approach you should closely monitor the power and vertical velocity required to remain on the proper glide path. If either of these appear abnormal, you should be alert for wind shear. Answer (A) is wrong because the amount of trim required will vary with how the aircraft is loaded. Changes in heading (answer B) indicate windy conditions and not necessarily the existence of wind shear.

9-60. Answer A. GFDICM 9B (AC 00-54)

Anytime you experience a sudden decrease in headwind, you will experience a performance decrease. This will equate to a loss of airspeed equal to the decrease in wind velocity and a corresponding loss of lift. Answer (B) is wrong because airspeed will decrease, not increase, and answer (C) is wrong because airspeed will change and groundspeed will remain unchanged until power is added and the original indicated airspeed value regained.

9-61. Answer C. GFDICM 9B (AW)

In order for precipitation to begin falling as a liquid and then freeze, rain typically must begin falling in air that is above freezing and continue falling through air that is below freezing. If rain begins falling in air that is freezing or below and continues into air that is above freezing (answers A and B), you would not experience freezing precipitation.

9-62   **I30**

Which statement is true concerning the hazards of hail?

A — Hail damage in horizontal flight is minimal due to the vertical movement of hail in the clouds.
B — Rain at the surface is a reliable indication of no hail aloft.
C — Hailstones may be encountered in clear air several miles from a thunderstorm.

9-63   **I30**

Hail is most likely to be associated with

A — cumulus clouds.
B — cumulonimbus clouds.
C — stratocumulus clouds.

9-64   **I30**

The most severe weather conditions, such as destructive winds, heavy hail, and tornadoes, are generally associated with

A — slow-moving warm fronts which slope above the tropopause.
B — squall lines.
C — fast-moving occluded fronts.

9-65   **I30**

Of the following, which is accurate regarding turbulence associated with thunderstorms?

A — Outside the cloud, shear turbulence can be encountered 50 miles laterally from a severe storm.
B — Shear turbulence is encountered only inside cumulonimbus clouds or within a 5-mile radius of them.
C — Outside the cloud, shear turbulence can be encountered 20 miles laterally from a severe storm.

9-66   **I30**

If airborne radar is indicating an extremely intense thunderstorm echo, this thunderstorm should be avoided by a distance of at least

A — 20 miles.
B — 10 miles.
C — 5 miles.

9-62. Answer C. GFDICM 9B (AW)

When hail is created in a thunderstorm, the existing updrafts can lift the hail to the top of the thunderstorm where strong upper-level winds can carry it several miles downwind. Answer (A) is wrong because hail can cause extensive damage to your aircraft in a very short period of time. Answer (B) is wrong because rain at the surface does not preclude hail. Hail is possible with any thunderstorm.

9-63. Answer B. GFDICM 9B (AW)

Hail is most commonly associated with cumulonimbus clouds (thunderstorms). Cumulus clouds (answer A) are not as likely to generate hail because the water droplets are too small. Answer (C) is wrong because stratocumulus clouds do not generate the updrafts necessary to produce hail.

9-64. Answer B. GFDICM 9B (AW)

A squall line is a narrow band of active thunderstorms which normally contains some of the most severe weather conditions. Slow-moving warm fronts typically do not extend above the tropopause (answer A), and they usually exhibit stable conditions. Answer (C) is wrong because occluded fronts are classified as either warm front occlusions or cold front occlusions, not fast-moving.

9-65. Answer C. GFDICM 9B (AW)

Thunderstorms typically contain many severe weather hazards including lightning, hail, turbulence, gusty surface winds, and tornados. These hazards are not confined to the cloud itself. For example, you can encounter turbulence in VFR conditions as far as 20 miles from the storm. Answer (A) is wrong because shear turbulence is not likely to occur 50 miles from the storm, and answer (B) is wrong because turbulence can exist outside the cumulonimbus cloud in excess of a 5-mile radius.

9-66. Answer A. GFDICM 9B (AW)

If the aircraft you are flying is equipped with airborne radar, you can use it to avoid thunderstorms. A good rule of thumb is to avoid any intense thunderstorm echoes by at least 20 miles. Any distance less than 20 miles (answers B and C) may not provide adequate separation.

9-67   **I30**

Which statement is true regarding squall lines?

A — They are always associated with cold fronts.
B — They are slow in forming, but rapid in movement.
C — They are nonfrontal and often contain severe, steady-state thunderstorms.

9-68   **I30**

Which statement is true concerning squall lines?

A — They form slowly, but move rapidly.
B — They are associated with frontal systems only.
C — They offer the most intense weather hazards to aircraft.

9-69   **I30**

Select the true statement pertaining to the life cycle of a thunderstorm.

A — Updrafts continue to develop throughout the dissipating stage of a thunderstorm.
B — The beginning of rain at the Earth's surface indicates the mature stage of the thunderstorm.
C — The beginning of rain at the Earth's surface indicates the dissipating stage of the thunderstorm.

9-70   **I30**

What visible signs indicate extreme turbulence in thunderstorms?

A —Base of the clouds near the surface, heavy rain, and hail.
B — Low ceiling and visibility, hail, and precipitation static.
C — Cumulonimbus clouds, very frequent lightning, and roll clouds.

9-71   **I30**

Which weather phenomenon signals the beginning of the mature stage of a thunderstorm?

A — The start of rain.
B — The appearance of an anvil top.
C — Growth rate of cloud is maximum.

9-72   **I30**

What feature is normally associated with the cumulus stage of a thunderstorm?

A — Roll cloud.
B — Continuous updraft.
C — Beginning of rain at the surface.

9-67. Answer C. GFDICM 9B (AW)
A squall line is a non-frontal, narrow band of active thunderstorms that typically contain some of the most intense weather hazards known to aircraft. They can develop ahead of a cold front in moist, unstable air, but they may develop in unstable air far removed from any front (answer A). Answer (B) is wrong because squall lines typically form rapidly and reach their maximum intensity during late afternoon.

9-68. Answer C. GFDICM 9B (AW)
See explanation for Question 9-67.

9-69. Answer B. GFDICM 9B (AW)
There are three stages in the life cycle of a thunderstorm; cumulus, mature, and dissipating. The cumulus stage is characterized by strong updrafts (answer A) reaching speeds in excess of 3,000 feet per minute. The mature stage signifies the beginning of downdrafts and can be identified by the presence of rain falling at the surface. The dissipating stage (answer C) consists primarily of downdrafts and the formation of an anvil cloud.

9-70. Answer C. GFDICM 9B (AC 00-24B)
Potentially hazardous turbulence is present in all thunderstorms. Some visual signs that can indicate extreme turbulence include the presence of cumulonimbus clouds, frequent lightning, and roll clouds. Answers (A) and (B) are wrong because the presence of low clouds, heavy rain, and hail do not necessarily indicate the presence of turbulence.

9-71. Answer A. GFDICM 9B (AW)
There are three stages in the life cycle of a thunderstorm; they are the cumulus stage, mature stage, and dissipating stage. The cumulus stage is characterized by strong updrafts reaching speeds in excess of 3,000 feet per minute causing a rapid growth rate (answer C). The mature stage signifies the beginning of downdrafts and can be identified by the presence of rain falling at the surface and the formation of a roll cloud. The dissipating stage consists primarily of downdrafts and the formation of an anvil (answer B).

9-72. Answer B. GFDICM 9B (AW)
See explanation for Question 9-71.

9-73   I30

During the life cycle of a thunderstorm, which stage is characterized predominately by downdrafts?

A — Mature.
B — Developing.
C — Dissipating.

9-74   I30

What minimum distance should exist between intense radar echoes before any attempt is made to fly between these thunderstorms?

A — 20 miles.
B — 30 miles.
C — 40 miles.

9-75   I31

Which in-flight hazard is most commonly associated with warm fronts?

A — Advection fog.
B — Radiation fog.
C — Precipitation-induced fog.

9-76   I31

Which is true regarding the use of airborne weather-avoidance radar for the recognition of certain weather conditions?

A — The radarscope provides no assurance of avoiding instrument weather conditions.
B — The avoidance of hail is assured when flying between and just clear of the most intense echoes.
C — The clear area between intense echoes indicates that visual sighting of storms can be maintained when flying between the echoes.

9-77   I31

A situation most conducive to the formation of advection fog is

A — a light breeze moving colder air over a water surface.
B — an air mass moving inland from the coastline during the winter.
C — a warm, moist air mass settling over a cool surface under no-wind conditions.

9-78   I31

Advection fog has drifted over a coastal airport during the day. What may tend to dissipate or lift this fog into low stratus clouds?

A — Nighttime cooling.
B — Surface radiation.
C — Wind 15 knots or stronger.

9-73. Answer C. GFDICM 9B (AW)
See explanation for Question 9-71.

9-74. Answer C. GFDICM 9B (AW)
If the aircraft you are flying is equipped with airborne radar, you can use it to avoid thunderstorms. A good rule of thumb is to avoid any intense thunderstorm echoes by at least 20 miles and never fly between two cells if they are less than 40 miles apart. When flying between cells, any distance less than 40 miles (answers A and B) may not provide adequate separation.

9-75. Answer C. GFDICM 9B (AW)
Precipitation-induced fog may form when precipitation falls through a layer of cooler air near the surface and evaporates, saturating the cool air. The conditions required to produce this type of fog are commonly associated with warm fronts. Advection fog (answer A) forms when a low layer of warm, moist air moves over a cooler surface, and radiation fog (answer B) forms over fairly level areas on clear, calm, humid nights.

9-76. Answer A. GFDICM 9B (AW)
Airborne weather radar is designed for avoiding severe weather, not for penetrating it. Weather radar detects drops of precipitation, not the minute drops associated with cloud formations. Therefore, weather radar provides no assurance of avoiding instrument meteorological conditions. Answer (B) is wrong because hail can occur several miles away from a thunderstorm. Since weather radar does not indicate cloud formations, there is no guarantee that visual sighting of storms (answer C) can be maintained when flying between echoes.

9-77. Answer B. GFDICM 9B (AW)
Advection fog is caused when a low layer of warm, moist air moves over a cooler land or water surface. It is most common along the coast where sea breezes transport air from the warm water to cool land. Cold air moving over water (answer A) will typically produce steam fog, and answer (C) identifies the conditions required to produce radiation fog (ground fog).

9-78. Answer C. GFDICM 9B (AW)
Once advection fog forms, winds of approximately 15 knots or stronger will usually lift the fog sufficiently to create stratus clouds. Nighttime cooling (answer A) and surface radiation (answer B) typically produce fog.

9-79   **I31**
What lifts advection fog into low stratus clouds?

A — Nighttime cooling.
B — Dryness of the underlying land mass.
C — Surface winds of approximately 15 knots or stronger.

9-80   **I31**
In what ways do advection fog, radiation fog, and steam fog differ in their formation or location?

A — Radiation fog is restricted to land areas; advection fog is most common along coastal areas; steam fog forms over a water surface.
B — Advection fog deepens as windspeed increases up to 20 knots; steam fog requires calm or very light wind; radiation fog forms when the ground or water cools the air by radiation.
C — Steam fog forms from moist air moving over a colder surface; advection fog requires cold air over a warmer surface; radiation fog is produced by radiational cooling of the ground.

9-81   **I31**
With respect to advection fog, which statement is true?

A — It is slow to develop, and dissipates quite rapidly.
B — It forms almost exclusively at night or near daybreak.
C — It can appear suddenly during day or night, and it is more persistent than radiation fog.

9-82   **I32**
A common location of clear air turbulence is

A — in an upper trough on the polar side of a jet stream.
B — near a ridge aloft on the equatorial side of a high-pressure flow.
C — south of an east/west oriented high-pressure ridge in its dissipating stage.

9-83   **I32**
The jet stream and associated clear air turbulence can sometimes be visually identified in flight by

A — dust or haze at flight level.
B — long streaks of cirrus clouds.
C — a constant outside air temperature.

9-79. Answer C. GFDICM 9B (AW)
See explanation for Question 9-78.

9-80. Answer A. GFDICM 9B (AW)
Radiation fog is typically restricted to land areas because water surfaces cool little from nighttime radiation. Because advection fog requires the movement of warm, moist air over a cooler land or water surface, it is most common along the coast. Steam fog occurs as cool air moves over warmer water, so its development is restricted to water surfaces. Answer (B) is wrong because advection fog typically lifts to create stratus clouds with winds stronger than 15 knots, and steam fog develops over water surfaces when air is blowing from a cold surface (either land or water) over warmer water. Answer (C) is inappropriate since the types of fog conflict with the formation descriptions.

9-81. Answer C. GFDICM 9B (AW)
A unique characteristic of advection fog is that it can form rapidly during the day or night, and it tends to be more persistent and extensive than radiation fog. Answer (A) is wrong because advection fog is quick to develop and dissipates slowly. Answer (B) is wrong because advection fog can form during the day or night.

9-82. Answer A. GFDICM 9B (AW)
Clear air turbulence (CAT) is often associated with a jet stream that is interacting with a large mountain range or deep low pressure system. It is commonly located in an upper trough on the polar or cold side of a jet stream where the wind speed gradient is greater. Answers (B) and (C) are wrong because CAT is not normally associated with either of the situations indicated.

9-83. Answer B. GFDICM 9B (AW)
Clear air turbulence associated with a jet stream can sometimes be visually identified in flight by long streaks of cirrus clouds. Answer (A) is wrong because dust or haze seldom rise to flight levels associated with the jet stream. Answer (C) is wrong because the temperature is not constant throughout the jet stream.

9-84 I35

The conditions most favorable to wave formation over mountainous areas are a layer of

A — stable air at mountaintop altitude and a wind of at least 20 knots blowing across the ridge.

B — unstable air at mountaintop altitude and a wind of at least 20 knots blowing across the ridge.

C — moist, unstable air at mountaintop altitude and a wind of less than 5 knots blowing across the ridge.

9-85 I41

What wind conditions would you anticipate when squalls are reported at your destination?

A — Peak gusts of at least 35 knots combined with a change in wind direction of 30° or more.

B — Sudden increases in windspeed of at least 16 knots to a sustained speed of 22 knots or more for at least 1 minute.

C — Rapid variations in windspeed of 15 knots or more between peaks and lulls.

9-86 I52

The minimum vertical wind-shear value critical for probable moderate or greater turbulence is

A — 4 knots per 1,000 feet.

B — 6 knots per 1,000 feet.

C — 8 knots per 1,000 feet.

9-87 I53

A pilot reporting turbulence that momentarily causes slight, erratic changes in altitude and/or attitude should report it as

A — light chop.

B — light turbulence.

C — moderate turbulence.

9-88 I53

When turbulence causes changes in altitude and/or attitude, but aircraft control remains positive, that should be reported as

A — light.

B — severe.

C — moderate.

9-84. Answer A. GFDICM 9B

The formation of a strong mountain wave requires stable air blowing across a ridge at a speed of at least 20 knots. Unstable air (answers B and C) does not support the formation of a mountain wave. In addition, the wind must be at least 20 knots (answer C).

9-85. Answer B. GFDICM 9B

A squall is defined as an abrupt windspeed increase of at least 16 knots to a sustained speed of 22 knots or more, lasting at least one minute.

9-86. Answer B. GFDICM 9B (AWS)

The tropopause data chart contains four panels: the observed tropopause data, a maximum wind prog, a height/vertical wind shear prog, and a high level significant weather prog. The height/vertical wind shear prog depicts the height of the tropopause in terms of pressure altitude and vertical wind shear in knots per 1,000 feet. As a general rule you should expect moderate or greater turbulence when the vertical wind shear is six knots or more.

9-87. Answer B. GFDICM 9B (AIM)

Light turbulence causes slight erratic changes in altitude or attitude and slight strain against seat belts. Light chop (answer A) is slight, rapid bumpiness without appreciable changes in altitude or attitude. Moderate turbulence (answer C) causes changes in altitude or attitude, but the aircraft remains in positive control at all times. There are usually changes in indicated airspeed and you will feel definite strains against the seat belt.

9-88. Answer C. GFDICM 9B (AIM)

See explanation for Question 9-87.

9-89   I53

Turbulence that is encountered above 15,000 feet AGL not associated with cumuliform cloudiness, including thunderstorms, should be reported as

A — severe turbulence.
B — clear air turbulence.
C — convective turbulence.

9-90   K02

Which type of jetstream can be expected to cause the greater turbulence?

A — A straight jetstream associated with a low-pressure trough.
B — A curving jetstream associated with a deep low-pressure trough.
C — A jetstream occurring during the summer at the lower latitudes.

9-91   K02

A strong wind shear can be expected

A — in the jetstream front above a core having a speed of 60 to 90 knots.
B — if the 5°C isotherms are spaced between 7° to 10° of latitude.
C — on the low-pressure side of a jetstream core where the speed at the core is stronger than 110 knots.

9-92   J25

The Low Level Wind Shear Alert System (LLWAS) provides wind data and software process to detect the presence of a

A — rotating column of air extending from a cumulonimbus cloud.
B — change in wind direction and/or speed within a very short distance above the airport.
C — downward motion of the air associated with continuous winds blowing with an easterly component due to the rotation of the Earth.

9-89. Answer B. GFDICM 9B (AIM)
Clear air turbulence (CAT) can take place at any altitude and its presence carries no visual warning. CAT may be caused by wind shear, convective currents, or obstructions to normal wind flow. According to the AIM, turbulence not associated with cumuliform clouds, including thunderstorms, should be reported as clear air turbulence preceded by the appropriate intensity. Severe turbulence (answer A) causes abrupt changes in altitude or attitude and usually large variations in indicated airspeed. The aircraft may be momentarily out of control, and occupants are usually forced violently against safety belts. Convective turbulence (answer C) is typically associated with convective activity and thunderstorms.

9-90. Answer B. GFDICM 9B (AC 00-30A)
The turbulence associated with a jet stream can be very strong, and because it often occurs in clear air, it is difficult to forecast accurately. As a rule of thumb, clear air turbulence can be expected when a curving jet steam is found north of a deep low pressure system. Although turbulence can be associated with a straight jet stream (answer A) and a jet stream occurring during the summer at lower latitudes (answer C), they typically do not cause the greatest turbulence.

9-91. Answer C. GFDICM 9B (AC 00-30A)
Strong clear air turbulence and strong wind shear can be expected on the low-pressure side of a jet stream core where the speed at the core is stronger than 110 knots. Answer (A) is wrong because strong wind shear is associated with jet streams of 110 knots or more at the core. Answer (B) is inappropriate.

9-92. Answer B. GFDICM 9B (AIM)
Wind shear is defined as a change in wind speed and/or direction in a short distance resulting in a tearing or shearing effect. It can exist in a horizontal or vertical direction and occasionally in both. Answer (A) describes a tornado, and answer (C) is a nonsensical distractor.

9-93 N33

One of the most dangerous features of mountain waves is the turbulent areas in and

A — below rotor clouds.
B — above rotor clouds.
C — below lenticular clouds.

9-94 H550

When turbulence is encountered during the approach to a landing, what action is recommended and for what primary reason?

A — Increase the airspeed slightly above normal approach speed to attain more positive control.
B — Decrease the airspeed slightly below normal approach speed to avoid overstressing the airplane.
C — Increase the airspeed slightly above normal approach speed to penetrate the turbulence as quickly as possible.

9-95 H550

Which type of approach and landing is recommended during gusty wind conditions?

A — A power-on approach and power-on landing.
B — A power-off approach and power-on landing.
C — A power-on approach and power-off landing.

9-96 H303

A pilot is entering an area where significant clear air turbulence has been reported. Which action is appropriate upon encountering the first ripple?

A — Maintain altitude and airspeed.
B — Adjust airspeed to that recommended for rough air.
C — Enter a shallow climb or descent at maneuvering speed.

9-97 H303

If severe turbulence is encountered during flight, the pilot should reduce the airspeed to

A — minimum control speed.
B — design-maneuvering speed.
C — maximum structural cruising speed.

9-93. Answer A. GFDICM 9B (AW)
There are three types of clouds associated with mountain wave activity. They are lenticular clouds, cap clouds, and rotor clouds. Lenticular clouds usually mark the crests of mountain waves. These clouds form in the updrafts and dissipate in the downdrafts so they have a stationary appearance as the wind blows through them. Rotor clouds may also form on the downwind side of the mountain and cap clouds may obscure the mountain peaks. One of the most dangerous features of mountain waves is the turbulent areas in and below rotor clouds. Although turbulence may be experienced when above a rotor cloud (answer B) and when below lenticulars (answer C), it is usually less severe.

9-94. Answer A. GFDICM 9B (AFH)
If you encounter turbulence while making an approach to landing, it is a good practice to make the approach at a slightly higher-than-normal airspeed to allow for more positive control of the airplane. Answer (B) is wrong because decreasing your airspeed would make the aircraft more difficult to control. Although increasing your approach speed will allow you to penetrate the turbulence faster (answer C), this is not the reason for doing it.

9-95. Answer A. GFDICM 9B (AFH)
When making an approach in gusty winds, it is best to make a power-on approach and landing at an airspeed slightly above normal. This will provide for better control of the aircraft throughout the landing. If you were to make a power-off approach and landing (answer B), you may not be able to maintain positive control. Answer (C) is wrong because you want to maintain positive control all the way to touchdown.

9-96. Answer B. GFDICM 9B (AFH)
Anytime you encounter turbulence, or expect to encounter turbulence, you should slow the airplane to maneuvering speed (V_A) or the recommended rough air penetration speed. If you do not reduce your airspeed (answer A), you run the risk of overstressing the aircraft. Answer (C) is wrong because the first action is to reduce speed; changing altitude after that also may be an appropriate action.

9-97. Answer B. GFDICM 9B (AFH)
See explanation for Question 9-96.

9-98   **I29**

Frost covering the upper surface of an airplane wing usually will cause

A — the airplane to stall at an angle of attack that is higher than normal.

B — the airplane to stall at an angle of attack that is lower than normal.

C — drag factors so large that sufficient speed cannot be obtained for takeoff.

9-99   **I30**

Which is the best technique for minimizing the wing-load factor when flying in severe turbulence?

A — Change power settings, as necessary, to maintain constant airspeed.

B — Control airspeed with power, maintain wings level, and accept variations of altitude.

C — Set power and trim to obtain an airspeed at or below maneuvering speed, maintain wings level, and accept variations of airspeed and altitude.

9-100   **J27**

Choose the correct statement regarding wake turbulence.

A — Vortex generation begins with the initiation of the takeoff roll.

B — The primary hazard is loss of control because of induced roll.

C — The greatest vortex strength is produced when the generating airplane is heavy, clean, and fast.

9-101   **J27**

During a takeoff made behind a departing large jet aircraft, the pilot can minimize the hazard of wingtip vortices by

A — being airborne prior to reaching the jet's flight-path until able to turn clear of its wake.

B — maintaining extra speed on takeoff and climbout.

C — extending the takeoff roll and not rotating until well beyond the jet's rotation point.

9-102   **J27**

Which procedure should you follow to avoid wake turbulence if a large jet aircraft crosses your course from left to right approximately 1 mile ahead and at your altitude?

A — Make sure you are slightly above the path of the jet.

B — Slow your airspeed to V_A and maintain altitude and course.

C — Make sure you are slightly below the path of the jet and perpendicular to the course.

9-98. Answer B. GFDICM 9B (FTP)

Frost interferes with the smooth flow of air over the wings and can cause early airflow separation. This results in a loss of lift, and the wing stalls at a lower than normal angle of attack. Answer (A) is wrong because early airflow separation causes the wing to stall at a lower (not higher) angle of attack. Drag (answer C) may increase due to surface roughness of the wings, but normally it is not enough to be noticeable. The aircraft should be able to reach takeoff speed; the danger is that it tends to stall during takeoff.

9-99. Answer C. GFDICM 9B (AIM)

Anytime you experience turbulence, or expect it, you should slow the aircraft to maneuvering speed or less. In addition, you should try to maintain a wings-level flight attitude and accept variations in airspeed and altitude. Answers (A) and (B) are wrong because it is best to adjust the power to a setting that will result in maneuvering speed or less and accept airspeed fluctuations.

9-100. Answer B. GFDICM 9B (AIM)

Large aircraft can produce wake turbulence that could induce uncontrolled roll rates in smaller aircraft. Vortex generation begins as soon as the aircraft's wing begins producing lift, not when it begins its takeoff roll (answer A). The greatest vortex strength is produced when the generating airplane is heavy, clean, and slow, not heavy, clean, and fast (answer C).

9-101. Answer A. GFDICM 9B (AIM)

If taking off behind a large aircraft, you can minimize the chance of flying into wake turbulence by making sure you lift off prior to the preceding aircraft's flightpath and remain above the flightpath until able to turn clear. Maintaining extra airspeed (answer B) will not minimize the hazard of wake turbulence. Delaying lift off until beyond the jet's rotation point (answer C) will take you through its wake turbulence.

9-102. Answer A. GFDICM 9B (AIM)

As wake turbulence is generated in flight, it tends to sink at a rate of 400 to 500 feet per minute. Because of this, anytime you anticipate crossing a large aircraft's flightpath, you should cross above its path. Answer (B) is wrong because slowing to V_A is not necessary if the vortices are avoided. Answer (C) is wrong because being below a large aircraft's flightpath will increase your chance of encountering wake turbulence.

9-103   J27
To avoid possible wake turbulence from a large jet aircraft that has just landed prior to your takeoff, at which point on the runway should you plan to become airborne?

A — Past the point where the jet touched down.
B — At the point where the jet touched down, or just prior to this point.
C — Approximately 500 feet prior to the point where the jet touched down.

9-104   J27
When landing behind a large aircraft, which procedure should be followed for vortex avoidance?

A — Stay above its final approach flightpath all the way to touchdown.
B — Stay below and to one side of its final approach flightpath.
C — Stay well below its final approach flightpath and land at least 2,000 feet behind.

9-105   J27
With respect to vortex circulation, which is true?

A — Helicopters generate downwash turbulence, not vortex circulation.
B — The vortex strength is greatest when the generating aircraft is flying fast.
C — Vortex circulation generated by helicopters in forward flight trail behind in a manner similar to wingtip vortices generated by airplanes.

9-106   J27
Which is true with respect to vortex circulation?

A — Helicopters generate downwash turbulence only, not vortex circulation.
B — The vortex strength is greatest when the generating aircraft is heavy, clean, and slow.
C — When vortex circulation sinks into ground effect, it tends to dissipate rapidly and offer little danger.

9-107   L52
During preflight in cold weather, crankcase breather lines should receive special attention because they are susceptible to being clogged by

A — congealed oil from the crankcase.
B — moisture from the outside air which has frozen.
C — ice from crankcase vapors that have condensed and subsequently frozen.

9-103. Answer A. GFDICM 9B (AIM)
When taking off behind a large aircraft that has just landed, you should plan on becoming airborne beyond the point where the large aircraft touched down. Beyond this point, the jet's wake turbulence will be greatly diminished. Becoming airborne at the large aircraft's touchdown point, or prior to (answers B and C), will increase your chance of encountering wake turbulence created by the jet while it was airborne.

9-104. Answer A. GFDICM 9B (AIM)
When landing behind a large aircraft, it is best to stay above its flight path all the way to touchdown. Since wake turbulence sinks after it is generated, staying below a large aircraft's flight path (answers B and C) will greatly increase your chance of encountering wake turbulence.

9-105. Answer C. GFDICM 9B (AIM)
In forward flight, departing or landing helicopters produce a pair of strong, high-speed trailing vortices similar to wingtip vortices of larger fixed-wing aircraft. Answer (A) is wrong because hovering helicopters generate downwash which produces high velocity outward vortices to a distance approximately three times the rotor diameter. When rotor downwash hits the surface, the resulting outward vortices have behavioral characteristics similar to wingtip vortices produced by fixed-wing aircraft. Answer (B) is incorrect because wingtip vortices are the strongest at high angles of attack and at faster airspeeds, the angle of attack is low.

9-106. Answer B. GFDICM 9B (AIM)
Whenever an airplane generates lift, air spills over the wingtips causing wingtip vortices. The greatest vortex strength occurs when the generating aircraft is heavy, clean and slow. Answer (A) is wrong because departing or landing helicopters produce a pair of strong, high-speed trailing vortices similar to wingtip vortices of larger fixed wing aircraft. Hovering helicopters also produce outward vortices when the rotor downwash hits the surface. Answer (C) is incorrect because vortices can remain in the touchdown zone for a period of time.

9-107. Answer C. GFDICM 9B (AC 91-13C)
Crankcase breather lines are susceptible to being clogged by ice formed when crankcase vapors condense after engine shutdown. The clogged lines prevent the release of air from the crankcase. Answer (A) is wrong because congealed oil is not likely to clog crankcase breather lines. Answer (B) is incorrect because moisture from the outside air usually is not substantial enough to clog crankcase breather lines.

9-108   **L52**

Which is true regarding preheating an aircraft during cold weather operations?

A — The cabin area as well as the engine should be preheated.

B — The cabin area should not be preheated with portable heaters.

C — Hot air should be blown directly at the engine through the air intakes.

9-108. Answer A. GFDICM 9B (AC 91-13C)

Preheating the cabin as well as the engine is recommended to ensure the proper operation of instruments, many of which are adversely affected by cold temperatures. Answer (B) is wrong because without preheating the cabin, instruments may not work properly. Answer (C) is incorrect because heat ducting should not be placed so it will blow hot air directly on combustible parts of the aircraft such as engine covers and flexible fuel, oil and hydraulic lines.

SECTION C
PRINTED REPORTS AND FORECASTS

METARs

1. An aviation routine weather report (METAR) is an observation of surface weather written in a standard format which typically contains 10 or more separate elements.

2. A non-routine aviation weather report (SPECI) is issued when a significant change in one or more of the elements of a METAR has occurred.

3. Prevailing visibility is the greatest distance an observer can see and identify objects through at least half of the horizon.

4. When a squall (SQ) is reported, you can expect a sudden increase in wind speed of at least 16 knots to a sustained wind speed of 22 knots or more for at least 1 minute.

5. Runway visual range (RVR) is based on what a pilot in a moving aircraft should see when looking down the runway. If included in a METAR, RVR is reported following prevailing visibility.

6. A ceiling is the height above ground level of the lowest layer of clouds aloft which is reported as broken (BKN) or overcast (OVC), or the vertical visibility (VV) into an obscuration. For example, VV008 indicates that the sky is obscured with a vertical visibility of 800 feet.

7. If the top of a layer is known, you can easily determine its thickness by adding the airport's elevation (MSL) to the height of the cloud base (AGL) found in a METAR observation, then subtract the height of the cloud tops.

8. The beginning of the remarks section is indicated by the code RMK. The remarks section reports weather considered significant to aircraft operations, which are not covered in the previous sections of the METAR.

Radar Weather Reports

9. Radar weather reports (SDs) define general areas of precipitation, particularly thunderstorms.

10. The abbreviation MT is used to denote maximum tops of the precipitation in the clouds. Heights are reported in hundreds of feet MSL followed by the radial and distance in nautical miles from the reporting location.

Pilot Weather Reports

11. The bases and tops of cloud layers, in-flight visibility, icing conditions, wind shear, and turbulence may be included in a pilot weather report (PIREP).

12. PIREPs are the best source for current weather between reporting stations.

Terminal Aerodrome Forecasts

13. Terminal aerodrome forecasts (TAFs) are issued 4 times per day, and predict the weather at a specific airport for a 24-hour period of time. A TAF should be your primary source of weather information for your destination.

14. In a TAF, the contraction VRB indicates that the wind direction is variable. A calm wind (3 knots or less) is indicated by 00000KT.

15. P6SM in a terminal aerodrome forecast implies that the prevailing visibility is expected to be greater than 6 statute miles.

16. The letters SKC are used in a terminal aerodrome forecast to indicate "sky clear."

17. The letters WS indicate that low-level wind shear which is not associated with convective activity may be present during the valid time of the forecast. For example, WS005/27050KT indicates that the wind at 500 feet AGL is 270° at 50 knots.

18. The term PROB40 2102 +TSRA in a terminal aerodrome forecast indicates that there is approximately a 40% probability of thunderstorms with heavy rain between 2100Z and 0200Z.

Aviation Area Forecasts

19. Aviation area forecasts are issued three times each day and generally include a total forecast period of 18 hours. They cover a geographical group of states or well known areas.

20. An aviation area forecast (FA) is a good source of information for weather at airports which do not have terminal aerodrome forecasts, as well as for enroute weather.

21. The VFR clouds and weather section of an aviation area forecast summarizes sky conditions, cloud heights, visibility, obstructions to vision, precipitation, and sustained surface winds of 20 knots or greater.

22. When the wind is forecast to be 20 knots or greater the categorical outlook in the aviation area forecast includes the contraction WND.

Winds and Temperatures Aloft Forecasts

23. An estimate of wind direction in relation to true north, wind speed in knots, and the temperature in degrees Celsius for selected altitudes can be found in the winds and temperatures aloft forecast (FD).

24. A winds and temperatures aloft forecast (FD) does not include winds within 1,500 feet of the station elevation. Likewise temperatures for the 3,000-foot level or for a level within 2,500 feet of the station elevation are omitted.

25. Wind direction and speed information on an FD are shown by a four-digit code. The first two digits are the wind direction in tens of degrees. Wind speed is shown by the second two digits. The last two digits indicate the temperature in degrees Celsius. All temperatures above 24,000 feet are negative and the minus sign is omitted.

26. To decode a forecast of winds between 100 and 199 knots, subtract 50 from the two-digit direction code and multiply by 10. Then, add 100 to the two-digit wind speed code. The code 9900 indicates the winds are light and variable.

Severe Weather

27. A convective outlook (AC) forecasts general thunderstorm activity for the next 24-hour period.

28. Severe weather watch bulletins (WW) are issued only when required. They outline areas of possible severe thunderstorms or tornadoes.

9-109   J25

The remarks section of the Aviation Routine Weather Report (METAR) contains the following coded information. What does it mean?

FZDZB42 WSHFT 30 FROPA

A — Freezing drizzle with cloud bases below 4,200 feet.

B — Freezing drizzle below 4,200 feet and wind shear.

C — Wind shift at three zero due to frontal passage.

9-109. Answer C. GFDICM 9C (AIM)

To help you develop a better picture of the weather, some METARs include a remarks section. The remarks are generally limited to operationally significant weather, and may include the beginning and ending times of certain weather phenomena. In this example, freezing drizzle (FZDZ) began at 42 minutes past the hour (B42), and a wind shift occurred at thirty minutes past the hour. The contraction for frontal passage (FROPA) may be added when there is reasonable certainty that the wind shift was the result of frontal passage. Answers (A) and (B) are wrong.

9-110   J25

What is meant by the Special METAR weather observation for KBOI?

SPECI KBOI 091854Z 32005KT 1 1/2SM RA BR OVC007 17/16 A2990 RMK RAB12

A — Rain and fog obscuring two-tenths of the sky; rain began at 1912Z.
B — Rain and mist obstructing visibility; rain began at 1812Z.
C — Rain and overcast at 1200 feet AGL.

9-111   J25

The station originating the following METAR observation has a field elevation of 3,500 feet MSL. If the sky cover is one continuous layer, what is the thickness of the cloud layer? (Top of overcast reported at 7,500 feet MSL).

METAR KHOB 151250Z 17006KT 4SM OVC005 13/11 A2998

A — 2,500 feet.
B — 3,500 feet.
C — 4,000 feet.

9-112   J25

What significant cloud coverage is reported by this pilot report?

KMOB
UA/OV 15NW MOB 1340Z/SK OVC 025/045 OVC 090

A — Three (3) separate overcast layers exist with bases at 250, 7,500 and 9,000 feet.
B — The top of the lower overcast is 2,500 feet; base and top of second overcast layer is 4,500 and 9,000 feet, respectively.
C — The base of the second overcast layer is 2,500 feet; top of second overcast layer is 7,500 feet; base of third layer is 9,000 feet.

9-113   I42

To best determine observed weather conditions between weather reporting stations, the pilot should refer to

A — pilot reports.
B — Area Forecasts.
C — prognostic charts.

9-110. Answer B. GFDICM 9C (AIM)

The last section of the METAR is the remarks section which reports operationally significant weather, and may include the beginning and ending times of certain weather phenomena. In this example, rain (RA) and mist (BR) are included in the body of the report with rain beginning at 12 minutes past the hour (RAB12) in the remarks. Answer (A) is wrong because fog (FG) is not mentioned and the rain began at 1812Z, not 1912Z. Answer (C) is wrong because cloud bases are reported in the body of the METAR and the base of the overcast is at 700 feet (OVC007) not 1,200 feet.

9-111. Answer B. GFDICM 9C (AIM)

The notation "OVC005" in the body of the report, indicates that the base of the overcast is at 500 feet AGL. The report of 7,500 feet overcast (probably from a pilot report) indicates the top of the overcast is at 7,500 feet MSL. To determine the thickness of the cloud layer, you must first add the height of the cloud base (500 feet AGL) and the field elevation (3,500 feet MSL) to determine the cloud base height MSL. By subtracting the base of the cloud layer (4,000 feet MSL) from the top of the cloud layer (7,500 feet MSL), you can determine the thickness of the layer is 3,500 feet (7,500 - 4,000 = 3,500 feet).

9-112. Answer B. GFDICM 9C (AIM)

In this example, the "UA" indicates routine PIREP information follows. The pilot reported the top of the lower overcast layer at 2,500 feet as indicated by the notation "SK OVC 025/." The rest of the notation, "/045 OVC 090," indicates that the base and top of the second layer at 4,500 feet and 9,000 feet MSL respectively. Answer (A) is wrong because three separate layers are not identified. Answer (C) is wrong because the base of the second layer is at 4,500 feet, not 2,500 feet. In addition, 7,500 feet is not indicated in the report.

9-113. Answer A. GFDICM 9C (AWS)

Pilot reports (PIREPs) are the only means of directly determining cloud tops, icing conditions, and turbulence. In addition, PIREPs are the best source for observed weather between reporting points. Area forecasts (answer B) and prognostic charts (answer C) contain forecast, not observed weather conditions.

9-114. I42
Which is true concerning the radar weather report (SD) for KOKC?

KOKC 1934 LN 8TRW++/+ 86/40 164/60 199/115 15W L2425 MT 570 AT 159/65 2 INCH HAIL RPRTD THIS CELL

A — There are three cells with tops at 11,500, 40,000, and 60,000 feet.

B — The line of cells is moving 060° with winds reported up to 40 knots.

C — The maximum tops of the cells is 57,000 feet located 65 NM southeast of the station.

9-115 J25
What is the meaning of the terms PROB40 2102 +TSRA as used in a Terminal Aerodrome Forecast (TAF)?

A — Probability of heavy thunderstorms with rain showers below 4,000 feet at time 2102.

B — Between 2100Z and 0200Z there is a forty percent (40%) probability of thunderstorms with heavy rain.

C — Beginning at 2102Z forty percent (40%) probability of heavy thunderstorms and rain showers.

9-116 J25
What does the contraction VRB in the Terminal Aerodrome Forecast (TAF) mean?

A — Wind speed is variable throughout the period.
B — Cloud base is variable.
C — Wind direction is variable.

9-117 J25
Which statement pertaining to the following Terminal Aerodrome Forecast (TAF) is true?

TAF
KMEM 091135Z 091515 15005KT 5SM HZ BKN060
    FM1600 VRB04KT P6SM SKC

A — Wind in the valid period implies surface winds are forecast to be greater than 5 KTS.

B — Wind direction is from 160° at 4 KTS and reported visibility is 6 statute miles.

C — SKC in the valid period indicates no significant weather and sky clear.

9-114. Answer C. GFDICM 9C (AWS)
When reading a radar weather report (SD), maximum tops are identified by the abbreviation "MT," followed by the radial and distance (in nautical miles) from the radar facility. This report indicates that the maximum tops are at 57,000 feet MSL located on the 159° radial (south-southeast) at 65 n.m. Answer (A) is wrong because the 40, 60, and 115 in the SD indicates the range of the echo pattern in nautical miles from the radar facility. Answer (B) is wrong because the cell movement is not indicated.

9-115. Answer B. GFDICM 9C (AIM)
The probability group (PROB40) in a TAF is used to indicate there is between a 30% and 49% probability of thunderstorms or precipitation events and associated conditions occurring in the forecast period. This is followed by beginning and ending time and then by the conditions that are expected. In this example, there is approximately a 40 percent probability of a thunderstorm and heavy rain between 2100Z and 0200Z. There is no mention of showers (SH). Thus, answer (A) is incorrect. Answer (C) is wrong because the intensity symbol (+) applies to precipitation. In the METAR/TAF code, the plus symbol is not applicable to thunderstorms.

9-116. Answer C. GFDICM 9C (AIM)
In a Terminal Aerodrome Forecast (TAF), the contraction "VRB" in the wind section indicates the wind direction is expected to be variable. Variable applies to the wind direction, not speed. Therefore, answer (A) is wrong. Answer (B) is wrong because sky condition is forecast with respect to amount, height, and type. "VV" is used to denote vertical visibility into an indefinite ceiling.

9-117. Answer C. GFDICM 9C (AIM)
In a Terminal Aerodrome Forecast (TAF), FM is used to indicate that a change in the existing weather is expected, with the hour of the expected change following "FM." In this example, at Memphis International from 1600Z until the end of the forecast period, the wind is forecast to be variable at 4 knots (VRB04KT), visibility greater than 6 statute miles (P6SM), and the sky is clear (SKC). Answer (A) is wrong because the wind is not forecast to be greater than 5 knots. Answer (B) is wrong because the wind is expected to be variable and visibility greater than 6 statute miles.

9-118   J25

The visibility entry in a Terminal Aerodrome Forecast (TAF) of P6SM implies that the prevailing visibility is expected to be greater than

A — 6 nautical miles.
B — 6 statute miles.
C — 6 kilometers.

9-118. Answer B. GFDICM 9C (AIM)

When the expected prevailing visibility is 6 miles or less it is included in the forecast, followed by "SM" to indicate statute miles. Visibilities greater than 6 statute miles are indicated in the forecast by Plus 6SM (P6SM).

9-119   J25

Terminal Aerodrome Forecasts (TAF) are issued how many times a day and cover what period of time?

A — Four times daily and are usually valid for a 24 hour period.
B — Six times daily and are usually valid for a 24 hour period including a 4-hour categorical outlook.
C — Four times daily and are valid for 12 hours including a 6-hour categorical outlook.

9-119. Answer A. GFDICM 9C (AIM)

TAFs generally are issued four times a day, beginning at 0000Z, 0600Z, 1200Z, and 1800Z. Each report is valid for a 24-hour period. The basic sequence of a TAF provides forecast wind, visibility, weather, and sky conditions. Answers (B) and (C) are wrong because a TAF does not specifically include a 4- or 6-hour categorical outlook.

9-120   I43

Which information section is contained in the Aviation Area Forecast (FA)?

A — Winds aloft, speed and direction.
B — VFR Clouds and Weather (VFR CLDS/WX).
C — In-Flight Aviation Weather Advisories.

9-120. Answer B. GFDICM 9C (AWS)

Issued three times each day for six regions in the contiguous U.S., an Aviation Area Forecast contains a heading section, precautionary statements section, a synopsis section, and a VFR Clouds and Weather section. Answer (A), is wrong because the speed and direction of winds aloft are contained in the Winds and Temperatures Aloft Forecast (FD). Answer (C) is wrong because In-Flight Aviation Weather Advisories are provided by ARTCC, terminal ATC, and FSS facilities and are not found in Aviation Area Forecasts (FAs).

9-121   I43

The section of the Aviation Area Forecast (FA) entitled VFR Clouds and Weather contains a summary of

A — forecast sky cover, cloud tops, visibility, and obstructions to vision along specific routes.
B — only those weather systems producing liquid or frozen precipitation, fog, thunderstorms, or IFR ceilings.
C — sky condition, cloud heights, visibility, obstructions to vision, precipitation, and sustained surface winds of 20 knots or greater.

9-121. Answer C. GFDICM 9C (AWS)

The VFR Clouds and Weather section of the area forecast describes the location and movement of frontal systems and circulation patterns. References to low ceilings and/or visibilities, strong winds, or other phenomena may be included. In addition, a forecast of conditions which meet marginal VFR (MVFR) criteria or better also is included. Answer (A) is wrong because the forecast specifies an area, not a specific route. Answer (B) is wrong because the VFR Clouds and Weather section includes clouds and weather which is significant to VFR flight and not ONLY "those weather systems producing liquid or frozen precipitation, fog, thunderstorms, or IFR ceilings."

9-122   I43

The Aviation Weather Center (AWC) prepares FA's for the contiguous U.S.

A — twice each day.
B — three times each day.
C — every 6 hours unless significant changes in weather require it more often.

9-122. Answer B. GFDICM 9C (AWS)

Aviation Area forecasts (FAs) are issued for six regions in the contiguous United States three times each day. A specialized FA for the Gulf of Mexico is issued twice a day (answer A) by the National Hurricane Center in Miami. The Weather Service Field Office in Honolulu issues FAs four times a day (every six hours) for the Hawaiian Islands (answer C).

9-123. I43

What values are used for Winds Aloft Forecasts?

A — True direction and MPH.
B — True direction and knots.
C — Magnetic direction and knots.

9-123. Answer B. GFDICM 9C (AWS)
Winds and temperatures aloft forecasts report wind direction in relation to true north and wind speed in knots. Answer (A) is wrong because miles per hour is not used to report wind direction in any aviation weather report. Answer (C) is wrong because true direction is used, not magnetic.

SECTION D
GRAPHIC WEATHER PRODUCTS
Surface Analysis Chart

1. The solid lines that depict sea level pressure patterns are called isobars. When they are close together, the pressure gradient is stronger and the wind velocities are stronger.

2. A surface analysis chart is a good source for general weather information over a wide area, depicting the actual positions of fronts, pressure patterns, temperatures, dewpoint, wind, weather, and obstructions to vision at the valid time of the chart.

3. A dashed line on a surface analysis chart indicates a weak pressure gradient.

Weather Depiction Chart

4. The weather depiction chart provides a graphic display of VFR and IFR weather, as well as the type of precipitation.

5. A ( ]) plotted to the right of a station circle on the weather depiction chart means the station is an automated observation location.

6. When total sky cover is FEW or scattered, the height shown on the weather depiction chart is the base of the lowest layer.

Radar Summary Chart

7. Radar summary charts are the only weather charts which show lines and cells of thunderstorms as well as other heavy precipitation. You can also determine the tops and bases of the echoes, the intensity of the precipitation, and the echo movement.

8. A radar summary chart is most effective when used in combination with other charts, reports, and forecasts.

Constant Pressure Analysis Chart

9. A constant pressure analysis chart provides observed winds aloft, temperature and dewpoint information. You can also use this chart to determine temperatures.

10. Hatching on a constant pressure analysis chart indicates wind speeds between 70 and 110 knots.

Winds and Temperatures Aloft Forecasts

11. An estimate of wind direction in relation to true north, wind speed in knots, and the temperature in degrees Celsius for selected altitudes can be found in the winds and temperatures aloft forecast (FD).

Low and High Level Significant Weather Prognostic Charts

12. A low-level significant weather prognostic chart depicts weather conditions forecast to exist at 12, and 24 hours in the future. This chart is valid up to 24,000 feet MSL.

13. In a high-level significant weather prognostic chart the areas enclosed in scalloped lines indicate that you should expect cumulonimbus clouds (CBs), icing, and moderate or greater turbulence.

14. A high-level significant weather prognostic chart forecasts clear air turbulence, tropopause height, sky coverage, embedded thunderstorms, and jet stream velocities between 24,000 feet MSL and 63,000 feet MSL.

Composite Moisture Stability Chart

15. A freezing level panel of the composite moisture stability chart is an analysis of observed freezing level data from upper air observations.

16. The difference found by subtracting the temperature of a parcel of air theoretically lifted from the surface to 500 millibars and the existing temperature at 500 millibars is called the lifted index.

9-124   I23
With regard to windflow patterns shown on a Surface Analysis Chart; when the isobars are

A — close together, the pressure gradient force is slight and wind velocities are weaker.
B — not close together, the pressure gradient force is greater and wind velocities are stronger.
C — close together, the pressure gradient force is greater and wind velocities are stronger.

9-125   I43
On a Surface Analysis Chart, the solid lines that depict sea-level pressure patterns are called

A — isobars.
B — isogons.
C — millibars.

9-126   I44
Dashed lines on a Surface Analysis Chart, if depicted, indicate that the pressure gradient is

A — weak.
B — strong.
C — unstable.

9-127   I44
Which chart provides a ready means of locating observed frontal positions and pressure centers?

A — Surface Analysis Chart.
B — Constant Pressure Analysis Chart.
C — Weather Depiction Chart.

9-128   I44
On a Surface Analysis Chart, close spacing of the isobars indicates

A — weak pressure gradient.
B — strong pressure gradient.
C — strong temperature gradient.

9-124. Answer C. GFDICM 9D (AW)
The closer the spacing of isobars, the stronger the pressure gradient force. The stronger the pressure gradient force, the greater the wind velocities. When the isobar spacing is not close together (answer B), the pressure gradient force is less and wind velocities are weaker. Answer (A) is wrong because the pressure gradient force and wind are strong when the isobars are close together.

9-125. Answer A. GFDICM 9D (AWS)
On surface analysis charts, points of equal pressure are connected with solid lines. These lines are referred to as isobars. Isogons (answer B) are lines that show points on the earth's surface that have the same magnetic declination, and millibars (answer C) is the metric unit of measure for pressure.

9-126. Answer A. GFDICM 9D (AWS)
On surface analysis charts, points of equal pressure are connected with solid lines. These lines are referred to as isobars. If the isobars on surface analysis charts are dashed the pressure gradient is weak. If the isobars are closely spaced, the pressure gradient is strong (answer B). There is no such thing as an unstable pressure gradient (answer C).

9-127. Answer A. GFDICM 9D (AWS)
In addition to depicting frontal positions and pressure centers, the surface analysis chart depicts such things as sea level pressure patterns, temperature and dewpoint, wind direction and speed, local weather, and obstructions to vision at the valid time of the chart. The constant pressure analysis chart (answer B) is wrong because it does not indicate frontal positions. Answer (C), the weather depiction chart, is incorrect because pressure centers are not shown.

9-128. Answer B. GFDICM 9D (AWS)
Close spacing of isobars indicates the pressure gradient is strong, while a weak pressure gradient (answer A) is identified by a dashed isobar. Temperature gradients (answer C) are not identified on surface analysis charts.

9-129   **I44**

The Surface Analysis Chart depicts

A — frontal locations and expected movement, pressure centers, cloud coverage, and obstructions to vision at the time of chart transmission.

B — actual frontal positions, pressure patterns, temperature, dewpoint, wind, weather, and obstructions to vision at the valid time of the chart.

C — actual pressure distribution, frontal systems, cloud heights and coverage, temperature, dewpoint, and wind at the time shown on the chart.

9-130   **I45**

Which provides a graphic display of both VFR and IFR weather?

A — Surface Weather Map.
B — Radar Summary Chart.
C — Weather Depiction Chart.

9-131   **I45**

When total sky cover is few or scattered, the height shown on the Weather Depiction Chart is the

A — top of the lowest layer.
B — base of the lowest layer.
C — base of the highest layer.

9-132   **I46**

What information is provided by the Radar Summary Chart that is not shown on other weather charts?

A — Lines and cells of hazardous thunderstorms.
B — Ceilings and precipitation between reporting stations.
C — Areas of cloud cover and icing levels within the clouds.

9-133   **I47**

Which weather chart depicts conditions forecast to exist at a specific time in the future?

A — Freezing Level Chart.
B — Weather Depiction Chart.
C — 12-Hour Significant Weather Prognostic Chart.

9-129. Answer B. GFDICM 9D (AWS)
See explanation for Question 9-127. Answer (A) is wrong because a surface analysis chart does not indicate expected or forecast conditions. Answer (C) is not correct because cloud heights are not shown.

9-130. Answer C. GFDICM 9D (AWS)
You can think of the weather depiction chart as an abbreviated version of the surface analysis chart. It provides a simplified station model and a graphic depiction of VFR, marginal VFR, and IFR weather conditions. For example, IFR conditions are indicated by shaded areas, MVFR conditions are identified with contoured lines without shading, and VFR areas have no contours. Neither the surface weather map (answer A) nor the radar summary chart (answer B) give a graphic display of these conditions.

9-131. Answer B. GFDICM 9D (AWS)
As with the hourly observation, the weather depiction chart indicates the base of the lowest layer of clouds. The top of the lowest layer (answer A) is reported by pilots in the form of pilot reports (PIREPs). Answer (C) is not correct because the base of the lowest (not highest) layer is reported.

9-132. Answer A. GFDICM 9D (AWS)
The radar summary chart provides a graphic depiction of areas of precipitation, individual thunderstorms cells, lines of cells, and areas of thunderstorm activity. The chart also shows size, shape, and intensity of returns, as well as the intensity trend and direction of movement. Information on ceilings (answer B) and areas of cloud cover and icing (answer C) are not shown on radar summary charts.

9-133. Answer C. GFDICM 9D (AWS)
The low-level significant weather prognostic chart depicts conditions forecast to exist 12 and 24 hours into the future. Both the freezing level chart (answer A) and the weather depiction chart (answer B) indicate reported conditions.

9-134   **I47**

What weather phenomenon is implied within an area enclosed by small scalloped lines on a U.S. High-Level Significant Weather Prognostic Chart?

A — Cirriform clouds, light to moderate turbulence, and icing.

B — Cumulonimbus clouds, icing, and moderate or greater turbulence.

C — Cumuliform or standing lenticular clouds, moderate to severe turbulence, and icing.

9-135   **I47**

The U.S. High-Level Significant Weather Prognostic Chart forecasts significant weather for what airspace?

A — 18,000 feet to 45,000 feet.

B — 24,000 feet to 45,000 feet.

C — 24,000 feet to 63,000 feet.

9-136   **I47**

What is the upper limit of the Low-Level Significant Weather Prognostic Chart?

A — 30,000 feet.

B — 24,000 feet.

C — 18,000 feet.

9-137   **I49**

A freezing level panel of the composite moisture stability chart is an analysis of

A — forecast freezing level data from surface observations.

B — forecast freezing level data from upper air observations.

C — observed freezing level data from upper air observations.

9-138   **I49**

The difference found by subtracting the temperature of a parcel of air theoretically lifted from the surface to 500 millibars and the existing temperature at 500 millibars is called the

A — lifted index.

B — negative index.

C — positive index.

9-134. Answer B. GFDICM 9D (AWS)

The high-level significant weather prognostic chart presents a forecast of thunderstorms, tropical cyclones, severe squalls, moderate or greater turbulence, widespread duststorms and sandstorms, tropopause heights, and the location of jet streams. The scalloped lines on this chart are used to enclose areas that have sandstorms, duststorms, and cumulonimbus clouds. Enclosed areas of cumulonimbus clouds also imply the presence of moderate or greater turbulence and icing conditions. Cirriform clouds, light turbulence (answer A), and standing lenticulars (answer C) are not indicated on the high-altitude significant weather prog.

9-135. Answer C. GFDICM 9D (AWS)

The high-level significant prog chart is valid from 400 millibars (24,000 feet) to 70 millibars (63,000 feet). Answers (A) and (B) are inappropriate.

9-136. Answer B. GFDICM 9D (AWS)

The low-level significant weather prog is prepared by the National Meteorological Center, and is valid for use up to 24,000 feet. Answer (A) is inappropriate and answer (C) represents the base of Class A airspace.

9-137. Answer C. GFDICM 9D (AWS)

The composite moisture stability chart contains four panels: stability, freezing level, precipitable water, and average relative humidity. The freezing level panel is an analysis of observed freezing level data from upper air observations. Answers (A) and (B) are wrong because the information on the chart is not forecast. In addition, answer (A) is wrong because the observations taken are upper air observations, not surface based.

9-138. Answer A. GFDICM 9D (AWS)

The stability panel of the composite moisture stability chart outlines areas of stable and unstable air. The lifted index is found by subtracting the temperature of a parcel of air that is theoretically lifted from the surface to 500 millibars (18,000 feet MSL) from the existing temperature at 500 millibars. The result can be zero, positive, or negative. A zero value indicates neutral stability, while a positive value means stable air. A negative value indicates the air is unstable. The greater the value, the greater the stability or instability. Answers (B) and (C) are wrong because negative and positive values are a part of the lifted index.

9-139   **I51**

Hatching on a Constant Pressure Analysis Chart indicates

A — hurricane eye.
B — windspeed 70 knots to 110 knots.
C — windspeed 110 knots to 150 knots.

9-139. Answer B. GFDICM 9D (AWS)
The constant pressure analysis chart is an upper air weather map on which all information is referenced to a specified pressure level. It is issued twice daily for each of five pressure altitude levels from 850 millibars (5,000 feet) to 200 millibars (39,000 feet). Cross-hatching is used on 300- and 200-millibar charts to denote wind speeds of 70 to 110 knots. A clear area within a hatched area indicates winds of 110 to 150 knots (answer C). Hurricane eyes (answer A) are not shown.

9-140   **I61**

What flight planning information can a pilot derive from Constant Pressure Analysis Charts?

A — Winds and temperatures aloft.
B — Clear air turbulence and icing conditions.
C — Frontal systems and obstructions to vision aloft.

9-140. Answer A. GFDICM 9D (AWS)
Each reporting location on a constant pressure chart includes information on the observed temperature and temperature/dewpoint spread, wind direction and speed, height of the pressure surface, and changes in height over the previous 12 hours. The constant pressure chart is most useful for quickly determining winds and temperatures aloft for your flight. The items indicated in answers (B) and (C) are not included on a constant pressure analysis chart.

9-141   **I51**

From which of the following can the observed temperature, wind, and temperature/dewpoint spread be determined at a specified altitude?

A — Stability Charts.
B — Winds Aloft Forecasts.
C — Constant Pressure Analysis Charts.

9-141. Answer C. GFDICM 9D (AWS)
See explanation for Question 9-140. Answers (A) and (B) are wrong because the stability chart does not indicate any of the listed items and the winds aloft forecast does not include the temperature/dewpoint spread.

SECTION E
SOURCES OF WEATHER INFORMATION

1. Enroute flight advisory service (EFAS) provides enroute aircraft with timely and meaningful weather advisories pertinent to the type of flight intended, route, and altitude.

2. EFAS is obtained by contacting flight watch, using the name of the ARTCC facility identification in your area, your aircraft identification, and name of the nearest VOR, on 122.0 MHz below FL180.

3. In-flight aviation weather advisories consisting of AIRMETs, SIGMETs, and convective SIGMETs are forecasts that advise enroute aircraft of the development of potentially hazardous weather, and information on volcanic eruptions that are occurring or expected to occur. All in-flight advisories in the contiguous U.S. are issued by the National Aviation Weather Advisory Unit in Kansas City, MO. All in-flight advisories use the same location identifiers (either VORs, airports, or well-known geographic areas) to describe the hazardous weather areas.

4. Convective SIGMETs contain either an observation and a forecast, or just a forecast, for tornadoes, significant thunderstorm activity, or hail 3/4 inch or greater in diameter.

5. A center weather advisory (CWA) is an unscheduled advisory issued by an ARTCC to alert pilots of existing or anticipated adverse weather conditions within the next two hours. A CWA may be issued prior to an AIRMET or SIGMET when PIREPs suggest AIRMET or SIGMET conditions exist. Even if adverse weather is not sufficiently intense or widespread for a SIGMET or AIRMET, a CWA may be issued if conditions are expected to affect the safe flow of air traffic within the ARTCC area of responsibility.

6. AIRMETs and CWAs provide an enroute pilot with information about moderate icing, moderate turbulence, winds of 30 knots or more at the surface, and extensive mountain obscurement.

7. Weather advisory broadcasts, including severe weather forecast alerts (AWW), convective SIGMETs, and SIGMETs, are provided by ARTCCs on all frequencies, except emergency, when any part of the area described is within 150 miles of the airspace under their jurisdiction.

8. The hazardous inflight weather advisory service (HIWAS) is a continuous broadcast of in-flight weather advisories over selected VORs of SIGMETs, convective SIGMETs, AIRMETs, AWWs, and CWAs.

9. A transcribed weather broadcast (TWEB) provides specific information concerning expected sky cover, cloud tops, visibility, weather, and obstructions to vision in a route format. To obtain continuous transcribed information, including winds aloft and route forecasts for a cross-country flight, you could monitor a TWEB on a low-frequency radio receiver. TWEB mostly has been replaced by HIWAS.

9-142   J25
The Hazardous Inflight Weather Advisory Service (HIWAS) is a broadcast service over selected VORs that provides

A — SIGMETs and AIRMETs at 15 minutes and 45 minutes past the hour for the first hour after issuance.
B — SIGMETs, CONVECTIVE SIGMETs and AIRMETs at 15 minutes and 45 minutes past the hour.
C — continuous broadcast of inflight weather advisories.

9-142. Answer C. GFDICM 9E (AIM 7-1-9)
HIWAS is a recorded summary of AIRMETs, SIGMETs, Convective SIGMETs, Servere Weather Forecast Weather Alerts (AWWs), Center Weather Advisories (CWAs), and urgent PIREPs that is continuously broadcast over selected VORs.

9-143   J25
The Telephone Information Briefing Service (TIBS) provided by AFSSs includes

A — continuous recording of meteorological and/or aeronautical information available by telephone.
B — recorded weather briefing service for the local area, usually within 50 miles and route forecasts.
C — weather information service on a common frequency (122.0 mHz).

9-143. Answer A. GFDICM 9E (AIM 7-1-7)
The Telephone Information Briefing Service (TIBS) provides continuous telephone recordings of meteorological and/or aeronautical information.

9-144   I43
In-Flight Aviation Weather Advisories include what type of information?

A — IFR conditions, turbulence, and icing within a valid period for the listed states.
B — Forecasts for potentially hazardous flying conditions for enroute aircraft.
C — State and geographic areas with reported ceilings and visibilities below VFR minimums.

9-144. Answer B. GFDICM 9B
In-Flight Aviation Weather Advisories are forecasts to advise enroute aircraft of potentially hazardous weather. Included are convective SIGMETs, SIGMETs, and AIRMETs, using VORs, airports, or other well known geographic areas to describe the location of hazardous weather along a route.

9-145   **J25**

What type of Inflight Weather Advisories provides an en route pilot with information regarding the possibility of moderate icing, moderate turbulence, winds of 30 knots or more at the surface and extensive mountain obscurement?

A — Convective SIGMETs and SIGMETs.
B — AIRMETs and Center Weather Advisories (CWA).
C — Severe Weather Forecast Alerts (AWW) and SIGMETs.

9-146   **J25**

What single reference contains information regarding expected a volcanic eruption, that is occurring or expected to occur?

A — Terminal Area Forecasts (TAF).
B — In-Flight Weather Advisories.
C — Weather Depiction Chart.

9-147   **I43**

Which forecast provides specific information concerning expected sky cover, cloud tops, visibility, weather, and obstructions to vision in a route format?

A — Transcribed Weather Broadcast.
B — Terminal Forecast.
C — Area Forecast.

9-148   **J25**

To obtain a continuous transcribed weather briefing including winds aloft and route forecasts for a cross-country flight, a pilot could monitor

A — a TWEB on a low-frequency and/or VOR receiver.
B — the regularly scheduled weather broadcast on a VOR frequency.
C — a high-frequency radio receiver tuned to En Route Flight Advisory Service.

9-149   **I43**

SIGMET's are issued as a warning of weather conditions which are hazardous

A — particularly to light airplanes.
B — to all aircraft.
C — particularly to heavy aircraft.

9-145. Answer B. GFDICM 9B
An AIRMET is an advisory of significant weather including moderate icing, moderate turbulence, sustained surface winds of 30 knots or more, ceilings less than 1000 feet and/or visibility less than 3 miles over 50 percent of the area, and extensive mountain obscuration. When appropriate Center Weather Advisories include AIRMETs.

9-146. Answer B. GFDICM 9B
In-Flight Weather Advisories include AIRMETs, SIGMETs, and Convective SIGMETs. Of these only SIGMETs report volcanic activity.

9-147. Answer A. GFDICM 9E (AIM 7-1-8)
Transcribed Weather Broadcasts (TWEBs) provide route-oriented data which is broadcast over designated NDB and VOR navigation facilities. Information contained in a TWEB forecast includes ceilings and sky cover, cloud tops, visibility, and obstructions to vision.

9-148. Answer A. GFDICM 9E (AIM 7-1-8)
Transcribed Weather Broadcasts (TWEBs) provide route-oriented data which is broadcast over designated NDB and VOR navigation facilities. Information contained in a TWEB forecast includes ceilings and sky cover, cloud tops, visibility, and obstructions to vision.

9-149. Answer B. GFDICM 9E (AIM 7-1-27)
SIGMETs (WSs) are issued for hazardous weather (other than convective activity) which is considered significant to all aircraft. SIGMET criteria include the following: severe, extreme, or clear air turbulence; severe icing, or wide spread duststorms, sandstorms, or volcanic ash lowering surface and/or in-flight visibilities to less than three miles.

9-150   **I43**
Which correctly describes the purpose of Convective SIGMET's (WST)?

A — They contain both an observation and a forecast of all thunderstorm and hailstone activity. The forecast is valid for 1 hour only.
B — They consist of an hourly observation of tornadoes, significant thunderstorm activity, and large hailstone activity.
C — They consist of either an observation and a forecast or just a forecast for tornadoes, significant thunderstorm activity, or hail greater than or equal to 3/4 inch in diameter.

9-151   **J25**
En route Flight Advisory Service (EFAS) is a service that provides en route aircraft with timely and meaningful weather advisories pertinent to the type of flight intended, route, and altitude. This information is received by

A — listening to en route VORs at 15 and 45 minutes past the hour.
B — contacting flight watch, using the name of the ARTCC facility identification in your area, your aircraft identification, and name of nearest VOR, on 122.0 MHz below 17,500 feet MSL.
C — contacting the AFSS facility in your area, using your airplane identification, and the name of the nearest VOR.

9-152   **J25**
Weather Advisory Broadcasts, including Severe Weather Forecast Alerts (AWW), Convective SIGMETs, and SIGMETs, are provided by

A — ARTCCs on all frequencies, except emergency, when any part of the area described is within 150 miles of the airspace under their jurisdiction.
B — AFSSs on 122.2 MHz and adjacent VORs, when any part of the area described is within 200 miles of the airspace under their jurisdiction.
C — selected low-frequency and/or VOR navigational aids.

9-150. Answer C. GFDICM 9E (AIM 7-1-5c)
A convective SIGMET (WST) is issued for hazardous convective weather. They include any of the following phenomena: tornadoes, lines of thunderstorms, embedded thunderstorms, thunderstorms over a wide area, hail greater than or equal to three-fourths of an inch in diameter, and/or wind gusts to 50 knots or greater.

9-151. Answer B. GFDICM 9E (AIM)
Answer (A) is wrong because (EFAS) En route Flight Advisory Service is available on a request basis and is transmitted on the discrete frequency of 122.0 MHz not over VORs. Answer (C) is partially correct, however, it does not specify what AFSS to contact or the communications frequency.

9-152. Answer A. GFDICM 9E (AIM)
According to the Aeronautical Information Manual, Weather Advisory Broadcasts are transmitted on all frequencies except 121.5 MHz when the area of adverse weather is within 150 miles, not 200 miles, of the area of the ARTCC's jurisdiction, therefore answer (B) is wrong. Answer (C) is wrong because TWEBs are broadcast on low-frequency (190-535 kHz), and/or VOR navigational aids.

FLIGHT CONSIDERATIONS

SECTION A
IFR EMERGENCIES

Chapter 10, Section A, covers IFR emergencies. Commercial pilots should also be familiar with these procedures. Because you have probably covered this material in your IFR training, there are only a few FAA test questions assigned to this section.

Distress and Urgency Conditions

1. The *Aeronautical Information Manual* defines an emergency as a condition of distress or urgency. Pilots in distress are threatened by serious and/or imminent danger and require immediate assistance. An urgency situation, such as low fuel quantity, requires timely but not immediate assistance.

2. In an emergency, you may deviate from any rule in FAR Part 91 to the extent necessary to meet the emergency. ATC may request a detailed report of an emergency when priority assistance has been given, even though no rules have been violated.

3. If you are disoriented while flying, a flight service specialist may be able to locate you with VHF/DF equipment. To use this service you must have an operative VHF two-way radio.

Communication Procedures

4. The frequency of 121.5 MHz may be used to declare an emergency in the event you are unable to contact ATC on other frequencies.

5. In a distress situation, begin your initial call with the word *"MAYDAY,"* preferably repeated three times. Use *"PAN-PAN"* in the same manner in an urgency situation.

6. Your transponder may be used to declare an emergency by squawking code 7700.

7. A special emergency is a condition of air piracy and should be indicated by squawking code 7500 on your transponder.

Minimum Fuel

8. If your remaining fuel quantity is such that you can accept little or no delay, you should alert ATC with a minimum fuel advisory. Declaring minimum fuel to ATC indicates an emergency situation is possible should any undue delay occur.

9. If the remaining usable fuel supply suggests the need for traffic priority to ensure a safe landing, you should declare an emergency due to low fuel and report fuel remaining in minutes.

Instrument Failure

10. During an instrument failure your first priority is to fly the airplane, navigate accurately, and then communicate with ATC.

Communication Failure

11. You can use your transponder to alert ATC to a radio communication failure by squawking code 7600.

12. During a communication failure in VFR conditions, remain in VFR conditions, land as soon as practicable, and call ATC.

Engine Failure

13. In the event of complete engine failure the pilot must first remember to fly the airplane and establish the recommended glide speed.

14. If a loss of power or system failure occurs and diverting to an alternate is the best course of action, quickly apply rule of thumb computations, estimates and other appropriate methods in order to quickly divert to the alternate.

15. If a total loss of engine power occurs at night, consider making an approach to unlighted areas if the condition of the nearby terrain is unknown. However, plan the landing to be as close to public access as possible to allow for rescue or help, if needed.

10-1   H574
After experiencing a powerplant failure at night, one of the primary considerations should include

A — turning off all electrical switches to save battery power for the landing.
B — planning the emergency approach and landing to an unlighted portion of an area.
C — maneuvering to, and landing on a lighted highway or road.

10-2   H574
When planning for an emergency landing at night, one of the primary considerations should include

A — selecting a landing area close to public access, if possible.
B — landing without flaps to ensure a nose-high landing attitude at touchdown.
C — turning off all electrical switches to save battery power for the landing.

10-3   H61
When diverting to an alternate airport because of an emergency, pilots should

A — rely upon radio as the primary method of navigation.
B — climb to a higher altitude because it will be easier to identify checkpoints.
C — apply rule-of-thumb computations, estimates, and other appropriate shortcuts to divert to the new course as soon as possible.

10-4   J22
To use VHF/DF facilities for assistance in locating your position, you must have an operative VHF

A — transmitter and receiver.
B — transmitter and receiver, and an operative ADF receiver.
C — transmitter and receiver, and an operative VOR receiver.

10-1. Answer B. GFDPMM (AFH)
Upon an airborne powerplant failure at night, one of the primary considerations should be to plan the emergency approach and landing to an unlighted area. Lighted areas typically indicate structures that may obstruct a landing area.

10-2. Answer A. GFDICM 10A (AFH)
When planning an emergency landing at night away from an airport, consider landing in an area close to public access. This may facilitate rescue or help, if needed.

10-3. Answer C. GFDICM 10A (AFH)
Because of the limitations in cockpit space and available equipment, and because the pilot's attention must be divided between solving the problem and operating the airplane, advantage must be taken of all possible short-cuts and rule-of-thumb computations when diverting to an alternate airport. Answer (A) is wrong because you should use all available methods of navigation when diverting, not just radio navigation. Answer (B) is wrong because the nature of the emergency may not allow you to climb.

10-4. Answer A. GFDICM 10A (AFH)
If you get disoriented while flying, a flight service specialist may be able to locate you with VHF direction finder (VHF/DF) equipment. To utilize these services, you must have an operative VHF two-way radio. Neither an ADF (answer B) nor a VOR (answer C) are required.

10-5   **H583**

A pilot's most immediate and vital concern in the event of complete engine failure after becoming airborne on takeoff is

A — maintaining a safe airspeed.
B — landing directly into the wind.
C — turning back to the takeoff field.

10-5. Answer A. GFDPMM M14 GFDICM 10A (AFH)
Anytime you experience an engine failure, your most immediate concern should be to establish the manufacturer's recommended glide speed. This speed will allow the aircraft to glide the farthest and remain in positive control. In an emergency situation, landing into the wind (answer B) is not always possible. Answer (C) is wrong because you should not turn back to the runway unless you have reached a safe maneuvering altitude.

SECTION B
IFR DECISION MAKING

Chapter 10, Section B, covers IFR decision making. Since this information is directed toward those preparing for an instrument rating, there are no commercial airplane FAA test questions assigned to this chapter.

Commercial decision making is covered in Chapter 13, Section B.

Safe Habit Patterns

1. Accidents are rarely attributed to a single cause, but are the result of a series of poor choices.

2. You should consider filing a flight plan for every flight, and you should close that flight plan only when a safe landing is assured.

3. Though you work closely with ATC, you remain the final authority as to the safety of the flight. You may also need to coordinate responsibility with other pilots that fly with you.

Personal Minimums Checklist

4. Developing a personal minimums checklist will assist you in determining the feasibility of a particular flight. You should take into account your currency and experience when deciding upon conditions in which you feel comfortable flying.

5. Five hazardous attitudes affect your decisions, and you should examine your choices to ensure that you make the proper response when one of these attitudes affects your flight.

Resource Use

6. Effective use of resources occurs when you understand and utilize all the people and equipment available to you during a flight.

7. Plan for each flight thoroughly before you leave the ground, including fuel requirements, alternates available, and missed approach instructions. It is also helpful to program any navigation information into your aircraft's equipment before engine start. The more you can rehearse ahead of time, the more prepared you will be in the event of a problem.

8. During a high workload situation, identify the most important tasks and make those a priority. Do not allow yourself to fixate on an extraneous issue.

SECTION C
IFR FLIGHT PLANNING

Chapter 10, Section C, of the Instrument Commercial Manual covers IFR flight planning. Much of this information is useful to both instrument and commercial pilots. Although this section emphasizes IFR operations, the calculations required for VFR and IFR flight planning are similar, and there are a number of FAA commercial questions assigned to this section.

Preflight Planning

1. Although weather information may be obtained from numerous sources including newspapers, television, and the internet, you should base any go/no-go decision on a flight service station or DUATS standard briefing.

2. The navigation log is a convenient way for you to complete your preflight planning, organize your flight, and provide you with a concise textual description of your flight.

3. During preflight preparation, weather report forecasts which are not routinely available at the local service outlet (AFSS) can best be obtained by means of contacting a weather forecast office (WFO).

4. The most current en route and destination weather information for an instrument flight should be obtained from the FSS/AFSS.

5. The hazardous inflight weather advisory service (HIWAS) is a broadcast service over selected VORs.

6. True course measurements on a sectional aeronautical chart should be made at a meridian near the midpoint of the course because the angles formed by meridians and the course line vary from point to point.

Descent Planning

7. If doing a time or fuel to descend problem, start by finding how long it will take to descend from the beginning altitude to the final altitude at the specified rate of descent. Once this time is computed, the fuel consumed can be calculated by multiplying the fuel flow by the time to descend. Remember to make sure the units of measurement are common or are converted when necessary.

8. If given groundspeed and fuel flow and asked to compute time enroute, use your flight computer or simply divide distance (n.m.) by groundspeed (knots). This gives you the time in hours. Multiply by 60 to get time in minutes. To find fuel required, multiply the time (in hours) by the fuel flow (in units per hour).

9. Some questions on the commercial test ask you to calculate wind speed and direction from course, heading, true airspeed and groundspeed. This is different than calculating groundspeed from winds, as you did on the private pilot test. Most newer electronic flight computers, as well as the classic E6B, can be used to perform these calculations.

10. If given a time and fuel to climb problem, first, find the time it takes to climb from the initial altitude to the enroute altitude at the specified rate. To calculate the fuel consumed, multiply this time by the fuel flow. Again, remember to make sure the units of measurement are common or are converted when necessary.

10-6   **I40**

During preflight preparation, weather report forecasts which are not routinely available at the local service outlet (AFSS) can best be obtained by means of contacting

A — pilot's automatic telephone answering service.
B — air route traffic control center.
C — weather forecast office (WFO).

10-6. Answer C. GFDICM 10C (AIM)

The weather forecast office prepares most weather forecasts that you use as a pilot. They are the logical source of additional information. PATWAS (answer A) is obsolete, having been replaced by TIBBS at AFSSs ARTCCs (answer B) do not have this information.

10-7   **I40**

The most current en route and destination weather information for an instrument flight should be obtained from the

A — ATIS broadcast.
B — Notices to Airmen publications.
C — AFSS.

10-8   **H317**

An airplane descends to an airport under the following conditions:

Cruising altitude	6,500 ft
Airport elevation	700 ft
Descends to	800 ft AGL
Rate of descent	500 ft/min
Average true airspeed	110 kts
True course	335°
Average wind velocity	060° at 15 kts
Variation	3°W
Deviation	+2°
Average fuel consumption	8.5 gal/hr

Determine the approximate time, compass heading, distance, and fuel consumed during the descent.

A — 10 minutes, 348°, 18 NM, 1.4 gallons.
B — 10 minutes, 355°, 17 NM, 2.4 gallons.
C — 12 minutes, 346°, 18 NM, 1.6 gallons.

10-7. Answer C. GFDICM 10C (AWS)

Of all the different ways there are to obtain current and forecast weather information, flight service stations (FSSs) and automated flight service stations (AFSS) are still the best sources for obtaining this information. Answer (A) is incorrect because an ATIS offers no forecast information for your departure or destination airports. You need a forecast at your destination for your intended time of arrival to make a responsible go, no-go decision. Answer (B) is incorrect because NOTAMs do not contain weather information at all.

10-8. Answer A. GFDICM 10C (PHB)

First, determine the total height of the descent from 6,500 feet minus the airport elevation of 700 feet and the traffic pattern altitude of 800 feet (6,500 ft - 1,500 ft. = 5,000 feet). The time to descend is determined by dividing the height of the descent by the rate of descent (5,000 ft. ÷ 500 ft/min = 10 minutes. Now, enter the following given information into your flight computer to calculate true heading, and groundspeed.

1. Wind 060° at 15 kts.

2. True course 335°

3. True airspeed 110 kts.

   True heading = 343°

   Groundspeed = 108 kts.

Determine compass heading by adding the variation and deviation to the true heading (343° + 5° = 348°). Determine the distance by entering the time of 10 minutes and a groundspeed of 108 knots to get 18.0 n.m. Determine fuel consumption by entering the time of 10 minutes and a fuel flow of 8.5 gallons per hour to get 1.4 gallons.

10-9   **H317**

An airplane descends to an airport under the following conditions:

Cruising altitude................................7,500 ft
Airport elevation.............................1,300 ft
Descends to.................................800 ft AGL
Rate of descent ....300 ft/min
Average true airspeed ....120 kts
True course ....165°
Average wind velocity ....240° at 20 kts
Variation..4°E
Deviation ....-2°
Average fuel consumption ....9.6 gal/hr

Determine the approximate time, compass heading, distance, and fuel consumed during the descent.

A — 16 minutes, 168°, 30 NM, 2.9 gallons.
B — 18 minutes, 164°, 34 NM, 3.2 gallons.
C — 18 minutes, 168°, 34 NM, 2.9 gallons.

10-10   **H317**

An airplane descends to an airport under the following conditions:

Cruising altitude...............................10,500 ft
Airport elevation.............................1,700 ft
Descends to.............................1,000 ft AGL
Rate of descent ....600 ft/min
Average true airspeed ....135 kts
True course ....263°
Average wind velocity ....330° at 30 kts
Variation..7°E
Deviation ....+3°
Average fuel consumption ....11.5 gal/hr

Determine the approximate time, compass heading, distance, and fuel consumed during the descent.

A — 9 minutes, 274°, 26 NM, 2.8 gallons.
B — 13 minutes, 274°, 28 NM, 2.5 gallons.
C — 13 minutes, 271°, 26 NM, 2.5 gallons.

10-9. Answer C. GFDICM 10C (PHB)

First, determine the total height of the descent from 7,500 feet minus the airport elevation of 1,300 feet and the traffic pattern altitude of 800 feet AGL. (7,500 ft. - 2,100 ft. = 5,400 ft.). The time to descend is determined by dividing the height of the descent by the rate of descent (5,400 ft. ÷ 300 ft./min. = 18 minutes). Now, enter the following given information into your flight computer to calculate true heading and groundspeed.

1. Wind 240° at 20 kts.

2. True course 165°

3. True airspeed 120 kts.

   True heading = 174°

   Groundspeed = 113 kts.

Determine compass heading by subtracting the variation and compass deviation from the true heading (174° - 6° = 168°). Determine the distance by entering the time of 18 minutes and the groundspeed of 113 knots into your flight computer to get 34 n.m. Determine fuel consumption by entering the time of 18 minutes and a fuel flow of 9.6 gallons per hour to get 2.9 gallons.

10-10. Answer C. GFDICM 10C (PHB)

First, determine the total height of the descent from 10,500 feet minus the airport elevation of 1,700 feet and the traffic pattern altitude of 1,000 feet (10,500 ft. - 2,700 ft. = 7,800 ft.). The time to descend is determined by dividing the height of the descent (7,800 ft. ÷ 600 ft./min. = 13 min.) Now, enter the following given information into your flight computer to calculated true heading and groundspeed.

1. Wind 330° at 30 kts.

2. True course 263°

3. True airspeed 135 kts.

   True heading = 275°

   Groundspeed = 120 kts.

Determine compass heading by subtracting the variation (7°E) and adding the deviation (+3°) to the true heading (275° - 4° = 271°). Determine the distance by entering the time of 13 minutes and a ground speed of 120 knots to get 26.1 n.m. Determine fuel consumption by entering the time of 13 minutes and a fuel flow of 11.5 gal/hr to get 2.5 gallons.

10-11   **H342**
If fuel consumption is 80 pounds per hour and ground-speed is 180 knots, how much fuel is required for an airplane to travel 460 NM?

A — 205 pounds.
B — 212 pounds.
C — 460 pounds.

10-12   **H342**
If an airplane is consuming 95 pounds of fuel per hour at a cruising altitude of 6,500 feet and the groundspeed is 173 knots, how much fuel is required to travel 450 NM?

A — 248 pounds.
B — 265 pounds.
C — 284 pounds.

10-13   **H342**
If an airplane is consuming 12.5 gallons of fuel per hour at a cruising altitude of 8,500 feet and the groundspeed is 145 knots, how much fuel is required to travel 435 NM?

A — 27 gallons.
B — 34 gallons.
C — 38 gallons.

10-14   **H342**
If an airplane is consuming 9.5 gallons of fuel per hour at a cruising altitude of 6,000 feet and the groundspeed is 135 knots, how much fuel is required to travel 490 NM?

A — 27 gallons.
B — 30 gallons.
C — 35 gallons.

10-15   **H342**
If an airplane is consuming 14.8 gallons of fuel per hour at a cruising altitude of 7,500 feet and the ground-speed is 167 knots, how much fuel is required to travel 560 NM?

A — 50 gallons.
B — 53 gallons.
C — 57 gallons.

10-11. Answer A. GFDICM 10C (PHB)
First, determine the time enroute by entering the groundspeed (180 kts.) and distance (460 n.m.) into your flight computer to get 2 hours 33 minutes. Then, enter the time (2:33:20) and fuel consumption rate (80 lbs/hr) into your flight computer to get 204.4 pounds of fuel. Answer (B) is incorrect because it would require a fuel consumption of 83 pounds per hour. Answer (C) is incorrect because it would require a fuel consumption rate of 180 pounds per hour.

10-12. Answer A. GFDICM 10C (PHB)
First, determine the time enroute by entering the groundspeed (173 kts.) and distance (450 n.m.) into your flight computer to get 2 hours 36 minutes. Then, enter the time (2:36:04) and fuel consumption rate (95 lbs/hr) into your flight computer to get 247.1 pounds of fuel. Answer (B) is incorrect because it would require a fuel consumption rate of 101.9 pounds per hour. Answer (C) is incorrect because it would require a fuel consumption rate of 109.2 pounds per hour.

10-13. Answer C. GFDICM 10C (PHB)
First, determine the time enroute by entering the groundspeed (145 kts.) and distance (435 n.m.) into your flight computer to get 3 hours even. Then, enter the time (3:00:00) and fuel consumption rate (12.5 lbs/hr) into your flight computer to get 37.5 gallons per hour. Answer (A) is incorrect because it would require a fuel consumption rate of 9 gallons per hour. Answer (B) is incorrect because it would require a fuel consumption rate of 11.3 gallons per hour.

10-14. Answer C. GFDICM 10C (PHB)
First, determine the time enroute by entering the groundspeed (135 kts.) and distance (490 n.m.) into your flight computer to get 3 hours 37 minutes. Then, enter the time (3:37:47) and fuel consumption rate (9.5 gal/hr) into your flight computer to get 34.5 gallons of fuel. Answer (A) is incorrect because it would require a fuel consumption rate of 7.4 gallons per hour. Answer (B) is incorrect because it would require a fuel consumption rate of 8.3 gallons per hour.

10-15. Answer A. GFDICM 10C (PHB)
First, determine the time enroute by entering the groundspeed (167 kts.) and distance (560 n.m.) into your flight computer to get 3 hours 21 minutes. Then, enter the time (3:21:12) and fuel consumption rate (14.8 gal/hr) into your flight computer to get 49.6 gallons of fuel. Answer (B) is incorrect because it would require a fuel consumption rate of 15.8 gallons per hour. Answer (C) is incorrect because it would require a fuel consumption rate of 17.0 gallons per hour.

10-16   **H342**

If fuel consumption is 14.7 gallons per hour and groundspeed is 157 knots, how much fuel is required for an airplane to travel 612 NM?

A — 58 gallons.
B — 60 gallons.
C — 64 gallons.

10-17   **H341**
GIVEN:

True course ....105°
True heading ....085°
True airspeed ....95 kts
Groundspeed...87 kts

Determine the wind direction and speed.

A — 020° and 32 knots.
B — 030° and 38 knots.
C — 200° and 32 knots.

10-18   **H341**
GIVEN:

True course ....345°
True heading ....355°
True airspeed ....85 kts
Groundspeed...95 kts

Determine the wind direction and speed.

A — 095° and 19 knots.
B — 113° and 19 knots.
C — 238° and 18 knots.

10-19   **H344**
True course measurements on a Sectional Aeronautical Chart should be made at a meridian near the midpoint of the course because the

A — values of isogonic lines change from point to point.
B — angles formed by isogonic lines and lines of latitude vary from point to point.
C — angles formed by lines of longitude and the course line vary from point to point.

10-16. Answer A. GFDICM 10C (PHB)
First, determine the time enroute by entering the groundspeed (157 kts.) and distance (612 n.m.) into your flight computer to get 3 hours 53 minutes. Then, enter the time (3:53:53) and fuel consumption rate (14.7 gal/hr) into your flight computer to get 57.3 gallons of fuel. Answer (B) is incorrect because it would require a fuel consumption rate of 15.4 gallons per hour. Answer (C) is incorrect because it would require a fuel consumption rate of 16.4 gallons per hour.

10-17. Answer A. GFDICM 10C (PHB)
Enter the given information into your flight computer to get a wind direction of 020° and a wind speed of 33 knots. Answer (A) is the closest. Answer (B) is incorrect because it would require a true heading of 082° and a groundspeed of 78 knots. Answer (C) is incorrect because it would require a true heading of 125° and a groundspeed of 92 knots.

10-18. Answer B. GFDICM 10C (PHB)
Enter the given information into your flight computer to get a wind direction of 112° and a wind speed of 19 knots. Answer (A) is incorrect because it would require a true heading of 357° and a groundspeed of 90 knots. Answer (C) is incorrect because it would require a true heading of 333° and a groundspeed of 89 knots.

10-19. Answer C. GFDPPM 9A (PHB)
Because lines of longitude (meridians) converge toward the poles, course measurement should be taken near the midpoint of the course rather than at the departure or destination point. This is because the angles formed by lines of longitude and your course line will vary from point to point. Answers (A) and (B) are incorrect because isogonic lines measure magnetic variation which is not used to determine true course.

10-20   H344
GIVEN:

Wind ....175° at 20 kts
Distance ....135 NM
True course ....075°
True airspeed ....80 kts
Fuel consumption ....105 lb/hr

Determine the time en route and fuel consumption.

A — 1 hour 28 minutes and 73.2 pounds.
B — 1 hour 38 minutes and 158 pounds.
C — 1 hour 40 minutes and 175 pounds.

10-21   H344
An airplane departs an airport under the following conditions:

Airport elevation...1,000 ft
Cruise altitude...9,500 ft
Rate of climb ....500 ft/min
Average true airspeed ....135 kts
True course ....215°
Average wind velocity ....290° at 20 kts
Variation...3°W
Deviation ....-2°
Average fuel consumption ....13 gal/hr

Determine the approximate time, compass heading, distance, and fuel consumed during the climb.

A — 14 minutes, 234°, 26 NM, 3.9 gallons.
B — 17 minutes, 224°, 36 NM, 3.7 gallons.
C — 17 minutes, 242°, 31 NM, 3.5 gallons.

10-20. Answer C. GFDICM 10C (PHB)
To solve this problem you must determine your groundspeed. To do this enter the wind direction (175°) and wind speed (20 kts.), true course (075°), and true airspeed (80 kts.) into your flight computer. Your groundspeed is 81 knots. To determine the estimated time enroute (ETE), divide the distance by your groundspeed. Your ETE is 1:40:00 (135 ÷ 81 = 1:40:00). To calculate your fuel consumption, multiply your ETE by the fuel consumption rate. The answer is 175 pounds (1:40:00 × 105 = 175).

10-21. Answer B. GFDICM 10C (PHB)
First, determine the total height of the climb from the airport elevation of 1,000 feet to the cruise altitude of 9,500 feet (9,500 ft. - 1,000 ft. = 8,500 feet). The time to climb is determined by dividing the height of the climb by the rate of climb (8,500 ft. ÷ 500 ft/min = 17.0 minutes). Now enter the following given information into your flight computer to calculate true heading, and groundspeed.

1. Wind 290° at 20 kts.

2. True course 215°

3. True airspeed 135 kts.

   True heading = 223°

   Groundspeed = 128 kts.

Determine compass heading by adding the variation (3°W) and subtracting the deviation (-2°) to the true heading (223° + 3° - 2° = 224°). Determine the distance by entering the time of 17 minutes and a groundspeed of 128 knots to get 36.4 n.m. Determine fuel consumption by entering the time of 17 minutes and a fuel flow of 13.0 gallons per hour to get 3.7 gallons.

10-22   **H344**

An airplane departs an airport under the following conditions:

Airport elevation .... 1,500 ft
Cruise altitude .... 9,500 ft
Rate of climb .... 500 ft/min
Average true airspeed .... 160 kts
True course .... 145°
Average wind velocity .... 080° at 15 kts
Variation .... 5°E
Deviation .... -3°
Average fuel consumption .... 14 gal/hr

Determine the approximate time, compass heading, distance, and fuel consumed during the climb.

A — 14 minutes, 128°, 35 NM, 3.2 gallons.
B — 16 minutes, 132°, 41 NM, 3.7 gallons.
C — 16 minutes, 128°, 32 NM, 3.8 gallons.

10-22. Answer B. GFDICM 10C (PHB)

First, determine the total height of the climb from the airport elevation of 1,500 feet to the cruise altitude of 9,500 feet (9,500 ft - 1,500 ft. = 8,000 feet). The time to climb is determined by dividing the height of the climb by the rate of climb (8,000 ft. ÷ 500 ft/min = 16.0 minutes). Now enter the following given information into your flight computer to calculate true heading, and groundspeed.

1. Wind 080° at 15 kts.

2. True course 145°

3. True airspeed 160 kts.

   True heading = 140°

   Groundspeed = 153 kts.

Determine compass heading by subtracting the variation (5°E) and deviation (-3°) to the true heading (140° - 8° = 132°). Determine the distance by entering the time of 16 minutes and a groundspeed of 153 knots to get 40.8 n.m. Determine fuel consumption by entering the time of 16 minutes and a fuel flow of 14.0 gallons per hour to get 3.7 gallons.

CHAPTER 11

ADVANCED SYSTEMS

SECTION A
HIGH-PERFORMANCE POWERPLANTS

Chapter 11, Section A, of the *Instrument/Commercial Manual* contains essential information for commercial pilots. It emphasizes reciprocating powerplant operations and procedures. You may have covered much of this material in your training for a private pilot certificate, in which case you may find this section a useful review.

Complex Airplanes

1. A complex airplane is one that has retractable landing gear, flaps, and a controllable pitch propeller, whereas, a high-performance airplane is one that has an engine of more than 200 horsepower.

2. Before increasing manifold pressure (MAP) or reducing r.p.m. on an aircraft that is equipped with a constant-speed propeller, you should verify that the resulting MAP will not cause engine damage.

3. To increase power on an engine equipped with a constant-speed propeller, first increase the engine r.p.m. by advancing the propeller control and then advance the throttle to increase MAP. To decrease power, first decrease the MAP by retarding the throttle and then decrease the engine r.p.m. by retarding the propeller control.

4. High engine oil temperature most likely is the indication of low oil level.

5. Crankshaft counterweights designed to reduce engine vibration can be detuned by rapidly opening and closing the throttle.

Operation of Fuel Systems

6. The ratio of the weight of fuel and the weight of air entering a cylinder is known as the fuel/air ratio. The best power mixture is that fuel/air ratio at which the most power can be obtained for any given throttle setting.

7. The application of carburetor heat enriches the fuel/air mixture, which can reduce power and decrease performance. It may be necessary to adjust the mixture control when applying carburetor heat.

8. An excessively rich mixture may cause spark plug fouling and a rough running engine at low r.p.m.

9. When using the fuel flow indicator, you should be aware of a malfunction that may occur if a fuel nozzle becomes obstructed by dirt or other foreign debris. With a blocked nozzle, the injection system's pressure will rise, causing the indicator to show a higher-than-normal fuel flow value. In response, you may be tempted to lean the mixture further in order to obtain the desired flow rate.

10. Fuel injection system vapor lock is caused by the fuel vaporizing in the injection system's lines and components. Without the flow of cooling air through the engine cowling, the engine's heat causes the fuel in the injection system to boil. The boiling fuel produces vapor that blocks fuel flow in the injection system.

11. Fuel injection systems have an alternate air source that provides unfiltered, heated intake air to the engine in the event the main air source is obstructed by impact ice.

Preignition and Detonation

12. Preignition and detonation are the result of abnormal ignition and combustion. Frequency and severity of these conditions can be greatly reduced by using the correct fuel/air mixture and by monitoring the engine instruments to maintain the proper engine operating temperatures.

13. Detonation is when the fuel air mixture in the cylinder instantaneously ignites instead of burning progressively and evenly.

14. Preignition is the uncontrolled firing of the fuel/air charge in advance of normal spark ignition. This can be the result of hot spots or glowing carbon particles within the cylinder.

15 Air-cooled reciprocating aircraft engines are dependent on the proper flow of lubricating oil to provide internal cooling. The circulation of the oil helps to disperse heat away from moving parts.

Propellers

16. The spiraling slipstream produced from a propeller around the fuselage of the aircraft strikes the left side of the vertical fin. This tends to cause the aircraft to turn left around the vertical axis, and roll to the right around the longitudinal axis.

17. Propeller efficiency is the ratio of thrust horsepower to brake horsepower. A fixed-pitch propeller achieves its peak efficiency at a specific airspeed and r.p.m. while an aircraft with a constant-speed propeller will automatically adjust the propeller blade angle for any given throttle setting to attain the optimum efficiency.

18. To obtain maximum power and thrust a controllable-pitch propeller should be set at a small angle of attack with a high r.p.m. setting.

11-1   **H307**
Before shutdown, while at idle, the ignition key is momentarily turned OFF. The engine continues to run with no interruption; this

A — is normal because the engine is usually stopped by moving the mixture to idle cut-off.
B — should not normally happen. Indicates a magneto not grounding in OFF position.
C — is an undesirable practice, but indicates that nothing is wrong.

11-1. Answer B. GFDPPM 2B (PHB)
An engine that continues running after the ignition switch is turned to OFF may have a disconnected ground wire in the ignition switch. Although it is normal procedure to stop the engine by moving the mixture to idle cutoff, the engine should not continue running with the ignition switch turned to OFF (answer A). Answer (C) is wrong because this check is a good operating practice which can identify a dangerous situation.

11-2   **H307**
Leaving the carburetor heat on during takeoff

A — leans the mixture for more power on takeoff.
B — will decrease the takeoff distance.
C — will increase the ground roll.

11-2. Answer C. GFDICM 11A (PHB)
Carburetor heat causes a slight decrease in engine power, because the heated air is less dense than the outside air that would have been entering the engine. Answer (A) is incorrect because adding carburetor heat enriches the mixture and causes a reduction in power. Answer (B) is not right because a decrease in engine power results in an increase in the takeoff distance.

11-3   **H307**
A way to detect a broken magneto primary grounding lead is to

A — idle the engine and momentarily turn the ignition off.
B — add full power, while holding the brakes, and momentarily turn off the ignition.
C — run on one magneto, lean the mixture, and look for a rise in manifold pressure.

11-3. Answer A. GFDPPM 2B (PHB)
To check the ignition system for a broken ground wire, idle the engine before shutting it down and momentarily turn the ignition switch to OFF, then, turn the switch back to both. If the engine continues to run without hesitation the ground wire is broken. This check should be accomplished in accordance with the manufacturer's recommendations in the Aircraft Flight Manual or the Pilot's Operating Handbook. Answer (B) is incorrect because attempting this check with the engine running at full power puts unnecessary stress on the engine. Neither the mixture, nor the manifold pressure, have anything to do with the ignition system of the aircraft (answer C).

11-4   H307

Fouling of spark plugs is more apt to occur if the aircraft

A — gains altitude with no mixture adjustment.
B — descends from altitude with no mixture adjustment.
C — throttle is advanced very abruptly.

11-4. Answer A. GFDICM 11A (PHB)
As altitude increases, the density of the air entering the carburetor decreases while the density of the fuel remains the same. This means that at higher altitudes the mixture becomes progressively richer. To maintain the correct fuel/air mixture, you must lean the mixture for flight at higher altitudes and you must remember to enrich the mixture during descent. Failure to do so may result in an excessively high engine operating temperatures and possible detonation (answer B). The throttle controls the amount of the fuel/air mixture entering the engine but can not alter the ratio of the mixture or directly cause fouled spark plugs (answer C).

11-5   H307

The most probable reason an engine continues to run after the ignition switch has been turned off is

A — carbon deposits glowing on the spark plugs.
B — a magneto ground wire is in contact with the engine casing.
C — a broken magneto ground wire.

11-5. Answer C. GFDPPM 2B (PHB)
The engine will continue to run with the ignition switch turned to the OFF position if a ground wire between the ignition switch and the magneto is broken. Carbon deposits glowing in the spark plugs may cause preignition (answer A), a situation where the glowing carbon ignites the fuel/air mixture prematurely as it enters the cylinder. Answer (B) is incorrect because a magneto ground wire in contact with the engine casing would prevent that magneto from firing.

11-6   H307

If the ground wire between the magneto and the ignition switch becomes disconnected, the engine

A — will not operate on one magneto.
B — cannot be started with the switch in the BOTH position.
C — could accidently start if the propeller is moved with fuel in the cylinder.

11-6. Answer C. GFDPPM 2B (PHB)
If the ground wire between the magneto and the ignition switch is disconnected, the magneto may send a current to the spark plugs if any rotation of the crankshaft/propeller occurs. A small amount of fuel in the cylinders is all that is needed to start the engine in this situation. The engine will operate on the magneto that has the broken ground wire between the ignition switch and the magneto (answer A) and both magnetos will operate with the ignition switch turned to the BOTH position (answer B).

11-7   H307

For internal cooling, reciprocating aircraft engines are especially dependent on

A — a properly functioning cowl flap augmenter.
B — the circulation of lubricating oil.
C — the proper freon/compressor output ratio.

11-7. Answer B. GFDPPM 2B (PHB)
Oil provides two important functions in an engine, lubrication and cooling by reducing friction and removing some of the heat from the cylinders. Answer (A) is incorrect because not all reciprocating engines have cowl flaps. Answer (C) is incorrect because freon and compressors are used in air conditioners for cooling the cabin and not engine cooling.

11-8   H307

The pilot controls the air/fuel ratio with the

A — throttle.
B — manifold pressure.
C — mixture control.

11-8. Answer C. GFDPPM 2B (AFH)
To maintain the proper fuel/air mixture, you must be able to adjust the amount of fuel that is mixed with the incoming air. This is a function of the mixture control. Answer (A) is incorrect because the throttle controls the quantity of the fuel/air mixture that enters the engine and not the ratio of fuel-to-air that enters the engine. Answer (B) is incorrect because manifold pressure is controlled by the throttle.

11-9   H308

Which statement best describes the operating principle of a constant-speed propeller?

A — As throttle setting is changed by the pilot, the prop governor causes pitch angle of the propeller blades to remain unchanged.

B — A high blade angle or increased pitch reduces the propeller drag and allows more engine power for takeoffs.

C — The propeller control regulates the engine RPM and in turn the propeller RPM.

11-10   H308

In aircraft equipped with constant-speed propellers and normally-aspirated engines, which procedure should be used to avoid placing undue stress on the engine components? When power is being

A — decreased, reduce the RPM before reducing the manifold pressure.

B — increased, increase the RPM before increasing the manifold pressure.

C — increased or decreased, the RPM should be adjusted before the manifold pressure.

11-11   H307

Detonation may occur at high-power settings when

A — the fuel mixture instantaneously ignites instead of burning progressively and evenly.

B — an excessively rich fuel mixture causes an explosive gain in power.

C — the fuel mixture is ignited too early by hot carbon deposits in the cylinder.

11-12   H307

Detonation can be caused by

A — using a lower grade of fuel than recommended.

B — low engine temperatures.

C — a "rich" mixture.

11-9. Answer C. GFDPPM 2B (AFH)

The propeller control is used to set the engine RPM, which is the same as setting the propeller RPM. Answer (A) is incorrect because when you set the propeller control to a specific RPM, a governor mounted on the engine and a mechanism inside the propeller hub automatically change the pitch of the propeller to maintain the corresponding RPM. Answer (B) is incorrect because a low blade angle and decreased pitch reduce propeller drag.

11-10. Answer B. GFDPPM 2B (AFH)

When increasing power in an airplane with a constant speed propeller, first increase the RPM by decreasing the propeller blade angle, then advance the throttle to increase manifold pressure. When decreasing power, first retard the throttle to reduce manifold pressure, then decrease RPM by increasing the propeller blade angle. Answers (A) and (C) are inappropriate because they do not follow the recommended sequence for adjusting power.

11-11. Answer A. GFDICM 11A (AFH)

Detonation is the uncontrolled, explosive combustion of fuel. Normally, fuel burns evenly and progressively inside the combustion chamber. Detonation causes the fuel to explode, producing excessive pressures and temperatures within the engine. An excessively rich mixture (answer B) decreases power. Answer (C) is incorrect because it describes preignition rather than detonation.

11-12. Answer A. GFDICM 11A

Detonation is the uncontrolled, explosive combustion of fuel. Detonation is caused by several conditions such as using a fuel grade lower than recommended, high engine temperatures, a heavy engine load at a low RPM, or using a fuel/air mixture that is too lean.

11-13   **H307**

The uncontrolled firing of the fuel/air charge in advance of normal spark ignition is known as

A — instantaneous combustion.
B — detonation.
C — pre-ignition.

11-13. Answer C. GFDICM 11A (AFH)

Preignition sometimes occurs when an excessively rich mixture causes residual fuel to form carbon deposits in the cylinder that are heated until they are glowing. Preignition can also occur from an excessively hot exhaust valve, or a cracked ceramic spark plug insulator, or almost any damage around the combustion chamber. These hot spots ignite the fuel/air mixture prematurely and cause a loss of performance, increase in operating temperatures and severe structural stresses on the engine. Instantaneous combustion (answer A) is part of the definition of detonation (answer B).

11-14   **H51**

Fuel/air ratio is the ratio between the

A — volume of fuel and volume of air entering the cylinder.
B — weight of fuel and weight of air entering the cylinder.
C — weight of fuel and weight of air entering the carburetor.

11-14. Answer B. GFDICM 11A (AFH)

Fuel and air are mixed in the carburetor prior to entering the cylinders. The throttle is used to regulate the amount of airflow. For this mixture to burn efficiently, the ratio of air-to-fuel must be maintained within a specific range, such as 12:1, or 12 pounds of air and 1 pound of fuel. Answer (A) is incorrect because the fuel-to-air mixture is not measured by volume. Answer (C) is not correct because the mixture of fuel-to-air is complete as it enters the engine not upon entering the carburetor.

11-15   **H307**

The mixture control can be adjusted, which

A — prevents the fuel/air combination from becoming too rich at higher altitudes.
B — regulates the amount of airflow through the carburetor's venturi.
C — prevents the fuel/air combination from becoming lean as the airplane climbs.

11-15. Answer A. GFDICM 11A (AFH)

The purpose of the mixture control is to prevent the mixture from becoming excessively rich at higher altitudes due to the decreasing density of the air. The mixture control specifically regulates the flow of fuel, not air (answer B). As an airplane climbs, failure to adjust the mixture will result in an excessively rich mixture, not lean (answer C).

11-16   **H307**

Which statement is true concerning the effect of the application of carburetor heat?

A — It enriches the fuel/air mixture.
B — It leans the fuel/air mixture.
C — It has no effect on the fuel/air mixture.

11-16. Answer A. GFDICM 11A (AC 65-12A)

Applying carburetor heat causes a slight decrease of engine power because the heated air is less dense than the outside air that would have been entering the engine. This enriches the mixture. When the same amount of fuel is mixed with less dense air (more fuel than air by weight), a richer mixture occurs. Answers (B) and (C) are wrong because the application of carburetor heat does affect the fuel/air mixture by making it richer.

11-17   **H51**

Detonation occurs in a reciprocating aircraft engine when

A — the spark plugs receive an electrical jolt caused by a short in the wiring.
B — the unburned fuel/air charge in the cylinders is subjected to instantaneous combustion.
C — there is an explosive increase of fuel caused by too rich a fuel/air mixture.

11-17. Answer B. GFDICM 11A

Detonation is the uncontrolled, explosive combustion of fuel. Normally, fuel burns evenly and progressively inside the combustion chamber. Detonation causes the fuel to explode, producing excessive pressures and temperatures within the engine.

11-18   **H66**

Propeller efficiency is the

A — ratio of thrust horsepower to brake horsepower.
B — actual distance a propeller advances in one revolution.
C — ratio of geometric pitch to effective pitch.

11-18. Answer A. GFDICM 11A (AFH)

Propeller efficiency is the ratio of thrust horsepower to brake horsepower. Propeller efficiency varies between 50% and 87%, depending on how much the propeller slips. Answer (B) is incorrect because the actual distance a propeller advances in one revolution is effective pitch, not propeller efficiency. Answer (C) is incorrect because it relates more to propeller slippage which is the difference between (not the ratio to) geometric pitch and effective pitch. Propeller slippage is reflected in overall propeller efficiency.

11-19   **H66**

A fixed-pitch propeller is designed for best efficiency only at a given combination of

A — altitude and RPM.
B — airspeed and RPM.
C — airspeed and altitude.

11-19. Answer B. GFDICM 11A (AFH)

A fixed-pitch propeller achieves peak efficiency only at a given combination of airspeed and r.p.m.

11-20   **H66**

The reason for variations in geometric pitch (twisting) along a propeller blade is that it

A — permits a relatively constant angle of incidence along its length when in cruising flight.
B — prevents the portion of the blade near the hub from stalling during cruising flight.
C — permits a relatively constant angle of attack along its length when in cruising flight.

11-20. Answer C. GFDICM 11A (AFH)

Unlike an airfoil which moves the air at a uniform rate, propellers are rotating airfoils, and sections near the tip travel at a much faster speed than the sections near the hub. To compensate for this, each small section of the propeller blade is set at a different angle of attack to the plane of rotation. The gradual decrease in the blade angle (the propeller twist) on sections further away from the hub, allows the propeller to provide a relatively constant angle of attack and uniform thrust throughout most of the blade length. Answer (A) is incorrect because twist provides a relatively constant angle of attack (not angle of incidence). Answer (B) is incorrect because the sections near the tips would stall before the sections near the hub if the propeller was not twisted.

11-21   **K20**

A detuning of engine crankshaft counterweights is a source of overstress that may be caused by

A — rapid opening and closing of the throttle.
B — carburetor ice forming on the throttle valve.
C — operating with an excessively rich fuel/air mixture.

11-21. Answer A. GFDICM 11A (AC 20-103)

Many aircraft engines are equipped with balance weights as part of the crankshaft assembly. These counterweights can be detuned by rapidly opening and closing the throttle or excessive speed or power settings. When these counterweights are detuned, crankshaft vibrations leading to engine and/or crankshaft failure can result. Carburetor ice (answer B) is wrong because it forms in the carburetor and has nothing to do with crankshaft counterweights. Answer (C) is wrong because operating with an excessively rich mixture causes sparkplug fouling, not engine stress.

11-22   **H51**

The best power mixture is that fuel/air ratio at which

A — cylinder head temperatures are the coolest.
B — the most power can be obtained for any given throttle setting.
C — a given power can be obtained with the highest manifold pressure or throttle setting.

11-22. Answer B. GFDICM 11A (AFH)

When setting the mixture, you want to achieve a fuel/air ratio that provides the most power for any given throttle setting. Flying with a fuel/air ratio that provides for the coolest cylinder head temperature (answer A) can cause sparkplug fouling and lead to engine roughness. Answer (C) is wrong because the highest manifold pressure or throttle setting is associated with maximum power.

11-23 **H307**
Applying carburetor heat will

A — not affect the mixture.
B — lean the fuel/air mixture.
C — enrich the fuel/air mixture.

11-24 **H307**
An abnormally high engine oil temperature indication may be caused by

A — a defective bearing.
B — the oil level being too low.
C — operating with an excessively rich mixture.

11-25 **H307**
What will occur if no leaning is made with the mixture control as the flight altitude increases?

A — The volume of air entering the carburetor decreases and the amount of fuel decreases.
B — The density of air entering the carburetor decreases and the amount of fuel increases.
C — The density of air entering the carburetor decreases and the amount of fuel remains constant.

11-26 **H307**
Unless adjusted, the fuel/air mixture becomes richer with an increase in altitude because the amount of fuel

A — decreases while the volume of air decreases.
B — remains constant while the volume of air decreases.
C — remains constant while the density of air decreases.

11-27 **H307**
The basic purpose of adjusting the fuel/air mixture control at altitude is to

A — decrease the fuel flow to compensate for decreased air density.
B — decrease the amount of fuel in the mixture to compensate for increased air density.
C — increase the amount of fuel in the mixture to compensate for the decrease in pressure and density of the air.

11-23. Answer C. GFDICM 11A (PHB)
When carburetor heat is applied, warm air is introduced into the carburetor. Since heated air is less dense, the mixture is enriched. Answers (A) and (B) are wrong because the mixture is enriched.

11-24. Answer B. GFDPPM 2B (PHB)
High oil temperature indications can be caused by several factors, including a low oil quantity, a plugged oil line, or a defective temperature gauge. A defective bearing (answer A), would not necessarily increase the oil temperature. Answer (C) is wrong because the engine temperature will decrease with an excessively rich mixture.

11-25. Answer C. GFDICM 11A (PHB)
As altitude increases, air becomes less dense. However, the density of the fuel entering the carburetor at altitude remains the same. If the mixture control is not changed, the mixture could be enriched enough to cause engine roughness, reduced power, and spark plug fouling. Answer (A) is wrong because the volume of both air and fuel are constant. It is the density of air that decreases. Answer (B) is wrong because the amount of fuel is the same. It should be noted that with fewer air molecules per given volume, and with the same number of fuel molecules, the fuel/air mixture (ratio) is increased, or enriched.

11-26. Answer C. GFDICM 11A (PHB)
See explanation for Question 11-25. As the air density decreases and the amount of fuel remains constant, the mixture becomes richer. Answers (A) and (B) are wrong because neither the amount of fuel nor the volume of air decrease.

11-27. Answer A. GFDICM 11A (PHB)
See explanation for Question 11-25. As the air density decreases with altitude, the fuel flow must be decreased to maintain the proper fuel/air ratio, or mixture. Answer (B) is wrong because the air density decreases, not increases, with altitude. Answer (C) is wrong because you would not increase the amount of fuel to compensate for the decrease in air density.

11-28   H307

At high altitudes, an excessively rich mixture will cause the

A — engine to overheat.
B — fouling of spark plugs.
C — engine to operate smoother even though fuel consumption is increased.

11-28. Answer B. GFDICM 11A (PHB)

A mixture that is too rich can foul the spark plugs, resulting in engine roughness. A mixture that is too lean can cause an engine to overheat (answer A). Answer (C) is wrong because the engine will not operate smoother with an excessively rich mixture.

11-29   H308

To establish a climb after takeoff in an aircraft equipped with a constant-speed propeller, the output of the engine is reduced to climb power by decreasing manifold pressure and

A — increasing RPM by decreasing propeller blade angle.
B — decreasing RPM by decreasing propeller blade angle.
C — decreasing RPM by increasing propeller blade angle.

11-29. Answer C. GFDICM 11A (AFH)

Anytime you decrease power on an engine with a constant-speed propeller, you should reduce the manifold pressure first with the throttle, and the RPM second by increasing the propeller blade angle. Answer (A) is wrong because you want to decrease RPM to achieve the climb power setting. Answer (B) is wrong because decreasing the propeller blade angle, increases RPM.

11-30   H308

To develop maximum power and thrust, a constant-speed propeller should be set to a blade angle that will produce a

A — large angle of attack and low RPM.
B — small angle of attack and high RPM.
C — large angle of attack and high RPM.

11-30. Answer B. GFDICM 11A (AFH)

To achieve maximum power and thrust from an aircraft equipped with a constant-speed propeller, you must use a low blade angle that develops a high RPM. Answer (A) is incorrect because this combination will not produce maximum power and thrust. Answer (C) is wrong because high RPM requires a small (not large) angle of attack.

11-31   H308

For takeoff, the blade angle of the controllable-pitch propeller should be set at a

A — small angle of attack and high RPM.
B — large angle of attack and low RPM.
C — large angle of attack and high RPM.

11-31. Answer A. GFDICM 11A (AFH)

See explanation for Question 11-30. During takeoff it is important that you obtain the maximum performance from your aircraft. To do this with a constant-speed propeller, you should use a small propeller blade angle resulting in a high RPM. If a large blade angle (answers B and C) and low RPM (answer B) were used, less than maximum performance and thrust would be obtained.

SECTION B
ENVIRONMENTAL AND ICE CONTROL SYSTEMS

Chapter 11, Section B, covers systems found in advanced aircraft that you may fly as a commercial pilot. Although this information is important, there are no commercial FAA test questions assigned.

Oxygen Systems

1. Make sure the oxygen system is filled with aviator's breathing oxygen. If you do not use this type of oxygen, it may contain too much moisture, which may cause valves and lines to freeze, possibly stopping the flow of oxygen.

Cabin Pressurization Systems

2. Pressurization is accomplished by pumping air into an aircraft that is adequately sealed to limit the rate at which air escapes from the cabin. By limiting the rate of airflow out of the cabin, the air pressure increases to produce a cabin environment equivalent to one encountered at a lower altitude.

Ice Control Systems

3. Anti-icing equipment prevents the formation of ice; de-icing equipment removes ice once it has formed. Common anti-icing systems include heated wings and propellers, as well as systems for applying anti-ice fluids to wings and propellers. De-icing equipment typically consists of inflatable boots on leading edges of airfoils, designed to break off accumulated ice.

SECTION C
RETRACTABLE LANDING GEAR

1. If there is moisture on the runway when taking off in freezing temperatures or possible ice accumulation climbing to or above the freezing level, it is wise to cycle the landing gear several times. Cycling the gear helps prevent ice from forming over the linkages and locking or sticking the gear in the retracted position.

2. V_{LE} is the maximum landing gear extended speed.

11-32   A02

14 CFR part 1 defines V_{LE} as

A — maximum leading edge flaps extended speed.
B — maximum landing gear operating speed.
C — maximum landing gear extended speed.

11-32. Answer C. GFDICM 11A (FAR 1.2)
V_{LE} is the maximum allowable speed with the landing gear extended. V_{LO} is the maximum landing gear operating speed.

11-33   L52

If necessary to take off from a slushy runway, the freezing of landing gear mechanisms can be minimized by

A — recycling the gear.
B — delaying gear retraction.
C — increasing the airspeed to V_{LE} before retraction.

11-33. Answer A. GFDICM 11C (AC 91-13C)
In cold weather, moisture can splash onto gear linkages and freeze. If moisture is unavoidable, cycle the landing gear several times after takeoff to prevent a solid bond of ice from adhering to movable parts. Answers (B) and (C) are wrong because delaying gear retraction after takeoff, can adversely affect climb performance. Also, delaying retraction may help the ice form a solid bond to movable parts and prevent retraction.

AERODYNAMICS AND PERFORMANCE LIMITATIONS

CHAPTER 12

SECTION A
ADVANCED AERODYNAMICS

Chapter 12, Section A is a review of basic aerodynamic principles and includes advanced aerodynamic topics appropriate for a commercial pilot.

Aerodynamic Fundamentals

1. The four fundamentals in maneuvering an aircraft are straight-and-level flight, turns, climbs, and descents.

2. Opposing forces are equal in unaccelerated flight.

3. When you initiate a climb or descent, you momentarily create an imbalance in the four forces, which causes the airplane to accelerate until the forces reach equilibrium again. For example, to climb you increase the angle of attack, creating an excess of lift. If thrust remains constant, the increase in induced drag slows the airplane. This reduced airspeed decreases the amount of lift, bringing lift and weight back into balance. Because the thrust vector is now inclined upward, a portion is acting to lift the airplane.

Lift

4. Lift is defined as the force acting perpendicular to the relative wind. Drag acts parallel to the flight path, in the same direction as the relative wind.

5. Lift results from relatively high pressure below the wing's surface and lower air pressure above the wing's surface.

6. There is a corresponding indicated airspeed for every angle of attack to generate sufficient lift to maintain altitude.

7. To generate the same amount of lift at a higher altitude, an airplane must be flown at either a higher angle of attack or a higher true airspeed.

8. When the angle of attack of a symmetrical airfoil is increased, the center of pressure will remain unaffected.

9. Flaps increase the coefficient of lift, allowing the wing to produce the same amount of lift at a lower airspeed. Flaps also lower the stall speed.

Drag

10. At high angles of attack, pressure increases below the wing, and the increase in lift is accompanied by an increase in induced drag.

11. Induced drag is a by-product of lift and is greatly affected by changes in airspeed.

12. Ground effect decreases induced drag and increases lift at a given angle of attack. An airplane leaving ground effect will experience an increase in drag and will require more thrust.

13. Parasite drag increases in proportion to the square of the airspeed, thus doubling the airspeed will quadruple parasite drag.

14. Total drag is lowest at the airspeed which produces the highest ratio of lift to drag (L/D$_{MAX}$). At airspeeds below L/D$_{MAX}$, total drag increases due to induced drag, and at speeds above L/D$_{MAX}$, total drag increases because of parasite drag.

15. The airspeed that gives the lowest total drag (L/D$_{MAX}$) will provide the best power-off glide range, as well as the greatest range. As aircraft weight decreases, the airspeed for L/D$_{MAX}$ also decreases.

Aircraft Stability

16. An airplane with positive static stability tends initially to return to equilibrium if disturbed. An airplane that remains in a new attitude without returning toward equilibrium or moving farther away from equilibrium displays neutral static stability. If an airplane initially tends to move away from equilibrium when disturbed, it has negative static stability.

17. Longitudinal dynamic stability is characterized by pitch oscillations that get smaller and eventually subside. Longitudinal dynamic instability is characterized by progressively steeper pitch oscillations.

18. Longitudinal stability involves the motion of the airplane controlled by the elevator.

Stalls and Spins

19. Total weight, load factor, power, and CG location affect stall speed.

20. Stalling speed is most affected by load factor. In any situation involving increased load factor, such as a rapid pullout from a dive, the stall speed increases.

21. Spin recovery may be difficult if the CG is too far aft and rotation is around the CG.

22. Rectangular wings have a tendency to stall first at the wing root, with the stall progression toward the wingtip.

Aerodynamics and Flight Maneuvers

23. To maintain altitude while airspeed is being reduced, the angle of attack must be increased.

24. Transitioning to a climb, angle of attack increases and lift momentarily increases.

25. Approximate gliding distance can be found by multiplying your altitude AGL by the L/D ratio. Glide ratios for various angles of attack are obtained from an L/D graph.

26. Load factor is the ratio between the lift generated by the wings at any given time divided by the total weight of the airplane. The design load factor takes into account the effects of acceleration on the contents of the airplane.

27. As the angle of bank is increased, the vertical component of lift decreases because more of the total lift is directed horizontally. To compensate for the loss of part of the vertical component of lift in a turn, you must increase the angle of attack by using elevator back pressure.

28. Load factor in turns increases at steeper bank angles, as does the stall speed. At a given bank angle, all airplanes experience the same load factor and the same percentage increase in stall speed over their wings-level stall speed. For example, any airplane in 60° banked coordinated, level turn experiences a 2-G load factor, which means the wings must support twice the weight of the loaded airplane.

29. A given airspeed and bank angle will produce a specific rate and radius of turn in any airplane. In a coordinated, level turn, an increase in airspeed will increase the radius and decrease the rate of turn. Load factor is directly related to bank angle, so the load factor for a given bank angle is the same at any airspeed.

30. V_{NO} is the maximum structural cruising speed during normal operations while V_{NE} is the never-exceed speed. Above V_{NE}, design limit load factors may be exceeded if gusts are encountered, causing structural damage or failure.

12-1   H303
The ratio between the total airload imposed on the wing and the gross weight of an aircraft in flight is known as

A — load factor and directly affects stall speed.
B — aspect load and directly affects stall speed.
C — load factor and has no relation with stall speed.

12-1. Answer A. GFDICM 12A (PHB)
The ratio of the load imposed on the wings and the airplane's actual weight is the effective weight, or load factor. If a load factor of three is imposed on a 3,000-pound airplane, the load on the airframe is 9,000 pounds. The term aspect load (answer B) is not correc terminology. Stall speed is directly related to airplane load factor (answer C). Stall speed increases by the square root of the load factor.

12-2   H303
Load factor is the lift generated by the wings of an airplane at any given time

A — divided by the total weight of the aircraft.
B — multiplied by the total weight of the aircraft.
C — divided by the basic empty weight of the aircraft.

12-3   H303
For a given angle of bank, in any airplane, the load factor imposed in a coordinated constant-altitude turn

A — is constant and the stall speed increases.
B — varies with the rate of turn.
C — is constant and the stall speed decreases.

12-4   H303
Airplane wing loading during a level coordinated turn in smooth air depends upon the

A — rate of turn.
B — angle of bank.
C — true airspeed.

12-5   H303
In a rapid recovery from a dive, the effects of load factor would cause the stall speed to

A — increase.
B — decrease.
C — not vary.

12-6   H303
If an aircraft with a gross weight of 2,000 pounds was subjected to a 60° constant-altitude bank, the total load would be

A — 3,000 pounds.
B — 4,000 pounds.
C — 12,000 pounds.

12-7   H303
While maintaining a constant angle of bank and altitude in a coordinated turn, an increase in airspeed will

A — decrease the rate of turn resulting in a decreased load factor.
B — decrease the rate of turn resulting in no change in load factor.
C — increase the rate of turn resulting in no change in load factor.

12-2. Answer A. GFDICM 12A (PHB)
Load factor is the ratio between the load imposed on the wings and the airplane's actual weight. The lift generated by the wings multiplied by the total weight of the airplane does not result in a relevant figure (answer B). Answer (C) is wrong because you must divide by the actual weight not the basic empty weight to get load factor.

12-3. Answer A. GFDICM 12A (AFH)
Load factor remains constant for a given bank angle in a constant altitude turn and stall speed increases in proportion to the square root of the load factor. These relationships are the same for all aircraft. The rate of turn is a function of bank angle and airspeed, and not load factor (answer B). Stall speed increases with increases in load factor (answer C).

12-4. Answer B. GFDICM 12A (AFH)
Load factor increases with an increase in bank angle. Rate of turn (answer A) is a function of airspeed and bank angle, and, in itself, is not directly related to wing loading. Wing loading is a function of bank angle and aircraft gross weight and is not directly related to airspeed (answer C).

12-5. Answer A. GFDICM 12A (AFH)
A rapid pull-up from a dive increases the load factor or "G" forces imposed on the airplane, and stall speed increases in proportion to the square root of the load factor. Stall speed does not decrease (answer B), or remain constant (answer C) with an increase in load factor.

12-6. Answer B. GFDICM 12A (AFH)
At a bank angle of 60°, the load factor is two Gs, which means that the wings are supporting twice the weight of the airplane, or 4,000 pounds. A bank angle of 50° would produce 1.5 Gs, or a total load of 3,000 pounds (answer A). A bank angle of 80° would produce 6 Gs, or a total load of 12,000 pounds (answer C).

12-7. Answer B. GFDICM 12A (AFH)
The rate of turn for a given bank angle varies with airspeed. If speed is increased at a constant bank angle, the rate of turn is reduced; however, changes in airspeed do not affect load factor. Answer (A) is incorrect because load factor does not vary with changes in airspeed. Answer (C) is incorrect because at a given bank angle, the rate of turn decreases with an increase in airspeed.

12-8   **H300**

Lift on a wing is most properly defined as the

A — force acting perpendicular to the relative wind.
B — differential pressure acting perpendicular to the chord of the wing.
C — reduced pressure resulting from a laminar flow over the upper camber of an airfoil, which acts perpendicular to the mean camber.

12-9   **H303**

While holding the angle of bank constant in a level turn, if the rate of turn is varied, the load factor would

A — remain constant regardless of air density and the resultant lift vector.
B — vary depending upon speed and air density provided the resultant lift vector varies proportionately.
C — vary depending upon the resultant lift vector.

12-10   **H300**

In theory, if the airspeed of an airplane is doubled while in level flight, parasite drag will become

A — twice as great.
B — half as great.
C — four times greater.

12-11   **H300**

As airspeed decreases in level flight below that speed for maximum lift/drag, total drag of an airplane

A — decreases because of lower parasite drag.
B — increases because of increased induced drag.
C — increases because of increased parasite drag.

12-12   **H303**

If the airspeed is increased from 90 knots to 135 knots during a level 60° banked turn, the load factor will

A — increase as well as the stall speed.
B — decrease and the stall speed will increase.
C — remain the same but the radius of turn will increase.

12-8. Answer A. GFDICM 12A (PHB)

Lift always acts perpendicular to the flight path, or relative wind, regardless of the wing's angle of attack. The production of lift requires relatively negative air pressure on the upper surface of the wing and positive air pressure on the bottom of the wing. The differential pressure does not clearly define the lifting force itself, and lift does not always act perpendicular to the chord of the wing (answer B). The lifting force does not always act perpendicular to the mean camber (answer C).

12-9. Answer A. GFDICM 12A (AFH)

Load factor varies with bank angle and is not affected by air density or the resultant lift vector. Answers (B) and (C) are incorrect because load factor is not affected by changes in airspeed or air density.

12-10. Answer C. GFDICM 12A (AFH)

Parasite drag varies proportionately to the square of the airspeed. Therefore if the airspeed is doubled, parasite drag increases four times. Both answers (A) and (B) are incorrect because parasite drag increases faster than the values specified.

12-11. Answer B. GFDICM 12A (AFH)

If all other factors remain constant, induced drag varies inversely with the square root of the airspeed. For example, if airspeed is reduced by half, induced drag increases by a factor of four. Parasite decreases with a decrease in airspeed (answer A), but the exponential increase is induced drag causes total drag to increase. Parasite drag increases with an increase in airspeed. It does not increase with a decrease in airspeed (answer C).

12-12. Answer C. GFDICM 12A (AFH)

The radius of turn for a given bank angle varies with airspeed. If speed is increased at a constant bank angle, the radius of turn is increased. Answers (A) and (B) are incorrect because changes in airspeed do not affect load factor, or stall speed.

12-13   **H303**

Baggage weighing 90 pounds is placed in a normal category airplane's baggage compartment which is placarded at 100 pounds. If this airplane is subjected to a positive load factor of 3.5 G's, the total load of the baggage would be

A — 315 pounds and would be excessive.
B — 315 pounds and would not be excessive.
C — 350 pounds and would not be excessive.

12-14   **H300**

(Refer to figure 1.) At the airspeed represented by point **A**, in steady flight, the airplane will

A — have its maximum lift/drag ratio.
B — have its minimum lift/drag ratio.
C — be developing its maximum coefficient of lift.

12-15   **H300**

(Refer to figure 1.) At an airspeed represented by point **B**, in steady flight, the pilot can expect to obtain the airplane's maximum

A — endurance.
B — glide range.
C — coefficient of lift.

12-13. Answer B. GFDICM 12A (PHB)

To find the weight of an object that is subject to a positive G force, multiply the weight of the object times the number of Gs. In this case, 90 pounds times 3.5 Gs equals 315 pounds. All airplanes are designed to meet certain strength requirements depending upon the intended use of the airplane. Normal aircraft are certificated with a maximum limit load factor of 3.8 positive Gs and 1.52 negative Gs. Answer (A) is incorrect because 315 pounds does not exceed the structural design limits. A G force of 3.89 (which exceeds the normal category limits of 3.8) would be required to create a 350 pound force from a 90 pound object (answer C).

12-14. Answer A. GFDICM 12A (AFH)

The intersection of the induced drag and parasite drag lines corresponds with a point on the total drag line where drag is at a minimum. This is also the point where the aircraft is operating at the best ratio of lift to drag, or L/D$_{MAX}$. The point of minimum lift/drag ratio (answer B) corresponds with the point on the total drag curve that represents the maximum cruise speed in level flight. The maximum coefficient of lift, CL$_{MAX}$, (answer C) corresponds with that point on the total drag curve just above a stall.

12-15. Answer B. GFDICM 12A (AFH)

Point **B** on figure 1 corresponds to the airspeed where the airplane obtains the maximum ratio of lift to drag, L/D$_{MAX}$. This point provides both maximum range and the best power-off glide speed. Any increase or decrease from that specified for L/D$_{MAX}$ will result in a reduced glide distance. Best endurance speed (answer A) occurs at the lowest point on the power-required curve, not the drag curve. The maximum coefficient of lift, CL$_{MAX}$, (answer C) corresponds with that point on the total drag curve just above a stall.

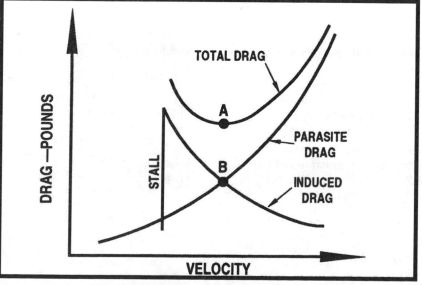

FIGURE 1.—Drag vs. Speed

12-16   **H300**

Which statement is true relative to changing angle of attack?

A — An increase in angle of attack will decrease pressure below the wing, and increase drag.

B — An increase in angle of attack will increase drag.

C — A decrease in angle of attack will increase pressure below the wing, and decrease drag.

12-17   **H305**

Which is true regarding the use of flaps during level turns?

A — The lowering of flaps increases the stall speed.

B — The raising of flaps increases the stall speed.

C — Raising flaps will require added forward pressure on the yoke or stick.

12-18   **H305**

One of the main functions of flaps during the approach and landing is to

A — decrease the angle of descent without increasing the airspeed.

B — provide the same amount of lift at a slower airspeed.

C — decrease lift, thus enabling a steeper-than-normal approach to be made.

12-19   **H55**

Name the four fundamentals involved in maneuvering an aircraft.

A — Power, pitch, bank, and trim.

B — Thrust, lift, turns, and glides.

C — Straight-and-level flight, turns, climbs, and descents.

12-20   **H55**

To increase the rate of turn and at the same time decrease the radius, a pilot should

A — maintain the bank and decrease airspeed.

B — increase the bank and increase airspeed.

C — increase the bank and decrease airspeed.

12-16. Answer B. GFDICM 12A

At higher angles of attack, more of the bottom surface of the wing is exposed to the relative wind which increases impact pressure. Induced drag also increases with an increase in angle of attack.

12-17. Answer B. GFDICM 12A (AFH)

Lowering flaps increases the coefficient of lift of the wing. It also lowers the stall speed. Therefore, raising the flaps increases the stall speed. Answer (A) is incorrect because it states flaps increase stall speed when the exact opposite is true. Answer (C) is incorrect because raising flaps decreases the coefficient of lift which must be compensated for by increasing back pressure on the yoke.

12-18. Answer B. GFDICM 12A (AFH)

Lowering flaps increases the coefficient of lift of the wing, which if all other variables remain constant, results in an overall increase in total lift produced by a wing. Answer (A) is incorrect because flaps allow you to increase your angle of descent without increasing airspeed. Answer (C) is incorrect because total lift increases with the use of flaps.

12-19. Answer C. GFDICM 12A (AFH)

The four fundamentals of flight include straight-and-level flight, climbs, turns, and descents. Answer (A) is incorrect because power and trim are cabin controls, and pitch is considered an axis of flight. Answer (B) is incorrect because thrust and lift are two of the four forces of flight, and glides are a derivative of fundamental descents.

12-20. Answer C. GFDICM 12A (AFH)

The rate of turn varies directly with bank angle and is inversely proportional to airspeed. The radius of turn is affected just the opposite by these two variables. Radius of turn varies directly with airspeed and is inversely proportional to bank angle. Maintaining the bank angle (answer A) will not contribute to an increase in rate of turn or decrease radius, therefore it is not the best choice. Answer (B) is incorrect because an increase in airspeed will decrease the rate of turn and increase the radius.

12-21   H55

Which is correct with respect to rate and radius of turn for an airplane flown in a coordinated turn at a constant altitude?

A — For a specific angle of bank and airspeed, the rate and radius of turn will not vary.

B — To maintain a steady rate of turn, the angle of bank must be increased as the airspeed is decreased.

C — The faster the true airspeed, the faster the rate and larger the radius of turn regardless of the angle of bank.

12-22   H55

Why is it necessary to increase back elevator pressure to maintain altitude during a turn? To compensate for the

A — loss of the vertical component of lift.

B — loss of the horizontal component of lift and the increase in centrifugal force.

C — rudder deflection and slight opposite aileron throughout the turn.

12-23   H55

To maintain altitude during a turn, the angle of attack must be increased to compensate for the decrease in the

A — forces opposing the resultant component of drag.

B — vertical component of lift.

C — horizontal component of lift.

12-24   H66

Stall speed is affected by

A — weight, load factor, and power.

B — load factor, angle of attack, and power.

C — angle of attack, weight, and air density.

12-25   H66

A rectangular wing, as compared to other wing planforms, has a tendency to stall first at the

A — wingtip, with the stall progression toward the wing root.

B — wing root, with the stall progression toward the wingtip.

C — center trailing edge, with the stall progression outward toward the wing root and tip.

12-21. Answer A. GFDICM 12A (AFH)

Airspeed and bank angle are the two variables in determining rate and radius of turn. If these variables remain constant, rate and radius of turn will remain constant. The rate of turn varies directly with bank angle and is inversely proportional to airspeed. By increasing bank angle and decreasing airspeed (answer B) the rate of turn will increase. Answer (C) is incorrect because angle of bank does affect rate and radius of turn.

12-22. Answer A. GFDICM 12A (AFH)

In a level turn the total vertical component of lift no longer directly opposes gravity. Back pressure must be added to increase the amount of lift to compensate for the lost portion of the vertical component of lift. The horizontal component of lift only exists during a turn (answer B). Rudder and aileron deflection in a turn have little to do with the need to increase back elevator pressure (answer C).

12-23. Answer B. GFDICM 12A (AFH)

See explanation for Question 12-22. Answer (A) is incorrect because the force opposing drag is thrust and is not directly related to the need to increase angle of attack in a turn. Answer (C), the horizontal component of lift is related to angle of bank with regard to turn rate and radius.

12-24. Answer A. GFDICM 12A (AFH)

The indicated stall speed is directly affected by weight, CG location, load factor, and power. Answers (B) and (C) are incorrect because exceeding the critical angle of attack is the only constant in every stall. Air density affects lift and drag but not stall speed.

12-25. Answer B. GFDICM 12A (AFH)

One desirable characteristic of a rectangular wing is it's tendency to stall at the wing root first. This provides for adequate stall warning and maintains aileron effectiveness. The tapered, pointed tip, and sweepback wings are examples of wings that first stall at the wing tip with the stall progression toward the wing root (answer A). Answer (C) is incorrect because the elliptical and moderate taper wings are examples of wings that first stall in the center of the trailing edge with the stall progressing toward the wing tip and root.

12-26   **H66**
By changing the angle of attack of a wing, the pilot can control the airplane's

A — lift, airspeed, and drag.
B — lift, airspeed, and CG.
C — lift and airspeed, but not drag.

12-26. Answer A. GFDICM 12A (AFH)
When you change the angle of attack of the wing, you also change lift and drag forces. In general, increasing the angle of attack increases both lift and drag. If drag is in-creased without changing thrust, airspeed will decrease in level flight. Thus, the pilot can directly affect lift, and indirectly change drag and airspeed by changing the angle of attack.

CG is determined by aircraft loading and not by angle of attack (answer B). Answer (C) is wrong because drag varies with angle of attack.

12-27   **H66**
The angle of attack of a wing directly controls the

A — angle of incidence of the wing.
B — amount of airflow above and below the wing.
C — distribution of pressures acting on the wing.

12-27. Answer C. GFDICM 12A (AFH)
There are regions of positive and negative pressure that move along the upper and lower surface of the wing as angle of attack is changed. The angle of incidence is the angle between the chordline of the wing and the longitu-dinal axis of the airplane (answer A). This angle is not affected by changes in angle of attack. Answer (B) is not correct because changing the angle of attack may alter the airflow around the wing but this is not as important as the distribution of the pressure patterns acting on the wing.

12-28   **H66**
In theory, if the angle of attack and other factors remain constant and the airspeed is doubled, the lift produced at the higher speed will be

A — the same as at the lower speed.
B — two times greater than at the lower speed.
C — four times greater than at the lower speed.

12-28. Answer C. GFDICM 12A (PHB)
Lift is directly proportional to the square of the velocity. Therefore doubling the airspeed will quadruple (four times) the amount of lift being produced. Answers (A) and (B) are inappropriate.

12-29   **H66**
An aircraft wing is designed to produce lift resulting from a difference in the

A — negative air pressure below and a vacuum above the wing's surface.
B — vacuum below the wing's surface and greater air pressure above the wing's surface.
C — higher air pressure below the wing's surface and lower air pressure above the wing's surface.

12-29. Answer C. GFDICM 12A (AFH)
Production of lift requires relatively negative air pressure on the upper surface of the wing and positive air pressure on the lower surface. Answer (A) is incorrect because some of the lift is provided by positive (not negative) pressure beneath the forward section of the wing. This is caused by airflow striking the bottom surface of the wing and is referred to as impact, or dynamic pressure. Answer (B) is incorrect because in order to produce lift in normal flight attitudes, air pressure must be less on the upper surface.

12-30   **H66**
On a wing, the force of lift acts perpendicular to and the force of drag acts parallel to the

A — chord line.
B — flight path.
C — longitudinal axis.

12-30. Answer B. GFDICM 12A (PHB)
Relative wind is parallel and opposite to the flight path of the airplane. Lift always acts perpendicular to the flight path (and to the relative wind), regardless of the wing's angle of attack. Also, drag acts opposite to the flight path. Answer (A) is incorrect because regardless of the angle between the chord line and the relative wind, lift always acts perpendicular to the flight path. Answer (C) is incorrect because the longitudinal axis deals more with the angle of incidence. The angle of incidence is formed by the wing's chord line and a line parallel to the longitudinal axis.

12-31   H66
Which statement is true, regarding the opposing forces acting on an airplane in steady-state level flight?

A — These forces are equal.
B — Thrust is greater than drag and weight and lift are equal.
C — Thrust is greater than drag and lift is greater than weight.

12-31. Answer A. GFDICM 12A (PHB)
Opposing aerodynamic forces are balanced in straight-and-level, unaccelerated flight. Lift opposes weight, thrust opposes drag, and the sum of opposing forces is zero. Answers (B) and (C) are incorrect because if thrust is momentarily greater than drag, the aircraft will accelerate until drag equals thrust.

12-32   H66
The angle of attack at which a wing stalls remains constant regardless of

A — weight, dynamic pressure, bank angle, or pitch attitude.
B — dynamic pressure, but varies with weight, bank angle, and pitch attitude.
C — weight and pitch attitude, but varies with dynamic pressure and bank angle.

12-32. Answer A. GFDICM 12A (AFH)
For a given airfoil, a stall will always occur at the same angle of attack regardless of weight, dynamic pressure, bank angle, or pitch attitude. However, the indicated stall speed required to achieve the critical stall angle of attack will vary. Answers (B) and (C) are incorrect because the indicated stall speed (not the angle of attack) is directly affected by weight, CG location, load factor, and power.

12-33   H66
In small airplanes, normal recovery from spins may become difficult if the

A — CG is too far rearward, and rotation is around the longitudinal axis.
B — CG is too far rearward, and rotation is around the CG.
C — spin is entered before the stall is fully developed.

12-33. Answer B. GFDICM 12A (AFH)
Distribution of weight is a critical factor in spin recovery. Spins with aft CG positions are flatter than ordinary spins and may be extremely difficult or even impossible to recover from. A flat spin is characterized by a near level pitch and roll attitude with the spin axis near the CG of the airplane. Although spins typically involve simultaneous rotation around both the vertical and longitudinal axes, answer (A) is incorrect because a forward, not rearward, CG tends to cause more rotation around the longitudinal axis. Answer (C) is incorrect because a stall must occur before a spin can develop.

12-34   H66
Recovery from a stall in any airplane becomes more difficult when its

A — center of gravity moves aft.
B — center of gravity moves forward.
C — elevator trim is adjusted nosedown.

12-34. Answer A. GFDICM 12A (AFH)
An airplane becomes less stable as the center of gravity moves aft. The airplane has less nose-down pitching moment. It is possible that the elevator would have insufficient authority to lower the nose and break the stall. Answer (B) is incorrect because a forward CG would make stall recovery easier. Answer (C) is incorrect because nosedown elevator trim would assist, not hamper, stall recovery.

12-35   H66
An airplane leaving ground effect will

A — experience a reduction in ground friction and require a slight power reduction.
B — experience an increase in induced drag and require more thrust.
C — require a lower angle of attack to maintain the same lift coefficient.

12-35. Answer B. GFDICM 12A (AFH)
During takeoffs or landings, when you are flying very close to the surface, the ground alters the three-dimensional airflow pattern around the airplane. This causes a reduction in upwash, downwash, and wingtip vortices, all of which contribute to induced drag. When an airplane climbs out of ground effect, these factors increase, thus increasing induced drag. To compensate for the increased induced drag, more thrust is required. Answer (A) is incorrect because as you leave ground effect, induced drag increases, thus requiring more thrust (not less) to compensate. Answer (C) is incorrect because a lower-than-normal angle of attack produces the same amount of lift when you are flying in ground effect. Therefore, when climbing out of ground effect, you need a higher angle of attack to maintain the same lift.

12-36   **H66**

If airspeed is increased during a level turn, what action would be necessary to maintain altitude? The angle of attack

A — and angle of bank must be decreased.
B — must be increased or angle of bank decreased.
C — must be decreased or angle of bank increased.

12-37   **H66**

The stalling speed of an airplane is most affected by

A — changes in air density.
B — variations in flight altitude.
C — variations in airplane loading.

12-38   **H66**

An airplane will stall at the same

A — angle of attack regardless of the attitude with relation to the horizon.
B — airspeed regardless of the attitude with relation to the horizon.
C — angle of attack and attitude with relation to the horizon.

12-39   **H66**

(Refer to figure 3.) If an airplane glides at an angle of attack of 10°, how much altitude will it lose in 1 mile?

A — 240 feet.
B — 480 feet.
C — 960 feet.

12-36. Answer C. GFDICM 12A (AFH)

If you increase airspeed in a level turn, your vertical component of lift will increase. To maintain the same vertical lift component and prevent a climb, you must compensate by either increasing the angle of bank (changing part of the vertical lift component to the horizontal lift component), and/or by decreasing the angle of attack. Answer (A) is not correct since decreasing the angle of attack will lower the coefficient of lift. However, decreasing the bank will change some of the horizontal lift component to the vertical lift component, thus offsetting all or part of the angle of attack adjustment. Answer (B) is not correct because increasing the angle of attack or decreasing the bank will increase the vertical lift component causing the aircraft to climb.

12-37. Answer C. GFDICM 12A (AFH)

The indicated stall speed can be affected by a number of things such as weight or load factor, center of gravity, and power. Answers (A) and (B) are incorrect because flight altitude (air density) influences your true airspeed and resulting groundspeed, not your indicated stalling airspeed.

12-38. Answer A. GFDICM 12A (AFH)

For a given airfoil, a stall will always occur at the same angle of attack regardless of weight, dynamic pressure, bank angle, or pitch attitude. Answer (B) is wrong because the indicated stall speed at the critical angle of attack will vary. Answer (C) is incorrect because angle of attack is the angle between the chord line of the airfoil and the direction of the relative wind, not the aircraft's attitude in relation to the horizon.

12-39. Answer B. GFDICM 12A (FTP)

Glide distance is determined by the aircraft's maximum lift-to-drag ratio. To find the L/D$_{MAX}$ value for a particular angle of attack, locate the horizontal base line at the bottom of the graph. These numbers correspond to the angle of attack in degrees. From zero, move right along the base line until you reach the number 10. Next, use the vertical reference line to move up the graph until you intersect the L/D$_{MAX}$ curve. The L/D ratio (11) can be determined by moving right along the horizontal reference line to the furthest right vertical line in bold. An 11:1 ratio means that for every 11 feet of horizontal glide distance, you will lose 1 foot in altitude. To find the total altitude lost in one mile, divide 5280 feet by the L/D ratio of 11. The answer is 480 feet (5280 ÷ 11 = 480). Answer (A) is incorrect since it is the value for altitude lost in 1/2 mile and answer (C) is the value for 2 miles.

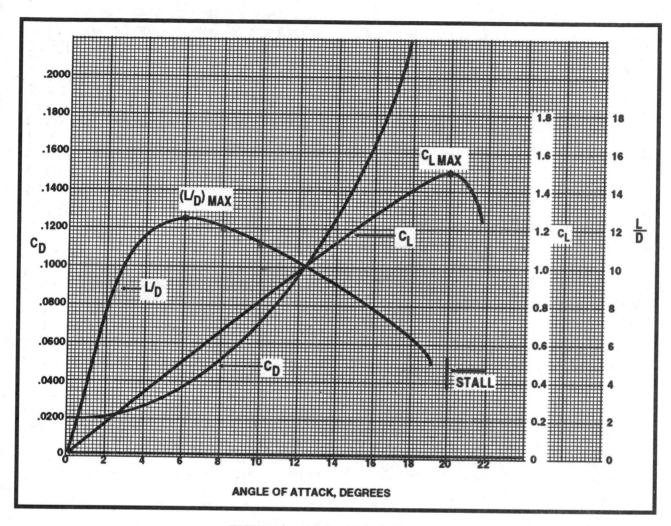

FIGURE 3.—Angle of Attack, Degrees.

12-40   **H66**

(Refer to figure 3.) How much altitude will this airplane lose in 3 statute miles of gliding at an angle of attack of 8°?

A — 440 feet.
B — 880 feet.
C — 1,320 feet.

12-40. Answer C. GFDICM 12A (FTP)

Glide distance is determined by the aircraft's maximum lift-to-drag ratio. To find the L/D$_{MAX}$ value for a particular angle of attack, locate the horizontal base line at the bottom of the graph. These numbers correspond to the angle of attack in degrees. From zero, move right along the base line until you reach the number eight. Next, use the vertical reference line to move up the graph until you intersect the L/D$_{MAX}$ curve. The L/D ratio (12) can be determined by moving right along the horizontal reference line to the furthest right vertical line in bold. A 12:1 ratio means that for every 12 feet of horizontal glide distance, you will lose 1 foot in altitude. To find the total altitude lost in one mile, divide 5280 feet by the L/D ratio of 12. The answer is 440 feet (5280 ÷ 12 = 440). To find the total altitude lost in 3 miles, multiply 440 feet by a factor of three (440 x 3 = 1320). Answer (A) is incorrect because it is the value for the altitude lost in one mile, not three miles. Answer (B) is incorrect because it is the value for the altitude lost in 2 miles, not 3 miles.

12-41   H66
(Refer to figure 3 on page 12-11.) The L/D ratio of a 2°
angle of attack is approximately the same as the L/D
ratio for a

A — 9.75° angle of attack.
B — 10.5° angle of attack.
C — 16.5° angle of attack.

12-41. Answer C. GFDICM 12A (FTP)
To find the L/D_{MAX} value for a particular angle of attack,
locate the horizontal base line at the bottom of the graph.
These numbers correspond to the angle of attack in
degrees. From zero, move right along the base line until
you reach the number two. Next, use the vertical reference line to move up the graph until you intersect the
L/D_{MAX} curve. Then move right until you reintersect the
back section of the L/D_{MAX} curve. Now, follow the vertical
reference line down to the corresponding angle of attack
(16.5°). Answer (A) is incorrect because it more closely
corresponds to using the coefficient of lift curve for determining the second angle of attack. Answer (B) is incorrect because it corresponds more to using the coefficient
of drag curve for determining the second angle of attack.

12-42   H66
If the same angle of attack is maintained in ground
effect as when out of ground effect, lift will

A — increase, and induced drag will decrease.
B — decrease, and parasite drag will increase.
C — increase, and induced drag will increase.

12-42. Answer A. GFDICM 12A (AFH)
An aircraft maintaining the same angle of attack when
entering ground effect will experience an increase in lift.
At the same time, upwash, downwash, and wingtip vortices decrease. Since these factors are associated with
induced drag, overall induced drag will decrease. Answer
(B) is incorrect because there will be an increase (not
decrease) in lift. Also, parasite drag is more a function of
aircraft speed, not angle of attack. Answer (C) is incorrect
because induced drag decreases in ground effect.

12-43   H66
What performance is characteristic of flight at maxi-
mum lift/drag in a propeller-driven airplane?
Maximum

A — gain in altitude over a given distance.
B — range and maximum distance glide.
C — coefficient of lift and minimum coefficient of
    drag.

12-43. Answer B. GFDICM 12A (FTP)
Flying your aircraft at L/D_{MAX} provides both maximum
range and the best power-off glide speed. Any decrease
or increase in airspeed from that specified for L/D_{MAX} will
result in reduced range or gliding distance. Answer (A) is
incorrect because maximum altitude gained over a given
distance, or V_X, occurs where the difference between
thrust available and thrust required is greatest. Answer
(C) is incorrect because your maximum coefficient of lift
occurs near a stall where induced drag is proportionally
high.

12-44   H66
Which is true regarding the forces acting on an aircraft
in a steady-state descent? The sum of all

A — upward forces is less than the sum of all down-
    ward forces.
B — rearward forces is greater than the sum of all for-
    ward forces.
C — forward forces is equal to the sum of all rearward
    forces.

12-44. Answer C. GFDICM 12A (AFH)
In a stabilized descent, the sum of the upward and
downward forces is zero. Likewise, forward and rearward forces are also balanced and a condition of equilibrium (similar to straight-and-level, unaccelerated
flight) exists. Answer (A) is incorrect because opposing
forces would not be balanced and the aircraft would be
accelerating. Answer (B) is incorrect because opposing
forces would not be balanced and the aircraft would be
slowing.

12-45   H66
Which is true regarding the force of lift in steady, unaccelerated flight?

A — At lower airspeeds the angle of attack must be less to generate sufficient lift to maintain altitude.
B — There is a corresponding indicated airspeed required for every angle of attack to generate sufficient lift to maintain altitude.
C — An airfoil will always stall at the same indicated airspeed; therefore, an increase in weight will require an increase in speed to generate sufficient lift to maintain altitude.

12-46   H303
During the transition from straight-and-level flight to a climb, the angle of attack is increased and lift

A — is momentarily decreased.
B — remains the same.
C — is momentarily increased.

12-47   H66
(Refer to figure 4 on page 12-14.) What is the stall speed of an airplane under a load factor of 2 G's if the unaccelerated stall speed is 60 knots?

A — 66 knots.
B — 74 knots.
C — 84 knots.

12-45. Answer B. GFDICM 12A (AFH)
For every angle of attack there is a corresponding indicated airspeed required to maintain altitude in steady, unaccelerated flight (all other factors being constant). Answer (A) is incorrect since lift varies in proportion to the square of the velocity. If you reduce airspeed by 1/2 without changing the angle of attack, lift will be reduced by a factor of four. Therefore, if lift is to be maintained, you must increase angle of attack to compensate for the reduction in airspeed. Answer (C) is incorrect because an airfoil will always stall at the same angle of attack. However, the airspeed which corresponds to that angle of attack varies with weight.

12-46. Answer C. GFDICM 12A (AFH)
Anytime there is a directional or velocity change in a flight path, an acceleration occurs. In order for an acceleration to occur there must be an imbalance in one or more of the four forces of flight. During the transition from straight-and-level flight to a climb, an increase in lift occurs when back elevator pressure is first applied. Because lift is momentarily greater then weight, the aircraft accelerates upwards. After the flight path is stabilized on the upward incline, the angle of attack and lift again stabilize at approximately the original value. Answer (A) is incorrect because a momentary decrease in lift will cause the aircraft to descend, not climb. Answer (B) is incorrect because a momentary change in lift is necessary to change the flight path.

12-47. Answer C. GFDICM 12A (AFH)
To find the increase in stall speed at a 2-G load factor, enter the chart on the left and locate the load factor. Next, move right using the horizontal reference lines as a guide until you intersect the load factor curve. A 2-G load factor intersects at the 60% bank angle. From that intersection point use the vertical reference lines as a guide to move up until you intersect the stall speed increase curve. To determine the percent increase in stall speed you again use the horizontal reference lines as a guide to move back to the left vertical base line. In this case, a 40% increase is indicated. Now, multiply the stall speed by a 140% ($60 \times 1.4 = 84$ knots). Answer (A) corresponds more to incorrectly stopping at the first curve and reading the percent increase as 10% ($60 \times 1.1 = 66$). Answer (B) is wrong because it corresponds more to a 1.6-G load factor and a 24% increase ($60 \times 1.24 = 74.4$).

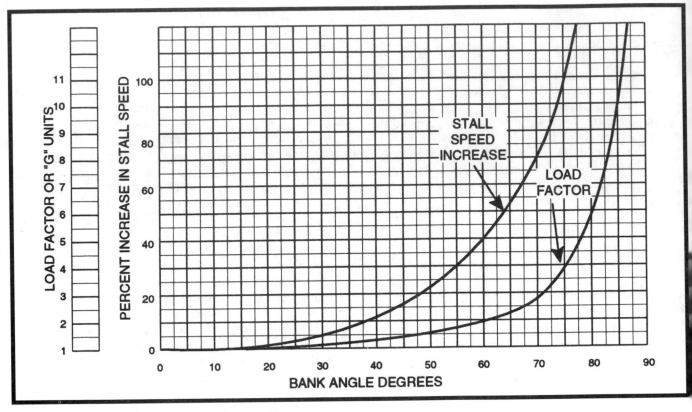

FIGURE 4.—Stall Speed/Load Factor.

12-48   H66

(Refer to figure 4 .) What increase in load factor would take place if the angle of bank were increased from 60° to 80°?

A — 3 G's.
B — 3.5 G's.
C — 4 G's.

12-48. Answer C. GFDICM 12A (AFH)

To find the increase in load factor from a 60° bank to a 80° bank, first locate the horizontal base line at the bottom of the graph. From zero move right along the base line until you reach 60°. Next, use the vertical reference lines as a guide to move up the graph until you intersect the load factor curve. Now, use the horizontal reference lines as a guide to read load factor from the scale on the left of the graph. In this case, there is a 2-G load factor at 60° of bank. Using the same procedure, you will find that the load factor at 80° of bank is approximately 6 G's. Finally, subtract the load factor at 60° bank from the load factor at 80° bank to find the increase (6 - 2 = 4). Answers (A) and (B) are incorrect because they indicate the increase in load factor from a 60° bank to a 80° bank to be less than 4 G's.

12-49   H66

To generate the same amount of lift as altitude is increased, an airplane must be flown at

A — the same true airspeed regardless of angle of attack.
B — a lower true airspeed and a greater angle of attack.
C — a higher true airspeed for any given angle of attack.

12-49. Answer C. GFDICM 12A (AFH)

In order to maintain lift at a higher altitude with the same angle of attack and wing area, a higher true airspeed is required because air density has decreased. Answers (A) and (B) are incorrect because flying at the same, or lower, true airspeed as altitude increases would generate less lift if angle of attack and wing area remain unchanged.

12-50   H66

To produce the same lift while in ground effect as when out of ground effect, the airplane requires

A — a lower angle of attack.
B — the same angle of attack.
C — a greater angle of attack.

12-50. Answer A. GFDICM 12A (AFH)

If an aircraft maintains the same angle of attack when entering ground effect, the aircraft will experience an increase in lift. At the same time, upwash, downwash, and wingtip vortices decrease. Therefore, a lower angle of attack is required to produce the same amount of lift in ground effect. Answer (B) is incorrect because there will be an increase (not decrease) in lift if the same angle of attack is used. Answer (C) is incorrect because the aircraft will experience an increase in lift with the same angle of attack. Lift will increase even more if you increase angle of attack in ground effect.

12-51   H66

As the angle of bank is increased, the vertical component of lift

A — decreases and the horizontal component of lift increases.
B — increases and the horizontal component of lift decreases.
C — decreases and the horizontal component of lift remains constant.

12-51. Answer A. GFDICM 12A (AFH)

As you increase bank, you are diverting part of the vertical lift component to the horizontal lift component. Answer (B) is incorrect because as bank increases, more of the vertical lift component is diverted to the horizontal lift component. Answer (C) is incorrect because as the vertical lift component is diverted to the horizontal lift component, the horizontal component increases; it does not remain constant.

12-52   H66

If the airplane attitude remains in a new position after the elevator control is pressed forward and released, the airplane displays

A — neutral longitudinal static stability.
B — positive longitudinal static stability.
C — neutral longitudinal dynamic stability.

12-52. Answer A. GFDICM 12A (AFH)

Longitudinal stability involves the pitching motion, or tendency, of the airplane to move about its lateral axis. After elevator control pressures are released following a pitch displacement, and the airplane remains in the new pitch attitude, the airplane is exhibiting neutral longitudinal static stability. Answer (B) is incorrect because if an airplane exhibits positive longitudinal static stability, it would have the tendency to return to the original pitch attitude. Answer (C) is wrong because neutral dynamic stability is indicated if the airplane attempts to return to its original state of equilibrium but the oscillations neither increase nor decrease in magnitude as time passes.

12-53   H66

Longitudinal dynamic instability in an airplane can be identified by

A — bank oscillations becoming progressively steeper.
B — pitch oscillations becoming progressively steeper.
C — Trilatitudinal roll oscillations becoming progressively steeper.

12-53. Answer B. GFDICM 12A (AFH)

Dynamic stability describes the time required for an airplane to respond to its static stability following a displacement from a condition of equilibrium. It is determined by the airplane's tendency to oscillate and damp out successive oscillations after initial displacement. If an aircraft is exhibiting longitudinal dynamic instability, it corrects itself but the aircraft enters a series of progressively steeper pitch oscillations. Answers (A) and (B) are incorrect because bank or roll involves lateral stability, not longitudinal stability.

12-54   **H66**
Longitudinal stability involves the motion of the airplane controlled by its

A — rudder.
B — elevator.
C — ailerons.

12-54. Answer B. GFDICM 12A (AFH)
Longitudinal stability involves the pitching motion, or tendency, of the airplane to move about its lateral axis and the elevator controls an airplane's pitching moment. Answer (A) is incorrect because the rudder and vertical stabilizer control movement about the vertical or yaw axis and influence directional stability. Answer (C) is incorrect because ailerons control roll or bank movement about the longitudinal axis which involves lateral stability.

12-55   **H66**
What changes in airplane longitudinal control must be made to maintain altitude while the airspeed is being decreased?

A — Increase the angle of attack to produce more lift than drag.
B — Increase the angle of attack to compensate for the decreasing lift.
C — Decrease the angle of attack to compensate for the increasing drag.

12-55. Answer B. GFDICM 12A (AFH)
Lift varies in proportion to the square of the velocity. If the wing area remains constant, as the velocity decreases, angle of attack must increase to maintain the same amount of lift. Answer (A) is incorrect because the opposing force to drag is thrust. Answer (C) is incorrect because if the angle of attack is decreased when speed is decreased, lift will decrease even further, resulting in a loss of altitude.

12-56   **H66**
If the airplane attitude initially tends to return to its original position after the elevator control is pressed forward and released, the airplane displays

A — positive dynamic stability.
B — positive static stability.
C — neutral dynamic stability.

12-56. Answer B. GFDICM 12A (AFH)
Static stability is the initial tendency of an airplane to return to a state of equilibrium following a displacement from that condition. If positive static stability is present, an airplane has a tendency to return to the original point of equilibrium. Answers (A) and (C) are incorrect because dynamic stability describes the time required for an airplane to respond to its static stability following a displacement. Positive dynamic stability (answer A) is the tendency to return to the original state directly or through a series of decreasing oscillations. Neutral dynamic stability (answer C), indicates that the airplane attempts to return to the original state, but the oscillations neither increase nor decrease in magnitude as time passes.

12-57   **H66**
A propeller, rotating clockwise as seen from the rear, creates a spiraling slipstream that tends to rotate the airplane to the

A — right around the vertical axis, and to the left around the longitudinal axis.
B — left around the vertical axis, and to the right around the longitudinal axis.
C — left around the vertical axis, and to the left around the longitudinal axis.

12-57. Answer B. GFDPPM 3C (AFH)
As the slipstream produced by a clockwise rotating propeller (as seen from the rear) wraps around the fuselage, some of it strikes the left side of the vertical fin. This tends to rotate the airplane to the left around the vertical axis. Because the vertical fin is above the longitudinal axis, the spiraling slipstream also tends to rotate the aircraft to the right around the longitudinal axis. Answers (A) and (C) are incorrect because airplanes tend to rotate left (not right) around the vertical axis, and right (not left) around the longitudinal axis.

12-58   N20
Which is true regarding aerodynamic drag?

A — Induced drag is created entirely by air resistance.
B — All aerodynamic drag is created entirely by the production of lift.
C — Induced drag is a by-product of lift and is greatly affected by changes in airspeed.

12-59   H66
Which maximum range factor decreases as weight decreases?

A — Altitude.
B — Airspeed.
C — Angle of attack.

12-60.   H312
Why should flight speeds above V_{NE} be avoided?

A — Design limit load factors may be exceeded, if gusts are encountered.
B — Excessive induced drag will result in structural failure.
C — Control effectiveness is so impaired that the aircraft becomes uncontrollable.

12-61.   A02
Maximum structural cruising speed is the maximum speed at which an airplane can be operated during

A — flight in smooth air.
B — normal operations.
C — abrupt maneuvers.

12-58. Answer C. GFDICM 12A (AFH)
There are two types of drag; induced and parasite. Induced drag is a by-product of lift and decreases as airspeed increases. Parasite drag is created by the disruption of the flow of air around the airplane's surfaces. Unlike induced drag, parasite drag increases with increases in airspeed. Answer (A) is incorrect because induced drag is directly related to the wing's angle of attack, not the resistance of the air. Answer (B) is wrong because parasite drag is not created by the production of lift.

12-59. Answer B. GFDICM 12A (AFH)
Maximum range is obtained when the lift to drag ratio is at its maximum (L/D_{MAX}). You should note that L/D_{MAX} is applicable only to a particular airplane in steady, unaccelerated flight at a specified weight and configuration. As fuel is burned, the weight decreases, which requires the values of airspeed and power required to be altered to achieve maximum range. Therefore, airspeed must decrease as weight decreases. Answer (A) is inappropriate since altitude has little effect on maximum range, and the angle of attack (answer C) must remain constant for maximum range to be achieved.

12-60. Answer A. GFDICM 12A
If you fly above the never-exceed speed, V_{NE}, you risk the possibility of exceeding limit load factors if gusts are encountered which can cause structural damage or failure.

12-61. Answer B. GFDICM 12A
Maximum structural cruising speed, V_{NO}, is the top speed of the normal operating range and corresponds to the upper limit of the green arc on the airspeed indicator. You should not exceed this speed in rough air.

SECTION B
PREDICTING PERFORMANCE

Factors Affecting Performance

1. Air density decreases with air temperature and altitude. As air density decreases, engine performance decreases for both piston and gas turbine engines.

2. A flight computer or a density altitude chart can be used to complete density altitude calculations based on pressure altitude and air temperature.

3. Stall speed is affected by angle of bank, gross weight, and gear and flap position. Stall speed increases with bank and, on most propeller airplanes, decreases with high power settings because of additional airflow over the wings. You can see this relationship in tables provided by aircraft manufacturers.

4. Headwind and crosswind components can be found using a wind component chart.

5. An uphill runway slope increases takeoff distance because the airplane accelerates more slowly.

The Pilot's Operating Handbook

6. To estimate takeoff ground roll and distance to clear a 50-foot obstacle, use the takeoff distance charts. Most takeoff distance charts include variables for surface condition, headwind, and airport altitude above sea level.

7. Climb performance charts provide information on time, fuel, and distance required to climb from one altitude to another. When using this chart you should remember to subtract the values for the starting altitude.

12-62   **H303**
(Refer to figure 2.) Select the correct statement regarding stall speeds.

A — Power-off stalls occur at higher airspeeds with the gear and flaps down.

B — In a 60° bank the airplane stalls at a lower airspeed with the gear up.

C — Power-on stalls occur at lower airspeeds in shallower banks.

12-63   **H303**
(Refer to figure 2.) Select the correct statement regarding stall speeds. The airplane will stall

A — 10 knots higher in a power-on 60° bank with gear and flaps up than with gear and flaps down.

B — 25 knots lower in a power-off, flaps-up, 60° bank, than in a power-off, flaps-down, wings-level configuration.

C — 10 knots higher in a 45° bank, power-on stall than in a wings-level stall.

12-62. Answer C. GFDICM 12B (PHB)
A careful examination of the stall speed table shows that stall speeds are lower with power on and higher with power off. This results from the induced airflow over the wings created by the propeller generating thrust. Answers (A) and (B) are incorrect because most airplanes stall at a lower airspeed with the gear and flaps down.

12-63. Answer A. GFDICM 12B (PHB)
According to the chart on figure 2 the difference between the stall speed with power on in a 60° bank with gear and flaps up, (76 kts.), and the stall speed with power on gear and flaps down (66 kts.) is 10 knots. Answer (B) is incorrect because the stall speed in a 60° bank turn will always be higher than the stall speed in wings-level flight. The increase in stall speed between wings level and a 45° bank is greater than 10 knots (answer C).

GROSS WEIGHT 2750 LBS		ANGLE OF BANK			
		LEVEL	30°	45°	60°
POWER		GEAR AND FLAPS UP			
ON	MPH KTS	62 54	67 58	74 64	88 76
OFF	MPH KTS	75 65	81 70	89 77	106 92
		GEAR AND FLAPS DOWN			
ON	MPH KTS	54 47	58 50	64 56	76 66
OFF	MPH KTS	66 57	71 62	78 68	93 81

FIGURE 2.—Stall Speeds.

12-64   **H66**
(Refer to figure 5 on page 12-20.) The horizontal line from point C to point E represents the

A — ultimate load factor.
B — positive limit load factor.
C — airspeed range for normal operations.

12-64. Answer B. GFDICM 12B (AFH)
The horizontal scale indicates speed (V), and the vertical scale is load factor (G). Speed is plotted against the load factor or G-loading. The curved lines extending upward and downward from the load factor of zero are the positive and negative lift capability lines, The horizontal line at 3.8 G's (point C to point E), and the line at -1.52 G's (point I through point G), indicate the positive and negative load factor limits, respectively. Some of the vertical lines are labeled to identify specific aircraft speeds and are labeled. Answer (A) is incorrect because at 3.8 G's the aircraft is at maximum acceptable limits. The ultimate load factor describes the point of actual structural failure. Answer (C) is incorrect because airspeed ranges are indicated on the graph by vertical lines.

12-65   **H66**
(Refer to figure 5 on page 12-20.) The vertical line from point E to point F is represented on the airspeed indicator by the

A — upper limit of the yellow arc.
B — upper limit of the green arc.
C — blue radial line.

12-65. Answer A. GFDICM 12B (AFH)
See explanation for Question 12-64. The vertical line from point E to point F represents the upper limit of the yellow arc and is marked on the airspeed indicator with a red line (V_{NE}). Answer (B) is incorrect because the upper limit of the green arc (maximum structural cruising speed) is indicated by point D to point G. Answer (C) is incorrect because a blue radial line indicates V_{YSE} (one engine inoperative best rate-of-climb) for multi-engine aircraft.

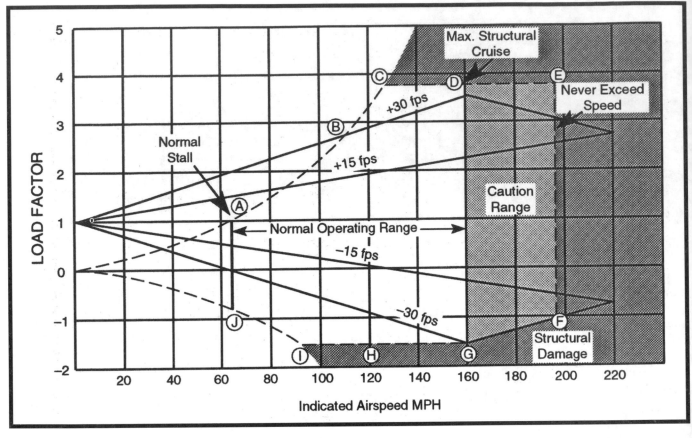

FIGURE 5.—Velocity vs. G-Loads.

12-66   H66
(Refer to figure 5.) The vertical line from point D to point G is represented on the airspeed indicator by the maximum speed limit of the

A — green arc.
B — yellow arc.
C — white arc.

12-66. Answer A. GFDICM 12B (AFH)
See explanation for Question 12-64. The vertical line from point D to point G represents the upper limit of the green arc and is the maximum structural cruising speed (V_{NO}). Answer (B) is incorrect because the yellow arc represents the caution range for smooth air operations, and the upper limit is identified by V_{NE} (the red line). Answer (C) is incorrect because the white arc represents the flap operating range which is not depicted.

12-67   H66
The performance tables of an aircraft for takeoff and climb are based on

A — pressure/density altitude.
B — cabin altitude.
C — true altitude.

12-67. Answer A. GFDICM 12B (AFH)
Performance charts generally present information in either table or graph format. Most charts require pressure altitude and temperature to determine performance. This means the charts reflect density altitude. Answer (B) is incorrect because cabin altitude has no effect on takeoff and climb performance. Answer (C) is incorrect because true altitude (the actual height of an object above mean sea level), is not used in performance charts.

12-68   **H66**

What effect would a change in ambient temperature or air density have on gas turbine engine performance?

A — As air density decreases, thrust increases.
B — As temperature increases, thrust increases.
C — As temperature increases, thrust decreases.

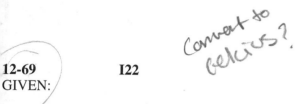

12-69   **I22**

GIVEN:

Pressure altitude................................12,000 ft
True air temperature ....+50 °F

From the conditions given, the approximate density altitude is

A — 11,900 feet.
B — 14,130 feet.
C — 18,150 feet.

12-70   **I22**

GIVEN:

Pressure altitude................................5,000 ft
True air temperature..........................+30°C

From the conditions given, the approximate density altitude is

A — 7,200 feet.
B — 7,800 feet.
C — 9,000 feet.

12-71   **I22**

GIVEN:

Pressure altitude................................6,000 ft
True air temperature..........................+30°F

From the conditions given, the approximate density altitude is

A — 9,000 feet.
B — 5,500 feet.
C — 5,000 feet.

12-68. Answer C. GFDICM 12B (FTP)

Density altitude is a factor which strongly affects the performance of gas-turbine engines. As ambient air temperatures increase, the density of the air decreases (increased density altitude). This results in less air-mass passing through the engine inlet and, therefore, a decrease in thrust. Answer (A) is wrong because thrust decreases with a decrease in air density. Answer (B) is wrong because an increase in air temperature causes a decrease in air density resulting in less thrust.

12-69. Answer B. GFDICM 12B (AFH)

This question requires you to compute density altitude. To do this use the following steps.

1. Enter pressure altitude (12,000 feet).
2. Enter the true air temperature (50°F/10°C).
3. Compute density altitude, 14,134 feet.

Answer (B) is the closest. Answer (A) is wrong because it represents the density altitude at 12,000 feet and standard temperature (-9.5°C). Answer (C) is wrong because it indicates the density altitude at 12,000 feet with a temperature of 50°C, not 50°F.

12-70. Answer B. GFDICM 12B (AFH)

This question requires you to compute density altitude. To do this use the following steps.

1. Enter pressure altitude (5,000 feet).
2. Enter the true air temperature (30°C/86°F).
3. Compute density altitude, 7,801 feet.

12-71. Answer B. GFDICM 12B (AFH)

This question requires you to compute density altitude. To do this use the following steps.

1. Enter pressure altitude (6,000 feet).
2. Enter the true air temperature (30°F/-1.1°C).
3. Compute density altitude, 5,496 feet.

Answer (B) is the closest. Answer (A), 9,000 feet, represents density altitude at 6,000 feet with a true temperature of 30°C, and answer (C), 5,000 feet, is inappropriate.

12-72   **I22**
GIVEN:

Pressure altitude...7,000 ft
True air temperature...+15°C

From the conditions given, the approximate density altitude is

A — 5,000 feet.
B — 8,500 feet.
C — 9,500 feet.

12-73   **H342**
(Refer to figure 8.)
GIVEN:

Fuel quantity...47 gal
Power-cruise (lean)....................................55 percent

Approximately how much flight time would be available with a night VFR fuel reserve remaining?

A — 3 hours 8 minutes.
B — 3 hours 22 minutes.
C — 3 hours 43 minutes.

12-74   **H342**
(Refer to figure 8.)
GIVEN:

Fuel quantity...65 gal
Best power-level flight ....55 percent

Approximately how much flight time would be available with a day VFR fuel reserve remaining?

A — 4 hours 17 minutes.
B — 4 hours 30 minutes.
C — 5 hours 4 minutes.

12-75   **H342**
(Refer to figure 8.) Approximately how much fuel would be consumed when climbing at 75 percent power for 7 minutes?

A — 1.82 gallons.
B — 1.97 gallons.
C — 2.15 gallons.

12-72. Answer B. GFDICM 12B (AFH)
This question requires you to compute density altitude. To do this use the following steps.

1. Enter pressure altitude (7,000 feet).
2. Enter the true air temperature (15°C/59°F).
3. Compute density altitude, 8,595 feet.

Answer (B) is the closest. Answer (A), 5,000 feet, represents density altitude at 7,000 feet with a true temperature of -30°C. Answer (C) represents density altitude at 7,000 feet with a true temperature of 20°C.

12-73. Answer B. GFDICM 12B (PHB)
Figure 8 is the Fuel Consumption vs. Brake Horsepower chart. Enter the chart at the cruise (lean) curve. Find where the curve intersects the 55% maximum continuous power line, and move horizontally to the corresponding point on the fuel flow axis, approximately 11.4 gal/hr. Now, compute time available by using the known fuel quantity of 47 gallons and the fuel flow rate of 11.4 gal/hr to get 4 hours and 7 minutes. FAR 91.151 requires a fuel reserve of 45 minutes at normal cruise speed for night VFR flying. Subtract 45 minutes from your total time of 4:07 to get approximately 3 hours and 22 minutes of flight time available.

12-74. Answer B. GFDICM 12B (PHB)
Find the best power level flight curve and proceed to where it intersects the 55% maximum continuous power line. From that point, move to the corresponding point on the fuel flow axis, 13 gallons per hour. Now, compute the time available using the total fuel quantity of 65 gallons and a fuel consumption rate of 13 gal/hr. The total flight time available is 5 hours. Part 91.151 requires 30 minutes of reserve fuel at normal cruise speed for day VFR flying. Subtract 30 minutes from 5 hours to get 4 hours and 30 minutes of fuel available after reserves.

12-75. Answer C. GFDICM 12B (PHB)
Find the takeoff and climb curve and follow it to where it intersects the vertical 75% maximum continuous power line. From that point, move to the corresponding point on the fuel flow axis, approximately 18.25 gal/hr. Now, compute total fuel consumed using 7 minutes and 18.25 gal/hr to get 2.13 gallons.

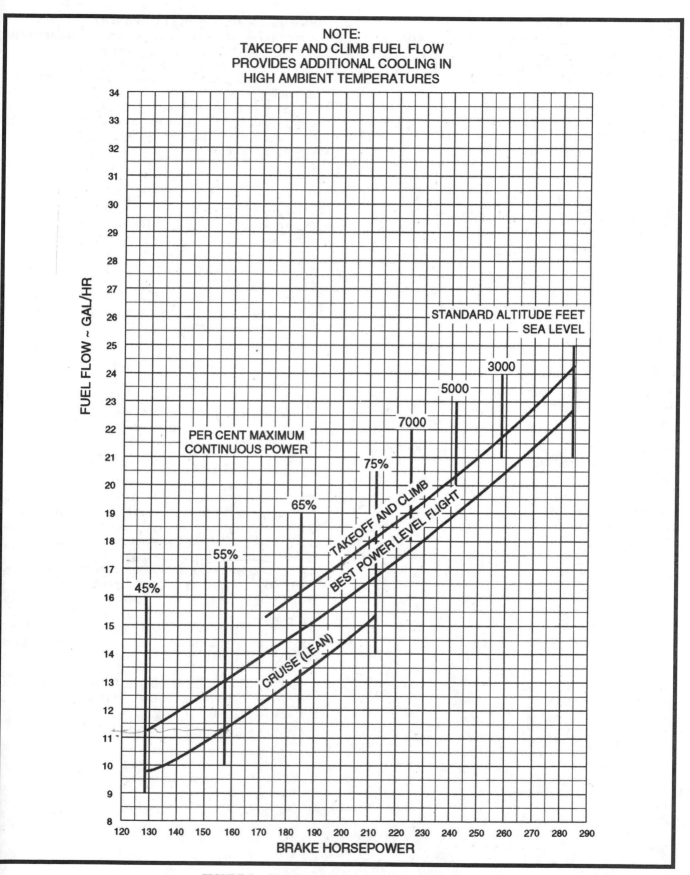

FIGURE 8.—Fuel Consumption vs. Brake Horsepower.

12-76   **H342**
(Refer to figure 8 on page 12-23.) Determine the
amount of fuel consumed during takeoff and climb at
70 percent power for 10 minutes.

A — 2.66 gallons.
B — 2.88 gallons.
C — 3.2 gallons.

12-77   **H342**
(Refer to figure 8 on page 12-23.) With 38 gallons of
fuel aboard at cruise power (55 percent), how much
flight time is available with night VFR fuel reserve still
remaining?

A — 2 hours 34 minutes.
B — 2 hours 49 minutes.
C — 3 hours 18 minutes.

12-78   **H317**
(Refer to figure 9.) Using a normal climb, how much
fuel would be used from engine start to 12,000 feet
pressure altitude?

Aircraft weight ....3,800 lb
Airport pressure altitude ....4,000 ft
Temperature ....26°C

A — 46 pounds.
B — 51 pounds.
C — 58 pounds.

12-76. Answer B. GFDICM 12B (PHB)
Follow the takeoff and climb curve to where it intersects
the 70% maximum continuous power line. Since this
line is not drawn on the chart, you must interpolate
between the 65% and 75% lines. Now move to the corresponding point on the fuel flow axis, approximately
17.2 gal/hr. You can now compute the amount of fuel
consumed using the fuel consumption rate of 17.2 gal/hr
and a time of 10 minutes to get 2.87 gallons consumed
in the takeoff and climb.

12-77. Answer A. GFDICM 12B (PHB)
Follow the cruise (lean) curve to where it intersects the
55% maximum continuous power line. Move horizontally
to the corresponding point on the fuel flow axis, approximately 11.4 gal/hr. Now you can compute total flight time
using 38 gallons of fuel and a fuel burn of 11.4 gal/hr to
get 3 hours and 20 minutes. Part 91.151 requires 45
minutes of reserve fuel for night VFR flying. Subtract 45
minutes from 3 hours 20 minutes to get 2 hours and 35
minutes, the closest answer is (A).

12-78. Answer C. GFDICM 12B (PHB)
Enter the table at the given aircraft weight of 3,800
pounds. Since the airport pressure altitude is 4,000 feet
and not sea level, you must find how much fuel would
be burned climbing from sea level to 4,000 feet (12 lbs.).
Fuel used from sea level to 12,000 feet is 51 pounds.
Therefore, fuel used from the airport to 12,000 feet is
the difference, or 39 pounds.

Note 2 states that you must increase time, fuel, and distance by 10% for each 10°C above standard temperature, (1% change for every 1°C). Standard temperature
at sea level is 15°C and the standard lapse rate is 2°C
per each 1,000-foot increase in altitude. Airport elevation is 4,000 feet and standard temperature should be
7°C (4,000 ft. × 2°C/1,000 ft. = 8°C) and (15°C - 8°C =
7°C). Since it is actually 26°C, there is a 19°C difference
(26°C - 7°C = 19°C). The 19°C difference means a 19%
increase in pounds of fuel used, according to Note 2.
Add 19% of 39 pounds (39 × .19 = 7.41), for a total of
46.41 lbs (39 + 7.41).

Note 1 tells you to add 12 pounds for engine start, taxi
and takeoff. Final result is 58.41 pounds; answer (C) is
the closest choice.

NORMAL CLIMB – 100 KIAS

CONDITIONS:
Flaps Up
Gear Up
2550 RPM
25 Inches MP or Full Throttle
Cowl Flaps Open
Standard Temperature

MIXTURE SETTING	
PRESS ALT	PPH
S.L. to 4000	108
8000	96
12,000	84

NOTES:
1. Add 12 pounds of fuel for engine start, taxi and takeoff allowance.
2. Increase time, fuel and distance by 10% for each 10 °C above standard temperature.
3. Distances shown are based on zero wind.

WEIGHT LBS	PRESS ALT FT	RATE OF CLIMB FPM	FROM SEA LEVEL		
			TIME MIN	FUEL USED POUNDS	DISTANCE NM
3800	S.L.	580	0	0	0
	2000	580	3	6	6
	4000	570	7	12	12
	6000	470	11	19	19
	8000	365	16	27	28
	10,000	265	22	37	40
	12,000	165	32	51	59
3500	S.L.	685	0	0	0
	2000	685	3	5	5
	4000	675	6	11	10
	6000	565	9	16	16
	8000	455	13	23	23
	10,000	350	18	31	33
	12,000	240	25	41	46
3200	S.L.	800	0	0	0
	2000	800	2	4	4
	4000	795	5	9	8
	6000	675	8	14	13
	8000	560	11	19	19
	10,000	445	15	25	27
	12,000	325	20	33	37

FIGURE 9.—Fuel, Time, and Distance to Climb

12-79   **H317**

(Refer to figure 9.) Using a normal climb, how much fuel would be used from engine start to 10,000 feet pressure altitude?

Aircraft weight ....3,500 lb
Airport pressure altitude ....4,000 ft
Temperature ....21°C

A — 23 pounds.
B — 31 pounds.
C — 35 pounds.

12-79. Answer C. GFDICM 12B (PHB)

See the explanation for Question 12-78. Enter the table at 3,500 pounds. You need to find two values, fuel used from sea level to 4,000 feet and sea level to 10,000 feet. These figures are 11 pounds and 31 pounds, respectively. The difference is 20 pounds. Standard temperature at 4,000 feet should be 7°C (4,000 ft. × 2°C/1,000 ft. = 8°C) and (15°C - 8°C = 7°C). Subtract 7°C from the given field temperature of 21°C, to get a 14°C difference, so you will add 14% to the fuel used. Multiply 14% times 20 pounds to get 2.8 pounds, then add these two figures to get 22.8 pounds. Add 12 pounds for start, taxi, and takeoff to get a final answer of 34.8 pounds. The closest answer is (C), 35 pounds.

MAXIMUM RATE OF CLIMB

CONDITIONS:
Flaps Up
Gear Up
2700 RPM
Full Throttle
Mixture Set at Placard Fuel Flow
Cowl Flaps Open
Standard Temperature

MIXTURE SETTING	
PRESS ALT	PPH
S.L.	138
4000	126
8000	114
12,000	102

NOTES:
1. Add 12 pounds of fuel for engine start, taxi and takeoff allowance.
2. Increase time, fuel and distance by 10% for each 10 °C above standard temperature.
3. Distances shown are based on zero wind.

WEIGHT LBS	PRESS ALT FT	CLIMB SPEED KIAS	RATE OF CLIMB FPM	FROM SEA LEVEL		
				TIME MIN	FUEL USED POUNDS	DISTANCE NM
3800	S.L.	97	860	0	0	0
	2000	95	760	2	6	4
	4000	94	660	5	12	9
	6000	93	565	9	18	14
	8000	91	465	13	26	21
	10,000	90	365	18	35	29
	12,000	89	265	24	47	41
3500	S.L.	95	990	0	0	0
	2000	94	885	2	5	3
	4000	93	780	5	10	7
	6000	91	675	7	16	12
	8000	90	570	11	22	17
	10,000	89	465	15	29	24
	12,000	87	360	20	38	32
3200	S.L.	94	1135	0	0	0
	2000	92	1020	2	4	3
	4000	91	910	4	9	6
	6000	90	800	6	14	10
	8000	88	685	9	19	14
	10,000	87	575	12	25	20
	12,000	86	465	16	32	26

FIGURE 10.—Fuel, Time, and Distance to Climb.

12-80   H317
(Refer to figure 10.) Using a maximum rate of climb, how much fuel would be used from engine start to 6,000 feet pressure altitude?
Aircraft weight ....3,200 lb
Airport pressure altitude ....2,000 ft
Temperature ....27°C

A — 10 pounds.
B — 14 pounds.
C — 24 pounds.

12-80. Answer C. GFDICM 12B (PHB)
See explanation for Question 12-78. Enter the table at 3,200 pounds aircraft weight. You need two figures, fuel used climbing from sea level to 2,000 feet and sea level to 6,000 feet, 4 pounds and 14 pounds of fuel respectively. The difference is 10 pounds of fuel used to climb from 2,000 feet to 6,000 feet. Standard temperature at 2,000 feet is 11°C (15°C - 2°C/1,000 ft. = 11°C). The actual temperature of 27°C is 16°C above standard, so you will increase the fuel used by 16%: (10 lbs × .16 = 1.6 lbs) and (10 lbs + 1.6 lbs = 11.6 lbs). Add 12 pounds for start, taxi, and takeoff (11.6 + 12 = 23.6). Answer (C) is the closest.

12-81   H317

(Refer to figure 10.) Using a maximum rate of climb, how much fuel would be used from engine start to 10,000 feet pressure altitude?

Aircraft weight ....3,800 lb
Airport pressure altitude ....4,000 ft
Temperature ....30°C

A — 28 pounds.
B — 35 pounds.
C — 40 pounds.

12-81. Answer C. GFDICM 12B (PHB)
See explanation for Question 12-78. Enter the table at 3,800 pounds and find the fuel used to climb from sea level to 4,000 feet and from sea level to 10,000 feet, 12 pounds and 35 pounds respectively. Then find the difference to determine fuel used to climb from 4,000 feet to 10,000 feet (35 lbs. - 12 lbs. = 23 lbs.). Fuel consumption increase due to nonstandard temperature is 23% (4,000 ft. x 2°C/1,000 ft. = 8°C) and (15°C - 8°C = 7°C) and (30°C - 7°C = 23°C). An increase of 23% times 23 pounds equals 5.29 pounds. Add this to 23 pounds to get 28.29. Now add 12 pounds for start up, taxi, and takeoff to obtain the final answer of 40.29. The closest answer is (C), 40 pounds.

12-82   H317

(Refer to figure 11 on page 12-28.) If the cruise altitude is 7,500 feet, using 64 percent power at 2,500 RPM, what would be the range with 48 gallons of usable fuel?

A — 635 miles.
B — 645 miles.
C — 810 miles.

12-82. Answer C. GFDICM 12B (PHB)
Enter the table at 7,500 feet under altitude and find the 2,500 RPM line. (Note, this is also 64% power). At this power setting, range in the far right column (based on 48 gallons with no reserve) is 810 miles. Answer (A) is incorrect because this would be the range at 38 gallons for different altitudes and power settings. Answer (B) is incorrect because this would be the range for 38 gallons at 7,500 feet.

12-83   H317

(Refer to figure 11 on page 12-28.) What would be the endurance at an altitude of 7,500 feet, using 52 percent power?

NOTE: (With 48 gallons fuel — no reserve.)

A — 6.1 hours.
B — 7.7 hours.
C — 8.0 hours.

12-83. Answer B. GFDICM 12B (PHB)
Enter the table at 7,500 feet altitude. Find 52% power then move across to the endurance column under 48 gallons to obtain the answer of 7.7 hours. Answer (A) is incorrect because it reflects the hours at 38 gallons. Answer (C) is incorrect since it reflects the hours at 10,000 feet altitude at 49% power.

12-84   H317

(Refer to figure 11 on page 12-28.) What would be the approximate true airspeed and fuel consumption per hour at an altitude of 7,500 feet, using 52 percent power?

A — 103 MPH TAS, 6.3 GPH.
B — 105 MPH TAS, 6.6 GPH.
C — 105 MPH TAS, 6.2 GPH.

12-84. Answer C. GFDICM 12B (PHB)
Enter the table at 7,500 feet and find 52 percent power. Move to the right and find 105 MPH TAS and 6.2 GPH. Answer (A) is wrong since it gives the TAS and GPH for 2,500 feet. The 6.6 in answer (B) is incorrect.

> Gross Weight- 2300 Lbs.
> Standard Conditions
> Zero Wind Lean Mixture

NOTE: Maximum cruise is normally limited to 75% power.

ALT.	RPM	% BHP	TAS MPH	GAL/ HOUR	38 GAL (NO RESERVE)		48 GAL (NO RESERVE)	
					ENDR. HOURS	RANGE MILES	ENDR. HOURS	RANGE MILES
2500	2700	86	134	9.7	3.9	525	4.9	660
	2600	79	129	8.6	4.4	570	5.6	720
	2500	72	123	7.8	4.9	600	6.2	760
	2400	65	117	7.2	5.3	620	6.7	780
	2300	58	111	6.7	5.7	630	7.2	795
	2200	52	103	6.3	6.1	625	7.7	790
5000	2700	82	134	9.0	4.2	565	5.3	710
	2600	75	128	8.1	4.7	600	5.9	760
	2500	68	122	7.4	5.1	625	6.4	790
	2400	61	116	6.9	5.5	635	6.9	805
	2300	55	108	6.5	5.9	635	7.4	805
	2200	49	100	6.0	6.3	630	7.9	795
7500	2700	78	133	8.4	4.5	600	5.7	755
	2600	71	127	7.7	4.9	625	6.2	790
	2500	64	121	7.1	5.3	645	6.7	810
	2400	58	113	6.7	5.7	645	7.2	820
	2300	52	105	6.2	6.1	640	7.7	810
10,000	2650	70	129	7.6	5.0	640	6.3	810
	2600	67	125	7.3	5.2	650	6.5	820
	2500	61	118	6.9	5.5	655	7.0	830
	2400	55	110	6.4	5.9	650	7.5	825
	2300	49	100	6.0	6.3	635	8.0	800

FIGURE 11.—Cruise and Range Performance.

PRESSURE ALTITUDE 18,000 FEET

CONDITIONS:
4000 Pounds
Recommended Lean Mixture
Cowl Flaps Closed

NOTE

For best fuel economy at 70% power or less, operate at 6 PPH leaner than shown in this chart or at peak EGT.

RPM	MP	20 °C BELOW STANDARD TEMP -41 °C			STANDARD TEMPERATURE -21 °C			20 °C ABOVE STANDARD TEMP -1 °C		
		% BHP	KTAS	PPH	% BHP	KTAS	PPH	% BHP	KTAS	PPH
2500	30	---	---	---	81	188	106	76	185	100
	28	80	184	105	76	182	99	71	178	93
	26	75	178	99	71	176	93	67	172	88
	24	70	171	91	66	168	86	62	164	81
	22	63	162	84	60	159	79	56	155	75
2400	30	81	185	107	77	183	101	72	180	94
	28	76	179	100	72	177	94	67	173	88
	26	71	172	93	67	170	88	63	166	83
	24	66	165	87	62	163	82	58	159	77
	22	61	158	80	57	155	76	54	150	72
2300	30	79	182	103	74	180	97	70	176	91
	28	74	176	97	70	174	91	65	170	86
	26	69	170	91	65	167	86	61	163	81
	24	64	162	84	60	159	79	56	155	75
	22	58	154	77	55	150	73	51	145	65
2200	26	66	166	87	62	163	82	58	159	77
	24	61	158	80	57	154	76	54	150	72
	22	55	148	73	51	144	69	48	138	66
	20	49	136	66	46	131	63	43	124	59

FIGURE 12.—Cruise Performance.

12-85   **H317**

(Refer to figure 12.)
GIVEN:

Pressure altitude...18,000 ft
Temperature...-21°C
Power...2400 RPM — 28" MP
Recommended lean mixture usable fuel.............425 lb

What is the approximate flight time available under the given conditions? (Allow for VFR day fuel reserve.)

A — 3 hours 46 minutes.
B — 4 hours 1 minute.
C — 4 hours 31 minutes.

12-85. Answer B. GFDICM 12B (PHB)
Enter the table at 2400 RPM. Move right along the line at 28 inches MP to the -21°C temperature columns. The corresponding fuel flow is 94 pounds per hour. Divide the usable fuel by the fuel flow to find total time (425 lbs ÷ 94 lb/hr = 4 hours 31 minutes). Subtract the day VFR fuel reserve of 30 minutes for a flight time of 4 hours 1 minute. Answer (A) is incorrect because this time is based on 100 PPH indicating you looked at the -41°C column instead of the -21°C column. Answer (C) is incorrect because the VFR day fuel reserve was not subtracted.

12-86   H317
(Refer to figure 12 on page 12-29.)
GIVEN:

Pressure altitude..18,000 ft
Temperature...-41°C
Power...2500 RPM - 26" MP
Recommended lean mixture usable fuel.............318 lb

What is the approximate flight time available under the given conditions? (Allow for VFR night fuel reserve.)

A — 2 hours 27 minutes.
B — 3 hours 12 minutes.
C — 3 hours 42 minutes.

12-87   H317
(Refer to figure 12 on page 12-29.)
GIVEN:

Pressure Altitude...18,000 ft
Temperature..-1°C
Power...2,200 RPM - 20" MP
Best fuel economy usable fuel............................344 lb

What is the approximate flight time available under the given conditions? (Allow for VFR day fuel reserve.)

A — 4 hours 50 minutes.
B — 5 hours 20 minutes.
C — 5 hours 59 minutes.

12-88   H342
(Refer to figure 13.)
GIVEN:

Aircraft weight..3,400 lb
Airport pressure altitude....................................6,000 ft
Temperature at 6,000 ft..10°C

Using a maximum rate of climb under the given conditions, how much fuel would be used from engine start to a pressure altitude of 16,000 feet?

A — 43 pounds.
B — 45 pounds.
C — 49 pounds.

12-86. Answer A. GFDICM 12B (PHB)
Enter the table at 2500 RPM. Move right along the line at 26 inches MP to the -41°C temperature columns. The corresponding fuel flow is 99 pounds per hour. Divide the usable fuel by fuel flow to find total time (318 lbs ÷ 99 lbs/hr = 3 hours 13 minutes). Subtract the night VFR fuel reserve of 45 minutes, for a flight time of 3 hours 28 minutes. Answer (A) is the closest. Answer (B) does not allow for the night VFR fuel reserve. Answer (C) is wrong because you would need a fuel flow of 71.5 PPH, which is not listed.

12-87. Answer C. GFDICM 12B (PHB)
Enter the table at 2200 RPM. Move right along the 20 inches of MP line to the -1°C columns and locate the fuel flow of 59 pounds per hour. To convert this to best economy subtract 6 pounds per hour to get 53 pounds of fuel burned per hour. Divide the usable fuel by fuel flow to find total time (344 lbs ÷ 53 lbs/hr = 6 hours 29 minutes). Subtract the day VFR fuel reserve of 30 minutes for a flight time of 5 hours 59 minutes. Answer (C) is closest. Answer (A) would require a MP of 22 inches. Answer (B) uses 20 inches MP but does not reflect best economy.

12-88. Answer A. GFDICM 12B (PHB)
To determine the fuel used, you must subtract the fuel indicated at 6,000 feet from the fuel used to climb to 16,000 feet. Begin by entering the table at the given aircraft weight of 3,400 pounds, and move right to the pressure altitude column. Since a 6,000-foot pressure altitude is not listed, you will have to interpolate between the 4,000 and 8,000-foot levels. This results in 14 pounds of fuel. The 16,000-foot pressure altitude indicates 39 pounds of fuel used. Subtract these two values to determine the fuel used. The result is 25 pounds of fuel (39 - 14 = 25).

Note 2 states that you must increase time, fuel, and distance by 10% for each 10°C above standard temperature (1% change for every 1°C). Standard temperature at sea level is 15°C and the standard lapse rate is 2°C per 1,000-foot increase in altitude. This means the standard temperature for an airport at 6,000 feet is 3°C (15°C - 12°C = 3°C). Since there is a 7°C difference between the actual temperature and standard, the fuel used must be increased by 7%. This increase results in a fuel usage of 26.75 pounds (25 x 1.07 = 26.75).

Note 1 indicates you need to add 16 pounds for engine start, taxi and takeoff. This increases the amount of fuel used to 42.75 pounds (26.75 + 16 = 42.75). Answer (A) is the closest.

MAXIMUM RATE OF CLIMB

CONDITIONS:
Flaps Up
Gear Up
2600 RPM
Cowl Flaps Open
Standard Temperature

PRESS ALT	MP	PPH
S.L. TO 17,000	35	162
18,000	34	156
20,000	32	144
22,000	30	132
24,000	28	120

NOTES:
1. Add 16 pounds of fuel for engine start, taxi and takeoff allowance.
2. Increase time, fuel and distance by 10% for each 10 °C above standard temperature.
3. Distances shown are based on zero wind.

WEIGHT LBS	PRESS ALT FT	CLIMB SPEED KIAS	RATE OF CLIMB FPM	FROM SEA LEVEL		
				TIME MIN	FUEL USED POUNDS	DISTANCE NM
4000	S.L.	100	930	0	0	0
	4000	100	890	4	12	7
	8000	100	845	9	24	16
	12,000	100	790	14	38	25
	16,000	100	720	19	52	36
	20,000	99	515	26	69	50
	24,000	97	270	37	92	74
3700	S.L.	99	1060	0	0	0
	4000	99	1020	4	10	6
	8000	99	975	8	21	13
	12,000	99	915	12	33	21
	16,000	99	845	17	45	30
	20,000	97	630	22	59	42
	24,000	95	370	30	77	60
3400	S.L.	97	1205	0	0	0
	4000	97	1165	3	9	5
	8000	97	1120	7	19	12
	12,000	97	1060	11	29	18
	16,000	97	985	15	39	26
	20,000	96	760	19	51	36
	24,000	94	485	26	65	50

FIGURE 13.—Fuel, Time, and Distance to Climb.

12-89   **H342**
(Refer to figure 13 on page 12-31.)
GIVEN:

Aircraft weight ....4,000 lb
Airport pressure altitude ....2,000 ft
Temperature at 2,000 ft...32°C

Using a maximum rate of climb under the given conditions, how much time would be required to climb to a pressure altitude of 8,000 feet?

A — 7 minutes.
B — 8.4 minutes.
C — 11.2 minutes.

12-90   **H342**
(Refer to figure 14.)
GIVEN:

Aircraft weight ....3,700 lb
Airport pressure altitude ....4,000 ft
Temperature at 4,000 ft...21°C

Using a normal climb under the given conditions, how much fuel would be used from engine start to a pressure altitude of 12,000 feet?

A — 30 pounds.
B — 37 pounds.
C — 46 pounds.

12-89. Answer B. GFDICM 12B (PHB)
To determine the time to climb, you must subtract the time indicated at 2,000 feet from the time to climb to 8,000 feet. Enter the table at 4,000 pounds and move to the pressure altitude column. Since a 2,000-foot pressure altitude is not listed, you will have to interpolate. This results in a time of 2 minutes. The 8,000-foot pressure altitude indicates a time to climb of 9 minutes. The difference is 7 minutes (9 - 2 = 7).

Note 2 states that you must increase time, fuel, and distance by 10% for each 10°C above standard temperature (1% change for every 1°C). Standard temperature at sea level is 15°C and the standard lapse rate is 2°C per 1,000-foot increase in altitude. This means the standard temperature for an airport at 2,000 feet is 11°C (15°C - 4°C = 11°C). Since there is a 21°C difference between the actual temperature and standard, the time to climb must be increased by 21%. This increase results in a time to climb of 8.47 minutes (7 x 1.21 = 8.47).

12-90. Answer C. GFDICM 12B (PHB)
To determine the fuel used, you must subtract the fuel indicated at 4,000 feet from the fuel used to climb to 12,000 feet. Begin by entering the table at the given aircraft weight of 3,700 pounds, and move right to the 4,000-foot pressure altitude line. Under these conditions, 12 pounds of fuel is indicated. The 12,000-foot altitude indicates 37 pounds of fuel used. Subtract these two values to determine the fuel used. The result is 25 pounds of fuel (37 - 12 = 25).

Note 2 states that you must increase time, fuel, and distance by 10% for each 7°C above standard temperature. Standard temperature at sea level is 15°C and the standard lapse rate is 2°C per 1,000-foot increase in altitude. This means the standard temperature for an airport at 4,000 feet is 7°C (15°C - 8°C = 7°C). Since there is a 14°C difference between the actual temperature and standard, the fuel used must be increased by 20%. This increase results in a fuel usage of 30 pounds (25 x 1.20 = 30).

Note 1 indicates you need to add 16 pounds for engine start, taxi and takeoff. This increases the amount of fuel used to 46 pounds (30 + 16 = 46).

NORMAL CLIMB – 110 KIAS

CONDITIONS:
Flaps Up
Gear Up
2500 RPM
30 Inches Hg
120 PPH Fuel Flow
Cowl Flaps Open
Standard Temperature

NOTES:
1. Add 16 pounds of fuel for engine start, taxi and takeoff allowance.
2. Increase time, fuel and distance by 10% for each 7 °C above standard temperature.
3. Distances shown are based on zero wind.

WEIGHT LBS	PRESS ALT FT	RATE OF CLIMB FPM	FROM SEA LEVEL		
			TIME MIN	FUEL USED POUNDS	DISTANCE NM
4000	S.L.	605	0	0	0
	4000	570	7	14	13
	8000	530	14	28	27
	12,000	485	22	44	43
	16,000	430	31	62	63
	20,000	365	41	82	87
	S.L.	700	0	0	0
3700	4000	665	6	12	11
	8000	625	12	24	23
	12,000	580	19	37	37
	16,000	525	26	52	53
	20,000	460	34	68	72
	S.L.	810	0	0	0
	4000	775	5	10	9
3400	8000	735	10	21	20
	12,000	690	16	32	31
	16,000	635	22	44	45
	20,000	565	29	57	61

FIGURE 14.—Fuel, Time, and Distance to Climb.

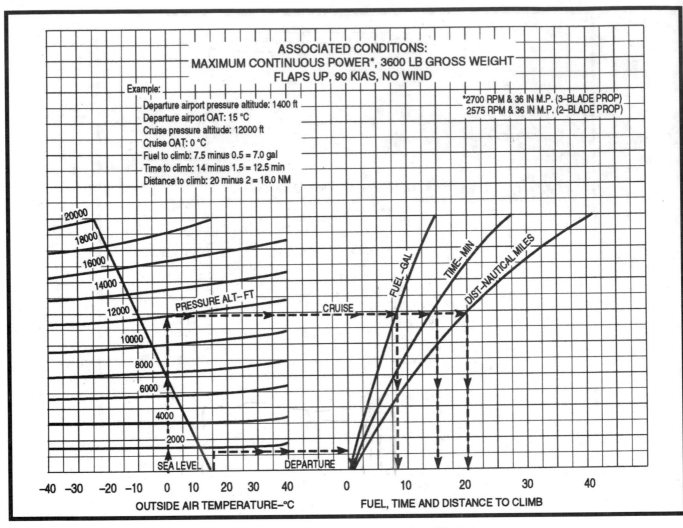

FIGURE 15.—Fuel, Time, and Distance to Climb.

12-91   H342
(Refer to figure 15.)
GIVEN:

Airport pressure altitude ....4,000 ft
Airport temperature...12°C
Cruise pressure altitude.......................................9,000 ft
Cruise temperature...-4°C

What will be the distance required to climb to cruise altitude under the given conditions?

A — 6 miles.
B — 8.5 miles.
C — 11 miles.

12-91. Answer B. GFDICM 12B (AFH)
To complete this problem, you must first determine the distance required to climb from sea level to 9,000 feet then subtract the distance required to climb from sea level to the airport elevation. Begin by entering the graph at the outside air temperature for the cruise altitude (-4°C). From this point proceed up the graph parallel to the vertical reference lines until you reach the corresponding point representing 9,000 feet (midway between the 8,000 and 10,000-foot lines). From this point move to the right, paralleling the horizontal reference lines until reaching the corresponding point on the reference line for distance. Now move downward, paralleling the vertical reference lines until reaching the horizontal axis and determine the corresponding distance (14 n.m.). Repeat the above steps for the temperature (12°C) and elevation (4,000 ft.) of the departure airport to determine that 5.5 nautical miles must be subtracted. The difference of these two figures (14 n.m. - 5.5 n.m. = 8.5 n.m.) represents the distance traveled climbing from 4,000 feet to 9,000 feet.

12-92   H317
What effect does an uphill runway slope have on take-off performance?

A — Increases takeoff speed.
B — Increases takeoff distance.
C — Decreases takeoff distance.

12-93   H317
(Refer to figure 31 on page 12-36.) Rwy 30 is being used for landing. Which surface wind would exceed the airplane's crosswind capability of 0.2 V_{SO}, if V_{SO} is 60 knots?

A — 260° at 20 knots.
B — 275° at 25 knots.
C — 315° at 35 knots.

12-94   H317
(Refer to figure 31 on page 12-36.) If the tower-reported surface wind is 010° at 18 knots, what is the crosswind component for a Rwy 08 landing?

A — 7 knots.
B — 15 knots.
C — 17 knots.

12-95   H317
(Refer to figure 31 on page 12-36.) The surface wind is 180° at 25 knots. What is the crosswind component for a Rwy 13 landing?

A — 19 knots.
B — 21 knots.
C — 23 knots.

12-96   H317
(Refer to figure 31 on page 12-36.) What is the head-wind component for a Rwy 13 takeoff if the surface wind is 190° at 15 knots?

A — 7 knots.
B — 13 knots.
C — 15 knots.

12-92. Answer B. GFDICM 12B (FTP)
When taking off on an uphill runway, aircraft accelera-tion is slower and the distance required to get airborne increases. If taking off on a downhill runway, aircraft acceleration will be enhanced and the distance required to get airborne will decrease (answer C). Runway slope has no effect on takeoff speed (answer A), although it would take longer (and more distance) to accelerate to takeoff speed.

12-93. Answer A. GFDICM 12B (AFH)
In this example, the aircraft's maximum crosswind component is 12 knots (.2 × 60 = 12). To determine which of the indicated choices exceeds this value, cal-culate the angle between the wind and the runway for each possible answer. Then, enter the chart in figure 31 with the result and the wind speed. A wind of 260° at 20 knots gives you a crosswind component of 13 knots. Answer (B) results in a crosswind component of 10 knots, and the crosswind component for answer (C) is approximately 9 knots.

12-94. Answer C. GFDICM 12B (AFH)
See explanation for Question 12-93. The angle between the wind and the runway is 70° (80° - 10° = 70°). Enter the chart on the 70° diagonal line and find the wind speed of 18 knots near the 20 knot arc. Drop straight down from there to find the crosswind compo-nent of 17 knots. A 7-knot crosswind component (answer A) would require a wind of 010° at 8 knots. A 15-knot crosswind component (answer B) would require a wind of 010° at 16 knots.

12-95. Answer A. GFDICM 12B (AFH)
See explanation for Question 12-94. The answer is 19 knots. Answer (B), 21 knots, would require a wind of 180° at 28 knots. Answer (C), 23 knots, would require a wind of 180° at 30 knots.

12-96. Answer A. GFDICM 12B (AFH)
The angle between the wind and the runway is 60° (190° - 130° = 60°). Enter the chart on the 60° diagonal line and go to the intersection of that line and the 15-knot arc. Now, move left to the vertical axis to find the headwind component. The answer is approximately 7 knots. A headwind component of 13 knots (answer B) would require a wind of 190° at 26 knots. A headwind component of 15 knots (answer C) would require a wind of 190° at 30 knots.

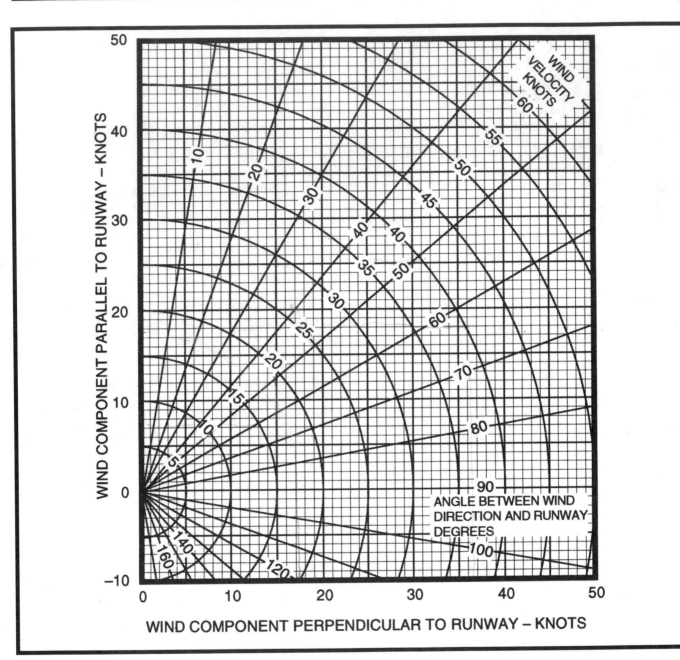

FIGURE 31.—Wind Component Chart.

12-97   **H317**
(Refer to figure 32 on page 12-38.)
GIVEN:

Temperature..75°F
Pressure altitude...6,000 ft
Weight ....2,900 lb
Headwind...20 kts

To safely take off over a 50-foot obstacle in 1,000 feet, what weight reduction is necessary?

A — 50 pounds.
B — 100 pounds.
C — 300 pounds.

12-97. Answer C. GFDICM 12B (PHB)
Enter the bottom, left side of the chart at 75°F and move up to the 6,000-foot pressure altitude line. Move right to the reference line, then move right an equal distance between the curved reference lines to intersect the 2,900 pound line. From this point move right horizontally to the second reference line. Now, move right to the headwind guidelines and parallel them to intersect 20 knots. Move horizontally to the total takeoff distance reference line. The total takeoff distance over a 50-foot obstacle is approximately 1,450 feet. To determine the takeoff weight that would reduce the total takeoff distance to 1,000 feet, enter the chart at 1,000 feet on the right side. Move horizontally to the 20-knot line, then move left with the sloping reference lines to the vertical reference line. Move horizontally until you intersect the 2,600 pound line. This point corresponds with the original mark on reference line number 1 and requires a weight reduction of 300 pounds.

12-98   **H317**
(Refer to figure 32 on page 12-38.)
GIVEN:
Temperature..50 °F
Pressure altitude ....2,000 feet
Weight ....2,700 lb
Wind ....Calm

What is the total takeoff distance over a 50-foot obstacle?

A — 650 feet.
B — 800 feet.
C — 1050 feet.

12-98. Answer B. GFDICM 12B (PHB)
Start at the 50°F position and move upward to where it intersects the 2,000-foot pressure altitude line. Move right, an equal distance along the reference lines, upward to intersect 2,700 pounds. Move horizontally across to the approximate total takeoff distance of 800 feet. A takeoff distance of 650 feet (answer A) results when the sea level pressure altitude is used. A takeoff distance of 1,050 feet results when a takeoff weight of approximately 2,900 pounds is used.

12-99   **H317**
(Refer to figure 32 on page 12-38.)
GIVEN:

Temperature..100°F
Pressure altitude...4,000 ft
Weight ....3,200 lb
Wind ....Calm

What is the ground roll required for takeoff over a 50-foot obstacle?

A — 1,180 feet.
B — 1,350 feet.
C — 1,850 feet.

12-99. Answer B. GFDICM 12B (PHB)
Start with 100°F, and follow the reference lines in the same manner described in Question 12-98. To find the ground roll, multiply the total takeoff distance (1,850 feet) by .73 as indicated in the heading portion of figure 32. The answer is approximately 1,350 feet. Answer (A), 1,180 feet, is incorrect since it is based on sea level pressure altitude. Answer (C) is wrong since it reflects total distance to clear the obstacle, not ground roll.

ASSOCIATED CONDITIONS:

POWER	TAKEOFF POWER SET BEFORE BRAKE RELEASE
FLAPS	20*
RUNWAY	PAVED, LEVEL, DRY SURFACE
TAKEOFF SPEED	IAS AS TABULATED

NOTE: GROUND ROLL IS APPROX. 73% OF TOTAL TAKEOFF DISTANCE OVER A 50 FT OBSTACLE

EXAMPLE:

OAT	75 °F
PRESSURE ALTITUDE	4000 FT
TAKEOFF WEIGHT	3100 LB
HEADWIND	20 KNOTS

TOTAL TAKEOFF DISTANCE OVER A 50 FT OBSTACLE	1350 FT
GROUND ROLL (73% OF 1350)	986 FT
IAS TAKEOFF SPEED	
LIFT-OFF	74 MPH
AT 50 FT	74 MPH

WEIGHT POUNDS	IAS TAKEOFF SPEED (ASSUMES ZERO INSTR. ERROR)			
	LIFT–OFF		50 FEET	
	MPH	KNOTS	MPH	KNOTS
3400	77	67	77	67
3200	75	65	75	65
3000	72	63	72	63
2800	69	60	69	60
2600	66	57	66	57
2400	63	55	63	55

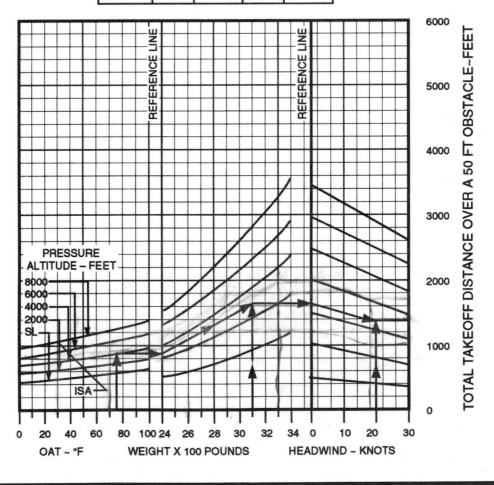

FIGURE 32.—Obstacle Take-off Chart.

12-100   **H317**
(Refer to figure 32.)
GIVEN:

Temperature...30°F
Pressure altitude...............................6,000 ft
Weight ....3,300 lb
Headwind...20 kts

What is the total takeoff distance over a 50-foot obstacle?

A — 1,100 feet.
B — 1,300 feet.
C — 1,500 feet.

12-101   **H317**
(Refer to figure 33 on page 12-40.)
GIVEN:

Weight ....4,000 lb
Pressure altitude...............................5,000 ft
Temperature ....30°C

What is the maximum rate of climb under the given conditions?

A — 655 ft/min.
B — 702 ft/min.
C — 774 ft/min.

12-100. Answer C. GFDICM 12B (PHB)
Start with 30°F, and follow the reference lines in the same manner described in Question 12-98. The answer is approximately 1,500 feet. Answer (A), 1,100 feet, reflects the approximate ground roll distance. Answer (B) reflects a pressure altitude of 4,000 feet.

12-101. Answer B. GFDICM 12B (PHB)
Enter the chart from the left at 4,000 pounds. Move right to the pressure altitude column. The pressure altitude of 5,000 feet does not appear on the chart. Since 5,000 feet is 1/4 of the difference between the 4,000-foot and 8,000-foot levels, you will need to interpolate by subtracting 25% of the difference from the climb rate at 4,000 feet. The temperature of 30°C also requires interpolation. The climb rate for 30°C falls directly between the climb rates for 20°C and 40°C. The interpolations are as follows:

Interpolate climb rate for 5,000 feet at 20°C
800 ft/min - 695 ft/min = 105
105 x 25% = 26.25
800 - 26.25 = 773.75 (774) ft/min

Interpolate climb rate for 5,000 feet at 40°C
655 ft/min - 555 ft/min = 100
100 x 25% = 25
655 - 25 = 630 ft/min

Interpolate climb rate for 5,000 feet at 30°C
774 ft/min - 630 ft/min = 144
144 x 50% = 72
774 - 72 = 702 ft/min

Answers (A) and (C) reflect intermediate solutions prior to the final interpolation.

CONDITIONS:
Flaps Up
Gear Up
2600 RPM
Cowl Flaps Open

PRESS ALT	MP	PPH
S.L. TO 17,000	35	162
18,000	34	156
20,000	32	144
22,000	30	132
24,000	28	120

WEIGHT LBS	PRESS ALT FT	CLIMB SPEED KIAS	RATE OF CLIMB – FPM			
			-20 °C	0 °C	20 °C	40 °C
4000	S.L.	100	1170	1035	895	755
	4000	100	1080	940	800	655
	8000	100	980	840	695	555
	12,000	100	870	730	590	---
	16,000	100	740	605	470	---
	20,000	99	485	355	---	---
	24,000	97	190	70	---	---
3700	S.L.	99	1310	1165	1020	875
	4000	99	1215	1070	925	775
	8000	99	1115	965	815	670
	12,000	99	1000	855	710	---
	16,000	99	865	730	590	---
	20,000	97	600	470	---	---
	24,000	95	295	170	---	---
3400	S.L.	97	1465	1320	1165	1015
	4000	97	1370	1220	1065	910
	8000	97	1265	1110	955	795
	12,000	97	1150	995	845	---
	16,000	97	1010	865	725	---
	20,000	96	730	595	---	---
	24,000	94	405	275	---	---

FIGURE 33.—Maximum Rate-of-Climb Chart.

12-102   **H317**
(Refer to figure 33.)
GIVEN:

Weight ....3,700 lb
Pressure altitude..............................22,000 ft
Temperature ....-10°C

What is the maximum rate of climb under the given conditions?

A — 305 ft/min.
B — 320 ft/min.
C — 384 ft/min.

12-102. Answer C. GFDICM 12B (PHB)
Enter the chart from the left at 3,700 pounds. Move right to the pressure altitude column. You will need to interpolate because the pressure altitude of 22,000 feet does not appear on the chart. Since the climb rate at 22,000 feet is 50% of the way between the rate at 20,000 and 24,000 feet, you will need to add one half of the difference between the respective rates to the climb rate at 24,000 feet. The temperature of -10°C also requires interpolation. The climb rate for -10°C falls directly between the climb rates for -20°C and 0°C. The interpolations are as follows:

Interpolate climb rate for 22,000 feet at -20°C
600 ft/min - 295 ft/min = 305
305 x 50% = 152.5
295 + 152.5 = 447.5 (448) ft/min

Interpolate climb rate for 22,000 feet at 0°C
470 ft/min - 170 ft/min = 300
300 x 50% = 150
170 + 150 = 320 ft/min

Interpolate climb rate for -10°C
448 ft/min - 320 ft/min = 128
128 x 50% = 64
320 + 64 = 384 ft/min

Answers (A) and (B) reflect the intermediate solutions prior to the final interpolation.

12-103   **H317**
(Refer to figure 34 on page 12-42.)
GIVEN:

Pressure altitude................................6,000 ft
Temperature ....+3°C
Power.....................................2,200 RPM — 22" MP
Usable fuel available..........................465 lb

What is the maximum available flight time under the conditions stated?

A — 6 hours 27 minutes.
B — 6 hours 39 minutes.
C — 6 hours 56 minutes.

12-103. Answer B. GFDICM 12B (PHB)
Enter the chart at the given power setting of 2,200 RPM and then go to the MP column and locate 22 in the manifold pressure (MP) column. Move directly across from the 22 to the standard temperature column (3°C) and locate the pounds per hour (PPH) column. These settings result in a fuel flow of 70 PPH. Divide your usable fuel (465 lbs) by 70 PPH to determine your available flight time. The answer is 6 hours 38 minutes and 34 seconds. Answer (B) is the closest. Answer (A) is the time available with a fuel flow of 72 PPH, and answer (C) is the time available with a 67 PPH fuel flow.

12-104   **H317**
(Refer to figure 34 on page 12-42.)
GIVEN:

Pressure altitude................................6,000 ft
Temperature ....-17°C
Power.....................................2,300 RPM — 23" MP
Usable fuel available..........................370 lb

What is the maximum available flight time under the conditions stated?

A — 4 hours 20 minutes.
B — 4 hours 30 minutes.
C — 4 hours 50 minutes.

12-104. Answer B. GFDICM 12B (PHB)
See explanation for Question 12-103. Your fuel flow is 82 pounds per hour (PPH). To determine your maximum available flight time, divide your usable fuel (370 lbs) by 82 PPH. The answer is 4 hours 30 minutes and 44 seconds. Answer (B) is closest. Answer (A) is the time available with a fuel flow of 85 PPH, and answer (C) is the time availalbe with a 77 PPH fuel flow.

PRESSURE ALTITUDE 6,000 FEET

CONDITIONS:
Recommended Lean Mixture
3800 Pounds
Cowl Flaps Closed

RPM	MP	20 °C BELOW STANDARD TEMP -17 °C			STANDARD TEMPERATURE 3 °C			20 °C ABOVE STANDARD TEMP 23 °C		
		% BHP	KTAS	PPH	% BHP	KTAS	PPH	% BHP	KTAS	PPH
2550	24	---	---	---	78	173	97	75	174	94
	23	76	167	96	74	169	92	71	171	89
	22	72	164	90	69	166	87	67	167	84
	21	68	160	85	65	162	82	63	163	80
2500	24	78	169	98	75	171	95	73	172	91
	23	74	166	93	71	167	90	69	169	87
	22	70	162	88	67	164	85	65	165	82
	21	66	158	83	63	160	80	61	160	77
2400	24	73	165	91	70	166	88	68	167	85
	23	69	161	87	67	163	84	64	164	81
	22	65	158	82	63	159	79	61	160	77
	21	61	154	77	59	155	75	57	155	73
2300	24	68	161	86	66	162	83	64	163	80
	23	65	158	82	62	159	79	60	159	76
	22	61	154	77	59	155	75	57	155	72
	21	57	150	73	55	150	71	53	150	68
2200	24	63	156	80	61	157	77	59	158	75
	23	60	152	76	58	153	73	56	154	71
	22	57	149	72	54	149	70	53	149	67
	21	53	144	68	51	144	66	49	143	64
	20	50	139	64	48	138	62	46	137	60
	19	46	133	60	44	132	58	43	131	57

FIGURE 34.—Cruise Performance Chart.

12-105   **H317**
(Refer to figure 34.)
GIVEN:

Pressure altitude...6,000 ft
Temperature...+13°C
Power..2,500 RPM — 23" MP
Usable fuel available..460 lb

What is the maximum available flight time under the
conditions stated?

A — 4 hours 58 minutes.
B — 5 hours 7 minutes.
C — 5 hours 12 minutes.

12-106   **H317**
(Refer to figure 35 on page 12-44.)
GIVEN:

Temperature...70°F
Pressure altitude...Sea level
Weight ....3,400 lb
Headwind..16 kts

Determine the approximate ground roll.

A — 689 feet.
B — 716 feet.
C — 1,275 feet.

12-107   **H317**
(Refer to figure 35 on page 12-44.)
GIVEN:

Temperature...85°F
Pressure altitude...6,000 ft
Weight ....2,800 lb
Headwind..14 kts

Determine the approximate ground roll.

A — 742 feet.
B — 1,280 feet.
C — 1,480 feet.

12-105. Answer C. GFDICM 12B (PHB)
Enter the table at 2,500 RPM and locate 23 in the manifold pressure (MP) column. Since there is no +13°C column, you must interpolate the fuel flow between 3°C and 23°C columns. The pertinent values are 90 and 87 pounds per hour (PPH), respectively. Interpolating for 13°C results in a fuel flow of 88.5 PPH. The maximum available flight time is 5 hours 11 minutes and 51 seconds. Answer (C) is the closest. Answer (A) represents the time available with a fuel flow of 93 PPH, and answer (B) is the time available with a 90 PPH fuel flow.

12-106. Answer A. GFDICM 12B (PHB)
Enter the chart from the bottom at 70°F and move vertically to the sea level pressure altitude line. From there, move right and parallel the reference lines to intersect 3,400 pounds. Move horizontally across to the next reference line, the move down the diagonal headwind guideline to intersect 16 knots. Next, move to the total landing distance reference line. The approximate landing distance is 1,300 feet. To determine the ground roll, multiply the total landing distance by .53 as indicated in the heading portion of figure 35. The answer is 689 feet. A ground roll of 716 feet (answer B) equals a total landing distance over a 50-foot obstacle of 1,350 feet which is too long considering the given conditions. Answer (C) is the approximately total landing distance over a 50-foot obstacle.

12-107. Answer A. GFDICM 12B (PHB)
Enter the chart at the 85°F and move to the 6,000-foot pressure altitude line. Proceed right and parallel the reference lines to intersect 2,800 pounds. From there move straight across to the next reference line and follow the headwind guideline to intersect 14 knots. Next, proceed to the landing distance reference line. The approximate landing distance is 1,400 feet. To determine the ground roll, multiply the total landing distance by .53 as indicated in the heading portion of figure 35. The answer is 742 feet. Answer (B) 1,280 feet, results from following the headwind guidelines to the end of the chart and not stopping at the 14-knot headwind component. Answer (C), 1,480 feet, is slightly longer than the correct total landing distance of 1,400 feet. Neither answer (B) or (C) are adjusted to ground roll distances.

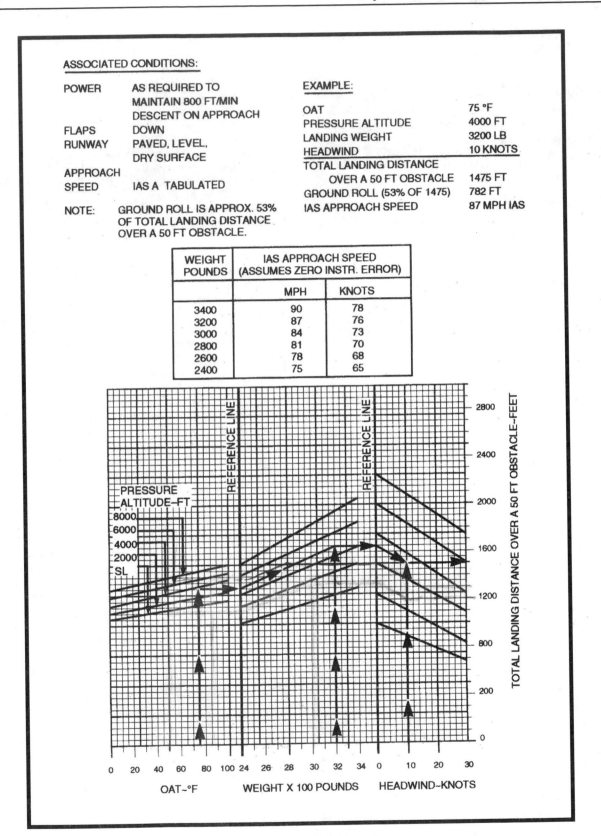

FIGURE 35.—Normal Landing Chart.

12-108   **H317**
(Refer to figure 35.)
GIVEN:

Temperature...50°F
Pressure altitude................................Sea level
Weight ....3,000 lb
Headwind...10 kts

Determine the approximate ground roll.

A — 425 feet.
B — 636 feet.
C — 836 feet.

12-108. Answer B. GFDICM 12B (PHB)
Enter chart at 50°F and follow the reference lines in the same manner described for the previous questions. To find the ground roll, multiply the total landing distance (1,200 feet) by .53 as indicated in the heading portion of figure 35. The answer is 636 feet. Answer (A), 425 feet, is the ground roll that corresponds to a total landing distance of 802 feet. Answer (C), 836 feet, is the total distance over a 50 foot obstacle resulting from following the headwind guidelines to the end of the chart and not correcting for ground roll.

12-109   **H317**
(Refer to figure 35.)
GIVEN:

Temperature..80°F
Pressure altitude..4,000 ft
Weight ....2,800 lb
Headwind..24 kts

What is the total landing distance over a 50-foot obstacle?

A — 1,125 feet.
B — 1,250 feet.
C — 1,325 feet.

12-109. Answer A. GFDICM 12B (PHB)
Enter the chart at the 80°F and follow the reference lines in the same manner described for the previous questions. The approximate landing distance over a 50-foot obstacle is 1,125 feet. Both answers (B) and (C) are landing distances resulting from a wind of less than 24 knots.

SECTION C
CONTROLLING WEIGHT AND BALANCE

Weight and Balance Limitations

1. For light general aviation airplanes, the maximum weight limit is specified as maximum weight, maximum certificated weight, or maximum gross weight.

2. Maximum ramp weight is what the airplane can weigh while on the ramp or during taxi. This is higher than maximum takeoff weight to allow for fuel used during engine start and taxi.

3. With the CG located near or in front of the forward CG limit, the tail-down force required to balance the airplane increases. This requires extra lift from the wings, and a higher angle of attack. For this reason, forward loading increases stall speed and reduces cruise performance.

4. While an aft CG can increase cruise performance, loading beyond the aft of limits is dangerous. The airplane can become difficult to control and may not be able to recover from a stall or spin.

Weight and Balance Documents

5. The empty weight of an airplane includes unusable fuel, hydraulic fluid, and undrainable oil, or, in some aircraft, all of the oil.

6. When using weight information published in a typical aircraft owner's manual, the empty weight of the actual aircraft may be higher than that shown in the manual because of additional installed equipment. This results in a lower useful load.

7. When the reference datum is located at or in front of the nose, all arms and moments will have positive values.

Weight and Balance Calculations

8. A moment is a twisting force calculated by multiplying a weight or other force by its distance from a specific reference.

9. To compute the loaded center of gravity (CG) of an aircraft, add up the moments and weights of each item and divide the total moment by the total weight. To determine the moment of an individual item, use a loading graph, or multiply its weight by its arm.

10. To determine the effects of fuel consumption on weight and balance, calculate the weight of fuel consumed for the specified period of time. Once the weight has been determined, deduct it from the original fuel weight and recompute the weight and balance for the airplane.

11. To perform weight and balance condition checks you can use a loading graph to locate the moment of all useful load items. Once the total weight and total moment are computed, determine if the moment and weight are within allowable limits by using a center of gravity envelope graph.

12. The weight shift formula calculates the amount of weight that must be moved a specific distance or determines the distance a specific weight must be moved to bring the CG within limits: Weight Moved ÷ Weight of Airplane = Distance CG Moves ÷ Distance between Arms.

12-110   H66
If an airplane is loaded to the rear of its CG range, it will tend to be unstable about its

A — vertical axis.
B — lateral axis.
C — longitudinal axis.

12-110. Answer B. GFDICM 12C (AFH)
With an aft CG, the airplane becomes more tail heavy and unstable in pitch, regardless of its speed. Pitch is the movement about the lateral axis. Answer (A) is incorrect because if the aircraft was unstable about the vertical axis, the aircraft would have a tendency to yaw. Answer (C) is incorrect because if the aircraft was unstable about the longitudinal axis the aircraft would have a tendency to roll. Neither of these tendencies is caused by an aft CG location.

12-111   H105
When computing weight and balance, the basic empty weight includes the weight of the airframe, engine(s), and all installed optional equipment. Basic empty weight also includes

A — all usable fuel and oil, but does not include any radio equipment or instruments that were installed by someone other than the manufacturer.
B — all usable fuel, full oil, hydraulic fluid, but does not include the weight of pilot, passengers, or baggage.
C — the unusable fuel, full operating fluids, and full oil.

12-111. Answer C. GFDICM 12C (PHB)
No empty weight definition differentiates between manufacturer-installed equipment and equipment added later, which requires modification of the empty weight and empty weight CG shown in aircraft documents. Empty weight includes unusable, but not usable, fuel.

12-112   H106
If all index units are positive when computing weight and balance, the location of the datum would be at the

A — centerline of the main wheels.
B — nose, or out in front of the airplane.
C — centerline of the nose or tailwheel, depending on the type of airplane.

12-112. Answer B. GFDICM 12C (PHB)
In order for all stations to be positive, the reference datum must be located at the nose or out in front of the airplane. Any reference datum aft of the nose will result in at least some stations being negative (answers A and C).

12-113   H106

The CG of an aircraft can be determined by which of the following methods?

A — Dividing total arms by total moments.
B — Multiplying total arms by total weight.
C — Dividing total moments by total weight.

12-114   H105

The CG of an aircraft may be determined by

A — dividing total arms by total moments.
B — dividing total moments by total weight.
C — multiplying total weight by total moments.

12-115   H106

GIVEN:

Weight A — 155 pounds at 45 inches aft of datum
Weight B — 165 pounds at 145 inches aft of datum
Weight C — 95 pounds at 185 inches aft of datum

Based on this information, the CG would be located how far aft of datum?

A — 86.0 inches.
B — 116.8 inches.
C — 125.0 inches.

12-116   H105

GIVEN:

Total Weight ....4,137 lb
CG location ....Station 67.8
Fuel consumption...............................13.7 gal/hr
Fuel CG..Station 68.0

After 1 hour 30 minutes of flight time, the CG would be located at station

A — 67.79.
B — 68.79.
C — 70.78.

12-117   H105

An aircraft is loaded with a ramp weight of 3,650 pounds and having a CG of 94.0, approximately how much baggage would have to be moved from the rear baggage area at station 180 to the forward baggage area at station 40 in order to move the CG to 92.0?

A — 52.14 pounds.
B — 62.24 pounds.
C — 78.14 pounds.

12-113. Answer C. GFDICM 12C (PHB)
Most aircraft weight and balance problems can be solved by using the formula: Weight × Arm = Moment. For example, an aircraft's center of gravity (CG) can be determined by arranging the formula to read: Arm (CG) = Moment ÷ Weight. Answers (A) and (B) do not reflect correct methods for determining CG.

12-114. Answer B. GFDICM 12C (PHB)
See explanation for Question 12-113.

12-115 Answer B. GFDICM 12C (PHB)
First, fill in the table by multiplying each weight by the arm to find the moment.

	WEIGHT (lbs)	ARM (in)	MOMENT (lb-in)
Weight A	155	45	6,975
Weight B	165	145	23,925
Weight C	95	185	17,575
Totals	415		48,475

The CG is the total moment divided by the total weight. The answer is 116.8 inches (48,475 ÷ 415 = 116.8).

12-116. Answer A. GFDICM 12C (PHB)
Subtract the weight and moment of the fuel burned from the aircraft's total weight and moment. In 1:30:00, you will burn 20.55 gallons of fuel (1:30:00 x 13.7 = 20.55), or 123.3 lbs. (20.55 × 6 = 123.3)

	WEIGHT (lbs)	ARM (in)	MOMENT (lb-in/100)
Total	4,137.0	67.8	2,804.88
Fuel 20.55 gal.	− 123.3	68.0	− 83.84
	4,013.7		2,721.04

The CG is the total moment divided by the total weight. The answer is 67.79 inches (272,104 ÷ 4,013.7 = 67.79).

12-117. Answer A. GFDICM 12C (PHB)
To determine how much baggage must be moved, use the weight shift formula:

$$\frac{\text{Weight Moved}}{\text{Weight of Airplane}} = \frac{\text{Distance CG Moves}}{\text{Dist. Btwn. Arms}}$$

The weight of the baggage is represented by "X." The distance between arms is 140 inches (180 - 40 = 140), and you want the CG to move 2.0 inches (94.0 - 92.0 =2.0).

$$\frac{X}{3,650} = \frac{2.0}{140}$$

You must move 52.14 pounds of baggage.

12-118   **H105**
GIVEN:

Total weight.......................................3,037 lb
CG location ....Station 68.8
Fuel consumption.......................12.7 gal/hr
Fuel CG.......................................Station 68.0

After 1 hour 45 minutes of flight time, the CG would be located at station

A — 68.77.
B — 68.83.
C — 69.77.

12-119   **H105**
(Refer to figure 38.)
GIVEN:

Empty weight (oil is included).........................1,271 lb
Empty weight moment (in-lb/1,000)..................102.04
Pilot and copilot ....400 lb
Rear seat passenger ....140 lb
Cargo...100 lb
Fuel...37 gal

Is the airplane loaded within limits?

A — Yes, the weight and CG is within limits.
B — No, the weight exceeds the maximum allowable.
C — No, the weight is acceptable, but the CG is aft of the aft limit.

12-118. Answer B. GFDICM 12C (PHB)
Subtract the weight and moment of the fuel burned from the aircraft's total weight and moment. In 1:45:00, you will burn 22.22 gallons of fuel (1:45:00 × 12.7 = 22.22), or 133.32 lbs. (22.22 × 6 = 133.32).

	WEIGHT (lbs)	ARM (in)	MOMENT (lb-in/100)
Total	3,037.0	68.8	2,089.45
Fuel 22.22 gal.	133.32	68.0	90.65
	2,903.68		1,998.80

The CG is the total moment divided by the total weight. The answer is 68.83 inches (199,880 ÷ 2,903.68 = 68.83).

12-119. Answer A. GFDICM 12C (PHB)
Refer to figure 38 to convert fuel to pounds. Add up the known weights, for a total of 1,933 pounds. Use the LOADING GRAPH and find the moment for each weight.

	WEIGHT (lbs)	MOMENT (lb-in/100)
Empty wt.	1,271	102.04
Pilot/Co-pilot	400	36.00
Rear seat	140	18.00
Cargo	100	11.50
Fuel	222	20.00
Totals	2,133	187.54

Total the moments and locate the maximum weight on the CENTER OF GRAVITY ENVELOPE graph. The intersection of the loaded weight and moment is in the upper portion of the normal category, but within the envelope.

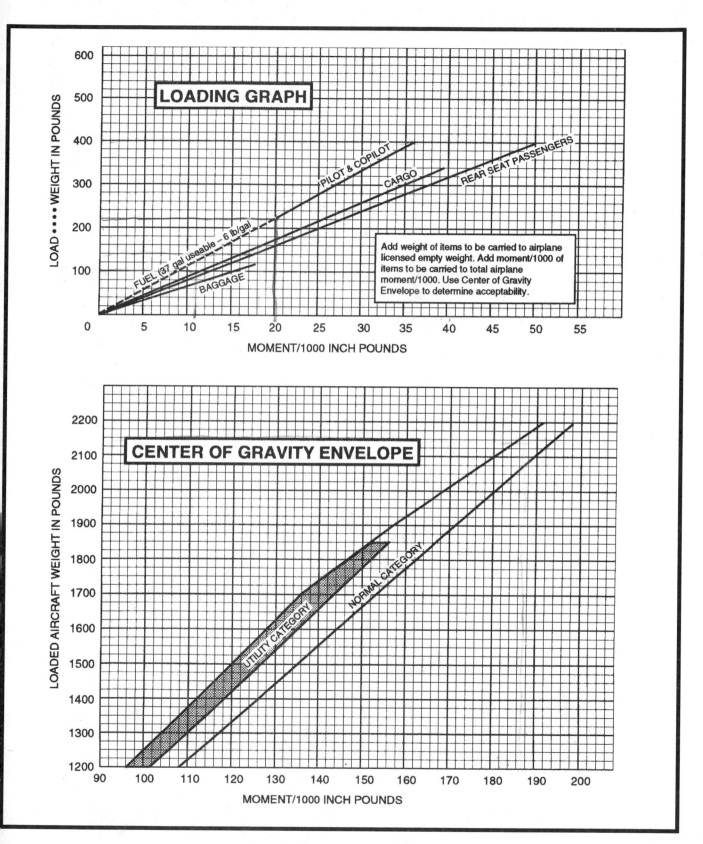

FIGURE 38.—Loading Graph and Center of Gravity Envelope.

COMMERCIAL FLIGHT CONSIDERATIONS

SECTION A
EMERGENCY PROCEDURES

Chapter 13, Section A of the *Instrument/Commercial Manual* covers emergency flight procedures for commercial pilots. You may find the following summary a useful review of some important procedures. However, there are no commercial FAA test questions assigned to this section.

Emergency Descent

1. An emergency descent is used to achieve the fastest practical rate of vertical descent to reach a safe altitude or landing during an emergency situation.

Emergency Approach and Landing

2. The best glide airspeed, found in the pilot's operating handbook, will maximize the distance you can glide and increase the number of available emergency landing areas. In some airplanes, the best glide speed may change as gross weight changes.

3. Key positions on downwind or base allow you to judge your gliding distance in the same manner you would during a normal traffic pattern.

Systems and Equipment Malfunctions

4. If you experience an in-flight emergency, follow the checklist procedures specified in the POH for your airplane and declare an emergency by radio.

5. A cabin or baggage compartment door opening in flight can be a major distraction. Despite the noise and confusion, it is important to maintain control of the airplane, particularly during departure.

SECTION B
COMMERCIAL DECISION MAKING

1. The **DECIDE** acronym stands for:

   Detect the fact that a change has occurred.
   Estimate the need to counter or react to the change.
   Choose a desirable outcome for the success of the flight.
   Identify actions which could successfully control the change.
   Do the necessary action to adapt to the change.
   Evaluate the effect of the action.

2. Aeronautical decision making (ADM) is a systematic approach to the mental process used by pilots to consistently determine the best course of action for a given set of circumstances.

3. Good cockpit stress management begins with good life stress management. To help you manage cockpit stress, you should avoid situations that degrade your ability to handle cockpit responsibilities.

4. Some behavioral traps that experienced pilots fall into are the need to complete a flight as planned, please passengers, meet schedules, and demonstrate the "right stuff." The desire to demonstrate the "right stuff" can generate tendencies that lead to practices that are dangerous, often illegal, and may lead to a mishap. Commercial pilots are also just as prone to peer pressure, get-there-itis, loss of situational awareness, and operating without adequate fuel reserves.

5. Identifying hazardous attitudes through an inventory is an early part of the ADM process. There are five hazardous attitudes and corresponding antidotes. The five types of hazardous attitudes and their antidotes are:

Anti-authority — "ATC says there are thunderstorm cells reported ahead, but I don't believe those doomsayers."

ANTIDOTE: ATC is trying to help; they may have information I do not.

Invulnerability — "I have weather radar and a lightning detector on board, so I'll be safe."

ANTIDOTE: These devices have important limitations to consider.

Macho — "I'm tough; I can handle a little turbulence."

ANTIDOTE: There's more than a little turbulence inside a thunderstorm cell.

Impulsivity — "I have to try that lighter spot before it closes up."

ANTIDOTE: Wait a minute — that hole is not big enough to allow me 20 miles of separation.

Resignation — "There's nothing I can do to control the aircraft now."

ANTIDOTE: I can maintain a safe airspeed.

13-1   L05
Risk management, as part of the Aeronautical Decision Making (ADM) process, relies on which features to reduce the risks associated with each flight?

A — The mental process of analyzing all information in a particular situation and making a timely decision on what action to take.
B — Application of stress management and risk element procedures.
C — Situational awareness, problem recognition, and good judgment.

13-1. Answer C. GFDICM 13B (AC 60-22)
Risk management is the part of the decision making process which relies on situational awareness, problem recognition, and good judgment to reduce risks associated with each flight.

13-2   L05
Aeronautical Decision Making (ADM) is a

A — systematic approach to the mental process used by pilots to consistently determine the best course of action for a given set of circumstances.
B —decision making process which relies on good judgment to reduce risks associated with each flight.
C — mental process of analyzing all information in a particular situation and making a timely decision on what action to take.

13-2. Answer A. GFDICM 13B (AC 60-22)
All these are good answers, but the FAA defines ADM as a systematic approach to the mental process used by aircraft pilots to consistently determine the best course of action in response to a given set of circumstances.

13-3   L05
The Aeronautical Decision Making (ADM) process identifies the steps involved in good decision making. One of these steps includes a pilot

A — making a rational evaluation of the required actions.
B — developing the "right stuff" attitude.
C —identifying personal attitudes hazardous to safe flight.

13-3. Answer C. GFDICM 13B (AC 60-22)
These steps are:

1. Identifying personal attitudes hazardous to safe flight.
2. Learning behavior modification techniques.
3. Learning how to recognize and cope with stress.
4. Developing risk assessment skills.
5. Using all resources in a multicrew situation.
6. Evaluating the effectiveness of one's ADM skills.

13-4 L05
Examples of classic behavioral traps that experienced pilots may fall into are: trying to

A — assume additional responsibilities and assert PIC authority.
B — promote situational awareness and then necessary changes in behavior.
C — complete a flight as planned, please passengers, meet schedules, and demonstrate the "right stuff."

13-5 L05
The basic drive for a pilot to demonstrate the "right stuff" can have an adverse effect on safety, by

A — a total disregard for any alternative course of action.
B — generating tendencies that lead to practices that are dangerous, often illegal, and may lead to a mishap.
C — allowing events, or the situation, to control his or her actions.

13-6 L05
Most pilots have fallen prey to dangerous tendencies or behavior problems at some time. Some of these dangerous tendencies or behavior patterns which must be identified and eliminated include:

A — Deficiencies in instrument skills and knowledge of aircraft systems or limitations.
B — Performance deficiencies from human factors such as, fatigue, illness or emotional problems.
C — Peer pressure, get-there-itis, loss of positional or situation awareness, and operating without adequate fuel reserves.

13-7 L05
An early part of the Aeronautical Decision Making (ADM) process involves

A — taking a self-assessment hazardous attitude inventory test.
B — understanding the drive to have the "right stuff."
C — obtaining proper flight instruction and experience during training.

13-4. Answer C. GFDICM 13B (AC 60-22)
Pilots, particularly those with considerable experience, as a rule always try to complete a flight as planned, please passengers, meet schedules, and generally demonstrate that they have the "right stuff." The FAA says that the basic drive to demonstrate the "right stuff" can have an adverse effect on safety and can impose an unrealistic assessment of piloting skills under stressful conditions.

13-5. Answer B. GFDICM 13B (AC 60-22)
The basic drive to demonstrate the "right stuff" ultimately may lead to practices that are dangerous and often illegal, and may lead to a mishap. All experienced pilots have fallen prey to, or have been tempted by, one or more of these tendencies in their flying careers. Answers A and C, while accurate, are not complete. Answer A is associated with one of these adverse tendencies, get-there-itis. Answer C is associated with another of these tendencies, getting behind the aircraft.

13-6. Answer C. GFDICM 13B (AC 60-22)
The FAA lists the following and identifies them as dangerous tendencies:

1. Peer pressure
2. Mind set
3. Get-there-itis
4. Duck-under syndrome
5. Scud running
6. Continuing visual flight rules (VFR) into instrument conditions
7. Getting behind the aircraft
8. Loss of positional or situation awareness
9. Operating without adequate fuel reserves
10. Descent below the minimum enroute altitude
11. Flying outside the envelope
12. Neglect of flight planning, preflight inspections, checklists, etc.

13-7. Answer A. GFDICM 13B (AC 60-22)
The self-assessment hazardous attitude inventory test presents a number of scenarios, each with five answer choices designed to analyze your motivation for making various decisions. Even if none of the answer choices is acceptable to you, the exercise forces you to rank them from the most likely reason to least likely reason for carrying out the action.

13-8   **L05**

Hazardous attitudes which contribute to poor pilot judgment can be effectively counteracted by

A — early recognition of hazardous thoughts.
B — taking meaningful steps to be more assertive with attitudes.
C — redirecting that hazardous attitude so that appropriate action can be taken.

13-9   **L05**

What are some of the hazardous attitudes dealt with in Aeronautical Decision Making (ADM)?

A — Antiauthority (don't tell me), impulsivity (do something quickly without thinking), macho (I can do it).
B — Risk management, stress management, and risk elements.
C — Poor decision making, situational awareness, and judgment.

13-10   **L05**

When a pilot recognizes a hazardous thought, he or she then should correct it by stating the corresponding antidote. Which of the following is the antidote for MACHO?

A — Follow the rules. They are usually right.
B — Not so fast. Think first.
C — Taking chances is foolish.

13-11   **L05**

What is the first step in neutralizing a hazardous attitude in the ADM process?

A — Recognition of invulnerability in the situation.
B — Dealing with improper judgment.
C — Recognition of hazardous thoughts.

13-12   **L05**

What should a pilot do when recognizing a thought as hazardous?

A — Avoid developing this hazardous thought.
B — Develop this hazardous thought and follow through with modified action.
C — Label that thought as hazardous, then correct that thought by stating the corresponding learned antidote.

13-8. Answer C. GFDICM 13B (AC 60-22)

Hazardous attitudes which contribute to poor pilot judgment can be effectively counteracted by redirecting that hazardous attitude so that appropriate action can be taken. Recognition of hazardous thoughts is the first step in neutralizing them in the ADM process.

13-9. Answer A. GFDICM 13B (AC 60-22)

Answers B and C are incorrect because they are not examples of attitudes. The five hazardous attitudes and their antidotes are:

ATTITUDE: Antiauthority: Don't tell me.
ANTIDOTE: Follow the rules. They are usually right.
ATTITUDE: Impulsivity: Do something quickly.
ANTIDOTE: Not so fast. Think first.
ATTITUDE: Invulnerability: It won't happen to me.
ANTIDOTE: It could happen to me.
ATTITUDE: Macho: I can do it.
ANTIDOTE: Taking chances is foolish.
ATTITUDE: Resignation: What's the use?
ANTIDOTE: I'm not helpless. I can make a difference.

13-10. Answer C. GFDICM 13B (AC 60-22)

Answer A is the antidote for the antiauthority hazardous attitude. Answer B is the antidote for the impulsivity hazardous attitude.

13-11. Answer C. GFDICM 13B (AC 60-22)

Hazardous attitudes which contribute to poor pilot judgment can be effectively counteracted by redirecting that hazardous attitude so that appropriate action can be taken. Recognition of hazardous thoughts is the first step in neutralizing them in the ADM process.

13-12. Answer C. GFDICM 13B (AC 60-22)

When a pilot recognizes a thought as hazardous, the pilot should label that thought as hazardous, then correct that thought by stating the corresponding antidote. Antidotes should be memorized for each of the hazardous attitudes so that they automatically come to mind when needed.

13-13   **L05**

To help manage cockpit stress, pilots must

A — be aware of life stress situations that are similar to those in flying.

B — condition themselves to relax and think rationally when stress appears.

C — avoid situations that will degrade their abilities to handle cockpit responsibilities.

13-14   **L05**

What does good cockpit stress management begin with?

A — Knowing what causes stress.

B — Eliminating life and cockpit stress issues.

C — Good life stress management.

13-15   **L05**

The passengers for a charter flight have arrived almost an hour late for a flight that requires a reservation. Which of the following alternatives best illustrates the ANTIAUTHORITY reaction?

A — Those reservation rules do not apply to this flight.

B — If the pilot hurries, he or she may still make it on time.

C —The pilot can't help it that the passengers are late.

13-13. Answer C. GFDICM 13B (AC 60-22)

Here are some of the tips the FAA offers for managing cockpit stress:

1. Avoid situations that distract you from flying the aircraft.

2. Reduce your workload to reduce stress levels. This will create a proper environment in which to make good decisions.

3. If an emergency does occur, be calm. Think for a moment, weigh the alternatives, then act.

4. Maintain proficiency in your aircraft; proficiency builds confidence. Familiarize yourself thoroughly with your aircraft, its systems, and emergency procedures.

5. Know and respect your own personal limits.

6. Do not let little mistakes bother you until they build into a big thing. Wait until after you land, then "debrief" and analyze past actions.

7. If flying is adding to your stress, either stop flying or seek professional help to manage your stress within acceptable limits.

13-14. Answer C. GFDICM 13B (AC 60-22)

Good cockpit stress management begins with good life stress management. Answer A is part of this, but is incomplete; knowledge of the causes of stress does not by itself help manage stress. Answer B is incorrect because it is not necessarily possible to eliminate stress issues; you must instead manage stress. Many of the stress coping techniques practiced for life stress management are not usually practical in flight. Rather, you must condition yourself to relax and think rationally when stress appears.

13-15. Answer A. GFDICM 13B (AC 60-22)

The Anti-authority attitude is demonstrated by a lack of respect for the regulations and/or rules applicable to the flight. Answer B is an example of the impulsivity reaction; the need to make a quick decision even if it is not a good decision. Answer C is an example of the resignation attitude.

13-16   **L05**

While conducting an operational check of the cabin pressurization system, the pilot discovers that the rate control feature is inoperative. He knows that he can manually control the cabin pressure, so he elects to disregard the discrepancy and departs on his trip. He will just handle the system himself. Which of the following alternatives best illustrates the INVULNERABILITY reaction?

A —What is the worst that could happen.
B —He can handle a little problem like this.
C —It's too late to fix it now.

13-17   **L05**

The pilot and passengers are anxious to get to their destination for a business presentation. Level IV thunderstorms are reported to be in a line across their intended route of flight. Which of the following alternatives best illustrates the IMPULSIVITY reaction?

A — They want to hurry and get going, before things get worse.
B — A thunderstorm won't stop them.
C —They can't change the weather, so they might as well go.

13-18   **L05**

While on an IFR flight, a pilot emerges from a cloud to find himself within 300 feet of a helicopter. Which of the following alternatives best illustrates the "MACHO" reaction?

A —He is not too concerned; everything will be alright.
B —He flies a little closer, just to show him.
C —He quickly turns away and dives, to avoid collision.

13-19   **L05**

When a pilot recognizes a hazardous thought, he or she then should correct it by stating the corresponding antidote. Which of the following is the antidote for ANTI-AUTHORITY?

A —Not so fast. Think first.
B —It won't happen to me. It could happen to me.
C —Don't tell me. Follow the rules. They are usually right.

13-20   **L05**

A pilot and friends are going to fly to an out-of-town football game. When the passengers arrive, the pilot determines that they will be over the maximum gross weight for take-off with the existing fuel load. Which of the following alternatives best illustrates the RESIGNATION reaction?

A —Well, nobody told him about the extra weight.
B —Weight and balance is a formality forced on pilots by the FAA.
C —He can't wait around to de-fuel, they have to get there on time.

13-16. Answer A. GFDICM 13B (AC 60-22)
The invulnerability attitude is that bad things cannot happen to you. Answer B is an example of the macho attitude. Answer C is an example of resignation.

13-17. Answer A. GFDICM 13B (AC 60-22)
Impulsivity is the need to make a quick decision without fully weighing the consequences. Answer B is an example of the invulnerability hazardous attitude. Answer C is an example of resignation.

13-18. Answer B. GFDICM 13B (AC 60-22)
Part of the macho attitude is the predisposition to take chances. Answer A is an example of the invulnerability attitude. Answer C is an example of an impulsive reaction.

13-19. Answer C. GFDICM 13B (AC 60-22)
This is a statement of the attitude (don't tell me) and the antidote (follow the rules; they are usually right). Answer A is the antidote for the impulsivity attitude. Answer B is a statement of the invulnerability attitude (it won't happen to me) and the antidote (it could happen to me).

13-20. Answer A. GFDICM 13B (AC 60-22)
Resignation occurs when a pilot proceeds with an inappropriate course of action with the attitude that it is not his/her responsibility, or that nothing can be done about the situation. Answer B is an example of the anti-authority attitude. Answer C is an example of an impulsive reaction.

13-21 **L05**

Which of the following is the final step of the Decide Model for effective risk management and Aeronautical Decision Making?

A —Estimate.
B —Evaluate.
C —Eliminate.

13-22 **L05**

Which of the following is the first step of the Decide Model for effective risk management and Aeronautical Decision Making?

A —Detect.
B —Identify.
C —Evaluate.

13-23 **L05**

The Decide Model is comprised of a 6-step process to provide a pilot a logical way of approaching Aeronautical Decision Making. These steps are:

A —Detect, estimate, choose, identify, do, and evaluate.
B —Determine, evaluate, choose, identify, do, and eliminate.
C —Determine, eliminate, choose, identify, detect, and evaluate.

13-21. Answer B. GFDICM 13B (AC 60-22)
There are six steps:

1. Detect. The decision maker detects the fact that change has occurred.
2. Estimate. The decision maker estimates the need to counter or react to the change.
3. Choose. The decision maker chooses a desirable outcome (in terms of success) for the flight.
4. Identify. The decision maker identifies actions which could successfully control the change.
5. Do. The decision maker takes the necessary action.
6. Evaluate. The decision maker evaluates the effect(s) of his action countering the change.

13-22. Answer A. GFDICM 13B (AC 60-22)
There are six steps:

1. Detect. The decision maker detects the fact that change has occurred.
2. Estimate. The decision maker estimates the need to counter or react to the change.
3. Choose. The decision maker chooses a desirable outcome (in terms of success) for the flight.
4. Identify. The decision maker identifies actions which could successfully control the change.
5. Do. The decision maker takes the necessary action.
6. Evaluate. The decision maker evaluates the effect(s) of his action countering the change.

13-23. Answer A. GFDICM 13B (AC 60-22)
Explanation of the six steps:

1. Detect. The decision maker detects the fact that change has occurred.
2. Estimate. The decision maker estimates the need to counter or react to the change.
3. Choose. The decision maker chooses a desirable outcome (in terms of success) for the flight.
4. Identify. The decision maker identifies actions which could successfully control the change.
5. Do. The decision maker takes the necessary action.
6. Evaluate. The decision maker evaluates the effect(s) of his action countering the change.

CHAPTER 14

COMMERCIAL MANEUVERS

Chapter 14 covers the performance maneuvers required for the commercial pilot airplane practical test. There are two commercial FAA test questions assigned.

1. During a crosswind takeoff, use the rudder to maintain directional control, turn the ailerons into the wind, and lift off at a slightly higher-than-normal speed.

2. When touching down with a crosswind, make sure the flight path and the aircraft's longitudinal axis are both parallel to the runway.

14-1   **H525**

With regard to the technique required for a crosswind correction on takeoff, a pilot should use

A — aileron pressure into the wind and initiate the lift-off at a normal airspeed in both tailwheel- and nosewheel-type airplanes.

B — right rudder pressure, aileron pressure into the wind, and higher than normal lift-off airspeed in both tricycle- and conventional-gear airplanes.

C — rudder as required to maintain directional control, aileron pressure into the wind, and higher than normal lift-off airspeed in both conventional- and nosewheel-type airplanes.

14-2   **H550**

A proper crosswind landing on a runway requires that, at the moment of touchdown, the

A — direction of motion of the airplane and its lateral axis be perpendicular to the runway.

B — direction of motion of the airplane and its longitudinal axis be parallel to the runway.

C — downwind wing be lowered sufficiently to eliminate the tendency for the airplane to drift.

14-1. Answer C. GFDPMM M11 (AFH)
During a crosswind takeoff, the rudder should be used to maintain directional control, the ailerons positioned into the wind, and lift off should be initiated at a slightly higher-than-normal speed. Answer (A) is wrong because lift off should be made at a slightly higher speed. Answer (B) is wrong because you should use rudder to maintain the runway centerline. Depending on conditions, either left or right rudder may be required.

14-2. Answer B. GFDPMM M14 (AFH)
With either the crab or wing-low method of drift correction, the flight path and the aircraft's longitudinal axis must be parallel to the runway at touchdown. Answer (A) is incorrect because the direction of motion cannot be at a 90° angle to the runway. Answer (C) is wrong because if the downwind wing were lowered, the airplane would drift downwind and not maintain runway alignment.

FEDERAL AVIATION REGULATIONS

SECTION A
14 CFR PART 1 — DEFINITIONS AND ABBREVIATIONS

1. A "commercial operator" is a person who, for compensation or hire, engages in air commerce through the carriage of persons or property by aircraft, other than as an air carrier. To determine if an operation is for compensation or hire you must determine whether the flight is incidental to other business being conducted or whether it is, in itself, an enterprise for profit or benefit.

2. The term "operate", as referred to by the FARs, is defined as the use or approval of the use of an aircraft for the purpose of air navigation, with or without the right of legal control.

3. "Operational control" differs from "operate" in that the person initiating, conducting, or terminating the flight has the authority to do so.

15-1   A01
Regulations which refer to "commercial operators" relate to that person who

A — is the owner of a small scheduled airline.
B — for compensation or hire, engages in the carriage by aircraft in air commerce of persons or property, as an air carrier.
C — for compensation or hire, engages in the carriage by aircraft in air commerce of persons or property, other than as an air carrier.

15-2   A01
Regulations which refer to "operate" relate to that person who

A — acts as pilot in command of the aircraft.
B — is the sole manipulator of the aircraft controls.
C — causes the aircraft to be used or authorizes its use.

15-3   A01
Regulations which refer to the "operational control" of a flight are in relation to

A — the specific duties of any required crewmember.
B — acting as the sole manipulator of the aircraft controls.
C — exercising authority over initiating, conducting, or terminating a flight.

15-1. Answer C. (FAR 1.1)
"Commercial Operator," means a person who, for compensation or hire, engages in the carriage by aircraft in air commerce of persons or property, other than as an air carrier or foreign air carrier. Answers (A) and (B) are incorrect because they imply that only airlines or air carriers can be classified as commercial operators.

15-2. Answer C. (FAR 1.1)
"Operate," with respect to aircraft, means use, cause to use, or authorize to use aircraft, for the purpose of air navigation including the piloting of aircraft, with or without the right of legal control (as owner, lessee, or otherwise). Answer (A) is wrong because the PIC may not be the same person as the operator. Answer (B) is inappropriate because it relates to the criteria for logging pilot-in-command time according to FAR 61.51.

15-3. Answer C. (FAR 1.1)
"Operational Control," with respect to a flight, means the exercise of authority over initiating, conducting, or terminating a flight. Answer (A) relates to the general term of crewmember, a person assigned to perform a duty in an aircraft during flight time. Answer (B) describes the conditions for logging of pilot-in-command time according to FAR 61.51.

15-4   **A150**
If an airplane category is listed as utility, it would mean that this airplane could be operated in which of the following maneuvers?

A — Any maneuver except acrobatics or spins.
B — Limited acrobatics, including spins (if approved).
C — Limited acrobatics, excluding spins.

15-4. Answer B. (FAR 23.3)
An airplane in the utility category can conduct limited acrobatics, including spins. Answer (A) is incorrect because it describes normal category. Answer (C) is incorrect because spins are included, not excluded.

SECTION B
14 CFR PART 61 — CERTIFICATION: PILOTS AND FLIGHT INSTRUCTORS

Commercial Pilot Requirements and Limitations

1. A commercial pilot, like any pilot, is required to have the appropriate certificate in his/her possession when acting as pilot in command or as a required crewmember.

2. A second-class medical is required to exercise commercial privileges and allows you to exercise these privileges for 12 calendar months from the month of issue.

3. When an action has been taken against a pilot for violating any Federal or State statutes relating to the operation of a motor vehicle while intoxicated, impaired, or under the influence of alcohol or a drug, then the pilot must submit a written report to the FAA, Civil Aviation Security Division (AFC-700), within 60 days of the action. If a pilot commits the act of operating an aircraft while intoxicated, impaired, or under the influence of alcohol or a drug, then any of the pilot's certificates, ratings, or authorizations may be suspended or revoked. In addition, committing the act is grounds for denial of an application for a certificate, rating, or authorization issued under Part 61 for a period of up to 1 year after the date of that act.

4. A type rating is required to act as PIC of any aircraft having a maximum certificated takeoff weight of more than 12,500 pounds.

5. A complex airplane has retractable landing gear, flaps, and a controllable-pitch propeller. In order to act as pilot-in-command of a complex airplane, you are required to have received and logged ground and flight training, and received a logbook endorsement of competency. A high performance airplane has an engine with more than 200 horsepower. To act as pilot-in-command of a high-performance airplane, you must also obtain training and a logbook endorsement stating that you are proficient to operate such an airplane.

Commercial Currency

6. To act as pilot in command of an aircraft carrying passengers, you must have made at least three takeoffs and three landings in an aircraft of the same category and class, and if a type rating is required, of the same type, within the preceding 90 days.

7. To meet the recency of experience requirements to act as pilot in command carrying passengers at night, you must have made at least three takeoffs and three landings to a full stop within the preceding 90 days in the same category, class and, if a type rating is required, type of aircraft to be used. The three takeoffs and landings required to act as pilot in command at night must be done during the time period from 1 hour after sunset to 1 hour before sunrise. If these requirements are not met, the latest time passengers may be carried is 1 hour after official sunset.

8. To act as pilot in command of an aircraft, you must show, by logbook endorsement, the satisfactory completion of a flight review or completion of a pilot proficiency check within the preceding 24 calendar months.

15-5   **A20**

Commercial pilots are required to have a valid and appropriate pilot certificate in their physical possession or readily accessible in the aircraft when

A — acting as pilot in command.
B — piloting for hire only.
C — carrying passengers only.

15-6   **A20**

Which of the following are considered aircraft class ratings?

A — Transport, normal, utility, and acrobatic.
B — Airplane, rotorcraft, glider, and lighter-than-air.
C — Single-engine land, multi-engine land, single-engine sea, and multi-engine sea.

15-7   **A20**

Does a commercial pilot certificate have a specific expiration date?

A — No, it is issued without a specific expiration date.
B — Yes, it expires at the end of the 24th month after the month in which it was issued.
C — No, but commercial privileges expire if a flight review is not satisfactorily completed each 12 months.

15-8   **A20**

A second-class Medical Certificate issued to a commercial pilot on April 10, this year, permits the pilot to exercise which of the following privileges?

A — Commercial pilot privileges through April 30, next year.
B — Commercial pilot privileges through April 10, 2 years later.
C — Private pilot privileges through, but not after, March 31, next year.

15-9   **A20**

When is the pilot in command required to hold a category and class rating appropriate to the aircraft being flown?

A — On flights when carrying another person.
B — On practical tests given by an examiner or FAA inspector.
C — All solo flights.

15-5. Answer A. (FAR 61.3)
You must have a current pilot certificate and medical certificate readily available and in your physical possession or readily accessible in the aircraft any time you act as pilot in command (PIC). It makes no difference whether you are carrying passengers or flying for hire.

15-6. Answer C. (FAR 61.5)
Single-engine land, multi-engine land, single-engine sea, and multi-engine sea are airplane class ratings placed on a pilot certificate. Answer (A) lists aircraft certification categories and is incorrect. Answer (B) is incorrect because it lists aircraft categories for pilot certification, not class ratings.

15-7. Answer A. (FAR 61.19)
Any pilot certificate (other than a student pilot certificate) issued under FAR Part 61 is issued without a specific expiration date. Answer (B) refers more to a flight instructor certificate and is incorrect. Answer (C) is incorrect because no pilot can act as PIC unless that person has completed a flight review within the preceding 24 calendar months.

15-8. Answer A. (FAR 61.23)
To exercise the privileges of a commercial pilot, that person also must hold at least a second-class medical certificate that was issued within the past 12 calendar months. Answer (B) is incorrect because only private pilot privileges can be exercised after 12 calendar months from the issue date for first or second class medical certificates. Also, all medical certificates expire at the end of the appropriate calendar month. Answer (C) is incorrect because 3rd class privileges expire at the end of 24 months, not the end of the 23rd month after issuance.

15-9. Answer A. (FAR 61.31)
To act as pilot in command (other than authorized student pilot solo activity), you must hold a pilot certificate with the appropriate category, class, and type rating (if a class and type rating is required) that applies to the aircraft. Answer (B) is incorrect because an applicant for a practical test is not rated until after the successful completion of that test. Answer (C) is incorrect because a person can conduct solo operations without an appropriate certificate, if that person receives, from an appropriately rated CFI, an additional category solo logbook endorsement under FAR 61.87.

15-10   **A20**
Unless otherwise authorized, the pilot in command is required to hold a type rating when operating any

A — aircraft that is certificated for more than one pilot.
B — aircraft of more than 12,500 pounds maximum certificated takeoff weight.
C — multi-engine airplane having a gross weight of more than 12,000 pounds.

15-10. Answer B. (FAR 61.31)
According to FAR 61.31, a person may not act as pilot in command of a large aircraft unless he or she hold a type rating for that aircraft. According to FAR Part 1, "Large Aircraft" means an aircraft of more than 12,500 pounds, maximum certificated takeoff weight. Answer (A) is incorrect because an aircraft requiring more then one crewmember does is not necessarily require the PIC to be type rated. Answer (C) is incorrect because multi-engine aircraft (other than turbojet) with gross weights between 6,000 and 12,500 pounds normally do not require a type rating.

15-11   **A20**
To act as pilot in command of an airplane that is equipped with retractable landing gear, flaps, and controllable-pitch propeller, a person is required to

A — make at least six takeoffs and landings in such an airplane within the preceding 6 months.
B — receive and log ground and flight training in such an airplane, and obtain a logbook endorsement of certifying proficiency.
C — hold a multi-engine airplane class rating.

15-11. Answer B. (FAR 61.31)
No person may act as pilot in command of a complex airplane (an airplane that has retractable landing gear, flaps, and a controllable pitch propeller) unless that person has received and logged ground and flight training from an authorized instructor in a complex airplane, or flight simulator that is representative of a complex airplane, and has received a one-time endorsement in the logbook from the instructor who certifies that the person is proficient to operate a complex airplane. Answer (A) is incorrect because there is no minimum number of takeoffs and landings, either for the initial endorsement or to continue to exercise the privileges of this endorsement. Answer (C) is incorrect because a multi-engine rating is not required for flying aircraft with retractable landing gear.

15-12   **A20**
What flight time may a pilot log as second in command?

A — Only that flight time during which the second in command is the sole manipulator of the controls.
B — All flight time while acting as second in command in aircraft configured for more than one pilot.
C — All flight time when qualified and occupying a crewmember station in an aircraft that requires more than one pilot.

15-12. Answer C. (FAR 61.51)
A pilot may log second in command time if qualified in accordance with the second-in-command requirements of FAR 61.55, and occupies a crewmember station in an aircraft that requires more than one pilot by the aircraft's type certificate, or if he/she holds the appropriate category, class, and instrument rating (if an instrument rating is required for the flight) for the aircraft being flown, and more than one pilot is required under the type certification of the aircraft or the regulations under which the flight is being conducted. Answer (A) is incorrect because being the sole manipulator of the flight controls is not a requirement for logging second in command. Answer (B) is not very specific, and does not agree with the wording in the regulation the way Answer (C) does.

15-13   **A20**
What flight time must be documented and recorded by a pilot exercising the privileges of a commercial certificate?

A — Flight time showing training and aeronautical experience to meet requirements for a certificate, rating or flight review.
B — Only flight time for compensation or hire with passengers aboard which is necessary to meet the recent flight experience requirements.
C — All flight time flown for compensation or hire.

15-13. Answer A. (FAR 61.51)
According to the regulation, "Each person must document and record the following flight time in a manner acceptable to the Administrator. This includes any time that is training and aeronautical experience used to meet the requirements for a certificate, rating, or flight review and aeronautical experience required for meeting the recent flight experience requirements." Answers (B) and (C) are incorrect because they limit the requirements for logging of flight time to flight time flown for compensation or hire.

15-14   **A20**

If a pilot does not meet the recency of experience requirements for night flight and official sunset is 1900 CST, the latest time passengers should be carried is

A — 1959 CST.
B — 1900 CST.
C — 1800 CST.

15-14. Answer A. (FAR 61.57b)
No person may act as pilot in command of an aircraft carrying passengers during the period beginning 1 hour after sunset and ending 1 hour before sunrise (as published in the American Air Almanac), unless that person meets night experience requirements.

15-15   **A20**

Prior to carrying passengers, the pilot in command must have accomplished the required takeoffs and landings in

A — the same category, class, and type of aircraft (if a type rating is required).
B — any category aircraft.
C — the same category and class of aircraft to be used.

15-15. Answer A. (FAR 61.57)
No person may act as pilot in command of an aircraft carrying passengers unless that person has made at least three takeoffs and three landings within the preceding 90 days, and the required takeoffs and landings were performed in an aircraft of the same category, class, and type (if a type rating is required). Answer (B) is incorrect because the takeoffs and landings must be in the same category of aircraft as well as class and type (if required). Answer (C) is incomplete because it does not include type of aircraft (if type rating is required).

15-16   **A20**

No pilot may act as pilot in command of an aircraft under IFR or in weather conditions less than the minimums prescribed for VFR unless that pilot has, within the past 6 months, performed and logged under actual or simulated instrument conditions, at least

A — six instrument approaches, holding procedures, intercepting and tracking courses, or passed an instrument proficiency check in an aircraft that is appropriate to the aircraft category.
B — six instrument flights and six approaches.
C — three instrument approaches and logged 3 hours of instruments.

15-16. Answer A. FAR 61.57
Six instrument approaches are required, as well as holding procedures, intercepting and tracking courses, or passing an instrument competency check in an aircraft that is appropriate to the aircraft category. There is no minimum instrument time required.

15-17   **A20**

To act as pilot in command of an aircraft operated under 14 CFR part 91, a commercial pilot must have satisfactorily accomplished a flight review or completed a proficiency check within the preceding

A — 12 calendar months.
B — 6 calendar months.
C — 24 calendar months.

15-17. Answer C. (FAR 61.56)
No person (not just a commercial pilot) may act as pilot in command of an aircraft unless, within the preceding 24 calendar months, they have satisfactorily completed a flight review, a pilot proficiency check, or one or more phases of an FAA-sponsored pilot proficiency award program.

15-18   **A20**

Pilots, who change their permanent mailing address and fail to notify the FAA Airmen Certification Branch of this change, are entitled to exercise the privileges of their pilot certificate for a period of

A — 30 days.
B — 60 days.
C — 90 days.

15-18. Answer A. (FAR 61.60)
After changing your permanent mailing address, you may not exercise the privileges of a pilot or flight instructor certificate after 30 days unless the FAA Airman Certification Branch has been notified in writing. Answer (B) exceeds the 30 day requirement and corresponds more to the Prerequisites for Flight Test requirements found under FAR 61.39. Answer (C) exceeds the 30 day limit and corresponds more to Recent Flight Experience requirements found under FAR 61.57.

15-19   A21
To act as pilot in command of an airplane towing a glider, the tow pilot is required to have

A — a logbook endorsement from an authorized glider instructor certifying receipt of ground and flight training in gliders, and be proficient with techniques and procedures for safe towing of gliders.
B — at least a private pilot certificate with a category rating for powered aircraft, and made and logged at least three flights as pilot or observer in a glider being towed by an airplane.
C — a logbook record of having made at least three flights as sole manipulator of the controls of a glider being towed by an airplane.

15-20   A21
To act as pilot in command of an airplane towing a glider, a pilot must have accomplished, within the preceeding 12 months, at least

A — three actual glider tows under the supervision of a qualified tow pilot.
B — three actual or simulated glider tows while accompanied by a qualified tow pilot.
C — ten flights as pilot in command of an aircraft while towing a glider.

15-21   A24
What limitation is imposed on a newly certificated commercial pilot - airplane, if that person does not hold an instrument rating? The carriage of passengers

A — for hire on cross-country flights is limited to 50 NM for night flights, but not limited for day flights.
B — or property for hire on cross-country flights at night is limited to a radius of 50 NM.
C — for hire on cross-country flights in excess of 50 NM, or for hire at night is prohibited.

15-22   A20
To act as pilot-in-command of an airplane with more than 200 horsepower, a person is required to

A — receive and log ground and flight training from a qualified pilot in such an airplane.
B — receive and log ground and flight training from an authorized instructor in such an airplane.
C — obtain an endorsement from a qualified pilot stating that the person is proficient to operate such an airplane.

15-19. Answer A. (FAR 61.69)
No person may act as pilot in command of an aircraft towing a glider unless he or she has an endorsement in his or her pilot logbook from a person authorized to give flight instruction in gliders, certifying that the pilot has received ground and flight instruction in gliders and is familiar with the techniques and procedures essential to the safe towing of gliders. Answer (B) incorrectly states the requirement to have made three flights as pilot-in-command of a glider being towed by an aircraft within the previous 12 months; flying as an observer does not meet this requirement. Answer (C) is incorrect because these three flights must be in a towplane, not a glider.

15-20. Answer B. (FAR 61.69)
Three actual or simulated glider tows while accompanied by a qualified pilot are required within the previous 12 months, or at least three flights as pilot in command of a glider towed by an aircraft. Answer (A) is incorrect because actual glider tows are not required; simulated glider tows are acceptable. Answer (C) refers to a regulation under which those making 10 flights as PIC in a towplane prior to May 16, 1967 are exempt from some of these requirements. It would need to state this additional qualifying information to be considered a correct answer.

15-21. Answer C. (FAR 61.133b)
Commercial night operations and flights of more than 50 NM require an instrument rating. Answers (A) and (B) are incorrect because commercial night flights with passengers are totally prohibited to non-instrument rated pilots.

15-22. Answer B. GFDPPM 1B (FAR 61.31f)
No person may act as PIC of a high-performance airplane unless the person has received and logged ground and flight training from an authorized instructor in a high-performance airplane and has been found proficient in the operation and systems of the airplane. Additionally, you must have a high-performance endorsement in your logbook from an authorized instructor.

15-23   **A20**

To serve as pilot in command of an airplane that is certified for more than one pilot crewmember, and operated under part 91, a person must

A — complete a flight review within the preceding 24 calendar months.

B — receive and log ground and flight training from an authroized flight instructor.

C — complete a pilot-in-command proficiency check within the preceding 12 calendar months in an airplane that is type certificated for more than one pilot.

15-24   **A20**

To serve as second in command of an airplane that is certificated for more than one pilot crewmember, and operated under part 91, a person must

A — within the last 12 months become familiar with the required information, and perform and log pilot time in the type of airplane for which privileges are requested.

B — receive and log flight training from an authorized flight instructor in the type of airplane for which privileges are requested.

C — hold at least a commercial pilot certificate with an airplane category rating.

15-25   **A24**

A person with a Commercial Pilot certificate may act as pilot in command of an aircraft for compensation or hire, if that person

A — is qualified in accordance with 14 CFR part 61 and with the applicable parts that apply to the operation.

B — is qualified in accordance with 14 CFR part 61 and has passed a pilot competency check given by an authorized check pilot.

C — holds appropriate category, class ratings, and meets the recent flight experience requirements of 14 CFR part 61.

12-23. Answer C. (FAR 61.58)

A PIC proficiency check in any airplane requiring more than one pilot is required within the preceding 12 calendar months, and a check in the same type of aircraft is required within the preceding 24 months. Answer (A) is incorrect because it describes the flight review required of all pilots and does not address the specific requirements for operating an airplane certified for more than one pilot crewmember. Answer (B) is incorrect because the flight training specified does not necessarily meet the specific requirements of the PIC check.

15-24. Answer A. FAR 61.55

A private pilot certificate is the minimum required, with an instrument rating for IFR operations. Three takeoffs and landings are required within the previous 12 months, plus engine-out and other procedures.

15-25. Answer A. (FAR 61.133)

The person must be qualified under part 61 and under part 91, 119, 121, 135, or other applicable FARs. Answer (B) is incorrect because a competency check is not necessarily required, and answer (C) is incorrect because the conditions listed here may not be sufficient to act as PIC of an aircraft for hire.

15-26   A24

A person with a commercial pilot certificate may act as pilot in command of an aircraft carrying persons or property for compensation or hire, if that person

A — holds appropriate category, class ratings, and meets the recent flight experience requirements of 14 CFR part 61.

B — is qualified in accordance with 14 CFR part 61 and with the applicable parts that apply to the operation.

C — is qualified in accordance with 14 CFR part 61 and has passed a pilot competency check given by an authorized check pilot.

15-26. Answer B. (FAR 61.133)

The person must be qualified under part 61 and under part 91, 119, 121, 135, or other applicable FARs. Answer (A) is incorrect because the conditions listed here may not be sufficient to act as PIC of an aircraft for hire. Answer (C) is incorrect because a competency check is not necessarily required.

15-27   A20

To act as pilot in command of a tailwheel airplane, without prior experience, a pilot must

A — log ground and flight training from an authorized instructor.

B — pass a competency check and receive an endorsement from an authorized instructor.

C — receive and log flight training from an authorized instructor.

15-27. Answer C. (FAR 61.31)

A pilot must receive flight training and a one-time instructor endorsement. Answers (A) and (B) are incorrect because ground instruction and a competency check are not required.

15-28   A20

A pilot convicted of operating a motor vehicle while either intoxicated by, impaired by, or under the influence of alcohol or a drug is required to provide a

A — written report to the FAA Civil Aeromedical Institute (CAMI) within 60 days after the motor vehicle action.

B — written report to the FAA Civil Aviation Security Division (AMC-700) not later than 60 days after the conviction.

C — Notification of the conviction to an FAA Aviation Medical Examiner (AME) not later than 60 days after the motor vehicle action.

15-28. Answer B. (FAR 61.15)

When a pilot is convicted of operating a motor vehicle while either intoxicated or impaired by alcohol or a drug, the pilot must notify the FAA Civil Aviation Security Division, in writing, not later than 60 days after the conviction.

15-29   A20

A pilot convicted of a motor vehicle offense involving alcohol or drugs is required to provide a written report to the

A — nearest FAA Flight Standards District Office (FSDO) within 60 days after such action.

B — FAA Civil Aeromedical Institute (CAMI) within 60 days after the conviction.

C — FAA Civil Aviation Security Division (AMC-700) within 60 days after such action.

15-29. Answer C. (FAR 61.15)

When a pilot is convicted of operating a motor vehicle while either intoxicated or impaired by alcohol or a drug, the pilot must notify the FAA Civil Aviation Security Division, in writing, not later than 60 days after the conviction.

15-30   A20

A pilot convicted for the violation of any Federal or State statute relating to the process, manufacture, transportation, distribution, or sale of narcotic drugs is grounds for

A — a written report to be filed with the FAA Civil Aviation Security Division (AMC-700) not later than 60 days after the conviction.

B — notification of this conviction to the FAA Civil Aeromedical Institute (CAMI) within 60 days after the conviction.

C — Suspension or revocation of any certificate, rating, or authorization issued under 14 CFR part 61.

15-31   A20

A pilot convicted of operating an aircraft as a crewmember under the influence of alcohol, or using drugs that affect the person's faculties, is grounds for a

A — written report to be filed with the FAA Civil Aviation Security Division (AMC-700) not later than 60 day after the conviction.

B — written notification to the FAA Civil Aeromedical Institute (CAMI) within 60 days after the conviction.

C — Denial of an application for an FAA certificate, rating, or authorization issued under 14 CFR part 61.

15-30. Answer C. (FAR 61.15)

A pilot convicted for the violation of any Federal or State statute relating to the process, manufacture, transportation, distribution, or sale of narcotic drugs is grounds for: the denial of an application for any certificate, rating, or authorization issued under CFR 14 Part 61 for a period of up to 1 year after the date of final conviction; or the suspension or revocation of any certificate, rating, or authorization issued under 14 CFR part 61. A written report is required to be submitted to the FAA Civil Aviation Security Division (AMC-700) when there is an offense involving the operation of a motor vehicle while intoxicated or impaired by alcohol or drugs.

15-31. Answer C. (FAR 61.15)

A person convicted of operating an aircraft as a required crewmember while under the influence of alcohol, or while using drugs that affect the person's faculties, is grounds for denial of an application for an FAA certificate, or rating, or authorization issued under FAR Part 61 for a period of up to one year after the date of that act. It is also grounds for suspension or revocation of any certificate, rating, or authorization issued under Part 61. Answer (A) is incorrect because a written report is required to be submitted within 60 days to the FAA Civil Aviation Security Division (AMC-700) when there is an offense involving the operation of a motor vehicle while intoxicated or impaired by alcohol or drugs.

SECTION C
14 CFR PART 91 — GENERAL OPERATING AND FLIGHT RULES

Pilot-in-Command Responsibility

1. The pilot in command is the final authority as to the operation of an aircraft. If an in-flight emergency requires immediate action, the pilot in command may deviate from the FARs to the extent required to meet that emergency. A written report is not required unless requested by the FAA.

Aircraft Documents

2. In addition to a valid airworthiness certificate, operating limitations and the registration certificate must also be on board an aircraft during flight.

Dropping Objects

3. Objects may be dropped from an aircraft if precautions are taken to avoid injury or damage to persons or property on the surface.

Preflight Planning

4. FAR 91.103 requires that a pilot in command, before beginning a flight, become familiar with all available information concerning that flight. For a flight under IFR or a flight not in the vicinity of an airport, this information must specifically include weather reports and forecasts, fuel requirements, alternatives available if the planned flight cannot be completed, and any known traffic delays of which the pilot in command has been advised by ATC. For any flight, the PIC must determine the runway lengths at airports of intended use, and takeoff and landing distance information for the aircraft.

Aircraft Equipment

5. Flight crewmembers are required to keep their safety belts and shoulder harnesses fastened during takeoffs and landings. Safety belts must stay fastened while enroute.

6. The pilot in command must brief the passengers on the use of safety belts and notify them to fasten their safety belts during taxi, takeoff and landing. Passengers must have their safety belts fastened during taxi, takeoffs and landings.

7. When the ELT has been in use for more than 1 cumulative hour, or if 50 percent of the useful life of the batteries expires, the batteries must be replaced or recharged.

8. An ATC transponder must be inspected, tested, and found to comply with FAA standards every 24 calendar months.

9. All operations within Class C airspace must be in an aircraft equipped with a 4096-code transponder with Mode C encoding capability.

10. During the period from sunset to sunrise, except in Alaska, lighted position lights must be displayed on an aircraft.

Supplemental Oxygen

11. Supplemental oxygen must be used by required crewmembers when operating an aircraft at cabin pressure altitudes above 12,500 feet MSL up to and including 14,000 feet MSL, for flight time at those altitudes that exceeds 30 minutes. Above 14,000 feet MSL, required crewmembers must use oxygen continuously.

12. Above cabin pressure altitudes of 15,000 feet MSL each person on board the aircraft must be provided with supplemental oxygen.

Aircraft Categories

13. Unless specifically authorized, no person may operate a restricted category aircraft or an aircraft that has an experimental certificate over a densely populated area or in a congested airway.

Special Flight Rules

14. No person may operate an aircraft in formation flight except by prior arrangement with the pilot in command of each aircraft.

15. No person may operate an aircraft in acrobatic flight when over any congested area of a city, town or settlement, in Class D airspace, or Class E airspace designated for Federal Airways. Acrobatic flight is also prohibited below 1,500 feet AGL, or when flight visibility is less than 3 statute miles.

16. With certain exceptions, each occupant must wear an approved parachute when intentionally pitching the nose of the aircraft up or down more than 30° or when exceeding 60° of bank. A chair-type parachute must have been packed by a certificated and appropriately rated parachute rigger within the preceding 120 days.

Airspeed

17. Unless otherwise authorized, the maximum indicated airspeed at which you may operate an aircraft below 10,000 feet MSL is 250 knots. This is also the maximum indicated airspeed within Class B airspace.

18. Under Class B airspace, or in a VFR corridor through a Class B area, you may not operate at an indicated airspeed of more than 200 knots.

ATC Clearances

19. When an ATC clearance has been obtained, you may not deviate from that clearance, unless you obtain an amended clearance. The exception to this regulation is in an emergency.

20. If given priority by ATC because of an emergency, you must submit a detailed report of that emergency within 48 hours to the manager of the ATC facility, if requested to do so.

Maintenance

21. The responsibility for ensuring that maintenance personnel make the appropriate entries in the aircraft maintenance records, indicating the aircraft has been approved for return to service, lies with the owner or operator.

22. Completion of an annual inspection and the return of the aircraft to service should always be indicated by an appropriate notation in the aircraft maintenance records.

23. If an alteration or repair substantially affects an aircraft's operation in flight, that aircraft must be flown by an appropriately rated private pilot and approved for return to service before being operated with passengers aboard.

24. No person may operate an aircraft unless, within the preceding 12 calendar months, it has had an annual inspection.

25. To determine the expiration date of the last annual inspection, a person should refer to the aircraft maintenance records.

26. You may not operate an aircraft carrying any person for hire, or give flight instruction for hire in an aircraft you provide, unless, within the preceding 100 hours of time in service, the aircraft has received an annual or 100-hour inspection. The aircraft may be flown beyond the 100 hours if it is being transported to a place where service can be completed. However, the next 100 hour inspection must be completed within 100 hours of the original expiration time.

27. The owner or operator of an aircraft must keep a record of current status of applicable airworthiness directives in the aircraft maintenance records.

15-32 B07

What action must be taken when a pilot in command deviates from any rule in 14 CFR Part 91?

A — Upon landing, report the deviation to the nearest FAA Flight Standards District Office.
B — Advise ATC of the pilot in command's intentions.
C — Upon the request of the Administrator, send a written report of that deviation to the Administrator.

15-32. Answer C. (FAR 91.3)
The pilot in command (PIC) of an aircraft is directly responsible for, and is the final authority as to, the operation of the aircraft. This regulation gives the PIC authority to deviate from any rule in order to meet the requirements of an emergency. However, the pilot in command is required to submit a written report of the deviation, upon request of the Administrator. Answer (A) is wrong because a written report is not required unless requested. Answer (B) is wrong because your priority is to meet the requirements of the emergency to ensure the safety of the flight; while you should communicate your intentions to ATC as soon as possible, you may not have time to do this prior to your deviation.

15-33 B07

Who is responsible for determining if an aircraft is in condition for safe flight?

A — A certificated aircraft mechanic.
B — The pilot in command.
C — The owner or operator.

15-33. Answer B. (FAR 91.7)
According to FAR Part 91.7, no person may operate an aircraft unless it is in an airworthy condition. The pilot in command of a civil aircraft is responsible for determining whether that aircraft is in condition for safe flight. The pilot in command shall discontinue the flight when unairworthy mechanical, electrical, or structural conditions occur. Answers (A) and (C) are wrong because they indicate the pilot in command does not make the final decision.

15-34 B07

When operating a U.S.-registered civil aircraft, which document is required by regulation, to be available in the aircraft?

A — A manufacturer's Operations Manual.
B — A current, approved Airplane Flight Manual.
C — An Owner's Manual.

15-34. Answer B. (FAR 91.9)
No person may operate a civil aircraft without complying with the operating limitations specified in the approved Airplane or Rotorcraft Flight Manual, markings, and placards, or as otherwise prescribed by the certifying authority of the country of registry. Answers (A) and (C) may not meet all the requirements for this flight manual.

15-35   B07

A pilot in command (PIC) of a civil aircraft may not allow any object to be dropped from that aircraft in flight

A — if it creates a hazard to persons and property.
B — unless the PIC has permission to drop any object over private property.
C — unless reasonable precautions are taken to avoid injury to property.

15-36   B08

When is preflight action required, relative to alternatives available, if the planned flight cannot be completed?

A — IFR flights only.
B — any flight not in the vicinity of an airport.
C — any flight conducted for hire or compensation.

15-37   B08

The required preflight action relative to weather reports and fuel requirements is applicable to

A — any flight conducted for compensation or hire.
B — any flight not in the vicinity of an airport.
C — IFR flights only.

15-38   B08

Before beginning any flight under IFR, the pilot in command must become familiar with all available information concerning that flight. In addition, the pilot must

A — be familiar with all instrument approaches at the destination airport.
B — list an alternate airport on the flight plan and confirm adequate takeoff and landing performance at the destination airport.
C — be familiar with the runway lengths at airports of intended use, and the alternatives available if the flight cannot be completed.

15-35. Answer A. (FAR 91.15)

According to FAR 91.15, no pilot in command of a civil aircraft may allow any object to be dropped in flight that creates a hazard to persons or property. The regulation provides an exception, that an object may be dropped if reasonable precautions are taken to avoid injury or damage to persons or property. Answer (B) is wrong because private property is not specified as an exception. Answer (C) is wrong because the pilot in command must take reasonable precaution to avoid injury to persons and property, not just property.

15-36. Answer B. (FAR 91.103)

Each pilot in command shall, before beginning a flight, become familiar with all available information concerning that flight. For a flight under IFR or not in the vicinity of an airport, this information must include weather reports and forecasts, fuel requirements, alternatives available if the planned flight cannot be completed, and any known traffic delays of which the pilot in command has been advised by ATC. Answer (A) incorrectly limits the preflight action to IFR flights. Answer (C) incorrectly limits the preflight action to flights for hire or compensation.

15-37. Answer B. (FAR 91.103)

Each pilot in command shall, before beginning a flight, become familiar with all available information concerning that flight. For a flight under IFR or not in the vicinity of an airport, this information must include weather reports and forecasts, fuel requirements, alternatives available if the planned flight cannot be completed, and any known traffic delays of which the pilot in command has been advised by ATC. Answer (A) incorrectly limits the preflight action to flights for hire or compensation. Answer (C) incorrectly limits the preflight action to IFR flights.

15-38. Answer C. (FAR 91.109)

Each pilot in command shall, before beginning a flight, become familiar with all available information concerning that flight. This includes flights under IFR, and alternatives available if the planned flight cannot be completed. In addition, for any flight, the pilot must be familiar with runway lengths at airports of intended use, as well as takeoff and landing distance information. Answers (A) and (B) provide an incomplete listing of the pertinent preflight actions required for an IFR flight and are incorrect.

15-39   B08

Before beginning any flight under IFR, the pilot in command must become familiar with all available information concerning that flight. In addition, the pilot must

A — list an alternate airport on the flight plan, and confirm adequate takeoff and landing performance at the destination airport.
B — be familiar with all instrument approaches at the destination airport.
C — be familiar with the runway lengths at airports of intended use, weather reports, fuel requirements, and alternatives available, if the planned flight cannot be completed.

15-39. Answer C. (FAR 91.103)

Regulations specifically require the pilots know runway lengths at airports of intended use for ALL flights. The remaining items listed in Answer (C) are required for IFR flights and for flights not in the vicinity of an airport. Answer (A) is incorrect because an alternate airport is not required on all IFR flight plans. Although you should be familiar with the information in Answer (B), it comes under "all available information" and is not specifically mentioned in the regulation.

15-40   B08

Required flight crewmembers' safety belts must be fastened

A — only during takeoff and landing.
B — while the crewmembers are at their stations.
C — only during takeoff and landing when passengers are aboard the aircraft.

15-40. Answer B. (FAR 91.105)

During takeoffs and landings, and while enroute, each required flight crewmember shall keep their safety belt fastened while at the crewmember station. Answer (A) applies to the use of shoulder harnesses and is incorrect. Answer (C) is incorrect, because passengers have no bearing on the safety belt and shoulder harness requirements for crewmembers.

15-41   B08

Each required flight crewmember is required to keep his or her shoulder harness fastened

A — during takeoff and landing only when passengers are aboard the aircraft.
B — while the crewmembers are at their stations, unless he or she is unable to perform required duties.
C — during takeoff and landing, unless he or she is unable to perform required duties.

15-41. Answer C. (FAR 91.105)

Each required flight crewmember of a U.S.-registered civil aircraft shall, during takeoff and landing, keep his or her shoulder harness fastened while at his or her assigned duty station, unless the crewmember would be unable to perform required duties with the shoulder harness fastened. Answer (A) is incorrect because this requirement is not affected by the presence or lack of passengers. Answer (B) is incorrect because shoulder harnesses, unlike safety belts, are not required to be fastened throughout the flight.

15-42   B08

With U.S.-registered civil airplanes, the use of safety belts is required during movement on the surface, takeoffs, and landings for

A — safe operating practice, but not required by regulations.
B — each person over 2 years of age on board.
C — commercial passenger operations only.

15-42. Answer B. (FAR 91.105, 91.107)

In addition to the required use of seat belts and shoulder harnesses for crewmembers, no pilot may cause to be moved on the surface, takeoff, or land a U.S. registered civil aircraft unless the pilot in command of that aircraft ensures that each person on board has been notified to fasten his or her safety belt and, if installed, shoulder harness. In addition, the safety belt and shoulder harness must be properly secured about each person more than 2 years of age. Answer (A) and (C) are incorrect, because safety belt use is required, not recommended, for non-commercial operations as well as commercial operations.

15-43   B12

Which is required to operate an aircraft towing an advertising banner?

A —Approval from ATC to operate in Class E airspace.
B — A certificate of waiver issued by the Administrator.
C — A safety link at each end of the towline which has a breaking strength not less than 80 percent of the aircraft's gross weight.

15-44   B07

Portable electronic devices which may cause interference with the navigation or communication system may not be operated on a U.S.- registered civil aircraft being flown

A — along Federal airways.
B — within the U.S.
C — in air carrier operations.

15-45   B07

Portable electronic devices which may cause interference with the navigation or communication system may not be operated on U.S.-registered civil aircraft being operated

A — under IFR.
B — in passenger carrying operations.
C — along Federal airways.

15-46   B10

If weather conditions are such that it is required to designate an alternate airport on your IFR flight plan, you should plan to carry enough fuel to arrive at the first airport of intended landing, fly from that airport to the alternate airport, and fly thereafter for

A — 30 minutes at slow cruising speed.
B — 45 minutes at normal cruising speed.
C — 1 hour at normal cruising speed.

15-43. Answer B. (FAR 91.311)

According to FAR 91.311, no pilot of a civil aircraft may tow anything with that aircraft (other than gliders), except in accordance with the terms of a certificate of waiver issued by the Administrator. Answer (A) is incorrect because air traffic control has no authority to issue an aircraft waiver for towing banners. Answer (C) corresponds more to glider towline safety link requirements found in FAR 91.309 and is incorrect.

15-44. Answer C. (FAR 91.21)

No person may operate or allow the operation of, any portable electronic device on U.S. registered civil aircraft which is operated by a holder of an air carrier operating certificate, or any other aircraft while it is operated under IFR. Answer (A) is incorrect because there are no restrictions to operating portable electronic devices on federal airways, as long as the flight is not an air carrier operation or an IFR flight. Answer (B) is incorrect because Part 91 VFR operations are not required to comply with this regulation.

15-45. Answer A. (FAR 91.21)

No person may operate or allow the operation of, any portable electronic device on U.S. registered civil aircraft which is operated by a holder of an air carrier operating certificate, or any other aircraft while it is operated under IFR. Answer (B) is incorrect because this restriction does not apply to non air carrier passenger carrying operations under VFR. Answer (C) is incorrect because there are no restrictions to operating portable electronic devices on federal airways, as long as the flight is not an air carrier operation or an IFR flight.

15-46. Answer B. (FAR 91.167)

If an alternate airport is required on your IFR flight plan, you may not operate a civil aircraft in IFR conditions unless it carries enough fuel to fly to the first airport of intended landing, fly from that airport to the alternate airport, and fly thereafter for 45 minutes at normal cruising speed (30 minutes for helicopters). Answer (A) is not correct because it corresponds to the day VFR reserve requirements for airplanes. In addition, it specifies slow cruising speed, not normal cruising speed. Answer (C) corresponds more to the weather forecast requirements for determining the need for an alternate airport and is not correct.

15-47   B11

In accordance with14 CFR part 91, supplemental oxygen must be used by the required minimum flightcrew for that time exceeding 30 minutes while at cabin pressure altitudes of

A — 10,500 feet MSL up to and including 12,500 feet MSL.

B — 12,000 feet MSL up to and including 18,000 feet MSL.

C — 12,500 feet MSL up to and including 14,000 feet MSL.

15-48   B11

What are the oxygen requirements when operating at cabin pressure altitudes above 15,000 feet MSL?

A — The flightcrew and passengers must be provided with supplemental oxygen.

B — Oxygen must be available for the flightcrew.

C — Oxygen is not required at any altitude in a balloon.

15-49   B11

Which is required equipment for powered aircraft during VFR night flights?

A — Anticollision light system.

B — Gyroscopic direction indicator.

C — Gyroscopic bank-and-pitch indicator.

15-50   B11

Which is required equipment for powered aircraft during VFR night flights?

A — Flashlight with red lens if the flight is for hire.

B — An electric light if the flight is for hire.

C — Sensitive altimeter adjustable for barometric pressure.

15-51   B11

Approved flotation gear, readily available to each occupant, is required on each aircraft if it is being flown for hire over water,

A — more than 50 statute miles from shore.

B — beyond power-off gliding distance from shore.

C — in amphibious aircraft beyond 50 NM from shore.

15-47. Answer C. (FAR 91.211)

No person may operate a civil aircraft of U.S. registry at cabin pressure altitudes above 12,500 feet MSL up to and including 14,000 feet MSL, unless the required minimum flight crew is provided with, and uses, supplemental oxygen for that part of the flight at those altitudes that is more than 30 minutes in duration. Answer (A) incorrectly includes the altitudes between 10,500 and 12,500 feet MSL while excluding the altitudes between 12,500 and 14,000 feet MSL. Answer (B) is wrong because most of this altitude block requires the continuous use of oxygen.

15-48. Answer A. (FAR 91.211)

No person may operate a civil aircraft of U.S. registry at cabin pressure altitudes above 14,000 feet MSL unless the required minimum flight crew uses supplemental oxygen. Above 15,000 each occupant must be provided with supplemental oxygen. Answer (B) is incorrect because oxygen is mandatory for flight crewmembers above 14,000, not 15,000, feet MSL. Answer (C) is incorrect because a balloon is not excluded from oxygen requirements.

15-49. Answer A. (FAR 91.205)

In addition to the instrument and equipment required for day VFR, night VFR also requires position lights, anticollision lights, landing light (only during operations for hire), an adequate source of electrical energy, and a spare set of fuses when applicable. Answers (B) and (C) are incorrect because the gyroscopic instruments are only required for IFR flight.

15-50. Answer B. (FAR 91.205)

In addition to the instrument and equipment required for day VFR, night VFR also requires position lights, anticollision lights, an electric landing light when the flight is operated for hire, an adequate source of electrical energy, and a spare set of fuses when applicable. Answer (A) is not a required item for night VFR. Answer (C) corresponds to the altimeter requirement for IFR flight and is incorrect.

15-51. Answer B. (FAR 91.205b)

If the aircraft is operated for hire over water and beyond power-off gliding distance from shore, approved flotation gear must be readily available to each occupant, and the aircraft must have at least one pyrotechnic signaling device on board. Answer (C) is incorrect because this regulation makes no distinction between amphibious and non-amphibious aircraft.

15-52   **B11**

Approved flotation gear, readily available to each occupant, is required on each airplane if it is being flown for hire over water,

A — more than 50 statute miles from shore.
B — in amphibious aircraft beyond 50 NM from shore.
C — beyond power-off gliding distance from shore.

15-53   **B12**

Which is true with respect to operating limitations of a "restricted" category airplane?

A — A pilot of a "restricted" category airplane is required to hold a commercial pilot certificate.
B — A "restricted" category airplane is limited to an operating radius of 25 miles from its home base.
C — No person may operate a "restricted" category airplane carrying passengers or property for compensation or hire.

15-54   **B12**

Which is true with respect to operating limitations of a "primary" category airplane?

A — A "primary" category airplane is limited to a specified operating radius from its home base.
B — No person may operate a "primary" category airplane carrying passengers or property for compensation or hire.
C — A pilot of a "primary" category airplane must hold a commercial pilot certificate when carrying passengers for compensation or hire.

15-55   **B12**

The carriage of passengers for hire by a commercial pilot is

A — not authorized in a "utility" category aircraft.
B — authorized in "restricted" category aircraft.
C — not authorized in a "limited" category aircraft.

15-56   **B11**

The maximum cumulative time that an emergency locator transmitter may be operated before the rechargeable battery must be recharged is

A — 30 minutes.
B — 45 minutes.
C — 60 minutes.

15-52. Answer C. (FAR 91.205b)
If the aircraft is operated for hire over water and beyond power-off gliding distance from shore, approved flotation gear must be readily available to each occupant, and the aircraft must have at least one pyrotechnic signaling device on board. Answer (B) is incorrect because this regulation makes no distinction between amphibious and non-amphibious aircraft.

15-53. Answer C. (FAR 91.313)
No person may operate a restricted category civil aircraft carrying persons or property for compensation or hire. Answer (A) is incorrect because no minimum certificate is specified by the regulation beyond what is required to operate a nonrestricted aircraft. Answer (B) is incorrect because there are no restrictions on the distance a restricted category aircraft can be operated from its home base.

15-54. Answer B. (FAR 91.325)
No person may operate a primary category civil aircraft carrying persons or property for compensation or hire. Answer (A) is incorrect because there are no restrictions on the distance a primary category aircraft can be operated from its home base. Answer (C) is incorrect because, although a commercial certificate is normally required when carrying passengers for hire, this activity is not authorized in a primary category aircraft.

15-55. Answer C. (FAR 91.313, 91.315)
FAR 91.315 simply states that no person may operate a limited category civil aircraft carrying persons or property for compensation or hire. There are no exceptions mentioned. Answer (A) is incorrect because there are no restrictions preventing the carriage of passengers in utility category aircraft. Answer (B) is incorrect because FAR 91.313 says carrying passenger for hire is NOT authorized in a restricted category aircraft. Special purpose operations allow the carrying of persons or material if necessary to accomplish that operation, and are not considered to be the carriage of persons or property for compensation or hire for the purpose of that regulation. Some of these operations include crop dusting, seeding, spraying, and banner towing.

15-56. Answer C. (FAR 91.207)
Batteries used in the emergency locator transmitter must be replaced or recharged (if appropriate) when the transmitter has been in use more than 1 cumulative hour. Answers (A) and (B) are less than the minimum cumulative time prescribed by the FARs.

15-57   **B07**

No person may operate a large civil aircraft of U.S. registry which is subject to a lease, unless the lessee has mailed a copy of the lease to the FAA Aircraft Registration Branch, Technical Section, Oklahoma City, OK, within how many hours of its execution?

A — 24.
B — 48.
C — 72.

15-58   **B08**

Which is true with respect to formation flights? Formation flights are

A — authorized when carrying passengers for hire with prior arrangement with the pilot in command of each aircraft in the formation.
B — not authorized when visibilities are less than 3 SM.
C — not authorized when carrying passengers for hire.

15-59   **B08**

Which is true with respect to operating near other aircraft in flight? They are

A — not authorized, when operated so close to another aircraft they can create a collision hazard.
B — not authorized, unless the pilot in command of each aircraft is trained and found competent in formation.
C — authorized when carrying passengers for hire, with prior arrangement with the pilot in command of each aircraft in the formation.

15-60   **B08**

Which is true with respect to formation flights? Formation flights are

A — not authorized, except by arrangement with the pilot in command of each aircraft.
B — not authorized, unless the pilot in command of each aircraft is trained and found competent in formation.
C — authorized when carrying passengers for hire, with prior arrangement with the pilot in command of each aircraft in the formation.

15-57. Answer A. (FAR 91.23)

A copy of the lease or contract that complies with the requirements involving a U.S. registered large civil aircraft must be mailed within 24 hours. Answer (B) corresponds more to the requirement for the lessee who is not a citizen of the United States to contact the FSDO prior to the first flight and is incorrect.

15-58. Answer C. (FAR 91.111)

No person may operate an aircraft, carrying passengers for hire, in formation flight. Answer (A) is incorrect because, while pilots must make arrangements with each other to fly formation, it cannot be done when either of the aircraft is carrying passengers for hire. Answer (B) is incorrect because there are no regulations limiting formation flight operations to 3 s.m. visibility or more.

15-59. Answer A. (FAR 91.111)

Regulations on formation flight specifically prohibit operation so close to another aircraft as to create a collision hazard. Although special training for formation flight is a good idea, answer (B) is incorrect because this training is not required by FAA regulations. Answer (C) is incorrect; while it is true pilots must make arrangements with each other to fly formation, it cannot be done when any of the aircraft is carrying passengers for hire.

15-60. Answer A. (FAR 91.111)

Pilots must make prior arrangements with each other to fly formation. Although special training for formation flight is a good idea, answer (B) is incorrect because this training is not required by FAA regulations. Answer (C) is incorrect because formation flight is prohibited when any of the aircraft is carrying passengers for hire.

15-61   B08
While in flight a helicopter and an airplane are converging at a 90° angle, and the helicopter is located to the right of the airplane. Which aircraft has the right-of-way, and why?

A — The helicopter, because it is to the right of the airplane.
B — The helicopter, because helicopters have the right-of-way over airplanes.
C — The airplane, because airplanes have the right-of-way over helicopters.

15-62   B08
Two aircraft of the same category are approaching an airport for the purpose of landing. The right-of-way belongs to the aircraft

A — at the higher altitude.
B — at the lower altitude, but the pilot shall not take advantage of this rule to cut in front of or to overtake the other aircraft.
C — that is more maneuverable, and that aircraft may, with caution, move in front of or overtake the other aircraft.

15-63   B08
During a night operation, the pilot of aircraft #1 sees only the green light of aircraft #2. If the aircraft are converging, which pilot has the right-of-way? The pilot of aircraft

A — #2; aircraft #2 is to the left of aircraft #1.
B — #2; aircraft #2 is to the right of aircraft #1
C — #1; aircraft #1 is to the right of aircraft #2.

15-64   B08
A pilot flying a single-engine airplane observes a multiengine airplane approaching from the left. Which pilot should give way?

A — The pilot of the multiengine airplane should give way; the single-engine airplane is to its right.
B — The pilot of the single-engine airplane should give way; the other airplane is to the left.
C — Each pilot should alter course to the right.

15-61. Answer A. (FAR 91.113)
Because helicopters and airplanes are considered to have the same maneuverability, neither one has the right of way over the other. When two aircraft with the same maneuverability are converging at approximately the same altitude (except head-on, or nearly so) the aircraft to the other's right has the right-of-way. In this case, it is the helicopter that has the right of way because it is on the right. Answers (B) and (C) are incorrect because in terms of the right-of-way rules, airplane and rotorcraft are given the same status for giving way to less maneuverable categories of aircraft.

15-62. Answer B. (FAR 91.113)
When two or more aircraft are approaching an airport for the purpose of landing, the aircraft at the lower altitude has the right-of-way, but it shall not take advantage of this rule to cut in front of another aircraft on final approach, or to overtake that aircraft. Answer (A) is incorrect because the aircraft at the lower (not higher) altitude has the right of way. Answer (C) is incorrect because, generally, the right-of-way rules dictate that the least maneuverable (not most maneuverable) aircraft has the right of way. In addition, the regulation specifically prohibits an aircraft in this situation from overtaking another aircraft on final.

15-63. Answer C. (FAR 91.113)
If aircraft #1 sees only the green light of aircraft #2, it would be looking at the right wingtip. Aircraft #1 has the right-of-way, since it is to the right of aircraft #2.

15-64. Answer A. (FAR 91.113)
When two aircraft of the same category are converging, that is, on intersecting courses, the aircraft to the right has the right of way. Answer (B) is incorrect because it says the aircraft to the left has the right of way. Answer (C) is incorrect because this course of action is appropriate for aircraft approaching head on, not on intersecting courses.

15-65   **B08**

Airplane A is overtaking airplane B. Which airplane has the right-of-way?

A — Airplane B; the pilot should expect to be passed on the left.
B — Airplane B; the pilot should expect to be passed on the right.
C — Airplane A; the pilot should alter course to the right to pass.

15-66   **B08**

An airplane is overtaking a helicopter. Which aircraft has the right-of-way?

A — Helicopter; the pilot should expect to be passed on the right.
B — Airplane; the airplane pilot should alter course to the left to pass.
C — Helicopter; the pilot should expect to be passed on the left.

15-67   **B12**

What is the minimum altitude and flight visibility required for acrobatic flight?

A — 1,500 feet AGL and 3 miles.
B — 2,000 feet MSL and 2 miles.
C — 3,000 feet AGL and 1 mile.

15-68   **B11**

If not equipped with required position lights, an aircraft must terminate flight

A — at sunset.
B — 30 minutes after sunset.
C — 1 hour after sunset.

15-69   **B11**

If an aircraft is not equipped with an electrical or anticollision light system, no person may operate that aircraft

A — after dark.
B — 1 hour after sunset.
C — after sunset to sunrise.

15-70   **B08**

The minimum flight visibility for VFR flight increases to 5 statute miles beginning at an altitude of

A — 14,500 feet MSL.
B — 10,000 feet MSL if above 1,200 feet AGL.
C — 10,000 feet MSL regardless of height above ground.

15-65. Answer B. (FAR 91.113)
When one aircraft is overtaking another, regardless of the categories of each aircraft, the aircraft being overtaken has the right of way over the aircraft that is passing. The faster aircraft should pass on the right. You can immediately eliminate Answer (C) because, in addition to being wrong, it does not make sense; it prescribes evasive action for the aircraft it says has the right of way. Answer (A) incorrectly states that the overtaking aircraft is expected to pass on the left.

15-66. Answer A. (FAR 91.113)
When one aircraft is overtaking another, regardless of the categories of each aircraft, the aircraft being overtaken has the right of way over the aircraft that is passing. The faster aircraft should pass on the right. You can immediately eliminate Answer (B) because, in addition to being wrong, it does not make sense; it prescribes evasive action for the aircraft it says has the right of way. Answer (C) incorrectly states that the overtaking aircraft is expected to pass on the left.

15-67. Answer A. (FAR 91.303)
No person may operate an aircraft in acrobatic flight below an altitude of 1,500 feet above the surface, or when flight visibility is less than three statute miles. Answers (B) and (C) are incorrect since the minimum altitudes are above, and the flight visibilities are below regulation requirements.

15-68. Answer A. (FAR 91.209)
No person may, during the period from sunset to sunrise operate an aircraft unless it has lighted position lights. Answer (B) is incorrect because it corresponds more to the end of evening civil twilight and logging of night flight. Answer (C) corresponds more to the recent flight experience requirements for night operations and is incorrect.

15-69. Answer C. (FAR 91.205, 91.209)
If an aircraft does not have approved position lights, it may not be operated after sunset. The regulation is clear that anticollision lights are required starting at sunset.

15-70. Answer B. (FAR 91.155)
When in airspace above 10,000 feet MSL and more than 1,200 feet above the surface, the visibility is 5 statute miles, regardless of the type of airspace. Answer (A) is incorrect since 14,500 feet MSL corresponds more to the segment of Class E airspace that blankets the 48 contiguous states. Answer (C) is wrong because, when within 1,200 feet above the surface, the visibility is no more than three miles, and if it is Class G airspace during the day, the visibility could be as low as one statute mile.

15-71   **B08**

What is the minimum flight visibility and proximity to cloud requirements for VFR flight, at 6,500 feet MSL, in Class C, D, and E airspace?

A — 1 mile visibility; clear of clouds.

B — 3 miles visibility; 1,000 feet above and 500 feet below.

C — 5 miles visibility; 1,000 feet above and 1,000 feet below.

15-72   **B09**

VFR cruising altitudes are required to be maintained when flying

A — at 3,000 feet or more AGL; based on true course.

B — more than 3,000 feet AGL; based on magnetic course.

C — at 3,000 feet or more above MSL; based on magnetic heading.

15-73   **B10**

Except when necessary for takeoff or landing or unless otherwise authorized by the Administrator, the minimum altitude for IFR flight is

A — 2,000 feet over all terrain.

B — 3,000 feet over designated mountainous terrain; 2,000 feet over terrain elsewhere.

C — 2,000 feet above the highest obstacle over designated mountainous terrain; 1,000 feet above the highest obstacle over terrain elsewhere.

15-74   **B13**

Who is primarily responsible for maintaining an aircraft in an airworthy condition?

A — The lead mechanic responsible for that aircraft.

B — Pilot in command or operator.

C — Owner or operator of the aircraft.

15-75   **B13**

Assuring compliance with an Airworthiness Directive is the responsibility of the

A — pilot in command and the FAA certificated mechanic assigned to that aircraft.

B — pilot in command of that aircraft.

C — owner or operator of that aircraft.

15-71. Answer B. (FAR 91.155)

When flying in Class C, Class D, or Class E airspace below 10,000 feet MSL, visibility must be at least 3 statute miles and the aircraft must maintain at least 1,000 feet above, 500 feet below, and 2,000 feet horizontal cloud separation. Answer (A) is incorrect because 1 mile visibility and clear of clouds is the requirement for operations in Class G airspace when within 1,200 feet of the surface. Answer (C) is incorrect since it corresponds to VFR minimums for Class E airspace when more than 1,200 feet above the surface and at or above 10,000 feet MSL.

15-72. Answer B. (FAR 91.159)

Anytime you fly in level cruising flight above 3,000 feet AGL, you must follow the VFR east/ west cruising altitudes. The VFR cruising altitudes are based on magnetic course. Answer (A) is incorrect because the cruising altitudes are based on magnetic (not true) course. Answer (C) is incorrect because the minimum altitude where you must comply with the VFR cruising rule is based on altitude above the surface (not mean sea level).

15-73. Answer C. (FAR 91.177)

Except when necessary for takeoff or landing, no person may operate an aircraft under IFR below an altitude of 2,000 feet above the highest obstacle within a horizontal distance of 4 nautical miles from the course to be flown in mountainous areas, or in other than mountainous areas, 1,000 feet above the highest obstacle within a horizontal distance of 4 nautical miles from the course to be flown. Answers (A) and (B) are higher than the prescribed minimum altitudes and are incorrect.

15-74. Answer C. (FAR 91.403)

The owner or operator is responsible for maintaining the aircraft in an airworthy condition. The pilot in command is responsible for making sure the airplane is airworthy before flying it.

15-75. Answer C. (FAR 91.403)

Compliance with Airworthiness Directives (FAR Part 39) is a function of maintaining an aircraft in an airworthy condition. Therefore, it is the owner or operator of an aircraft who is primarily responsible for maintaining the aircraft in an airworthy condition. Answers (A) and (B) are incorrect because the pilot in command is only responsible for determining if the aircraft is in an airworthy condition prior to flight. In addition, the mechanic (answer A) is only responsible for the work he or she performed on the aircraft.

15-76   B13

After an annual inspection has been completed and the aircraft has been returned to service, an appropriate notation should be made

A — on the airworthiness certificate.
B — in the aircraft maintenance records.
C — in the FAA-approved flight manual.

15-76. Answer B. (FAR 91.407, 91.409)

According to FAR 91.409 no person may operate an aircraft unless, within the preceding 12 calendar months, it has had an annual inspection in accordance with FAR Part 43. FAR 91.407 states that no person may operate any aircraft following maintenance unless it has been returned to service by an authorized mechanic. FAR Part 43.9 states that each person who maintains, performs preventive maintenance, rebuilds, or alters an aircraft, airframe, aircraft engine, propeller, appliance, or component part shall make an entry in the maintenance record. Since an annual inspection is one of the requirements for maintaining an aircraft, an aircraft maintenance logbook entry is required. Answer (A) is incorrect because an airworthiness certificate may only be amended or modified upon application to the Administrator. Answer (C) is incorrect since an FAA-approved flight manual or pilot's operating handbook does not include maintenance records.

15-77   B13

A standard airworthiness certificate remains in effect as long as the aircraft receives

A — required maintenance and inspections.
B — an annual inspection.
C — an annual inspection and a 100-hour inspection prior to their expiration dates.

15-77. Answer A. (FAR 91.407)

Airworthiness certificates are effective as long as the maintenance, preventive maintenance, and alterations are performed in accordance with Parts 43 and 91. Part 43 requires that an appropriate return to service statement entry is recorded in aircraft maintenance records. Answers (B) and (C) are incorrect because an annual inspection is not valid until the required return to service entries are made in the aircraft maintenance records.

15-78   B13

If an aircraft's operation in flight was substantially affected by an alteration or repair, the aircraft documents must show that it was test flown and approved for return to service by an appropriately-rated pilot prior to being operated

A — under VFR or IFR rules.
B — with passengers aboard.
C — for compensation or hire.

15-78. Answer B. (FAR 91.407)

No person may carry any person in an aircraft that has been maintained, rebuilt, or altered in a manner that may have appreciable changed its flight characteristics or substantially affect its operation in flight until an appropriately rated pilot with at least a private pilot certificate flies the aircraft to make an operational check and logs the flight in the aircraft records. Answer (A) is wrong because a private pilot or better is already authorized to fly the aircraft to make an operational check. Answer (C) is incorrect because regardless of the flight operation, all passengers who are not crewmembers are prohibited until an operational check has been made.

15-79   B13

Which is correct concerning preventive maintenance, when accomplished by a pilot?

A — A record of preventive maintenance is not required.
B — A record of preventive maintenance must be entered in the maintenance records.
C — Records of preventive maintenance must be entered in the FAA-approved flight manual.

15-79. Answer B. (FAR 43.9)

FAR Part 43.9 states that each person who maintains, performs preventive maintenance, rebuilds, or alters and aircraft part shall make an entry in the maintenance record. This includes the pilot if he or she performs preventative maintenance. Answer (A) is incorrect because work performed by a pilot is not exempt from the requirements specified in FAR Part 43. Answer (C) is incorrect because an FAA-approved flight manual or pilot's operating handbook does not include maintenance records.

15-80   **B13**

An aircraft carrying passengers for hire has been on a schedule of inspection every 100 hours of time in service. Under which condition, if any, may that aircraft be operated beyond 100 hours without a new inspection?

A — The aircraft may be flown for any flight as long as the time in service has not exceeded 110 hours.

B — The aircraft may be dispatched for a flight of any duration as long as 100 hours has not been exceeded at the time it departs.

C — The 100-hour limitation may be exceeded by not more than 10 hours if necessary to reach a place at which the inspection can be done.

15-81   **B13**

Which is true concerning required maintenance inspections?

A — A 100-hour inspection may be substituted for an annual inspection.

B — An annual inspection may be substituted for a 100-hour inspection.

C — An annual inspection is required even if a progressive inspection system has been approved.

15-82   **B13**

An ATC transponder is not to be used unless it has been tested, inspected, and found to comply with regulations within the preceding

A — 30 days.
B — 12 calendar months.
C — 24 calendar months.

15-83   **B13**

Aircraft maintenance records must include the current status of the

A — applicable airworthiness certificate.
B — life-limited parts of only the engine and airframe.
C — life-limited parts of each airframe, engine, propeller, rotor, and appliance.

15-80. Answer C. (FAR 91.409)

The 100-hour limitation may be exceeded by not more than 10 hours while enroute to reach a place where the inspection can be done. The excess time used to reach a place where the inspection can be performed must be included in computing the next 100 hours of time in service. Answers (A) and (B) are incorrect because the 100-hour limitation may only be exceeded when the aircraft is enroute to reach a place where the 100-hour inspection can be done.

15-81. Answer B. (FAR 91.409)

No person may operate an aircraft carrying any person (other than required crewmembers) for hire, and no person may give flight instruction for hire in an aircraft which that person provides, unless within the preceding 100 hours of time in service the aircraft has received an annual or 100-hour inspection, and the aircraft has been approved for return to service in accordance with FAR Part 43. Answer (A) is incorrect because an annual inspection may be substituted for a 100-hour, not vice versa. The main difference between the 100-hour and the annual inspection is that a 100-hour can be accomplished and signed off by an A&P mechanic while an IA (an A&P mechanic who has obtained Inspection Authorization) is required to perform an annual inspection. In addition, the requirement to record a specific annual inspection entry is still there. Answer (C) is incorrect because progressive inspection procedures accomplish the same thing as the annual/100-hour inspections but with a different method.

15-82. Answer C. (FAR 91.413)

No person may use an ATC transponder unless within the preceding 24 calendar months, that ATC transponder has been tested and inspected. Answers (A) and (B) are inappropriate in that 30 days applies to VOR checks and 12 calendar months applies to annual inspections for aircraft.

15-83. Answer C. (FAR 91.417)

Aircraft maintenance records must contain the current status of life-limited parts of each airframe, engine, propeller, rotor, and appliance. Answer (A) is incorrect because the records must include the current status of applicable ADs, not the Airworthiness Certificate. Answer (B) is incorrect because the current status must include more than the engine and airframe.

15-84   **B13**

Which is true relating to Airworthiness Directives (AD's)?

A — AD's are advisory in nature and are, generally, not addressed immediately.
B — Noncompliance with AD's renders an aircraft unairworthy.
C — Compliance with AD's is the responsibility of maintenance personnel.

15-85   **B13**

A new maintenance record being used for an aircraft engine rebuilt by the manufacturer must include previous

A — operating hours of the engine.
B — annual inspections performed on the engine.
C — changes as required by Airworthiness Directives.

15-86   **B13**

If an ATC transponder installed in an aircraft has not been tested, inspected, and found to comply with regulations within a specified period, what is the limitation on its use?

A — Its use is not permitted.
B — It may be used when in Class G airspace.
C — It may be used for VFR flight only.

15-87   **B07**

What person is directly responsible for the final authority as to the operation of the airplane?

A — Certificate holder.
B — Pilot in command.
C — Airplane owner/operator.

15-88   **B08**

Operating regulations for U.S.-registered civil airplanes require that during movement on the surface, takeoffs, and landings, a safety belt and shoulder harness (if installed) must be properly secured about each

A — flight crewmember only.
B — person on board.
C — flight and cabin crewmembers.

15-84. Answer B. (FAR 91.403, 91.417)
FAR Part 91.403 states that the owner or operator of an aircraft is primarily responsible for maintaining that aircraft in an airworthy condition and in compliance with Part 39, Airworthiness Directives. Answer (A) is incorrect because ADs are regulatory directives. Answer (C) is incorrect because compliance is the responsibility of the owner or operator.

15-85. Answer C. (FAR 91.421)
Each manufacturer or agency that rebuilds an engine and grants zero time to an engine, shall enter in the new record, each change made as required by airworthiness directives. Answers (A) and (B) are not required in the maintenance record for a rebuilt aircraft engine.

15-86. Answer A. (FAR 91.413)
No person may use an ATC transponder unless it has been tested and inspected within the preceding 24 months. Answers (B) and (C) are incorrect because transponder operation without inspection compliance is not authorized for use in any airspace.

15-87. Answer B. (FAR 91.3)
The pilot in command of an aircraft is directly responsible for, and is the final authority as to, the operation of that aircraft.

15-88. Answer B. (FAR 91.105, 91.107)
Each person must occupy an approved seat or berth with a safety belt and, if installed, shoulder harness, properly secured about him or her during movement on the surface, takeoff, and landing. There are exceptions for children under 2 years of age, and flight crewmembers do not have to wear shoulder harnesses if those harnesses prevent the crew from performing their duties.

15-89   B08

No person may operate an aircraft in simulated instrument flight conditions unless the

A — other control seat is occupied by at least an appropriately rated commercial pilot.
B — pilot has filed an IFR flight plan and received an IFR clearance.
C — other control seat is occupied by a safety pilot, who holds at least a private pilot certificate and is appropriately rated.

15-89. Answer C. (FAR 91.109)
No person may operate a civil aircraft in simulated instrument flight unless the other control seat is occupied by a safety pilot who possesses at least a private pilot certificate with category and class ratings appropriate to the aircraft being flown. The safety pilot must have adequate vision forward and to each side of the aircraft, or a competent observer in the aircraft that adequately supplements the vision of the safety pilot. Answer (A) is incorrect because a commercial pilot certificate is not required of a safety pilot. Answer (B) is incorrect because simulated instrument flights are not required to be conducted under IFR; in practice they are frequently conducted under VFR with simulated clearances in which the controller specifically reminds the pilot to maintain VFR.

15-90   B08

If the minimum safe speed for any particular operation is greater than the maximum speed prescribed in 14 CFR part 91, the

A — operator must have a Memorandum of Agreement (MOA) with the controlling agency.
B — aircraft may be operated at that speed.
C — operator must have a Letter of Agreement with ATC.

15-90. Answer B. (FAR 91.117)
The speed limit is 200 KIAS in most Class C and D airspace, under Class B airspace and in VFR corridors through Class B airspace. It is 250 KIAS elsewhere below 10,000 feet MSL. If the minimum safe speed for your aircraft is higher, then use that speed. Answers (A) and (C) are incorrect because no special authorization is required to operate an aircraft at its minimum safe speed.

15-91   B08

After an ATC clearance has been obtained, a pilot may not deviate from that clearance, unless the pilot

A — requests an amended clearance.
B — is operating VFR on top.
C —receives an amended clearance or has an emergency.

15-91. Answer C. (FAR 91.123)
Even when operating VFR-on-top, you can deviate from a clearance only if you request AND RECEIVE an amended clearance. Exceptions are emergencies and TCAS alerts requiring immediate action.

15-92   B08

When approaching to land at an airport, without an operating control tower, in Class G airspace, the pilot should

A —make all turns to the left, unless otherwise indicated.
B — fly a left-hand traffic pattern at 800 feet AGL.
C — enter and fly a traffic pattern at 800 feet AGL.

15-92. Answer A. (FAR 91.126)
Airplane pilots must make all turns to the left unless the airport displays approved light signals or visual markings indicating that turns should be made to the right, in which case right turns are mandatory. Answers (B) and (C) are incorrect because traffic pattern altitudes are not specified in regulations.

15-93   B08

When weather information indicates that abnormally high barometric pressure exists, or will be above _____ inches of mercury, flight operations will not be authorized contrary to the requirements published in NOTAMs.

A — 32.00
B — 31.00
C — 30.50

15-93. Answer B. (FAR 91.144)
When any information indicates that the barometric pressure on the route of flight currently exceeds or will exceed 31 inches of mercury, no one may operate an aircraft or initiate a flight contrary to any NOTAM published under this section or in violation of requirements established by the Administrator.

15-94   B10

For an airport with an approved instrument approach procedure to be listed as an alternate airport on an IFR flight plan, the forecasted weather conditions at the time of arrival must be at or above the following weather minimums.

A — Ceiling 600 feet and visibility 2 NM for precision.
B — Ceiling 800 feet and visibility 2 SM for nonprecision.
C — Ceiling 800 feet and visibility 2 NM for non-precision.

15-94. Answer B. (FAR 91.169)
The requirement is 600-2 if a precision approach is available, 800-2 for nonprecision approaches, and basic VFR below the MEA if no approaches are available. Answers (A) and (C) incorrectly state visibility in NM.

15-95   B10

For an airport without an approved instrument approach procedure to be listed as an alternate airport on an IFR flight plan, the forecasted weather conditions at the time of arrival must have at least a

A — ceiling of 2,000 feet and visibility 3 SM.
B — ceiling and visibility that allows for a descent, approach, and landing under basic VFR.
C — ceiling of 1,000 feet and visibility 3 NM.

15-95. Answer B. (FAR 91.169)
The requirement is 600-2 if a precision approach is available, 800-2 for nonprecision approaches, and basic VFR below the MEA if no approaches are available. No specific ceiling and visibility is mentioned for airports without published approaches, and it is unlikely the values in Answers (A) and (C) would not meet the requirement for VFR below the MEA at most airports.

15-96   B10

Pilots are not authorized to land an aircraft from an instrument approach unless the

A — flight visibility is at, or exceeds the visibility prescribed in the approach procedure being used.
B — flight visibility and ceiling are at, or exceeds the minimums prescribed in the approach being used.
C — visual approach slope indicator and runway references are distinctly visible to the pilot.

15-96. Answer A. (FAR 91.175)
You must have the required flight visibility, and be able to identify approach lights, runway lights, or one of the other references listed in FAR 91.175. Plus, you must be able to make a normal descent to a landing. Answer (B) is incorrect because regulations do not specify any required ceiling for landing from an approach; only visibility. Keep in mind that if you are in the clouds, you will not have any visibility. Answer (C) is incorrect because these exact items are not required to be distinctly visible; they are part of a list of references, any one of which will meet the requirement if visible.

15-97   B10

On an instrument approach where a DH or MDA is applicable, the pilot may not operate below, or continue the approach unless the

A — aircraft is continuously in a position from which a descent to a normal landing, on the intended runway, can be made.
B — approach and runway lights are distinctly visible to the pilot.
C — flight visibility and ceiling are at, or above, the published minimums for that approach.

15-97. Answer A. (FAR 91.175)
You must have the required flight visibility, and be able to identify approach lights, runway lights, or one of the other references listed in FAR 91.175. Plus, you must be able to make a normal descent to a landing. Answer (B) is incorrect because it says both approach and runway lights must be visible when actually only one of these items OR any one of a number of other items are required to be distinctly visible. Answer (C) is incorrect because regulations do not specify any required ceiling for landing from an approach; only visibility. Keep in mind that if you are in the clouds, you will not have any visibility.

15-98   B10

A pilot performing a published instrument approach is not authorized to perform a procedure turn when

A — receiving a radar vector to a final approach course or fix.
B — maneuvering at minimum safe altitudes.
C — maneuvering at radar vectoring altitudes.

15-98. Answer A. (FAR 91.175)
With radar vectors to a final approach course or fix, a timed approach from a holding fix, or an approach procedure which specifies "NoPT," you may not make a procedure turn unless it is cleared by ATC. Answers (B) and (C) address factors that have nothing to do with whether procedure turns are authorized.

15-99   B10
The pilot in command of an aircraft operated under IFR, in controlled airspace, not in radar contact, shall report by radio as soon as possible when

A — passing FL 180.
B — passing each designated reporting point, to include time and altitude.
C — changing control facilities.

15-100   B10
The pilot in command of an aircraft operated under IFR, in controlled airspace, shall report as soon as practical to ATC when

A — climbing or descending to assigned altitudes.
B — experiencing any malfunctions of navigational, approach, or communications equipment, occurring in flight.
C — requested to contact a new controlling facility.

15-101   B12
No person may operate an aircraft that has an experimental airworthiness certificate

A — under instrument flight rules (IFR).
B — when carrying property for hire.
C — when carrying persons or property for hire.

15-102.   J15
For IFR operations off established airways, ROUTE OF FLIGHT portion of an IFR flight plan should list VOR navigational aids which are no more than

A — 80 miles apart.
B — 70 miles apart.
C — 40 miles apart.

15-99. Answer B. (FAR 91.183)
IFR flights in controlled airspace must continuously monitor the appropriate frequency and, when not in radar contact, report the time and altitude of passing each designated reporting point. In addition, pilots are obligated to report any unforecast weather conditions encountered and any other information relating to the safety of flight. Answer (A) is incorrect because, even though an IFR clearance is required at or above FL 180, regulations do not require reports passing through this altitude, unless it is specifically requested by ATC.

15-100. Answer B. (FAR 91.187)
The pilot in command of each aircraft operated in controlled airspace under IFR shall report as soon as practical to ATC any malfunctions of navigational, approach, or communication equipment occurring in flight. This report shall include the

(1) Aircraft identification;
(2) Equipment affected;
(3) Degree to which the capability of the pilot to operate under IFR in the ATC system is impaired; and
(4) Nature and extent of assistance desired from ATC.
While Answers (A) and (C) reflect standard operating procedures, they are not explicitly listed as required reports in the regulations.

15-101. Answer C. (FAR 91.319)
No person may carry passengers or property for hire in an experimental aircraft. Answer (A) is incorrect because IFR not-for-hire operations can be approved. Answer (B) is obviously incorrect because regulations never prohibit carrying property for hire without also prohibiting carrying persons for hire.

15-102. Answer A. AIM 5-1-7(3),c,3
An operational service volume has been established for each class in which adequate signal coverage and frequency protection can be assured. To facilitate use of VOR, VORTAC, or TACAN aids, consistent with their operational service volume limits, pilot use of such aids for defining a direct route of flight in controlled airspace should not exceed the 80 NM apart when operating off established airways below 18,000 feel MSL.

SECTION D
NTSB 830 — AIRCRAFT ACCIDENT AND INCIDENT REPORTING

Accidents

1. If an aircraft is involved in an accident which results in substantial damage to the aircraft, the nearest NTSB field office must be notified immediately.

2. Aircraft wreckage may be moved prior to the time the NTSB takes custody only to protect the wreckage from further damage.

3. The operator of an aircraft that has been involved in an accident is required to file an accident report within 10 days or after 7 days if an overdue aircraft is still missing.

Incidents Requiring Immediate Notification:

4. In-flight fire

5. Aircraft collide in flight

6. Flight control system malfunction or failure

7. Inability of any required flight crewmember to perform normal flight duties as a result of injury or illness

8. Failure of structural components of a turbine engine excluding compressor and turbine blades and vanes

9. Damage to property, other than the aircraft, estimated to exceed $25,000 for repair (including materials and labor) or fair market value in the event of total loss, whichever is less

10. An overdue aircraft that is believed to be involved in an accident

Notification

11. The operator of an aircraft that has been involved in an incident is required to submit a report to the nearest NTSB field office when requested.

15-103   G10
Notification to the NTSB is required when there has been substantial damage

A — which requires repairs to landing gear.
B — to an engine caused by engine failure in flight.
C — which adversely affects structural strength or flight characteristics.

15-104   G11
NTSB Part 830 requires an immediate notification as a result of which incident?

A — Engine failure for any reason during flight.
B — Damage to the landing gear as a result of a hard landing.
C — Any required flight crewmember being unable to perform flight duties because of illness.

15-103. Answer C. (NTSB 830.2)
"Substantial damage," means damage or failure which adversely affects the structural strength, performance, or flight characteristics of the aircraft, and which would normally require major repair or replacement of the affected component. The definition specifically states that, among other things, engine failure and damage limited to one engine (answer B) or damage to landing gear (answer A) are not considered substantial damage.

15-104. Answer C. (NTSB 830.5)
The operator of an aircraft shall immediately, and by the most expeditious means available, notify the nearest National Transportation Safety Board field office when any required flight crewmember is unable to perform flight duties because of illness. Answers (A) and (B) do not require immediate notification.

15-105   G11
Which incident would require that the nearest NTSB field office be notified immediately?

A — In-flight fire.
B — Ground fire resulting in fire equipment dispatch.
C — Fire of the primary aircraft while in a hanger which results in damage to other property of more than $25,000.

15-106   G11
Which airborne incident would require that the nearest NTSB field office be notified immediately?

A — Cargo compartment door malfunction or failure.
B — Cabin door opened in-flight.
C — Flight control system malfunction or failure.

15-107   G11
During flight, a fire, which was extinguished, burned the insulation from a transceiver wire. What action is required by regulations?

A — No notification or report is required.
B — A report must be filed with the avionics inspector at the nearest FAA Flight Standards District Office within 48 hours.
C — An immediate notification by the operator of the aircraft to the nearest NTSB field office.

15-108   G11
When should notification of an aircraft accident be made to the NTSB if there was substantial damage and no injuries?

A — Immediately.
B — Within 10 days.
C — Within 30 days.

15-109   G13
The operator of an aircraft that has been involved in an incident is required to submit a report to the nearest field office of the NTSB

A — within 7 days.
B — within 10 days.
C — only if requested to do so.

15-110   G13
How many days after an accident is a report required to be filed with the nearest NTSB field office?

A — 2 days.
B — 7 days.
C — 10 days.

15-105. Answer A. (NTSB 830)
The operator of an aircraft shall immediately, and by the most expeditious means available, notify the nearest National Transportation Safety Board field office when an in-flight fire occurs. Answers (B) does not require immediate notification since this fire did not occur during flight. Answer (C) does not require immediate notification because the fire did not occur in flight and damage does not exceed $50,000.

15-106. Answer C. (NTSB 830)
The operator of an aircraft shall immediately, and by the most expeditious means available, notify the nearest National Transportation Safety Board field office when there is a flight control system malfunction or failure. Answers (A) and (B) are not even mentioned in the NTSB regulations.

15-107. Answer C. (NTSB 830.5)
Immediate notification to the nearest NTSB field office is required when a fire in flight occurs.

15-108. Answer A. (NTSB 830.2, 830.5)
NTSB 830.5 specifies that immediate notification is required when an accident occurs. "Aircraft Accident" means an occurrence associated with the operation of an aircraft which takes place between the time any person boards the aircraft with the intention of flight and all such persons have disembarked, and in which the aircraft receives substantial damage. Answer (B), 10 days, is the time limit for filing a formal accident report. Answer (C), 30 days, applies to the definition of fatal injury where death occurs within 30 days of the injury.

15-109. Answer C. (NTSB 830.15)
A report on an incident for which immediate notification is required shall be filed only if requested by an authorized representative of the board. Answer (A) is incorrect because it refers to a mandatory report for overdue and still missing aircraft. Answer (B) refers to a mandatory report for aircraft involved in an accident, not an incident.

15-110. Answer C. (NTSB 830.15)
The operator of an aircraft shall file a report within 10 days after an accident. Answer (B) refers to filing a report for overdue and still missing aircraft and is incorrect.

APPENDIX 1

SUBJECT MATTER KNOWLEDGE CODES

To determine the knowledge area in which a particular question was incorrectly answered, compare the subject matter code(s) on the Federal Aviation Administration Airmen Computer Test Report to the following subject matter outline. The total number of test items missed may differ from the number of subject matter codes shown on the test report, since you may have missed more than one question in a certain subject matter code.

Title 14 of the Code of Federal Regulations (14 CFR) part 1-Definitions and Abbreviations

- A01   General Definitions
- A02   Abbreviations and Symbols

14 CFR part 21-Certification Procedures for Products and Parts

- A100   General
- A102   Type Certificates
- A104   Supplemental Type Certificates
- A108   Airworthiness Certificate
- A110   Approval of Materials, Part, Processes, and Appliances
- A112   Export Airworthiness Approvals
- A114   Approval of Engines, Propellers, Materials, Parts, and Appliances Import
- A117   Technical Standard Order Authorizations

14 CFR part 23-Airworthiness Standards: Normal, Utility, Acrobatic, and Commuter Category Aircraft

- A150   General
- A151   Flight
- A152   Structure
- A153   Design and Construction
- A154   Powerplant
- A155   Equipment
- A157   Operating Limitations and Information
- A159   Appendix G: Instructions for Continued Airworthiness

14 CFR part 27-Airworthiness Standards: Normal Category Rotorcraft

- A250   General
- A253   Flight
- A255   Strength Requirements
- A257   Design and Construction
- A259   Powerplant
- A261   Equipment
- A263   Operating Limitations and Information
- A265   Appendix A: Instructions for Continued Airworthiness

14 CFR part 39-Airworthiness Directives

- A13   General
- A14   Airworthiness Directives

14 CFR part 45-Identification and Registration Marking

- A400   General
- A401   Identification of Aircraft and Related Products
- A402   Nationality and Registration Marks

14 CFR part 61-Certification: Pilots, Flight Instructors, and Ground Instructors

- A20   General
- A21   Aircraft Ratings and Pilot Authorizations
- A22   Student Pilots
- A23   Private Pilots
- A24   Commercial Pilots
- A25   Airline Transport Pilots
- A26   Flight Instructors
- A27   Ground Instructors
- A29   Recreational Pilot

14 CFR part 71-Designation of Class A, Class B, Class C, Class D, and Class E Airspace Areas; Airways; Routes; and Reporting Points

- A60   General-Class A Airspace
- A61   Class B Airspace
- A64   Class C Airspace
- A65   Class D Airspace
- A66   Class E Airspace

14 CFR part 91-General Operating and Flight Rules

B07   General
B08   Flight Rules-General
B09   Visual Flight Rules
B10   Instrument Flight Rules
B11   Equipment, Instrument, and Certificate Requirements
B12   Special Flight Operations
B13   Maintenance, Preventive Maintenance, and Alterations
B14   Large and Turbine-powered Multiengine Airplanes
B15   Additional Equipment and Operating Requirements for Large and Transport Category Aircraft
B16   Appendix A-Category II Operations: Manual, Instruments, Equipment, and Maintenance
B17   Foreign Aircraft Operations and Operations of U.S.-Registered Civil Aircraft Outside of the U.S.

14 CFR part 97-Standard Instrument Approach Procedures

B97   General

14 CFR part 105-Parachute Jumping

C01   General
C02   Operating Rules
C03   Parachute Equipment

14 CFR part 119-Certification: Air Carriers and Commercial Operators

C20   General
C21   Applicability of Operating Requirements to Different Kinds of Operations Under Parts 121, 125, and 135
C22   Certification, Operations Specifications, and Certain Other Requirements for Operations Conducted Under Parts 121 or 135

14 CFR part 121-Operating Requirements: Domestic, Flag, and Supplemental Operations

D01   General
D02   Certification Rules for Domestic and Flag Air Carriers
D03   Certification Rules for Supplemental Air Carriers and Commercial Operators
D04   Rules Governing all Certificate Holders Under This Part
D05   Approval of Routes: Domestic and Flag Air Carriers
D06   Approval of Areas and Routes for Supplemental Air Carriers and Commercial Operators
D07   Manual Requirements
D08   Aircraft Requirements
D09   Airplane Performance Operating Limitations
D10   Special Airworthiness Requirements
D11   Instrument and Equipment Requirements
D12   Maintenance, Preventive Maintenance, and Alterations
D13   Airman and Crewmember Requirements
D14   Training Program
D15   Crewmember Qualifications
D16   Aircraft Dispatcher Qualifications and Duty Time Limitations: Domestic and Flag Air Carriers
D17   Flight Time Limitations and Rest Requirements: Domestic Air Carriers
D18   Flight Time Limitations: Flag Air Carriers
D19   Flight Time Limitations: Supplemental Air Carriers and Commercial Operators
D20   Flight Operations
D21   Dispatching and Flight Release Rules
D22   Records and Reports
D23   Crewmember Certificate: International
D24   Special Federal Aviation Regulation SFAR No. 14

NTSB 830-Rules Pertaining to the Notification and Reporting of Aircraft Accidents or Incidents and Overdue Aircraft, and Preservation of Aircraft Wreckage, Mail, Cargo, and Records

G10   General
G11   Initial Notification of Aircraft Accidents, Incidents, and Overdue Aircraft
G12   Preservation of Aircraft Wreckage, Mail, Cargo, and Records
G13   Reporting of Aircraft Accidents, Incidents, and Overdue Aircraft

AC 61-13-Basic Helicopter Handbook

H70   General Aerodynamics
H71   Aerodynamics of Flight
H72   Loads and Load Factors
H73   Function of the Controls
H74   Other Helicopter Components and Their Functions
H75   Introduction to the Helicopter Flight Manual
H76   Weight and Balance
H77   Helicopter Performance
H78   Some Hazards of Helicopter Flight
H79   Precautionary Measures and Critical Conditions

H80   Helicopter Flight Maneuvers
H81   Confined Area, Pinnacle, and Ridgeline Operations
H82   Glossary

FAA-H-8083-1-Aircraft Weight and Balance Handbook

H100   Why is Weight and Balance Important?
H101   Weight Control
H102   Effects of Weight
H103   Weight Changes
H104   Stability and Balance Control
H105   Weight and Balance Theory
H106   Weight and Balance Documents
H107   Requirements
H108   Equipment for Weighing
H109   Preparation for Weighing
H110   Determining the Center of Gravity
H111   Empty-Weight Center of Gravity Formulas
H112   Determining the Loaded Weight and CG
H113   Multiengine Airplane Weight and Balance Computations
H114   Determining the Loaded CG
H115   Equipment List
H116   Weight and Balance Revision Record
H117   Weight Changes Caused by a Repair or Alteration
H118   Empty-Weight CG Range
H119   Adverse-Loaded CG Checks
H120   Ballast
H121   Weighing Requirements
H122   Locating and Monitoring Weight and CG Location
H123   Determining the Correct Stabilizer Trim Setting
H124   Determining CG Changes Caused by Modifying the Cargo
H125   Determining Cargo Pallet Loads with Regard to Floor Loading Limits
H126   Determining the Maximum Amount of Payload That Can Be carried
H127   Determining the Landing Weight
H128   Determining the Minutes of Fuel Dump Time
H129   Weight and Balance of Commuter Category Airplanes
H130   Determining the Loaded CG of a Helicopter
H131   Using an Electronic Calculator to Solve Weight and Balance Problems
H132   Using an E6-B Flight Computer to Solve Weight and Balance Problems
H133   Using a Dedicated Electronic Computer to Solve Weight and Balance Problems
H134   Typical Weight and Balance Problems
H135   Glossary

FAA-H-8083-9-Aviation Instructor Handbook

H200   Learning Theory
H201   Definition of Learning
H202   Characteristics of Learning
H203   Principles of Learning
H204   Level of Learning
H205   Learning Physical Skills
H206   Memory
H207   Transfer of Learning
H208   Control of Human Behavior
H210   Human Needs
H211   Defense Mechanisms
H212   The Flight Instructor as a Practical Psychologists
H213   Basic Elements
H214   Barriers of Effective Communication
H215   Developing Communications Skills
H216   Preparation
H217   Presentation
H218   Application
H219   Review and Evaluation
H220   Organizing Material
H221   Lecture Method
H222   Cooperative or Group Learning Method
H223   Guided Discussion Method
H224   Demonstration-Performance Method
H225   Computer-Based Training Method
H226   The Instructor as a Critic
H227   Evaluation
H228   Instructional Aid Theory
H229   Reasons for Use of Instructional Aids
H230   Guidelines for Use of Instructional Aids
H231   Types of Instructional Aids
H232   Test Preparation Material
H233   Aviation Instructor Responsibilities
H234   Flight Instructor Responsibilities
H235   Professionalism
H236   The Telling-and-Doing Technique
H237   Integrated Flight Instruction
H238   Obstacles to Learning During Flight Instruction
H239   Positive Exchange of Flight Controls
H240   Use of Distractions
H241   Aeronautical Decision Making
H242   Factors Affecting Decision Making
H243   Operational Pitfalls
H244   Evaluating Student Decision Making
H245   Course of Training
H246   Blocks of Learning
H247   Training Syllabus
H248   Lesson Plans
H249   Growth and Development
H250   Sources of Material
H251   Appendix A-Sample Test Items
H252   Appendix B-Instructor Endorsements
H253   Glossary

AC 61-23-Pilot's Handbook of Aeronautical Knowledge

H300   Forces Acting on the Airplane in Flight
H301   Turning Tendency (Torque Effect)
H302   Airplane Stability
H303   Loads and Load Factors
H304   Airplane Structure
H305   Flight Control Systems
H306   Electrical System
H307   Engine Operation
H308   Propeller
H309   Starting the Engine
H310   Exhaust Gas Temperature Gauge
H311   Aircraft Documents, Maintenance, and Inspections
H312   The Pitot-Static System and Associated Instruments
H313   Gyroscopic Flight Instruments
H314   Magnetic Compass
H315   Weight Control
H316   Balance, Stability, and Center of Gravity
H317   Airplane Performance
H318   Observations
H319   Service Outlets
H320   Weather Briefings
H321   Nature of the Atmosphere
H322   The Cause of Atmospheric Circulation
H323   Moisture and Temperature
H324   Air Masses and Fronts
H325   Aviation Weather Reports, Forecasts, and Weather Charts
H326   Types of Airports
H327   Sources for Airport Data
H328   Airport Markings and Signs
H329   Airport Lighting
H330   Wind Direction Indicators
H331   Radio Communications
H332   Air Traffic Services
H333   Wake Turbulence
H334   Collision Avoidance
H335   Controlled Airspace
H336   Uncontrolled Airspace
H337   Special Use Airspace
H338   Other Airspace Areas
H339   Aeronautical Charts
H340   Latitude and Longitude
H341   Effect of Wind
H342   Basic Calculations
H343   Pilotage
H344   Dead Reckoning
H345   Flight Planning
H346   Charting the Course
H347   Filing a VFR Flight Plan
H348   Radio Navigation
H349   Obtaining a Medical Certificate
H350   Health Factors Affecting Pilot Performance
H351   Environmental Factors which Affect Pilot Performance

FAA-H-8083-11 Balloon Flying Handbook

H400   History
H401   Physics
H402   Basic Balloon Terms
H403   Balloon Components
H404   Support Equipment
H405   Choosing a Balloon
H406   Flight Planning
H407   Preflight Operations
H408   Checklists
H409   Crew
H410   Chase
H411   Inflation
H412   Launch
H413   Approach to Landing
H414   Landing
H415   Standard Burn
H416   Level Flight
H417   Use of Instruments
H418   Ascents and Descents
H419   Maneuvering
H420   Winds Above
H421   Winds Below
H422   Contour Flying
H423   Radio Communications
H424   Deflation
H425   Preparing for Pack-up
H426   Legal Considerations
H427   Propane Management and Fueling
H428   Tethering
H429   Emergency Procedures
H430   Regulations
H431   Maintenance
H432   Earning a Pilot Certificate
H433   Practical Test Standards
H434   Skill Development
H435   What is a Good Instructor
H436   Aeronautical Decision Making
H437   Types of Decisions
H438   Effectiveness of ADM
H439   Glossary

FAA-H-8083-3-Airplane Flying Handbook

H501   Choosing a Flight School
H502   Instructor/Student Relationship
H503   Role of the FAA
H504   Flight Standards District Offices (FSDO's)
H505   Study Habits
H506   Study Materials
H507   Collision Avoidance
H509   Pilot Assessment
H510   Preflight Preparation and Flight Planning
H511   Airplane Preflight Inspection
H512   Minimum Equipment Lists (MEL's) and Operations with Inoperative Equipment
H513   Cockpit Management

H514 Use of Checklists
H515 Ground Operations
H516 Taxiing
H517 Taxi Clearances at Airports with an
      Operating Control Tower
H518 Before Takeoff Check
H519 After-landing
H520 Postflight
H522 Terms and Definitions
H523 Prior to Takeoff
H524 Normal Takeoff
H525 Crosswind Takeoff
H526 Short-field Takeoff and Climb
H527 Soft-field Takeoff and Climb
H528 Rejected Takeoff
H529 Noise Abatement
H531 Integrated Flight Instruction
H532 Attitude Flying
H533 Straight-and-level Flight
H534 Turns
H535 Climbs
H536 Descents
H538 Slow Flight
H539 Stalls
H540 Spins
H541 Spin Procedures
H542 Aircraft Limitations
H543 Weight and Balance Requirements
H545 Maneuvering by Reference to Ground
      Objects
H546 Performance Maneuvers
H548 Airport Traffic Patterns and Operations
H549 Normal Approach and Landing
H550 Crosswind Approach and Landing
H551 Short-field Approach and Landing
H552 Soft-field Approach and Landing
H553 Power-off Accuracy Approaches
H554 Faulty Approaches and Landings
H555 Final Approaches
H556 Roundout (Flare)
H557 Touchdown
H559 Basic Instrument Training
H560 Basic Instrument Flight
H561 Use of Navigation Systems
H562 Use of Radar Services
H564 Night Vision
H565 Night Illusions
H566 Pilot Equipment
H567 Airplane Equipment and Lighting
H568 Airport and Navigation Lighting Aids
H569 Preparation and Preflight
H570 Starting, Taxiing, and Runup
H571 Takeoff and Climb
H572 Orientation and Navigation
H573 Approaches and Landings
H574 Night Emergencies
H576 VOR Navigation
H577 VOR/DME RNAV

H578 LORAN-C Navigation
H579 Global Positioning System (GPS)
H580 Radar Services
H582 Systems and Equipment Malfunctions
H583 Emergency Approaches and Landings
      (Actual)
H585 Airplane Systems
H586 Pressurized Airplanes
H587 Oxygen Systems
H588 Physiological Altitude Limits
H589 Regulatory Requirements
H591 Multiengine Performance Characteristics
H592 The Critical Engine
H593 Vmc for Certification
H594 Performance
H595 Factors in Takeoff Planning
H596 Accelerates/Stop Distance
H597 Propeller Feathering
H598 Use of Trim Tabs
H599 Preflight Preparation
H600 Checklist
H601 Taxiing
H602 Normal Takeoffs
H603 Crosswind Takeoffs
H604 Short-field or Obstacle Clearance Takeoff
H605 Stalls
H606 Emergency Descent
H607 Approaches and Landings
H608 Crosswind Landings
H609 Short-field Landing
H610 Go-around Procedure
H611 Engine Inoperative Emergencies
H612 Engine Inoperative Procedures
H613 Vmc Demonstrations
H614 Engine Failure Before Lift-off (Rejected
      Takeoff)
H615 Engine Failure After Lift-off
H616 Engine Failure En Route
H617 Engine Inoperative Approach and Landing
H618 Types of Decisions
H619 Effectiveness of ADM

Understanding the Gyroplane -The Abbott Co.

H650 Magic of Rotor Blades
H651 Behind the Power Curve
H652 Beating P.I.O.

FAA-H-8083-21-Rotorcraft Flying Handbook

H700 Glossary
Helicopter
H701 Introduction to the Helicopter
H702 General Aerodynamics
H703 Aerodynamics of Flight
H704 Autorotation
H705 Helicopter Flight Controls
H706 Helicopter Systems

H707 Engines
H708 Transmission System
H709 Main Rotor System
H710 Fuel Systems
H711 Electrical Systems
H712 Hydraulics
H713 Stability Augmentations Systems
H714 Autopilot
H715 Environmental Systems
H716 Anti-Icing Systems
H717 Rotorcraft Flight Manual
H718 Operating Limitations
H719 Weight and Balance
H720 Performance
H721 Performance Charts
H722 Basic Flight Maneuvers
H723 Minimum Equipment Lists
H724 Rotor Safety Considerations
H725 Vertical Takeoff to a Hover
H726 Hovering
H727 Taxiing
H728 Turns
H729 Normal Takeoff
H730 Ground Reference Maneuvers
H731 Traffic Patterns
H732 Approaches
H733 Go-Around
H734 Noise Abatement Procedures
H735 Advance Flight Maneuvers
H736 Reconnaissance Procedures
H737 Maximum Performance Takeoff
H738 Running/Rolling Takeoff
H739 Rapid Deceleration (Quick Stop)
H740 Steep Approach to a Hover
H741 Shallow Approach and Running/Roll-On
      Landing
H742 Slope Operations
H743 Confined Area Operations
H744 Pinnacle and Ridgeline Operations
H745 Helicopter Emergencies
H746 Autorotation
H747 Height/Velocity Diagram
H748 Retreating Blade Stall
H749 Ground Resonance
H750 Dynamic Rollover
H751 Low G Conditions and Mast Bumping
H752 Low Rotor RPM and Blade Stall
H753 Recovery From Low Rotor RPM
H754 Systems Flight Diversion Malfunctions
H755 Lost Procedures
H756 Emergency Equipment and Survival Gear
H757 Attitude Instrument Flying
H758 Flight Instruments
H759 Night Operations
H760 Aeronautical Decision Making

Gyroplanes

H761 Introduction to the Gyroplane
H762 Aerodynamics of the Gyroplane

H763 Autorotations
H764 Rotor Disc Regions
H765 Retreating Blade Stall
H766 Rotor Force
H767 Stability
H768 Horizontal Stabilizer
H769 Propeller Thrust Line
H770 Gyroplane Flight Controls
H771 Cyclic Control
H772 Gyroplanes Systems
H773 Semirigid Rotor Systems
H774 Fully Articulated Rotor System
H775 Prerotator
H776 Rotorcraft Flight Manual
H777 Weight and Balance
H778 Performance
H779 Height/Velocity Diagram
H780 Gyroplane Flight Operations
H781 Taxi
H782 Blade Flap
H783 Takeoff
H784 Jump Takeoff
H785 Basic Flight Maneuvers
H786 Ground Reference Maneuvers
H787 Flight at Slow Airspeeds
H788 High Rate of Descent
H789 Landings/Crosswind
H790 Go Around
H791 Gyroplane Emergencies
H792 Aborted Takeoff
H793 Lift-Off at Low Airspeed and High Angle of
      Attack
H794 Pilot-Induced Oscillation (PIO)
H795 Buntover (Power Pushover)
H796 Ground Reference
H797 Emergency Approach and Landing
H798 Aeronautical Decision Making

FAA-H-8083-15 - Instrument Flying Handbook

Human Factors
H800 Sensory Systems
H801 Spatial Disorientation
H802 Optical Illusions
H803 Physiological and Psychological Factors
H804 Medical Factors
H805 Aeronautical Decision Making
H806 Crew/Cockpit Resource Management
Aerodynamics
H807 Basic Aerodynamics
Flight Instruments
H808 Pitot Static
H809 Compass
H810 Gyroscopic
H811 Flight Director
H812 Systems Preflight
Airplane Attitude Instrument Flying
H813 Fundamental Skills

Airplane Basic Flight Maneuvers
H814 Straight-and-level Flight
H815 Straight Climbs and Descents
H816 Turns
H817 Approach to Stall
H818 Unusual Attitude Recoveries
H819 Instrument Takeoff
H820 Instrument Flight Patterns
Helicopter Attitude Instrument Flying
H821 Instrument Flight
H822 Straight-and-level
H823 Straight Climbs
H824 Straight Descents
H825 Turns
H826 Unusual Attitude Recoveries
H827 Emergencies
H828 Instrument Takeoff
Navigation Systems
H829 Basic Radio Principals
H830 Nondirectional Beacon (NDB)
H831 Very High Frequency Omnidirectional
       Range (VOR)
H832 Distance Measuring Equipment (DME)
H833 Area Navigation (RNAV)
H834 Long Range Navigation (LORAN)
H835 Global Positioning System (GPS)
H836 Inertia Navigation System (INS)
H837 Instrument Landing System (ILS)
H838 Microwave Landing System (MLS)
H839 Flight Management Systems (FMS)
H840 Head-up Display (HUD)
H841 Radar Navigation (Ground Based)
National Airspace System
H842 IFR Enroute Charts
H843 U.S. Terminal Procedures Publications
H844 Instrument Approach Procedures
Air Traffic Control Systems
H845 Communications Equipment
H846 Communications Procedures
H847 Communications Facilities
IFR Flight
H848 Planning
H849 Clearances
H850 Departures
H851 Enroute
H852 Holding
H853 Arrival
H854 Approaches
H855 Flying Experience
H856 Weather Conditions
H857 Conducting an IFR Flight
Emergency Operations
H858 Unforecast Adverse Weather
H859 Aircraft System Malfunction
H860 Communication/Navigation System
       Malfunction
H861 Loss of Situational Awareness
Glossary
H862 Glossary

Gyroplane Flight Training Manual-Jean-Pierre Harrison

H660 General Aerodynamics
H661 Aerodynamics of Flight
H662 Rotor RPM During Autorotations
H663 Function of the Controls
H664 Some Hazards of Gyroplane Flight
H665 Precautionary Measures and Critical
       Conditions
H666 Gyroplane Flight Maneuvers

AC 61-27-Instrument Flying Handbook

I01 Training Considerations
I02 Instrument Flying: Coping with Illusions in
      Flight
I03 Aerodynamic Factors Related to
      Instrument Flying
I04 Basic Flight Instruments
I05 Attitude Instrument Flying-Airplanes
I06 Attitude Instrument Flying-Helicopters
I07 Electronic Aids to Instrument Flying
I08 Using the Navigation Instruments
I09 Radio Communications Facilities and
      Equipment
I10 The Federal Airways System and
      Controlled Airspace
I11 Air Traffic Control
I12 ATC Operations and Procedures
I13 Flight Planning
I14 Appendix: Instrument Instructor Lesson
      Guide-Airplanes
I15 Segment of En Route Low Altitude Chart

AC 00-6-Aviation Weather

I20 The Earth's Atmosphere
I21 Temperature
I22 Atmospheric Pressure and Altimetry
I23 Wind
I24 Moisture, Cloud Formation, and
      Precipitation
I25 Stable and Unstable Air
I26 Clouds
I27 Air Masses and Fronts
I28 Turbulence
I29 Icing
I30 Thunderstorms
I31 Common IFR Producers
I32 High Altitude Weather
I33 Arctic Weather
I34 Tropical Weather
I35 Soaring Weather
I36 Glossary of Weather Terms

AC 00-45-Aviation Weather Services

I54   The Aviation Weather Service Program
I55   Aviation Routine Weather Report (METAR)
I56   Pilot and Radar Reports, Satellite Pictures, and Radiosonde Additional Data (RADATs)
I57   Aviation Weather Forecasts
I58   Surface Analysis Chart
I59   Weather Depiction Chart
I60   Radar Summary Chart
I61   Constant Pressure Analysis Charts
I62   Composite Moisture Stability Chart
I63   Winds and Temperatures Aloft Chart
I64   Significant Weather Prognostic Charts
I65   Convective Outlook Chart
I66   Volcanic Ash Advisory Center Products
I67   Turbulence Locations, Conversion and Density Altitude Tables, Contractions and Acronyms, Station Identifiers, WSR-88D Sites, and Internet Addresses

AIM-Aeronautical Information Manual

J01   Air Navigation Radio Aids
J02   Radar Services and Procedures
J03   Airport Lighting Aids
J04   Air Navigation and Obstruction Lighting
J05   Airport Marking Aids and Signs
J06   Airspace-General
J07   Class G Airspace
J08   Controlled Airspace
J09   Special Use Airspace
J10   Other Airspace Areas
J11   Service Available to Pilots
J12   Radio Communications Phraseology and Techniques
J13   Airport Operations
J14   ATC Clearance/Separations
J15   Preflight
J16   Departure Procedures
J17   En Route Procedures
J18   Arrival Procedures
J19   Pilot/Controller Roles and Responsibilities
J20   National Security and Interception Procedures
J21   Emergency Procedures-General
J22   Emergency Services Available to Pilots
J23   Distress and Urgency Procedures
J24   Two-Way Radio Communications Failure
J25   Meteorology
J26   Altimeter Setting Procedures
J27   Wake Turbulence
J28   Bird Hazards, and Flight Over National Refuges, Parks, and Forests
J29   Potential Flight Hazards
J30   Safety, Accident, and Hazard Reports

J31   Fitness for Flight
J32   Type of Charts Available
J33   Pilot Controller Glossary

Other Documents

J34   Airport/Facility Directory
J35   En Route Low Altitude Chart
J36   En Route High Altitude Chart
J37   Sectional Chart
J39   Terminal Area Chart
J40   Instrument Departure Procedure Chart
J41   Standard Terminal Arrival (STAR) Chart
J42   Instrument Approach Procedures
J43   Helicopter Route Chart

ADDITIONAL ADVISORY CIRCULARS

K01   AC 00-24, Thunderstorms
K02   AC 00-30, Atmospheric Turbulence Avoidance
K03   AC 00-34, Aircraft Ground Handling and Servicing
K04   AC 00-54, Pilot Wind Shear Guide
K05   AC 00-55, Announcement of Availability: FAA Order 8130.21A
K06   AC 43-4, Corrosion Control for Aircraft
K11   AC 20-34, Prevention of Retractable Landing Gear Failures
K12   AC 20-32, Carbon Monoxide (CO) Contamination in Aircraft-Detection and Prevention
K13   AC 20-43, Aircraft Fuel Control
K20   AC 20-103, Aircraft Engine Crankshaft Failure
K23   AC 20-121, Airworthiness Approval of Airborne Loran-C Navigation Systems for Use in the U.S. National Airspace System
K26   AC 20-138, Airworthiness Approval of Global Positioning System (GPS) Navigation Equipment for Use as a VFR and IFR Supplemental Navigation System
K40   AC 25-4, Inertial Navigation Systems (INS)
K45   AC 39-7, Airworthiness Directives
K46   AC 43-9, Maintenance Records
K47   AC 43.9-1, Instructions for Completion of FAA Form 337
K48   AC 43-11, Reciprocating Engine Overhaul Terminology and Standards
K49   AC 43.13-1, Acceptable Methods, Techniques, and Practices-Aircraft Inspection and Repair
K50   AC 43.13-2, Acceptable Methods, Techniques, and Practices-Aircraft Alterations
K80   AC 60-4, Pilot's Spatial Disorientation
L05   AC 60-22, Aeronautical Decision Making
L10   AC 61-67, Stall Spin Awareness Training

L15 AC 61-107, Operations of Aircraft at Altitudes Above 25,000 Feet MSL and/or MACH numbers (Mmo) Greater Than .75

L25 FAA-G-8082-11, Inspection Authorization Knowledge Test Guide

L34 AC 90-48, Pilots' Role in Collision Avoidance

L42 AC 90-87, Helicopter Dynamic Rollover

L44 AC 90-94, Guidelines for Using Global Positioning System Equipment for IFR En Route and Terminal Operations and for Nonprecision Instrument Approaches in the U.S. National Airspace System

L45 AC 90-95, Unanticipated Right Yaw in Helicopters

L50 AC 91-6, Water, Slush, and Snow on the Runway

L52 AC 91-13, Cold Weather Operation of Aircraft

L53 AC 91-14, Altimeter Setting Sources

L57 AC 91-43, Unreliable Airspeed Indications

L59 AC 91-46, Gyroscopic Instruments-Good Operating Practices

L61 AC 91-50, Importance of Transponder Operation and Altitude Reporting

L62 AC 91-51, Effect of Icing on Aircraft Control and Airplane Deice and Anti-Ice Systems

L70 AC 91-67, Minimum Equipment Requirements for General Aviation Operations Under FAR Part 91

L80 AC 103-4, Hazard Associated with Sublimation of Solid Carbon Dioxide (Dry Ice) Aboard Aircraft

L90 AC 105-2, Sport Parachute Jumping

M01 AC 120-12, Private Carriage Versus Common Carriage of Persons or Property

M02 AC 120-27, Aircraft Weight and Balance Control

M08 AC 120-58, Pilot Guide for Large Aircraft Ground Deicing

M13 AC 121-195-1, Operational Landing Distances for Wet Runways; Transport Category Airplanes

M35 AC 135-17, Pilot Guide — Small Aircraft Ground Deicing

M51 AC 20-117, Hazards Following Ground Deicing and Ground Operations in Conditions Conducive to Aircraft Icing

M52 AC 00-2, Advisory Circular Checklist

Soaring Flight Manual — Jeppesen Sanderson, Inc.

N20 Sailplane Aerodynamics

N21 Performance Considerations

N22 Flight Instruments

N23 Weather for Soaring

N24 Medical Factors

N25 Flight Publications and Airspace

N26 Aeronautical Charts and Navigation

N27 Computations for Soaring

N28 Personal Equipment

N29 Preflight and Ground Operations

N30 Aerotow Launch Procedures

N31 Ground Launch Procedures

N32 Basic Flight Maneuvers and Traffic

N33 Soaring Techniques

N34 Cross-Country Soaring

Flight Instructor Manual-Balloon Federation of America

O10 Flight Instruction Aids

O11 Human Behavior and Pilot Proficiency

O12 The Flight Check and the Designated Examiner

Balloon Digest-Balloon Federation of America

O150 Balloon-Theory and Practice

O155 Structure of the Modern Balloon

O160 Lift-off to Landing

O165 Weather for the Balloonist

O170 Propane and Fuel Management

O171 Chemical and Physical Properties

O172 Tanks

O173 Burners

O174 Hoses

O175 Refueling

O176 Fuel Contamination

O177 Heat Tapes (Coils)

O178 Nitrogen Pressurization

O179 Repairs and Maintenance

Powerline Excerpts-Balloon Federation of America

O30 Excerpts

Balloon Ground School-Balloon Publishing Co.

O220 Balloon Operations

How To Fly A Balloon-Balloon Publishing Co.

O250 Basic Terminology

O251 History

O252 Physics

O253 Equipment

O254 Checklists

O255 Flight Planning

O256 Preflight Operations

O257 The Standard Burn

O258 Inflation

O259 Launch

O260 Level Flight

O261 Ascents and Descents

O262 Contour Flying

O263 Maneuvering
O264 Approach to Landing
O265 Landings
O266 Deflation
O267 The Chase
O268 Landowners Relations
O269 Recovery and Pack-up
O270 Propane: Management and Fueling
O271 Tethering
O272 Emergency Procedures
O273 Skill Development
O274 Crew
O275 What is a Good Instructor
O276 Regulations
O277 Maintenance
O278 Earning a Pilot Certificate
O279 Radio Communications
O280 Appendix 1: Glossary

Goodyear Airship Operations Manual

P01 Buoyancy
P02 Aerodynamics
P03 Free Ballooning
P04 Aerostatics
P05 Envelope
P06 Car
P07 Powerplant
P08 Airship Ground Handling
P11 Operating Instructions
P12 History
P13 Training

The Parachute Manual-Para Publishing

P31 Regulations
P32 The Parachute Rigger Certificate
P33 The Parachute Loft
P34 Parachute Materials
P35 Personnel Parachute Assemblies
P36 Parachute Component Parts
P37 Maintenance, Alteration, and
      Manufacturing Procedures
P38 Design and Construction
P39 Parachute Inspecting and Packing
P40 Glossary/Index

The Parachute Manual, Vol. II-Para Publishing

P51 Parachute Regulations
P52 The Parachute Rigger's Certificate
P53 The Parachute Loft
P54 Parachute Materials
P55 Personnel Parachute Assemblies
P56 Parachute Component Parts
P57 Maintenance, Alteration, and
      Manufacturing
P58 Parachute Design and Construction

P59 Parachute Inspection and Packing
P60 Appendix
P61 Conversion Tables
P62 Product/Manufacturer — Index
P63 Name and Manufacture — Index
P64 Glossary-Index

FAA Accident Prevention Program Bulletins

V01 FAA-P-8740-2, Density Altitude
V02 FAA-P-8740-5, Weight and Balance
V03 FAA-P-8740-12, Thunderstorms
V04 FAA-P-8740-19, Flying Light Twins Safely
V05 FAA-P-8740-23, Planning your Takeoff
V06 FAA-P-8740-24, Tips on Winter Flying
V07 FAA-P-8740-25, Always Leave Yourself
      an Out
V08 FAA-P-8740-30, How to Obtain a Good
      Weather Briefing
V09 FAA-P-8740-40, Wind Shear
V10 FAA-P-8740-41, Medical Facts for Pilots
V11 FAA-P-8740-44, Impossible Turns
V12 FAA-P-8740-48, On Landings, Part I
V13 FAA-P-8740-49, On Landings, Part II
V14 FAA-P-8740-50, On Landings, Part III
V15 FAA-P-8740-51, How to Avoid a Midair
      Collision
V16 FAA-P-8740-52, The Silent Emergency

FTP-Flight Theory for Pilots-Jeppesen Sanderson, Inc.

W01 Introduction
W02 Air Flow and Airspeed Measurement
W03 Aerodynamic Forces on Airfoils
W04 Lift and Stall
W05 Drag
W06 Jet Aircraft Basic Performance
W07 Jet Aircraft Applied Performance
W08 Prop Aircraft Basic Performance
W09 Prop Aircraft Applied Performance
W10 Helicopter Aerodynamics
W11 Hazards of Low Speed Flight
W12 Takeoff Performance
W13 Landing Performance
W14 Maneuvering Performance
W15 Longitudinal Stability and Control
W16 Directional and Lateral Stability and Control
W17 High Speed Flight

Fly the Wing-Iowa State University Press/Ames, Second Edition

X01 Basic Aerodynamics
X02 High-Speed Aerodynamics
X03 High-Altitude Machs
X04 Approach Speed Control and Target
      Landings

X05   Preparation for Flight Training
X06   Basic Instrument Scan
X07   Takeoffs
X08   Rejected Takeoffs
X09   Climb, Cruise, and Descent
X10   Steep Turns
X11   Stalls
X12   Unusual Attitudes
X14   Maneuvers At Minimum Speed
X15   Landings: Approach Technique and
         Performance
X16   ILS Approaches
X17   Missed Approaches and Rejected Landings
X18   Category II and III Approaches
X19   Nonprecision and Circling Approaches
X20   Weight and Balance
X21   Flight Planning
X22   Icing
X23   Use of Anti-ice and Deice
X24   Winter Operation
X25   Thunderstorm Flight
X26   Low-Level Wind Shear

Practical Test Standards

Z01   FAA-S-8081-6, Flight Instructor Practical
         Test Standards for Airplane
Z02   FAA-S-8081-7, Flight Instructor Practical
         Test Standards for Rotorcraft
Z03   FAA-S-8081-8, Flight Instructor Practical
         Test Standards for Glider

NOTE: AC 00-2, Advisory Circular Checklist, transmits the status of all FAA advisory circulars (AC's), as well as FAA internal publications and miscellaneous flight information, such as Aeronautical

Information Manual, Airport/Facility Directory, knowledge test guides, practical test standards, and other material directly related to a certificate or rating. To obtain a free copy of AC 00-2, send your request to:

U.S. Department of Transportation
Subsequent Distribution Office, SVC-121.23
Ardmore East Business Center
3341 Q 75 Ave.
Landover, MD 20785

CROSS-REFERENCE LISTING OF QUESTIONS

APPENDIX 2

Appendix 2 is a numerical listing of all airplane questions in the Commercial Pilot Computer Test. The listing includes the FAA Test question number, Jeppesen test question number, and the answer. The cross-reference listing is to the right of the answer. It refers to the chapter and the page in the *Commercial Pilot Exam Test Guide* where the question is answered.

Example: 09-004   329   C   9-3

This indicates that the answer to FAA question number 329, which is Jeppesen test question 9-4, is A. The question is answered in Chapter 9, on page 9-3 of the Test Guide.

FAA Number	Question Number	Answer	Page		FAA Number	Question Number	Answer	Page		FAA Number	Question Number	Answer	Page
001	15-103	C	15-27		038	15-019	A	15-6		088	15-058	C	15-17
002	15-104	C	15-27		039	15-020	B	15-6		089	15-059	A	15-17
003	15-105	A	15-28		045	15-021	C	15-6		090	15-060	A	15-17
004	15-106	C	15-28		049	03-002	B	3-4		091	15-061	A	15-18
005	15-107	C	15-28		050	15-032	C	15-11		092	15-062	B	15-18
006	15-108	A	15-28		051	15-033	B	15-11		093	15-063	C	15-18
007	15-109	C	15-28		053	15-034	B	15-11		094	15-064	A	15-18
008	15-110	C	15-28		054	15-035	A	15-12		095	15-065	B	15-19
009	03-001	B	3-3		056	15-036	B	15-12		096	15-066	A	15-19
011	15-001	C	15-1		057	15-037	B	15-12		097	03-006	B	3-4
012	15-002	C	15-1		058	15-038	C	15-12		098	03-007	A	3-5
013	15-003	C	15-1		059	15-039	C	15-13		099	15-067	A	15-19
014	02-001	B	2-2		060	15-040	B	15-13		100	15-068	A	15-19
015	02-002	A	2-2		061	15-041	C	15-13		101	15-069	C	15-19
016	02-003	C	2-2		062	15-042	B	15-13		105	03-008	A	3-5
017	02-004	B	2-2		065	15-043	B	15-14		106	03-009	B	3-5
018	11-032	C	11-9		066	15-044	C	15-14		107	03-010	A	3-5
019	02-005	A	2-3		067	15-045	A	15-14		108	15-070	B	15-19
020	02-006	B	2-3		070	15-046	B	15-14		110	15-071	B	15-20
022	15-004	B	15-2		071	03-003	A	3-4		113	03-011	A	3-5
023	15-005	A	15-3		072	03-004	A	3-4		114	03-012	B	3-6
024	15-006	C	15-3		073	02-018	C	2-7		115	03-013	C	3-6
025	15-007	A	15-3		074	15-047	C	15-15		116	15-072	B	15-20
026	15-008	A	15-3		075	15-048	A	15-15		117	15-073	C	15-20
027	15-009	A	15-3		076	15-049	A	15-15		118	15-074	C	15-20
028	15-010	B	15-4		077	15-050	B	15-15		119	15-075	C	15-20
029	15-011	B	15-4		078	15-051	B	15-15		120	15-076	B	15-21
030	15-012	C	15-4		079	15-052	C	15-16		121	15-077	A	15-21
031	15-013	A	15-4		081	15-053	C	15-16		122	15-078	B	15-21
032	15-014	A	15-5		082	15-054	B	15-16		123	15-079	B	15-21
033	15-015	A	15-5		083	15-055	C	15-16		124	15-080	C	15-22
035	15-016	A	15-5		084	15-056	C	15-16		125	15-081	B	15-22
036	15-017	C	15-5		085	15-057	A	15-17		126	15-082	C	15-22
037	15-018	A	15-5		087	03-005	A	3-4		127	15-083	C	15-22

FAA Number	Question Number	Answer	Page	FAA Number	Question Number	Answer	Page	FAA Number	Question Number	Answer	Page
128	15-084	B	15-23	195	11-002	C	11-2	250	12-050	A	12-15
129	15-085	C	15-23	196	11-003	A	11-2	251	12-051	A	12-15
130	15-086	A	15-23	197	11-004	A	11-3	252	12-052	A	12-15
131	15-022	B	15-6	198	11-005	C	11-3	253	12-053	B	12-15
132	15-023	C	15-7	199	11-006	C	11-3	254	12-054	B	12-16
133	15-024	A	15-7	200	11-007	B	11-3	255	12-055	B	12-16
134	15-087	B	15-23	201	11-008	C	11-3	256	12-056	B	12-16
135	15-088	B	15-23	202	02-008	C	2-3	257	12-064	B	12-19
137	15-089	C	15-24	203	02-009	B	2-3	258	12-065	A	12-19
138	15-090	B	15-24	204	12-062	C	12-18	259	12-066	A	12-20
141	02-007	C	2-3	205	12-063	A	12-18	260	12-067	A	12-20
142	15-091	C	15-24	206	12-017	B	12-6	261	11-018	A	11-6
143	15-092	A	15-24	207	12-018	B	12-6	262	11-019	B	11-6
145	03-014	C	3-6	208	11-009	C	11-4	263	11-020	C	11-6
146	03-015	C	3-6	209	11-010	B	11-4	264	12-057	B	12-16
147	03-016	B	3-6	210	11-011	A	11-4	294	02-011	C	2-4
148	03-017	B	3-7	211	11-012	A	11-4	295	02-012	A	2-4
149	03-018	C	3-7	212	11-013	C	11-5	296	02-013	B	2-4
150	03-019	B	3-7	213	11-014	B	11-5	297	11-021	A	11-6
151	15-093	B	15-24	214	11-015	A	11-5	298	05-001	C	5-1
152	02-019	B	2-8	215	11-016	A	11-5	306	12-058	C	12-17
153	02-020	C	2-8	216	11-017	B	11-5	324	11-022	B	11-6
154	15-094	B	15-25	217	12-019	C	12-6	325	12-068	C	12-21
155	15-095	B	15-25	218	12-020	C	12-6	326	09-001	A	9-3
156	15-096	A	15-25	219	12-021	A	12-7	327	09-002	A	9-3
157	15-097	A	15-25	220	12-022	A	12-7	328	09-003	C	9-3
158	15-098	A	15-25	221	12-023	B	12-7	329	09-004	A	9-3
159	15-099	B	15-26	222	12-024	A	12-7	330	02-014	A	2-4
160	15-100	B	15-26	223	12-025	B	12-7	331	12-069	B	12-21
161	15-025	A	15-7	224	12-026	A	12-8	332	12-070	B	12-21
162	15-026	B	15-8	225	12-027	C	12-8	333	12-071	B	12-21
164	15-027	C	15-8	226	12-028	C	12-8	334	12-072	B	12-22
165	15-101	C	15-26	227	12-029	C	12-8	335	09-005	C	9-3
168	15-028	B	15-8	228	12-030	B	12-8	336	09-006	A	9-3
169	15-029	C	15-8	229	12-031	A	12-9	337	09-007	A	9-4
170	15-030	C	15-9	230	12-032	A	12-9	338	09-008	B	9-4
171	15-031	C	15-9	231	12-033	B	12-9	339	09-124	C	9-32
176	12-001	A	12-2	232	12-034	A	12-9	340	09-009	A	9-4
177	12-002	A	12-3	233	12-110	B	12-46	341	09-010	A	9-4
178	12-003	A	12-3	234	02-010	A	2-4	342	09-011	C	9-4
179	12-004	B	12-3	235	12-035	B	12-9	343	09-012	B	9-5
180	12-005	A	12-3	236	12-036	C	12-10	344	09-013	B	9-5
181	12-006	B	12-3	237	12-037	C	12-10	345	09-014	B	9-5
182	12-007	B	12-3	238	12-038	A	12-10	346	09-015	A	9-5
183	12-008	A	12-4	239	12-039	B	12-10	347	09-016	C	9-5
184	12-009	A	12-4	240	12-040	C	12-11	348	09-017	C	9-6
185	09-045	B	9-13	241	12-041	C	12-12	349	09-046	B	9-14
186	12-010	C	12-4	242	12-042	A	12-12	350	09-047	A	9-14
187	12-011	B	12-4	243	12-043	B	12-12	351	09-048	C	9-14
188	12-012	C	12-4	244	12-044	C	12-12	352	09-018	C	9-6
189	12-013	B	12-5	245	12-045	B	12-13	353	09-019	C	9-6
190	12-014	A	12-5	246	12-046	C	12-13	354	09-020	C	9-6
191	12-015	B	12-5	247	12-047	C	12-13	355	09-021	B	9-6
192	12-016	B	12-6	248	12-048	C	12-14	356	09-022	C	9-7
194	11-001	B	11-2	249	12-049	C	12-14	357	09-023	B	9-7

FAA Number	Question Number	Answer	Page
358	09-024	A	9-7
359	09-025	B	9-7
360	09-026	C	9-7
361	09-027	B	9-7
362	09-028	B	9-8
363	09-029	C	9-8
364	09-049	B	9-14
365	09-030	B	9-8
366	09-031	B	9-8
367	09-032	A	9-8
368	09-033	B	9-8
369	09-034	C	9-9
370	09-035	C	9-9
371	09-036	C	9-9
372	09-037	B	9-9
373	09-038	B	9-9
374	09-050	C	9-14
375	09-051	C	9-14
376	09-052	C	9-15
377	09-053	C	9-15
378	09-054	B	9-15
379	09-055	A	9-15
380	09-056	C	9-15
381	09-057	A	9-16
382	09-058	B	9-16
383	09-059	C	9-16
384	09-060	A	9-16
385	09-061	C	9-16
386	09-062	C	9-17
387	09-063	B	9-17
388	09-064	B	9-17
389	09-065	C	9-17
390	09-066	A	9-17
391	09-067	C	9-18
392	09-068	C	9-18
393	09-069	B	9-18
394	09-070	C	9-18
395	09-071	A	9-18
396	09-072	B	9-18
397	09-073	C	9-19
398	09-074	C	9-19
399	09-075	C	9-19
400	09-076	A	9-19
401	09-077	B	9-19
402	09-078	C	9-19
403	09-079	C	9-20
404	09-080	A	9-20
405	09-081	C	9-20
406	09-039	B	9-10
407	09-082	A	9-20
408	09-083	B	9-20
409	09-040	B	9-10
410	09-041	A	9-10
413	09-042	A	9-10
417	09-043	B	9-10

FAA Number	Question Number	Answer	Page
418	09-084	A	9-21
423	10-006	C	10-4
424	10-007	C	10-5
425	09-142	C	9-36
426	09-143	A	9-36
427	09-109	C	9-27
428	09-110	B	9-28
429	09-111	B	9-28
430	09-085	B	9-21
431	09-112	B	9-28
432	09-113	A	9-28
433	09-114	C	9-29
434	09-115	B	9-29
435	09-116	C	9-29
436	09-117	C	9-29
437	09-118	B	9-30
438	09-119	A	9-30
439	09-120	B	9-30
440	09-121	C	9-30
441	09-144	B	9-36
442	09-145	B	9-37
443	09-146	B	9-37
444	09-122	B	9-30
445	09-147	A	9-37
446	09-148	A	9-37
447	09-149	B	9-37
448	09-150	C	9-38
449	09-123	B	9-31
450	09-125	A	9-32
451	09-126	A	9-32
452	09-127	A	9-32
453	09-128	B	9-32
454	09-129	B	9-33
455	09-130	C	9-33
456	09-131	B	9-33
457	09-132	A	9-33
458	09-133	C	9-33
459	09-134	B	9-34
460	09-135	C	9-34
461	09-136	B	9-34
463	09-137	C	9-34
464	09-138	A	9-34
465	09-139	B	9-35
466	09-140	A	9-35
467	09-141	C	9-35
468	09-086	B	9-21
469	09-087	B	9-21
470	09-088	C	9-21
471	09-089	B	9-22
472	09-090	B	9-22
473	09-091	C	9-22
474	09-092	B	9-22
475	09-093	A	9-23
476	12-073	B	12-22
477	12-074	B	12-22

FAA Number	Question Number	Answer	Page
478	12-075	C	12-22
479	12-076	B	12-24
480	12-077	A	12-24
481	12-078	C	12-24
482	12-079	C	12-25
483	12-080	C	12-26
484	12-081	C	12-27
485	12-082	C	12-27
486	12-083	B	12-27
487	12-084	C	12-27
488	12-085	B	12-29
489	12-086	A	12-30
490	12-087	C	12-30
491	10-008	A	10-5
492	10-009	C	10-6
493	10-010	C	10-6
494	10-011	A	10-7
495	10-012	A	10-7
496	10-013	C	10-7
497	10-014	C	10-7
498	10-015	A	10-7
499	10-016	A	10-8
500	10-017	A	10-8
501	10-018	B	10-8
502	05-002	C	5-2
503	05-003	C	5-2
504	10-019	C	10-8
506	10-020	C	10-9
507	12-088	A	12-30
508	12-089	B	12-32
509	12-090	C	12-32
510	12-091	B	12-34
511	10-021	B	10-9
512	10-022	B	10-10
513	03-020	C	3-7
514	03-021	C	3-7
515	09-044	A	9-13
516	10-001	B	10-2
517	10-002	A	10-2
518	02-021	C	2-8
519	02-022	A	2-8
520	02-023	C	2-9
521	02-024	C	2-9
522	02-025	C	2-11
523	02-026	A	2-11
524	02-027	C	2-11
525	02-028	C	2-11
526	10-003	C	10-2
527	10-004	A	10-2
528	12-059	B	12-17
529	02-029	A	2-11
530	02-030	A	2-12
531	02-031	B	2-13
532	02-032	A	2-13
533	02-033	C	2-13

FAA Number	Question Number	Answer	Page	FAA Number	Question Number	Answer	Page	FAA Number	Question Number	Answer	Page
534	02-034	B	2-13	607	03-034	A	3-13	681	14-002	B	14-1
535	02-035	B	2-13	608	03-035	B	3-13	682	05-004	A	5-3
536	02-036	C	2-14	610	03-036	A	3-13	683	11-030	B	11-8
537	02-037	C	2-14	611	03-037	C	3-13	684	11-031	A	11-8
538	02-038	C	2-14	624	02-015	A	2-5	685	09-096	B	9-23
539	02-039	B	2-15	625	02-016	C	2-5	686	09-097	B	9-23
540	02-040	C	2-15	627	12-060	A	12-17	755	09-098	B	9-24
541	02-041	C	2-15	628	12-061	B	12-17	756	02-017	B	2-5
542	02-042	A	2-15	629	11-023	C	11-7	757	09-099	C	9-24
543	02-043	C	2-15	630	11-024	B	11-7	764	04-001	A	4-1
544	02-044	C	2-16	631	11-025	C	11-7	765	05-005	B	5-3
545	02-045	B	2-16	632	11-026	C	11-7	766	09-100	B	9-24
546	02-046	B	2-16	633	11-027	A	11-7	767	09-101	A	9-24
547	02-047	A	2-16	634	11-028	B	11-8	768	09-102	A	9-24
548	02-048	B	2-16	637	12-092	B	12-35	769	09-103	A	9-25
549	02-049	A	2-17	638	12-093	A	12-35	770	09-104	A	9-25
550	02-050	A	2-17	639	12-094	C	12-35	771	09-105	C	9-25
551	02-051	B	2-17	640	12-095	A	12-35	772	09-106	B	9-25
552	02-052	A	2-17	641	12-096	A	12-35	773	01-002	C	1-4
553	02-053	A	2-18	642	12-097	C	12-37	774	01-003	C	1-4
554	02-054	A	2-18	643	12-098	B	12-37	775	01-004	A	1-4
555	02-055	B	2-18	644	12-099	B	12-37	776	01-005	C	1-5
556	02-056	B	2-18	645	12-100	C	12-39	777	01-006	B	1-5
557	02-057	A	2-18	646	12-101	B	12-39	778	01-007	B	1-5
558	02-058	C	2-19	647	12-102	C	12-41	779	01-008	C	1-5
559	02-059	B	2-20	648	12-103	B	12-41	780	01-009	B	1-5
560	02-060	B	2-20	649	12-104	B	12-41	781	01-010	C	1-6
561	02-061	A	2-20	650	12-105	C	12-43	782	09-107	C	9-25
562	02-062	A	2-20	651	12-106	A	12-43	783	09-108	A	9-26
563	02-063	A	2-21	652	12-107	A	12-43	784	11-033	A	11-9
564	02-064	A	2-21	653	12-108	B	12-45	958	13-001	C	13-2
565	02-065	B	2-22	654	12-109	A	12-45	959	13-002	A	13-2
566	02-066	A	2-22	655	12-111	C	12-46	960	13-003	C	13-2
567	02-067	B	2-22	656	12-112	B	12-46	961	13-004	C	13-3
568	02-068	A	2-23	657	12-113	C	12-47	962	13-005	B	13-3
569	02-069	B	2-23	658	12-114	B	12-47	963	13-006	C	13-3
570	02-070	A	2-23	659	12-115	B	12-47	964	13-007	A	13-3
573	02-071	B	2-23	663	12-116	A	12-47	965	13-008	C	13-4
574	02-072	C	2-23	664	12-117	A	12-47	966	13-009	A	13-4
575	02-073	B	2-24	665	12-118	B	12-48	967	13-010	C	13-4
577	15-102	A	15-26	666	12-119	A	12-48	968	13-011	C	13-4
581	09-151	B	9-38	667	01-001	A	1-4	969	13-012	C	13-4
582	09-152	A	9-38	668	11-029	C	11-8	970	13-013	C	13-5
586	03-022	C	3-8	669	03-038	A	3-14	971	13-014	C	13-5
587	03-023	A	3-8	670	03-039	A	3-14	972	13-015	A	13-5
588	03-024	C	3-8	671	03-040	C	3-15	973	13-016	A	13-6
589	03-025	B	3-8	672	03-041	C	3-15	974	13-017	A	13-6
590	03-026	C	3-8	673	03-042	B	3-15	975	13-018	B	13-6
591	03-027	B	3-8	674	03-043	C	3-15	976	13-019	C	13-6
592	03-028	B	3-12	675	03-044	C	3-15	977	13-020	A	13-6
594	03-029	B	3-12	676	03-045	A	3-15	978	13-021	B	13-7
598	03-030	A	3-12	677	14-001	C	14-1	979	13-022	A	13-7
600	03-031	C	3-12	678	09-094	A	9-23	980	13-023	A	13-7
604	03-032	C	3-12	679	10-005	A	10-3				
606	03-033	C	3-12	680	09-095	A	9-23				

Multimedia Software Courses for FAA Exams

FliteSchool, PRIVATE PILOT & INSTRUMENT MULTIMEDIA SOFTWARE

The GFD FliteSchool Multimedia Software is a complete, interactive home study course for passing the FAA airman knowledge exams. FliteSchool Multimedia Software makes it easy, fast and fun to get a great score on your exam. You learn the material thoroughly and get the highest possible score on your exam while retaining what you learn. Only FliteSchool Multimedia software integrates the complete textual references of the GFD, Private, or Instrument/Commercial Manual, allowing you easy access to expanded information. Carefully selected graphics and computer animation are combined to help you understand difficult concepts. In addition, all FAA figures are contained on the CD-ROM for easy reference.

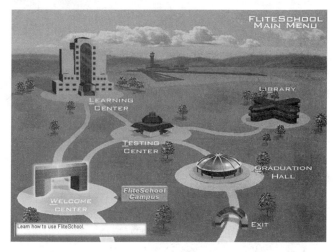

Computer Requirements:

- Pentium 100 MHz processor
- Windows 95, 98, or NT 4.0 with 16 MB RAM
- 6-speed or higher CD-ROM drive
- SVGA card with 1 MB (800X600X16 bit color) or higher video RAM
- SoundBlaster or Windows-compatible sound card
- 3 1/2" disk drive (for backing up student records)

Course	Item #	
Private Pilot	JS202001	$169.95
Instrument Pilot	JS202002	$179.95
Private Manual and FliteSchool	JS202505	$199.95
Instrument Manual and FliteSchool	JS201000	$229.95

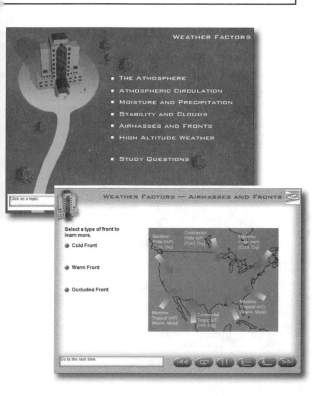

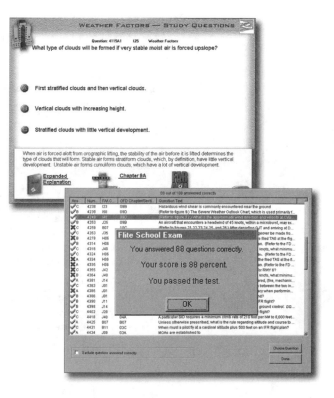

JeppPrep

JEPPPREP

Now students can prepare for their FAA knowledge exams on the internet. With the purchase of JeppPrep, you will receive a 60-day period of unlimited study for a particular FAA knowledge exam. A renewal can be purchased for each additional 30-day period for an additional charge. JeppPrep contains the latest FAA questions taken from the FAA database, so it is always current. Pilots can take practice FAA exams and review their performance once the exams are scored

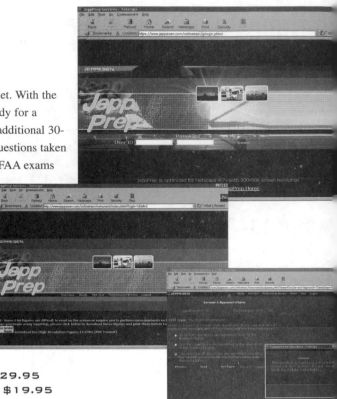

JeppPrep Features:

- Study actual FAA questions at your own pace, on your own time
- Review answers and explanations to actual FAA questions
- Take sample tests that emulate actual FAA knowledge tests
- Efficiently review the results of your practice tests
- Compare your performance on several tests
- Work with the most current FAA questions
- View or print the FAA figures and legends for FAA questions

ITEM NUMBER WB100500 JEPPPREP INITIAL ORDER $29.95
ITEM NUMBER WB100543 JEPPPREP 30-DAY RENEWAL $19.95

Jeppesen FlighTime Chart Series Videos

Now featuring the New Jeppesen Chart formats! Professionally designed and produced, the FlighTime Chart Video Series covers Jeppesen Enroute Charts, Approach Charts, and SIDs and STARs. Each video is designed to refresh and enhance pilot knowledge by explaining each Jeppesen chart and how to read them in detail. Effective for student and experienced pilot.

ITEM NUMBER JS200251 (VHS) $99.95

Approach Charts FlighTime video now includes a special "Video NOTAM" describing new RNAV (GPS) procedures!

ALSO AVAILABLE INDIVIDUALLY:

Approach Charts Includes a detailed introduction of Jeppesen's New Approach Chart Format featuring the Briefing Strip Concept. This totally new video provides an overview of the various types of information portrayed as well as in-depth explanations that go beyond the chart legend
ITEM NUMBER JS273268 (VHS) $37.95

Enroute Charts Completely new video that features the Jeppesen Four-Color Enroute Charts. Maximizes the usefulness of your Enroute Charts by thoroughly explaining chart data. Allows quick and easy in-flight identification of chart information.
ITEM NUMBER JS273269 (VHS) $37.95

SIDs and STARs Presents the unique characteristics of SID and STAR charts in an easily understandable format, allowing you to take advantage of these simplified procedures at busy terminal areas.
ITEM NUMBER JS273270 (VHS) $37.95

VISIT YOUR JEPPESEN DEALER OR CALL 1-800-621-5377
MAKE SURE TO CHECK OUT OUR WEB PAGE AT HTTP://WWW.JEPPESEN.COM
PRICES SUBJECT TO CHANGE.

ntroducing Jeppesen Flight Bags

THE CAPTAIN FLIGHT BAG

he Jeppesen *Captain Flight Bag* is the most versatile bag available. The
eadset bags can be removed and attached together to form a dual headset bag.
he removable Transceiver/GPS bag can be worn on your belt. The flexible
esign allows you to add or subtract components to match your flying needs.
he roomy interior has a 4-way custom divider that can hold four Jeppesen
nders. An exterior zippered pocket provides a convenient storage space to
lp pilots organize their supplies. Two large zippered storage pockets can
ld glasses, charts, pilot operating handbooks and other miscellaneous
cessories. Carry your supplies in comfort with a wide cushioned
oulder strap. 12″x22½″x8″

THE CAPTAIN FLIGHT BAG (BLACK OR BLUE)
ITEM NUMBER JS621214 (BLACK) $139.95
ITEM NUMBER JS621251 (BLUE) $139.95

THE NAVIGATOR FLIGHT BAG

The *Navigator Flight Bag* includes all of the features and benefits of the Captain Flight Bag,
except the removable Transceiver/GPS bag and the two zippered exterior storage pockets.
Instead, it includes two exterior pockets for easy access to sectional and world aeronautical
charts. 12″x22½″x8″

THE NAVIGATOR FLIGHT BAG (BLACK OR BLUE)
ITEM NUMBER JS621213 (BLACK) $99.95
ITEM NUMBER JS621250 (BLUE) $99.95

HE PROTECTOR HEADSET BAGS

e *Protector Headset Bags* are constructed of fully padded 600 denier poly for extra
otection. Each bag comes with its own snap-on handle grip for comfort. Large enough to fit
e ANR headsets (12″x2¾″x8″). Offered in both a single and dual configuration. Designed to
the Core Captain Flight Bag.

HE PROTECTOR HEADSET BAGS (BLACK)
SINGLE JS621220 $17.95
DUAL JS621219 $35.95

THE STUDENT PILOT FLIGHT BAG

The *Student Pilot Flight Bag* is designed for new student pilots. Numerous outside pockets will
organize charts, flight computer, fuel tester, plotter, pens and pencils, flashlight and much more.
Additional features include a wide removable shoulder strap for comfort and a reinforced bottom.
10″x5½″x17″

THE STUDENT PILOT FLIGHT BAG (BLACK)
ITEM NUMBER JS621212 $41.95

NEW! THE AVIATOR BAG

he Aviator Bag is constructed of fully padded vynlon for extra durability. Each bag includes
e headset bag and one Transceiver/GPS bag. The interior has a 2-way divider that can be
ed to separate your pilot accessories.

HE AVIATOR BAG (BLACK)
EM NUMBER JS621252 $79.95

VISIT YOUR JEPPESEN DEALER OR CALL 1-800-621-5377
MAKE SURE TO CHECK OUT OUR WEB PAGE AT HTTP://WWW.JEPPESEN.COM
PRICES SUBJECT TO CHANGE.

ECHSTAR PRO AND DATALINK

EPPESEN'S "NEXT GENERATION" VIATION COMPUTER

ppesen's innovative TechStar Pro is the first handheld flight computer and rsonal organizer. Combining the latest technology and ease of use, TechStar o gives you a 7-function aviation computer and an 8-function personal ganizer. All-in-one compact handheld unit. Students to Airline Transport Pilots, e it in the cockpit, home, office or classroom.

CHSTAR PRO
EM NUMBER JS505000 $99.95

ECHSTAR PRO ATALINK SOFTWARE ND CABLE

imple to use – Windows 3.1 or higher
ackup data on your TechStar Pro
dit, add and delete records from your
PC and then download the records
ave time when inputting data
ave different files for different trips

ATALINK
EM NUMBER JS505050 $12.95

DataLink sold separately.

FUEL TESTER

The last fuel tester you'll ever need! Strong, clear butyrate plastic resists cracking, breaking and yellowing. Works with both pin and petcock actuators. Removable splash guard prevents fuel spillage and attaches to side for flat, slimline storage. Solid bronze rod actuator prevents breaking and pushing down. Measures 8.25″ x 3.25″ x 1″.

FUEL TESTER
ITEM NUMBER JS628855 $13.95

JEPPSHADES

IFR FLIP-UP TRAINING GLASSES

• Replaces bulky, hard-to-use instrument training hoods • Improved design allows
better student/instructor interaction • Cockpit proven design works conveniently
under headsets • Universal adjusting strap reduces pressure on ears and temple
• Velcro™ strap fits comfortably under headsets • Flip-Up lens allows convenient
IFR/VFR flight transition • High quality polycarbonate lens is impact resistant

JEPPSHADES
ITEM NUMBER JS404311 $24.95

VFR/IFR KNEEBOARD

Our new kneeboard places information at your fingertips. It holds charts, flight computers/plotters, flashlight, pen, pilot notes and more. An elastic leg strap holds this unit comfortably in place with a Velcro closure. The metal clipboard (also available separately) contains valuable information for your VFR and IFR flight needs. An additional strap is included, allowing you to use the clipboard independent of the kneeboard. You're really getting two products in one.

KNEEBOARD/CLIPBOARD
ITEM NUMBER JS626003 $36.95

CLIPBOARD ONLY
ITEM NUMBER JS626001 $16.95

VISIT YOUR JEPPESEN DEALER OR CALL 1-800-621-5377
MAKE SURE TO CHECK OUT OUR WEB PAGE AT HTTP://WWW.JEPPESEN.COM
PRICES SUBJECT TO CHANGE.

Pilot Supplies